The vernacular workshop:
from craft to industry, 1400–1900

The vernacular workshop:
from craft to industry, 1400–1900

P S Barnwell, Marilyn Palmer & Malcolm Airs (eds)

Published in 2004 by the Council for British Archaeology
Bowes Morrell House, 111 Walmgate, York, YO1 9WA

Copyright © 2004 Authors, English Heritage and Council for
British Archaeology (English Heritage copyright applies to
Chapters 5, 6, 9, 10, 11, 12, and 14)

British Library cataloguing in Publication Data
A catalogue record for this book is available from the British Library
ISBN 1-902771-45-1

Cover designed by BP Design, York

Typeset by Archetype IT Ltd, www.archetype-it.com

Printed by Pennine Printing Services Ltd

The publisher asknowledges with gratitude a grant
from English Heritage towards the cost of publication

Front cover: Weavers' cottages, Chandler Lane, Honley, Holme Valley, West Yorkshire
(© English Heritage).

Contents

List of illustrations vi
List of tables ix
List of abbreviations. x
List of contributors xi
Acknowledgements. xii
Summaries – English, French and German xiii

1 The workshop: type of building or method of work? *Marilyn Palmer* 1

2 Making luxuries: the image and reality of luxury workshops in
18th-century London *Helen Clifford*. 17

3 The archaeology of the late and post-medieval workshop – a review and
proposal for a research agenda *Jane Grenville* 28

4 Late medieval workshops in East Anglia *Leigh Alston* 38

5 Transformations in Georgian London's silk-weaving workshop homes,
with a comparative detour to Lyons *Peter Guillery* 60

6 The Yorkshire textile loomshop: from weaver's cottage to the factory *Colum Giles*. 75

7 Domestic weaving premises in Lancashire: a contextual analysis *Geoffrey Timmins* 90

8 Outworking dynamism and stasis: Nottinghamshire's 19th-century
machine-made lace and framework knitting industries *Garry Campion*. 101

9 Domesticated factories and industrialised houses: the buildings of the
Northamptonshire boot and shoe industry *Adam Menuge* 122

10 Workshops of the Sheffield cutlery and edge-tool trades *Nicola Wray* 136

11 The workshops of Birmingham's Jewellery Quarter *John Cattell* 150

12 The Furness iron industry *Mark Bowden* 166

13 Workshops and cottages in the Ironbridge Gorge *Barrie Trinder* 173

14 Workshops, industrial production and the landscape *P S Barnwell* 179

Consolidated bibliography 183
Index *by Peter Rea* 192

List of illustrations

1.1	Tanners' workshops along the River Schwendi, Colmar, Upper Alsace (© Marilyn Palmer)	4
1.2	La Croix-Rousse from the Quai Saint-Vincent, Lyons (© Marilyn Palmer)	4
1.3	Halifax Piece Hall (© Crown Copyright. NMR)	5
1.4	New Tame fold, Saddleworth (© Marilyn Palmer)	5
1.5	Courtfield House, Trowbridge (© Marilyn Palmer)	6
1.6	A clothier's house, Holt, near Melksham (© Marilyn Palmer)	6
1.7	Part of the Rotes Haus, Monschau, Germany (© Marilyn Palmer)	7
1.8	North Street, Cromford (© Marilyn Palmer)	8
1.9	Yerbury Street, Trowbridge (© Marilyn Palmer)	9
1.10	Weavers' terrace, Kingswood (© Marilyn Palmer)	10
1.11	Weavers' houses, Bradley Green, near Wotton-under-Edge (© Marilyn Palmer)	10
1.12	Timber-framed house, Shepshed (© Marilyn Palmer)	10
1.13	Cottages, St Mary's Lane, Tewkesbury (© Marilyn Palmer)	11
1.14	Nailmakers' workshops, Dudley (Courtesy of Dudley Leisure Services)	12
1.15	Chainmakers' workshop, Mushroom Green, Dudley Wood (© Marilyn Palmer)	12
1.16	Maison Closset, Verviers, Belgium (© Marilyn Palmer)	13
1.17	Loom shop, Church Street, Bradford-on-Avon (© Marilyn Palmer)	14
1.18	The Green, Calne (© Marilyn Palmer)	14
1.19	Interior view of framework knitting workshop, Bushloe End, Wigston Magna (© Marilyn Palmer)	15
1.20	Cottage factories, Coventry (© Marilyn Palmer)	15
2.1	'Joyner's Work' from Moxon's *Mechanick Exercises . . .*, 1678 (© Bodleian Library, Oxford)	20
2.2	A goldsmith's work room, c1576 (© Worshipful Company of Goldsmiths, London)	21
2.3	Frontispiece from William Badcock, *A New Touchstone to Gold & Silverwares* (© Worshipful Company of Goldsmiths, London)	22
2.4	A goldsmith's workshop, 1701 (© Worshipful Company of Goldsmiths, London)	23
2.5	Invitation to Goldsmiths' Hall, 1741/2 (© Trustees of the Ashmolean Museum, Oxford)	24
2.6	Trade card of jeweller, goldsmith and toyman, c1770 (© The British Museum)	25
2.7	Trade card of goldsmith, clock and watchmaker, c1750 (© The British Museum)	26
3.1	Smelting complex, Rockley (By permission of the Society for Post Medieval Archaeology)	31
3.2	Reconstruction of iron-working structures, Minepit Wood (By permission of *Medieval Archaeology*)	32
3.3	Potter's House, Rodger Lane, Potovens, Wakefield (By permission of the Society for Post Medieval Archaeology)	34
3.4	Robert Glover's house of 1679, Potovens, Wakefield (By permission of the Society for Post Medieval Archaeology)	34
3.5	Allen House, Rosedale (By permission of the Society for Post Medieval Archaeology)	35
3.6	Bolsterstone Glasshouse, Stocksbridge (By permission of the Society for Post Medieval Archaeology)	36
4.1	26 Market Place, Lavenham (© David Clark)	40
4.2	Reconstruction, 26 Market Place, Lavenham (© Leigh Alston)	41
4.3	Reconstruction, 2 Nayland Road, Bures St Mary (© Leigh Alston)	42
4.4	Internal elevation, Antrim House, Haughley (© Leigh Alston)	43
4.5	Reconstructions, 40–43 Prentice Street, Lavenham (© Leigh Alston)	44
4.6	Reconstruction, Bildeston Hall, Bildeston (© Leigh Alston)	45
4.7	Reconstruction, 27 Cumberland Street, Woodbridge (© Leigh Alston)	46
4.8	Ground plan and internal elevation, 16 Fen Street, Nayland (© Leigh Alston)	47
4.9	Interior, 16 Fen Street, Nayland (© Leigh Alston)	48
4.10	31–39 Chapel Street, Bildeston (© Leigh Alston)	48
4.11	Woodbine Cottage, Kersey (© Leigh Alston)	48
4.12	Cordell Cottages, High Street, Long Melford (© Leigh Alston)	49
4.13	16–18 Birch Street, Nayland (© Leigh Alston)	50
4.14	6 High Street, Lavenham (© Leigh Alston)	52
4.15	Ground plan, Alston Court, Nayland (© Leigh Alston)	53
4.16	The Guildhall, Thaxted (© Leigh Alston)	55

List of illustrations vii

4.17	Ground plan and shop fronts, 1 Church Street, Coggeshall (© Leigh Alston)	56
4.18	Reconstruction, Cleo's Restaurant, Market Place, Debenham (© Leigh Alston)	57
4.19	Reconstruction, Cleo's Restaurant, Market Place, Debenham (© Leigh Alston)	58
5.1	Perspective reconstruction 113 and 115 Bethnal Green Road, Tower Hamlets (© English Heritage. NMR)	61
5.2	71–9 Sclater Street, Tower Hamlets (© Tower Hamlets Local History Library)	62
5.3	Plans of late 17th and early 18th-century houses in Bethnal Green (© English Heritage. NMR)	63
5.4	Plans of late 18th and early 19th-century houses in Bethnal Green (© English Heritage. NMR)	66
5.5	125 Brick Lane, Tower Hamlets (© London Metropolitan Archives)	67
5.6	34 and 36 Florida Street, Tower Hamlets (© English Heritage)	68
5.7	Early 19th-century cottages, Boundary Street Estate, Tower Hamlets (© London Metropolitan Archives)	69
5.8	5 Rue Major Martin, Lyons, France (© Peter Guillery)	70
5.9	Grande Rue de la Guillotiere, Lyons, France (© Peter Guillery)	71
5.10	La Maison des Canuts, Rue d'Ivry, Lyons, France (© Peter Guillery)	73
6.1	Schematic map of West Riding wool textile area (© R G Wilson)	76
6.2	Greenwood Lee, Heptonstall (© Crown Copyright. NMR)	77
6.3	Church Fold, Heptonstall (© English Heritage. NMR)	78
6.4	Lumb, Almondbury, near Huddersfield (© English Heritage. NMR)	80
6.5	Loomshop, Cliffe Ash, Golcar (© Crown Copyright. NMR)	81
6.6	Well House Fold, Golcar (© Crown Copyright. NMR)	82
6.7	Upper Well House, Golcar (© English Heritage. NMR)	82
6.8	Oldfield, Honley (© English Heritage. NMR)	83
6.9	Spring Grove, Linthwaite (© English Heritage. NMR)	84
6.10	New Hagg, Oldfield, Honley (© English Heritage. NMR)	85
6.11	Meltham Road, Honley (© English Heritage. NMR)	86
6.12	Sowerby Bridge Mills (© Crown Copyright. NMR)	87
7.1	Map of Lancashire towns (© Geoffrey G Timmins)	90
7.2	Mount Pleasant, Preston (Harris Library, Preston)	91
7.3	Plan of handloom weavers' cottages, 1795 (Turton Tower Museum)	91
7.4	Ordnance Survey map, Chorley, 1848 (Ordnance Survey)	92
7.5	Ordnance Survey map, Livesey, 1848 (Ordnance Survey)	93
7.6	Hand-loom weavers' cottage, New Houses, Livesey (© Greoffrey G Timmins)	94
7.7	Hand-loom weavers' cottages (© Greoffrey G Timmins)	95
7.8	Hill Top, Barrowford, near Colne (© Greoffrey G Timmins)	98
7.9	Wolfenden Street, Bolton (© Greoffrey G Timmins)	99
8.1	Extracts from map of Nottinghamshire, 1836 (NAO)	102
8.2	Map of Nottingham, 1831 (NAO)	103
8.3	Housing and workshops, Mansfield Road, Nottingham (© Garry Campion)	105
8.4	Ordnance Survey map, Mansfield Road and North Sherwood Street, Nottingham, 1915 (Ordnance Survey)	106
8.5	Windles Square, Calverton (© Garry Campion)	107
8.6	Ordnance Survey map, west Calverton, 1889 (Ordnance Survey)	108
8.7	Ordnance Survey map, east Calverton, 1889 (Ordnance Survey)	108
8.8	Knitters' workshop, Chapel Street, Ruddington (© Garry Campion)	110
8.9	Ordnance Survey map, south Ruddington, 1900 (Ordnance Survey)	111
8.10	Ordnance Survey map, north Ruddington, 1900 (Ordnance Survey)	112
8.11	Rear view, Albert Street, Hucknall (© Garry Campion)	114
8.12	Ordnance Survey map, central and east Hucknall, 1880 (Ordnance Survey)	115
8.13	Ordnance Survey map, central and north Hucknall, 1880 (Ordnance Survey)	116
8.14	Ordnance Survey map, south and east Hucknall, 1880 (Ordnance Survey)	117
9.1	Contrasting images of the boot and shoe industry (By permission of Northampton Museum and Art Gallery)	123
9.2	Shoe factories, Long Buckby and Kettering (© English Heritage. NMR)	125
9.3	Ordnance Survey map, Kettering, 1899 (Ordnance Survey)	127
9.4	Outworker's workshop (© English Heritage. NMR)	128
9.5	41–3 Colwyn Road, Northampton (© English Heritage. NMR)	131
9.6	83 High Street South, Rushden (© English Heritage. NMR)	132
9.7	The Unicorn Works, 20–6 St Michaels Road, Northampton (© English Heritage. NMR)	133
9.8	Robert Street and Connaught Road, Northampton (© English Heritage. NMR)	134

10.1	Sheaf Works, Sheffield (© Bob Hawkins)	136
10.2	Globe Works, Sheffield (© English Heritage. NMR)	137
10.3	Perspective reconstruction of Sykehouse, Dungworth Green (© English Heritage. NMR)	138
10.4	Interior of a cutlers' wheel (© English Heritage. NMR)	139
10.5	Door and Window, Portland Works, Sheffield (© Crown Copyright. NMR)	141
10.6	Hand forge, Cyclops Works, Sheffield (© Sheffield Local Studies Library)	142
10.7	Redrawn insurance plans of Union and Soho grinding wheels (© English Heritage. NMR)	142
10.8	Rear wall of grinding hulls, Beehive Works, Milton Street, Sheffield (© Crown Copyright. NMR)	143
10.9	Garden Street, Sheffield (© Crown Copyright. NMR)	144
10.10	Anglo Works, Trippet Lane, Sheffield (© English Heritage. NMR)	145
10.11	Challenge Works, 94 Arundel Street, Sheffield (© Crown Copyright. NMR)	146
10.12	Franklin Cottage, Stannington (© English Heritage. NMR)	147
11.1	Map of the Jewellery Quarter (© English Heritage. NMR)	151
11.2	View of part of the centre of the Jewellery Quarter (© Crown Copyright. NMR)	152
11.3	Elkington and Co's electro-plating and gilding factory, Newhall Street, c1843 (© English Heritage. NMR)	152
11.4	Workshop range at rear of Warstone Lane (© Crown Copyright. NMR)	153
11.5	Elevation and plan of a pair of 'three-quarter' houses, 1842 (© English Heritage. NMR)	154
11.6	Workshop range at rear of 94 Vyse Street (© English Heritage. NMR)	154
11.7	Former court of blind-back houses, Summer Lane (© English Heritage. NMR)	155
11.8	House of 1818 and adjoining workshops, Mary Street (© Crown Copyright. NMR)	155
11.9	Rear view 119–21 Branston Street (© English Heritage. NMR)	155
11.10	House and workshop development of 1885, Legge Lane (© English Heritage. NMR)	156
11.11	Two small factories of 1870–1, Warstone Lane (© English Heritage. NMR)	156
11.12	Jewellery factory of 1882, Warstone Lane (© English Heritage. NMR)	157
11.13	Late 19th-century purpose-built jewellery factory, cut-away drawing (© English Heritage. NMR)	158
11.14	Former factor's warehouse of c1839, Regent Parade (© English Heritage. NMR)	158
11.15	Parisian jewellery workshop from Diderot's *L'Encyclopedie*, 1763 (© English Heritage. NMR)	160
11.16	Craftsmen working in a small top-floor workshop, Spencer Street (© English Heritage. NMR)	160
11.17	Stamping battery, 94 Vyse Street (© English Heritage. NMR)	161
11.18	Top-floor press shop, 94 Vyse Street (© English Heritage. NMR)	162
11.19	Variety Works of 1881–2, Frederick Street (© English Heritage. NMR)	162
11.20	A double-width press shop, William Elliott's button-making factory, Regent Street (© English Heritage. NMR)	163
11.21	A stamp shop, Newman Brothers' coffin furniture factory, Fleet Street (© English Heritage. NMR)	164
12.1	Map showing places mentioned in text (© English Heritage. NMR)	167
12.2	Charcoal burners' and bark peelers' huts, 1901	168
12.3	Plan of bark peelers' hut, Roudsea Wood (© Crown Copyright. NMR)	169
12.4	Perspective reconstruction of Duddon Bridge iron works (© Crown Copyright. NMR)	170
13.1	Squatter cottages from the Broseley Estate Book (© Barrie Trinder)	175
13.2	Open settlement at Madeley Wood (© Barrie Trinder)	175
13.3	Cottage, Hodge Bower, Madeley (© Barrie Trinder)	177
13.4	Squatter cottage, The Stocking, Little Dawley (© Barrie Trinder)	178

List of tables

7.1	Bridegroom weaver proportions in selected Lancashire parishes, 1818–22.	92
7.2	Hand-loom weaving settlement at Livesey, 1851	94
7.3	Hand-loom weavers' settlement in Ribble Valley districts, 1851	95
8.1	Identified or possible extant outworking buildings – Mansfield Road, Nottingham	104
8.2	Identified or possible outworking buildings – North Sherwood Street, Nottingham	104
8.3	1841 census data for Mansfield Road and (North) Sherwood Street.	104
8.4	Nottingham directory evidence 1832–42	105
8.5	Identified or possible outworking buildings.	107
8.6	1881 Census figures – outworking activity	107
8.7	Trade directory entries.	109
8.8	Identified or possible outworking buildings.	110
8.9	1881 Census figures – outworking activity	111
8.10	Trade directory entries.	111
8.11	Identified or possible outworking buildings.	113
8.12	1881 Outworking activity	114
8.13	Trade directory data.	114
Appendix 8.1	1858 Wright's directory for Mansfield Road area.	119
Appendix 8.2	1881 Census breakdown of outworkers for Calverton, by street	120
Appendix 8.3	1881 Census breakdown of outworkers for Ruddington, by street	120
Appendix 8.4	1881 Census breakdown of outworkers for Hucknall, by street	121

List of abbreviations

BPP	British Parliamentary Papers
CBA	Council for British Archaeology
ERO	Essex Record Office
Ex	Exhibition date of probate documents
FWK	Framework Knitter(s)
HPL	Hucknall Public Library
HMSO	Her Majesty's Stationery Office
HRO	Herefordshire Record Office
IUP	Irish Universities Press
LRO	Lichfield Record Office
Med Arch	Medieval Archaeology
NAO	Nottingham Archives Office
NBR	National Buildings Record
NCL	Nottingham Central Library
NMR	National Monuments Record
NRO	Northamptonshire Record Office
OS	Ordnance Survey
PMA	Post-Medieval Archaeology
PRO	Public Record Office (now the National Archives)
RCHME	Royal Commission on the Historical Monuments of England
RFWKM	Ruddington Knitters' Museum
RVM	Ruddington Village Museum
SRO	Suffolk Record Office
SRR	Shropshire Records and Research
VCH	Victoria County History

List of contributors

Professor Malcolm Airs, Director of Studies, OUDCE, Rewley House, 1 Wellington Square, Oxford OX1 2JA

Leigh Alston, Architectural Historian, 4 Nayland Road, Bures St Mary, Suffolk CO8 5BX

Dr P S Barnwell, Head of Rural Research Policy, Historic Buildings and Areas Research Department, English Heritage, 37 Tanner Row, York YO1 6WP

Mark Bowden, Senior Investigator, Archaeology Department, English Heritage, NMRC, Great Western Village, Kemble Drive, Swindon SN2 2GZ

Dr Garry Campion, Lecturer in Industrial Archaeology, University College Northampton, 57 York Road, Paignton, South Devon TQ4 5NN

John Cattell, Head of Research and Analysis, Historic Buildings and Areas Research Department, English Heritage, NMRC, Great Western Village, Kemble Drive, Swindon SN2 2GZ

Dr Helen Clifford, Honorary Fellow, Department of History, University of Warwick, 37 Woodstock Road, Witney, Oxfordsire OX28 1EB

Colum Giles, Head of Urban Research Policy, Historic Buildings and Areas Research Department, English Heritage, 37 Tanner Row, York YO1 6WP

Jane Grenville, Head of Department of Archaeology, University of York, The Kings Manor, York YO1 2EP

Peter Guillery, Senior Investigator, Historic Buildings and Areas Research Department, English Heritage, 23 Savile Row, London W1S 2ET

Dr Adam Menuge, Senior Investigator and Team Leader, Historic Buildings and Areas Research Department, English Heritage, 37 Tanner Row, York YO1 6WP

Peter Neaverson, Honorary Research Fellow, School of Archaeology and Ancient History, University of Leicester, Leicester LE1 7RH

Professor Marilyn Palmer, Professor of Industrial Archaeology, Head of the School of Archaeology and Ancient History, University of Leicester, Leicester LE1 7RH

Geoffrey Timmins, Reader in Industrial History, University of Central Lancashire, 231 Bolton Road, Edgworth, Bolton BL7 0HY

Dr Barrie Trinder, Independent Historian, 6 Wheelwright House, High Street, Rothwell, Northamptonshire NN14 6LE

Nicola Wray, Investigator, Historic Buildings and Areas Research Department, English Heritage, 37 Tanner Row, York YO1 6WP

Acknowledgements

This volume presents a revised and edited version of the papers presented at a conference held at Rewley House, Oxford in October 2002 as part of a continuing series aimed at exploring new directions in the study of vernacular buildings. It was hosted by Oxford University Department for Continuing Education and the programme was planned in association with the Vernacular Architecture Group and the Association for Industrial Archaeology. The editors are grateful to all the contributors who helped to make the event such a stimulating multidisciplinary occasion and who have responded with such patience to the demands that we have made of them in preparing their papers for publication. In addition we owe a special debt to Peter Neaverson, Honorary Research Fellow in the School of Archaeology and Ancient History, University of Leicester, who compiled the consolidated bibliography with meticulous attention to detail.

Publication would not have been possible without the generous financial assistance of English Heritage and we gratefully acknowledge their support for the project. The Council for British Archaeology published the proceedings of the first conference in the series as *Vernacular buildings in a changing world* (ed Sarah Pearson and Bob Meeson: CBA Research Report 126, 2001) and we are delighted that they have again undertaken to provide a permanent record of what was acknowledged as an important conference.

Summaries

The best known of the surviving physical manifestations of Britain's contribution to the development of the factory system have recently been granted World Heritage status – the Derwent Valley of Derbyshire, New Lanark in Scotland, and Saltaire in West Yorkshire. However, a large proportion of industrial output – certainly before the late 18th century and then well into the second half of the 19th century – was not produced in large, impressive buildings such as those built by Arkwright, Robert Owen or Titus Salt, but in small, often undistinguished, buildings which blended into the environment and did not attract the attention of contemporary commentators in the same way as the new factories.

This volume arose from a conference held at the Department of Continuing Education in Oxford in 2002, when the Vernacular Architecture Group and the Association for Industrial Archaeology came together to evaluate the workshop both as a building type and as a workplace. Interest in these smaller manifestations of the period of industrialisation was stimulated both by economic historians' re-evaluation of the significance of workshops for the industrial economy and process of the 18th and 19th centuries, and by recording programmes carried out by English Heritage.

The workshop economy was frequently regional in scale, so that recording programmes could be carried out, for example, on the textile workers' housing of West Yorkshire, the little mesters' shops of Sheffield, the Birmingham Jewellery Quarter, or the boot and shoe workshops of Northamptonshire. In many cases, the buildings themselves form distinct types: the increased fenestration of weavers' or knitters' workshops; the backyard workshops with small chimneys in the boot and shoe areas; and the tall tenements of the silk-weaving districts of London. The workshop, though, is equally a method of work organisation that dates back to the late medieval period and continues to the present day. Papers in this volume explore the implications of this from the point of view both of entrepreneurs, for whom the workshop was a means of organising production, and of the workers, for whom it was, generally, a preferred method of work in which they retained at least some control over the speed, rhythm and intensity of the process of production.

The volume should be of interest to buildings historians and archaeologists, industrial archaeologists and social and economic historians who recognise that industrial production has involved both factory and workshop. It will also help conservation and planning staff in regional and local government to recognise the types of buildings which characterise the industrial economy of their areas and to include these more mundane buildings in conservation schemes. Above all, this volume should encourage economic historians and those who work with the historic environment to bring their insights together to create a new understanding of the organisation of particular industries, of methods of production, and of the work and life of those engaged in them.

Résumé

Les manifestations matérielles les plus connues existant encore de la contribution faite par la Grande-Bretagne au développement du système des usines ont été récemment inscrits sur la liste du Patrimoine Mondial – la Vallée de la Derwent au Derbyshire, le New Lanark en Ecosse, et Saltaire dans le West Yorkshire. Néanmoins, une grande partie de la production industrielle – en tout cas avant la fin du 18ème siècle et durant au moins jusqu'au milieu du 19ème siècle – n'avait pas été élaborée dans de grands bâtiments impressionnants tels que ceux construits par Arkwright, Robert Owen ou Titus Salt, mais dans de petits bâtiments, souvent très ordinaires, qui se fondaient à l'environnement et qui n'attiraient pas l'attention des commentateurs contemporains comme le faisaient les nouvelles usines.

Le présent volume est le fruit d'une conférence qui a eu lieu au Department of Continuing Education [Service de la Formation Permanente] à Oxford en 2002, lorsque le Vernacular Architecture Group [Groupe de l'Architecture locale] et l'Association for Industrial Archaeology [Association pour l'Archéologie industrielle] se sont réunis afin d'évaluer l'atelier à la fois comme type de bâtiment et lieu de travail. L'intérêt témoigné pour ces manifestations plus petites de la période d'industrialisation était accentué par la réévaluation faite par les historiens économiques concernant l'importance des ateliers pour l'économie et les processus industriels du 18ème et du 19ème siècle aussi bien que par les programmes de reconnaissance exécutés par English Heritage.

L'économie des ateliers était fréquemment à l'échelle régionale, et des programmes de reconnaissance pouvaient donc être effectués, par exemple, au niveau des logements des travailleurs du textile au West Yorkshire, des échoppes des petits maîtres de Sheffield, du Quartier des Bijoutiers de Birmingham, ou des ateliers de bottes et de chaussures du Northamptonshire. Dans de nombreux cas, les bâtiments eux-mêmes constituent des types distincts: la fenestration accrue dans les ateliers de tissage ou de tricot; les ateliers dans les arrière-cours équipés de petites cheminées dans les quartiers de la botte et de la chaussure; et les immeubles à plusieurs étages dans les quartiers de tissage de la soie de Londres. Il faut bien dire que l'atelier est également une méthode d'organisation du travail qui remonte à la fin de la période médiévale et qui continue de nos jours. Les communications contenues dans ce volume explorent les implications de ce fait à la fois du point de vue des entrepreneurs, pour lesquels l'atelier constituait une méthode d'organisation de la production, et du point de vue des travailleurs, pour lesquels c'était en général la méthode de travail qu'ils préféraient car ils gardaient encore un certain contrôle sur la vitesse, le rythme et l'intensité du processus de production.

Ce volume devrait intéresser les historiens du bâtiment et les archéologues, les archéologues industriels et les historiens sociaux et économiques qui reconnaissent que la production industrielle a entraîné la participation et de l'usine et de l'atelier. Il aidera également le personnel de planification et de sauvegarde employé par le gouvernement régional et local à reconnaître les types de bâtiments qui caractérisent l'économie industrielle de leurs régions, et à inclure ces bâtiments plus ordinaires dans leurs programmes de sauvegarde. Par-dessus tout, ce volume devrait encourager les historiens économiques et ceux qui travaillent avec l'environnement historique à rassembler leurs appréciations afin de créer une nouvelle compréhension de l'organisation d'industries particulières, des méthodes de production, et du travail et de la vie de ceux qui y participaient.

Zusammenfassung

Den bekanntesten physischen Überresten des Britischen Beitrags zur Entwicklung der Manufaktur wurden kürzlich der Rang des Weltkulturerbes gewährt – das Flußtal des Derwent, New Lanark in Schottland und Saltaire in West Yorkshire. Ein großer Anteil der industriellen Leistung – vor dem späten 18. Jahrhundert bis in die Mitte des 19. Jahrhunderts – wurde jedoch nicht in den großen, imposanten Gebäuden der Erbauer wie Arkwright, Robert Owen oder Titus Salt produziert, sondern in kleinen, bescheidenen Häusern, die sich so in die Umgebung einfügten, daß sie kaum die Aufmerksamkeit von zeitgenössischen Berichterstattern auf sich zogen, deren Interesse sich auf die neuen Fabrikgebäude konzentrierte.

Dieser Beitrag ist das Ergebnis einer Konferenz, die 2002 in der Department of Continuing Education [Abteilung für Erwachsenenbildung] in Oxford gehalten wurde. Die Vernacular Architecture Group 'Forschungsgruppe für regionaltypische Architektur von Kleinwerkstätten' und der Association for Industrial Archaeology [Bund der Industriellen Archäologen] trafen zusammen, um die Bedeutung der Werkstatt als Gebäudetyp und Arbeitsplatz näher zu erforschen. Das Interesse für diese eher bescheidenen Erscheinungsformen der Industrialisation wurde durch die Neubewertung der Bedeutsamkeit von Werkstätten für die industriellen Wirtschaftsprozesse des 18. und 19. Jahrhunderts geweckt, und Bestandsaufnahmen die von 'English Heritage' durchgeführt wurden.

Die Verbreitung von Kleinwerkstätten war häufig regional begrenzt, so daß Bestandsaufnahmen in bestimmten Lokalitäten durchgeführt werden konnten, zum Beispiel für die Wohnsiedlungen der Textilarbeiter in West Yorkshire, die kleinen Besteckschmieden in Sheffield, das Juwelierviertel von Birmingham, oder die Schustereien in Northamptonshire. In vielen Fällen haben die Gebäude selbst typische Architekturformen: die großen Fenster der Weber- und Strickerwerkstätten; die Hinterhofwerkstätten der Schusterviertel mit ihren kleinen Schornsteinen, die hohen Mietskasernen der Seidenweber Bezirke in London. Die Werkstatt ist ebenfalls eine Methode der Arbeitsorganisation, die ihren Ursprung im Mittelalter hatte und bis zur heutigen Zeit fortwährt. Die Abhandlungen in diesem Band untersuchen deren Begleiterscheinungen; einerseits vom Gesichtspunkt des Unternehmers, für den die Werkstatt ein Mittel war, um die Produktion zu organisieren, und andererseits die des Handwerkers, für den es gemeinhin die bevorzugte Arbeitsweise war, da er das Arbeitstempo, den Arbeitsrythmus und die Intensität des Produktionsprozesses selbst bestimmen konnte.

Dieser Band ist vor allem für Gebäudehistoriker, Archäologen, Industriearchäologen, und Sozial- und Wirtschaftshistoriker interessant, die anerkannt haben, daß industrielle Produktion nicht nur von Fabriken sondern auch von Kleinwerkstätten ausging. Er wird auch Denkmalschützern und Planern in regionalen und städtischen Ämtern helfen, die Gebäudetypen zu erkennen, die für die regionalen industriellen Wirtschaftszweige typisch sind, um auch die weniger auffälligen Gebäude der Kleinwerkstätten in den Denkmalschutz mit einzubeziehen. Vor allem soll dieser Band Wirtschaftshistoriker und Stadthistoriker dazu anregen ihre Erkenntnisse auszutauschen und damit zu einem neuen Verständnis der Organisation bestimmter Industrien, Produktionsmethoden, und das Leben und Schaffen deren Handwerker, führen soll.

1 The workshop: type of building or method of work? *by Marilyn Palmer*

Introduction

Monument types dating from the period of industrialisation in Britain have excited a great deal of interest in the last two decades, largely because of their rapid disappearance as a result of urban renewal and the demise of many of Britain's traditional industries. Particular attention has been given, therefore, to buildings and structures of the coal industry (Thornes 1994; Hughes *et al?*1994) and to textile mills (Giles & Goodall 1992; Williams & Farnie 1992; Calladine & Fricker 1993), categories of monument of which large numbers became redundant all at once and so were in danger of wholesale demolition. Meanwhile, the workshops in which a considerable proportion of Britain's industrial output was produced have mouldered quietly. Most of them are mundane functional buildings, with little architectural pretension, and hardly noticed in the urban and rural landscapes. However, economic historians' interest in continuity as well as discontinuity in methods of industrial production has coincided both with recording programmes of workshop structures of regional significance by English Heritage, and recognition by some academics of the importance of this class of building in understanding the nature of past industrial activity.

This volume brings together contributions by both archaeologists and architectural historians to the debate on both the origins of outworking practices and how far industrial production outside the factory continued to be of significance in the period of industrialisation. All the contributions seek not just to describe the building types but also to explain their function as part of the industrial organisation prevalent in the different industries of which they form a part. As Grenville has argued strongly in relation to the recording of smaller vernacular buildings, 'it is the act of explanation that raises research above mere data-gathering' (Grenville 2001, 15). In other words, while it is important to record structures in danger of decay or demolition, explaining how their style or plan-form related to their function in the broader historical context makes a real contribution to the debate on the origins and nature of the process of industrialisation.

The conference from which this volume emanates identified the workshop as a vernacular building. Without wishing to re-open the whole debate on the nature and meaning of vernacular architecture, we have briefly to consider the workshop in this light. Undoubtedly, the 16th- and 17th-century Suffolk cloth workshops discussed by Alston fall squarely into the vernacular tradition. Timber-framed, their previous industrial function is identified both from their plan-form and, for example, from marks in the timbers indicating the existence of pentices or awnings over the retail shops which frequently fronted loomshops. The claim for later workshops to be part of the vernacular tradition is that, since most pre-date 1850 or thereabouts (there are exceptions in industries such as hosiery and boot and shoe), the workshops tend to be built in the local vernacular style, using the building materials common in that area. They formed part of the local landscape and did not stand out from it in any way. However, few historians of vernacular architecture have paid much attention to such workplaces in their studies, a notable exception being Brunskill in his pioneering *Illustrated Handbook of Vernacular Architecture* (Brunskill 1971). He identified what he called 'minor industrial vernacular', dividing it into two groups: the first, early cottage industry, witnessed both the modification of a living room to accommodate simple machinery and the provision of a separate room as a workplace, while the second, later cottage industry, resulted in the provision of specialised buildings for particular crafts. Whereas the first group were largely rural, the second group included buildings in groups or short terraces which were erected in both the country and expanding towns (Brunskill 1971, 160–3).

However, as well as being a class of vernacular building, the kinds of workshops discussed in this volume are also the physical envelopes in which particular forms of work organisation took place. The primary purpose of this chapter is to examine workshops as workplaces, putting them in their social and economic context and demonstrating how they reveal both change and continuity in the gradual process of industrialisation. As most of this book is devoted to the English scene, an attempt will also be made to set this in its contemporary European context.

The definition of a workshop

Defining a workshop is not at all easy. The *Oxford English Dictionary* definition of a room, apartment or building in which manual or industrial work was carried on covers most of the types of building with which we will be concerned but does not help to differentiate between them. Many rooms in domestic buildings served as workplaces, as for example when weaving looms or stocking frames were placed in them from the medieval period onwards and family life went on around them. This type of workplace has been examined by Campion in his study of East Midland industries, where he used spatial analysis to try to analyse the potential conflict between working and living space in such situations (Campion 1996). It also applies to the tenements housing the silk workers of Lyons (Barre 2001, and see Guillery this volume). An 'apartment' could be taken to mean a dedicated room used as a workplace in a domestic building, such as the purpose-built houses incorporating workshops, most of which date from the last two decades of the 18th century and the first half of the 19th in various branches of the textile industries. These are considered by several authors in this volume. Finally, workshops were often placed in separate buildings where room was available or where the nature of the work made a domestic location impossible, as in the small metal industries. However, the part of the *OED* definition 'in which manual or industrial work was carried out' does not enable us to differentiate between a workshop and a factory in the later stages of the period we are considering. Is it, for example, essential that a workshop should be a place in which the work that was carried out did not make use of mechanical power but was wholly hand-powered? That is probably broadly true, but in the 19th century many of the buildings traditionally classified as workshops made some use of power, as in the engineering workshops where lathes and presses were driven from overhead line-shafting or, in the case of the Coventry cottage factories in the ribbon industry, power from a central steam engine was supplied to looms worked in domestic workshops. Is the workshop, then, a building that housed a particular form of work organisation? Perhaps the most satisfactory definition of workshop is a building or even a room housing skilled operatives working on a particular product: they might not control the actual product, which could well be marketed by someone else, but they did still control the processes of production. Within reason, they could control the rhythm and intensity of the process by which the product was manufactured, something that became impossible under the factory system. Workshop production, certainly in its later stages, depended on the sub-division of the production process into a number of distinct operations, each of which could be carried out by different operatives. Diderot's description of the eighteen different stages in the manufacture of a pin is well known (Diderot 1755, Vol 5, 'Epingle') and in this volume Menuge points out the different stages in the manufacture of boots and shoes. Workshop labour, then, usually resulted in a product being manufactured, but not all the preparation processes necessarily took place under that one roof: nailers produced nails in their workshops from rods of iron produced in rolling and slitting mills, while weavers – at least by the late 18th century – wove thread which had been spun elsewhere, even on spinning machines in a factory.

A workshop as referred to in most instances in this volume, then, is a room or building in which a skilled workman or woman had a degree of control over the rhythm and intensity of the processes undertaken to produce something which could be a finished article or only one part of that article, regardless of whether any mechanical power was used within the workshop. This definition will now be used to look more or less chronologically at the different kinds of work organisation which have taken place in workshops since 1400 and the ways in which the actual buildings reflect the nature of the work carried out.

Urban artisan production

At the beginning of the period covered in this volume, the majority of workshops were urban, albeit in small towns as in Suffolk (see Alston this volume). Manufacturing was generally carried out by skilled artisans in households where a significant proportion of the total household income was derived from the manufacture or processing of goods for sale. Many artisans were grouped into craft guilds by this time, partly to regulate entry into their crafts by means of apprenticeship but also to protect themselves against exploitation by the merchants or entrepreneurs often responsible for marketing the goods made, particularly if they were destined for the European market. Swanson has shown that in the later Middle Ages there were 56 different craft guilds in York whose ordinances regulating work have been recorded (Swanson 1989, 111). Most of the workshops in which the artisans operated were comparatively small, and guild ordinances frequently restricted the number of apprentices a master could take. In the mid-16th century, various regulating acts were passed, including one which restricted master weavers from owning more than two looms, suggesting that attempts to group weavers into larger workshops had been made (Jack of Newbury, for example) but was generally something to be resisted. This Act was invoked by weavers in both the West of England and West Yorkshire in the early 19th century as they fought to retain the small domestic workshop in the face of attempts made by clothiers to group looms together in large collective workshops (Palmer & Neaverson 2004).

Few, if any, medieval workshops remain in recognisable form, but as more and more archaeological excavations in towns take note of the existence of medieval and later deposits rather than stripping sites to get down to the Roman layers, we are getting better ideas of the layout and grouping of medieval workshops. This point is developed later in this volume by Grenville. However, in the market towns of Suffolk which have been spared much later development, timber-framed workshops surviving from the very important woollen industry of the 16th and 17th centuries can be identified, as is discussed here by Alston. Leech, then of RCHME, undertook in the late 1970s an important survey of late 17th- and early 18th-century houses incorporating workplaces for looms in the Somerset town of Frome. The Trinity area was developed as three major landowners leased land for building and over half the houses built on these plots were rented by people in the cloth trade. The style of houses, with the main ground floor room, or hall, occupying the whole street frontage, made housing a loom comparatively easy and many had an attic that doubtless served as a wool loft (Leech 1981).

The decline of the craft guilds in the 18th century did not, of course, mean the end of artisan production. Households of skilled workers continued to produce goods in small workshops, especially in trades where the raw materials were small in quantity and often valuable, as in the jewellery and small metal trades, and where the skill of the handicraft worker was paramount. Equipment was also small in size – the anvil, hammer, file and grindstone, followed later by the stamp and press – and could be fitted into the small urban workshop (see Berg 1994, 83). Eighteenth-century travellers such as Defoe in the 1720s and the Swedish 'industrial spy', Reinhold Rucker Angerstein in the years 1753–55, emphasised the continuing industrial nature of towns where the products of the countryside were still often processed for sale as well as specialist goods being produced. In Exeter, Angerstein viewed fulling mills, cloth presses, flour mills and a malt kiln as well as several iron manufactories (Angerstein 1753–55, 75–8). Nottingham 'echoed to the thumping and squeaking of stocking frames, which can be heard at all time, encouraging the people to be diligent and industrious' (Angerstein 1753–55, 194). Urban workshops still existed in considerable numbers: not all industry had migrated to the countryside, as is so often argued.

Urban artisan production in the 18th and 19th centuries is exemplified by the so-called 'toy' trades of Birmingham and other towns in the West Midlands – boxes, brassware, jewellery, buckles and buttons. In these towns, a multitude of small family firms, descendants of the medieval artisan household, operated in workshops in attics or erected in back gardens, as Cattell describes later in this volume. The heads of these small firms were often known as 'garret masters' or 'small masters', a name echoed in Sheffield by the use of the term 'little mesters' to describe the independent artisans who manufactured cutlery, edge tools and other metal goods in small urban workshops which have recently been recorded by English Heritage (see Wray in this volume). Maps of many 18th-century towns indicate the spread of industrial development in the form of workshops in various quarters of the town, often grouped by products. Tanning was still very much an urban industry, as urban excavations often indicate, and, to give a European example, the splendid tanner's quarter in Colmar in Alsace shown in Figure 1.1 was only saved from demolition about twenty years ago because of public protest. A further European example of the system of urban artisan production which has left some very distinctive buildings is the area of Lyons in France known as La Croix-Rousse. Lyons had a long-standing silk industry which was revived after the French Revolution, but experienced dramatic growth after the invention of a replacement for the draw-loom by Joseph-Marie Jacquard in 1804. The development of 'la colline de la Croix-Rousse' to the north of Lyons was encouraged by the city authorities, who provided roads but left it to developers to construct the large blocks with their distinctive windows which provided light for the tall looms. There was little restriction on the developers who provided the housing, so they built the blocks very tall and close together (Fig 1.2), resulting in the distinctive pattern on Croix-Rousse with many passage ways between and under buildings which, incidentally, saved the finished silk from getting wet when it was being taken to the merchants' quarters whose more elaborate houses occupied other squares nearby. This example has been taken up by Guillery later in the volume as a comparison with the silk-weavers' houses of Spitalfields in London.

Proto-industrialisation

The system of artisan production was not, however, by the 18th century confined to towns. Much has been written about the migration of industry from the town to the countryside and the growth of rural industry in some key regions, described by Mendels as ' proto-industrialisation' (Mendels 1972). He argued that proto-industrialisation was associated with the increasing demand for consumer goods from the 16th century onwards, which grew at such a pace that the traditional, guild-regulated urban production could not efficiently respond. Manufacturing, he argued, therefore spread to the countryside and was combined with agriculture in a system of dual economy. This created a favourable climate for the second phase of industrialisation or, as Mendels put it (1972, 245), 'prior proto-industrialization tended to induce the passage to modern industry'. The concept has been much criticised, but has nevertheless given rise to a great deal of research into rural industrialisation and helped to stimulate interest in the existence of the workshop. Importantly, from the point of view of this volume, two different systems of industrialisation in this phase have been identified, generally known as *kaufsystem* of artisan production and the *verlagsytem*, in which materials were put out to the workforce by merchant capitalists (see Berg, Hudson & Sonenscher 1983b, 19–24). Contrary to the widely-held belief that artisan production was an urban feature, it has been pointed out by several economic historians that the *kaufsystem* played a substantial role in rural industry, depending not only on the branch of industry in which it operated but also on the agricultural potential of the region in which it was carried out. Hudson has suggested that the reason the independent artisan survived in the woollen-producing area of the West Riding of Yorkshire because it was generally more fertile than the areas in which worsteds were produced on the putting-out or *verlagsystem* (Hudson 1983). Holdings

4 *The vernacular workshop*

Figure 1.1 Tanners' workshops along the River Schwendi in Colmar, Upper Alsace. The tall, narrow timber-framed buildings had a loft for drying skins. (© Marilyn Palmer)

Figure 1.2 Lyons, La Croix-Rousse from the Quai Saint-Vincent on the River Saône. The hill is dominated by the Maison Brunet tenement in Place Rouville, which was built in the 1820s and said to have a window for every day of the year. (© Marilyn Palmer)

The workshop: type of building or method of work? 5

Figure 1.3 The Halifax Piece Hall built between 1775 and 1779, to which yeoman clothiers brought their 'pieces' for purchase by merchants. (© Crown Copyright. NMR)

Figure 1.4 Farmers supplemented their income by building weavers' workshops grouped around their farmsteads, as here at New Tame fold in the parish of Saddleworth, now in Greater Manchester. (© Marilyn Palmer)

were often larger, and so the domestic clothier had a reasonably-sized plot that could cushion him against periods of bad trade and also helped him to accumulate capital. The small clothier could organise the production of cloth in his workshop, helped by his family, and take the finished product to the cloth halls of the area, such as the surviving one in Halifax (Fig 1.3). Hudson has also pointed out that this accumulation of capital on the part of the small clothiers enabled them to get together and build 'company mills' for fulling, scribbling, carding and slubbing, possibly even dyeing, in the late 18th and early 19th centuries, and so maintain their independence from the entrepreneur except for the final marketing (Hudson 1983, 133–40). Many of the farm-based workshops (Fig 1.4) in the West Riding may well therefore be representative of the survival of the independent artisan as described by Defoe in the 1720s rather than the putting-out system which has often been assumed to dominate

6 *The vernacular workshop*

Figure 1.5 Workshops forming part of a clothier's house: Courtfield House, Trowbridge, dating from the mid-18th century. (© Marilyn Palmer)

Figure 1.6 A fine clothier's house at Holt, near Melksham, rebuilt in the rococo style by John Phelps in the 1730s. Workshops and dyehouses, formerly in the adjacent garden were demolished in the 1880s but ponds associated with the dyehouse and some tall stone columns remain, the latter once supporting chains on which cloths were hung for tentering. (© Marilyn Palmer)

Figure 1.7 Part of the Rotes Haus in Monschau in Germany, built for the Scheibler family in the 1760s. The doorway to the workers' section of the building, marked by a pelican, can be seen on the left with an adjacent workshop on the right. (© Marilyn Palmer)

the rural textile industries. In reality, neither system of production was confined solely to either the countryside or the towns, because the towns themselves were so closely associated with their hinterlands. So, systems of artisan production in towns could result in the myriads of small workshops which dominate parts of Birmingham and Sheffield, and in the countryside could result in farm-based workshops, not just in the textile industries but also in the small metal trades, such as the many small forges for hand tools around Sheffield which are either attached to farm buildings or sited in gardens and yards (Wray *et al*, 2001).

Capitalist production

By contrast with artisan production, capitalist-dominated production is a form of industrial organisation which could result in very different forms of workshops. Two of these will next be considered, the first being the workshops provided by entrepreneurs which often formed part of their own homes for purposes of quality control, prevention of embezzlement, etc. The second type of workshop associated with capitalist production is the workshop that is characteristic of the *verlagsystem*, in which the entrepreneurs rarely financed the buildings themselves but provided the materials that were worked on within them and marketed the finished product. This type of workshop proliferated in the late 18th and early 19th centuries and can still be seen in large numbers in various regions associated with different industries.

The manufacture of textiles requires a great many preparation and finishing processes apart from the familiar spinning and weaving. As we have seen, manufacture by the independent artisan and his family was one way of getting these done in the woollen industry. Elsewhere, a capitalist system developed whereby the preparation, manufacture and finishing as well as the marketing was organised by clothiers. This was prevalent in the broadcloth industry of south-west England and in the worsted areas of West Yorkshire: the reasons for the co-existence of clothier-dominated and artisan production in the latter has been the subject of debate among economic historians (see Hudson 1983). Among the first distinctive buildings to develop in the woollen industry were the preparation and finishing workshops, usually forming part of the clothier's own house. In the south-west of England, the earliest references to such 'workhouses', as they were called, date from the 15th century. Insurance policies, deeds and rate books provide evidence of the existence of 'houses and workhouses under one roof', as at Courtfield House in Trowbridge (Fig 1.5), where workshop windows can clearly be seen under the eaves. Many of the elegant clothiers' houses in the Wiltshire towns of Trowbridge and Bradford-on-Avon once had dyeshops and finishing shops to the rear (Rogers 1976). An elegant clothiers house, the

8 *The vernacular workshop*

Figure 1.8 North Street, Cromford: the best-known row of workers' housing provided by Richard Arkwright in the 1770s for employees at his mills. The windows at eaves level indicate the workshops for weaving or knitting, thought originally to be linked together along the row. (© Marilyn Palmer)

Courts in Holt, had finishing shops attached and the posts which held the tenters for drying the fulled cloth still remain (Fig 1.6). The close physical relationship between the clothiers' houses and the industrial organisation they supervised remained into the factory age, with clothiers' houses continuing to exist alongside powered factories, for example at Lodgemore Mill in Gloucestershire.

This was a phenomenon which was common in Europe as well as England. Mende has shown that clothier families in Lower Saxony gained privileges from the Elector of Mainz to avoid guild restrictions, and began to build houses in towns such as Grossbartloff and Goettingen which had finishing shops and warehouses either incorporated into them or built alongside. As Mende has said, 'the 18th-century woollen and worsted manufacture was centred in the owners' residence. It was the heart of the business, enabling the owner to keep visual control over both the stages of manufacture and the quality of the products. An eye-catching attic or warehouse represented his wealth and economic potential, underlining the character of his residence as the heart of the factory and thus serving as a means of publicity' (Mende 2001, 62). Figure 1.7 is the Rotes Haus in Monschau, an ancient village in the winding gorge of the river Rur in the Eifel massif in Germany, centred upon fulling mills from the 16th century. Built for the Scheibler family around 1760, the Rotes Haus was a clothier's house incorporating both warehouse and workshops, the two separate entrances for the master and workforce identified by the Golden Helmet on the residential side and the Pelican on the commercial entrance. Workshops forming part of the entrepreneur's house also existed in other industries, such as the hosiery industry discussed by Campion later in this volume.

Elements of paternalism are evident here, perhaps another aspect of proto-industrialisation which is worth considering briefly. The *bruk* system in the Swedish iron industry is a good example, in which the iron furnaces often formed part of a rural estate that was organised in a paternalistic manner, the *brukspatroner* providing housing and social services. Workshops grew up in these estates, from which sprang the engineering workshops or machine shops which became so important by the 19th century (see Dahlström 2001). The system operated elsewhere: in

Figure 1.9 One of the weavers' houses planned by John Ching in the 1790s on Yerbury Street in Trowbridge. (© Marilyn Palmer)

France, many of the charcoal iron furnaces and their surrounding workshops, forges, etc. were built in the shadow of the chateau owning and organising the industry. The role of the landowner in industrialisation has recently been emphasised by a group of archaeologists in north-west England: the 'Manchester Methodology' attempts to relate the introduction of new building types into the archaeological record to the types of landowner who provided them (Nevell 2003). Within the UK, paternalism is evident in the cotton communities of the East Midlands, Cheshire, Scotland, etc, where paternalistic employers created new communities to provide workers for a new industry but in some instances also provided workshops, as in North Street in Cromford (Fig 1.8). In Belper in Derbyshire, Jedediah Strutt attracted female and child labour into his mills, but provided nailing workshops for many of the men, building up an industry which had existed prior to his construction of cotton spinning mills in the 1790s. How far such actions were paternalistic and how far merely good business practice is a matter of debate, but certainly many industrialists were responsible for much of the social framework of settlements surrounding their mills and factories.

The putting-out system

The question of paternalism leads us to a fuller consideration of the putting-out or *verlagsystem* in which materials were put out by merchant capitalists to workers in their own homes – or, we should say, rented homes. The capitalist or entrepreneur organised production, putting out parts of it to different groups of skilled workers – spinners, weavers, makers of nails, closers in the shoe trade and so on. Under this system, the workforce had less freedom in what they were able to produce than in the *kaufsytem* of artisan producers but still, to some extent, retained control of the intensity and rhythm of the processes of production. The classic exponents of the putting-out system have generally linked it to rural production, with merchant capitalists in urban centres taking advantage of cheap rural labour, but certainly by the 19th century it also operated in towns. The system could be described as dispersed production under capitalist control.

The textile industries, particularly those in the West of England and in the worsted producing areas of West Yorkshire, were largely organised on this system. In the West of England, the entrepreneur had put out both spinning and weaving to different groups of people in the 18th century – often those in the villages surrounding the principal finishing centres of Trowbridge, Bradford-on-Avon, Malmesbury and so on. The spinning process did not really need specially adapted premises, and generally became a factory-based industry from the last two decades of the 18th century. The great increase in yarn production following on from this resulted in an explosion of houses incorporating weaving shops being constructed from the first decade of the 19th century. Few of these were built by the weavers themselves: most were financed by people outside the industry, such as those in the retail trades, as a means of investment. For example, in Trowbridge a local glazier and plumber, John Ching, leased in the 1790s a close to build weavers' houses, which were needed 'from the great want of houses at Trowbridge and from the very flourishing state of the trade there'. He planned two rows of three-storey houses incorporating weaving shops, which were built in a slightly altered form from his original proposals (see Palmer & Neaverson 2003, 142) (Fig 1.9). In the South West, the weavers' houses were more scattered than those of West Yorkshire, being built in small terraces or as single-storey buildings attached to houses, often in squatter settlements where there was more room to spare (Fig 1.10). It is tempting to speculate that the single-storey weaving shops housed the broad looms characteristic of the West of England industry, and that the top-storey weaving shops accommodated the narrow looms for the newer cassimeres or fine, fancy cloths. It is, however, clear from various auction sale documents that many weavers had both types of looms to enable them to meet different orders from the firms to which they worked. In West Yorkshire, top-storey workshops

10 *The vernacular workshop*

Figure 1.10 A largely unaltered weavers' terrace off the Charfield Road at Kingswood in Gloucestershire, with weaving shops on the two lower floors. (© Marilyn Palmer)

Figure 1.11 A purpose-built row of weavers' houses in the hamlet of Bradley Green, near Wotton-under-Edge in Gloucestershire. The position of the four ground- and first-floor workshops is marked by the paired windows. (© Marilyn Palmer)

were more common and Caffyn has shown how many weavers' houses there were also financed by people outside the trade (Caffyn 1986). Equally, in Gloucestershire, a terraced row at Bradley Green near Wotton-under-Edge (Fig 1.11) resembles the weaving folds of West Yorkshire. Between Corner Farm and its outbuildings is a row of four early 19th-century rubble-built cottages with brick lintels over segmental-headed windows. The problem of combining domestic and functional space is solved here by placing one weaving shop with a pair of windows above that of the adjacent cottage, giving each a living room, small kitchen, two bedrooms and work-space for two broad looms.

Figure 1.12 A timber-framed house in the important hosiery village of Shepshed in Leicestershire. An extension has been added on the left and large windows inserted at front and rear. (© Marilyn Palmer)

Figure 1.13 Framework knitting occupied many people in Tewkesbury, Gloucestershire, in the 18th and 19th centuries. These late 18th-century cottages in St Mary's Lane, with unusual elongated windows to workshops on the first floor, have been restored by the Civic Trust. (© Marilyn Palmer)

With so many of these obvious weavers' domestic workshops existing in West Yorkshire, Timmins became puzzled by their lack in Lancashire until he carried out fieldwork with an adult education group and discovered the many cellar workshops in the county, particularly suited to the manufacture of cotton (Timmins 1977). The linen industry in Belgium presents us with another variant on the domestic workshop. Flax was very dusty raw material, even after the scutching process, and so houses were built with through passageways to allow the flax dust to escape when the material was being prepared before hand spinning.

The hosiery industry was mainly located in the East Midlands and was probably the branch of the textile industry which resisted the factory system for longest. The invention of the knitting frame c1589 introduced one of the earliest textile machines into the home environment. The workplaces which housed this machine reflect changes in the technology and organisation of the industry, indicating four phases of development. The first, dating from the late 17th century when the industry began to flourish in the East Midlands, was the insertion of large windows into workplaces in timber-framed houses, as in Shepshed in Leicestershire (Fig 1.12). Secondly, as with handloom weaving, rows of purpose-built houses were constructed in the late 18th or early 19th centuries, their workshops with large windows being placed on the ground, first or top floors. Figure 1.13 shows St Mary's Lane in Tewkesbury, an important hosiery centre outside the East Midlands. The third phase was the construction of garden workshops, generally in areas with plenty of land to spare as in the squatter settlements of the West Country woollen industry, while the final phase was the collective, non-powered workshop; the workshops of these latter two phases usually housed wide knitting frames which were not easily accommodated in a domestic environment (see Palmer 1994).

The division of labour for different parts of a production process was partly responsible for enabling the putting-out system to last well beyond the introduction of the factory system. As Menuge shows later in this volume, the boot and shoe industry of Northamptonshire is probably the one which most exemplifies the use of workshops in combination with small factories in the production process. In the nail and chain industry of the West Midlands, the simplicity of the tools required enabled workshop industry to continue. The nailer obtained iron rod either from the warehouse of a nailmaster or by means of a middleman, usually the notorious 'fogger' who exploited the nailers in hard times much as the bag hosier did in the stocking trade. The nailshop of

12 The vernacular workshop

Figure 1.14   Nailmakers' workshops to the rear of terraced houses in Dudley, West Midlands. (Courtesy of Dudley Leisure Services)

Figure 1.15   Chainmakers' workshop at Mushroom Green, Dudley Wood, West Midlands. Note the chimneys for the individual hand forges. (© Marilyn Palmer)

the Black Country is perhaps the most primitive of the all the domestic work premises so far considered (Fig 1.14). J E White, reporting to the Children's Employment Commission in 1864, said that ' the nailers' forges remain as they are described to have been in the neighbouring districts 20 years ago, small gloomy hovels adjoining the cottages with barely room for the two to half a dozen workers' (BPP 1864, 54). The small workshops, often placed at the ends of terraced rows or behind cottages, contained a hearth, anvil and the tommy hammer attached to its springy larch pole to provide the upward lift. Such simple set-ups enabled the nailers to work to order, adjusting the tools to make nails for special purposes. From the 1830s, they faced competition from the machine-made nail trade and their numbers declined, but once again it is obvious from documentary evidence that hand nailers hung on to their domestic way of life for as long as possible. The American Elihu Burritt said in 1868:

> I always love to walk about in the villages of the nail-makers. The clinking of hundreds of their little hammers supply the aria to the great concertos and oratorio of mechanical industry. They are poorly-paid and have to work long and hard to earn bread in competition with machinery. Indeed, it shows the superabundance and exigencies of labour that nails should be made at all by hand at this late day of mechanical improvements. But thousands of families in this district have inherited the trade from several generations of their ancestors, and they are born to it, apparently with a physical conformation to the work. Then thousands of cottages are equally conformed to it in their structure. For each has a little shop-room attached to it generally under the same roof. Thus the whole business becomes a domestic industry or house employment for the family, and frequently every member, male or female, young or old, has his or her rod in the fire all the day long and often far into the night (Burritt 1868, 228–9).

The chain industry did not really develop in the Black Country until the nail industry was beginning to succumb to competition from machine-made nails. What is surprising, therefore, is that, in the 1840s and 1850s, the chain industry developed on in workshops at all. A chainmaking workshop differed from a nailing workshop in that several workmen operated in the same building, each having his own hearth usually against the outer walls. From the exterior, then, the most obvious feature of the small, rectangular building is the number of chimneys on each side as can be seen in the surviving chainshop at Mushroom Green (Fig 1.15), now operated by the Black Country Society.

The chainshop exemplifies the final stage of workshop development, the collective, non-powered workplace, not incorporating domestic accommodation, where the processes were brought under one roof for purposes of supervision and quality control. The machines used were not yet powered, meaning that the worker still had some control over the intensity and rhythm of the process. This was true of the chainshop: it was also true of the loomshops introduced into the textile industries and the collective workshops in the hosiery industry. This production method may well have first been used in the woollen industry by Jack of Newbury, and William Stumpe who placed his looms in the aisles of Malmesbury Abbey in the 16th century. Figure 1.16 is the so-called Maison Closset in the town of Verviers, in Belgium, constructed in the late 17th century for the Peltzner family, and provides evidence for collective hand-powered textile production in a heavily fenestrated building which was converted into housing in 1924. The weavers of Gloucestershire and Wiltshire were very concerned, as suggested earlier,

Figure 1.16 The so-called Maison Closset in the town of Verviers, in Belgium, constructed in the late 17th century for the Peltzner family, housed collective hand-powered textile production. (© Marilyn Palmer)

about the development of loomshops in the first decade of the 19th century, and many were built (see Fig 1.17). Many of the clothiers argued, however, that it was not worth their while to provide buildings for looms when they could get the work done much more cheaply in the weavers' own homes (see Palmer & Neaverson 2003, 145). Loomshops in West Yorkshire were identified by the RCHME team, often forming part of the mill complex (Giles & Goodall 1992). Many of these buildings, though, certainly in the West Country, housed not looms but spinning jennies, even into the 19th century. Rogers has shown how workshops on The Green in Calne in Wiltshire (Fig 1.18) housed jennies, eventually driven by a horse-wheel (Rogers 1976, 84). The advent of the large workshop in the hosiery industry was largely brought about by the development of the wide frame for the production of shawls or several stockings at once, but by the mid-19th century, narrow stocking frames and glove frames were grouped in them too, as at Bushloe End near Leicester (Fig 1.19). The Sheffield cutlery and edge tool industry also made use of many large urban workshops, often in multiple occupation, where processes such as grinding were carried on (Wray in this volume).

Power, of course, was increasingly used in the 19th century, although the point being made in this chapter is for how long many workers resisted the break-up of the domestic system of production, whether artisan or putting out, that usually followed the introduction of mechanical power. The domestic workshop is evidence for worker resistance to life in the factory and a preference for the patterns of existence within the family, albeit on lower wages than workers would have received had they made a different choice. The Commissioners' reports of the mid-19th century emphasise the poverty of the weavers at a time when, in the south-west, the whole textile industry, not just handloom weaving, was in decline. Yet the weavers who worked in collective loomshops and earned a steady wage are described by the Gloucestershire Commissioner W A Miles, as the most discontented of the lot:

> The factory weavers, although earning the most money, are the most dissatisfied class, endeavouring by every means to underrate their earnings and condition, while the poorer outdoor weaver, who does not earn half the amount of these men . . . is patient in his sufferings and privations (BPP 1840–41, 437).

Why should this be so? The shop weavers resented

14   *The vernacular workshop*

Figure 1.17   A jenny or loom shop in Church Street, Bradford-on-Avon. It is now in the yard of the later Abbey Mill and both have been converted to housing. (© Marilyn Palmer)

Figure 1.18   The Green in Calne, Wiltshire, described by Pevsner as a spacious triangle with the wealthiest houses in Georgian Calne. There are several clothiers' houses here, while the large building with the tie rod ends was probably used for carding and spinning wool. (© Marilyn Palmer)

Figure 1.19 An interior view of the framework knitting workshop at Bushloe End in Wigston Magna, Leicestershire, showing the closely placed knitting frames. (© Marilyn Palmer)

Figure 1.20 Cottage factories built in 1857 by the Cash Brothers in Coventry. The top-floor workshops housed Jacquard looms, hence the very large windows. (© Marilyn Palmer.)

'the deprivation of their little messes, such as a cup of tea, or hot vegetables at dinner time . . . which in the factory is impracticable, owing the distance many of them live from the shop'. They also disliked 'the non-employment of their wives and children, who formerly could act as quillers, and occasionally, as regards the wife, relieve the man from the loom while he worked in his garden, or earned a trifle in another way' – to which Miles rather unkindly although probably justly added 'or went to the beershop and *lost* a trifle another way' (BPP 1840–41, 437).

When the home was also the workplace, the rhythm of family life provided an essential context for the domestic weaver, even though he was no longer an independent artisan but part of a capitalist economy. He lived within what was usually a large family, since weavers, along with other groups of workers who could earn a cash wage at an early age, tended to marry early and have large families (see also Mendels 1972, 250–2). What was euphemistically described by the relieving officer of the parish of Dilton Marsh in Wiltshire in 1840 as 'company-keeping' often resulted in pregnancy followed by marriage: the census returns show that weavers had often married and produced one or two children in their late teens. This undoubtedly led to overcrowded cottages: W A Miles commented on the untidy state of cottages in Cam in Gloucestershire in 1840, saying that it was 'an unavoidable consequence of large families and small cottages; thus you find them washing, drying, cooking, weaving, quilling and all the other necessary culinary and working duties performed in one small, confined apartment' (BPP 1840–41, 461). Yet this is the view of a man from a different walk of life and not that of the weavers themselves, who complained about the decline in wages but not about their living conditions.

The collective workshop was one step nearer the relentless system imposed within the factory by the use of the waterwheel or steam engine, which meant that the worker no longer had control over the rhythm and intensity of the process. However, there are a few examples of workshops that compromised between the need of the employers and the demands of the workers by making use of centrally-provided power. Some of these were in the small metal industries both in London and Birmingham. However, probably the most interesting examples of the compromise between the factory and the workshop are the silk weaving workshops or cottage factories of Coventry which date from the mid-19th century (Prest 1960, 96–112). Ten years or so after handloom weavers had destroyed the first steam-powered factory erected by Joseph Beck in 1830, neighbouring weavers began to co-operate in renting steam engines which were installed in nearby yards and the power was taken to their workshops by overhead shafting. The idea was adopted by a number of manufacturers who presumably saw this as a way of minimising the resistance to the introduction of new technology which they had previously encountered. Rows of purpose-built, three-storey weavers' houses were erected around a central engine house that supplied power to the looms housed in the top-floor workshops. According to the factory inspectors, there were 343 of these 'cottage factories' in existence by the 1860s, each separate weaver's house being classed as a factory because it was supplied with power. Because of the wartime destruction of much of Coventry, the only ones which now survive are some of the 'hundred houses' built alongside the Coventry Canal by the Quakers John and Joseph Cash in 1857 (Fig 1.20). The cottage factories represent an interesting combination of artisan determination to retain independence and entrepreneurial attempts at control of the workforce. It would be interesting to know why this system was not adopted in other weaving colonies which had access to coalfields, as in Yorkshire and Lancashire, but there is no evidence that this happened as far as the author is aware.

Conclusion

This chapter has attempted to outline the development of the workshop both as a distinctive type of building and as a particular form of industrial organisation. Within the non-powered workshop, the worker, to a greater or lesser degree, remained in control of the rhythm and intensity of work of the work carried out even if control of the actual product has been lost. Artisan production or the *kaufsystem* goes back to the towns of the late medieval period, but continued late into the 19th century in towns such as Sheffield and Birmingham as well as in the rural areas of the West Yorkshire worsted industry. The growth of merchant capital was partly responsible for the other type of industrial organisation, the *verlagsystem* or putting-out system, which took advantage of the division of labour which the production of an article entails, for example between weaving and spinning; between clicking, closing and lasting in the boot and shoe industries; and between the production of rods of iron and the manufacture of nails. The construction of the workshops themselves was not generally undertaken by either the worker or the entrepreneur, certainly in the last decades of the 18th and the 19th centuries, but by speculative builders who followed local styles of construction. However, capitalist control of the processes of production was sometimes tempered by paternalism, as in the ironworks of Sweden, America and France as well as the paternalistic cotton spinning communities of Arkwright, Strutt, David Dale and Robert Owen. I have elsewhere referred to the survival of the workshop system beyond the introduction of the factory as a contribution to the archaeology of resistance, the buildings indicating how this particular group of artisans cherished their illusory independence and resisted integration into the factory system for as long as possible (Palmer & Neaverson 2003, 127). Preliminary research suggests that workshop survival was more common in Britain than in Europe or America, where at least in the textile industries machinery was accepted rather more readily than in Britain (Palmer & Neaverson 2001b, 52). The cherished independence of the workforce was, of course, largely illusory, despite their tenacity in clinging on to their domestic workplaces: they had become essentially a dispersed industrial workforce, albeit one resisting the final step of accepting powered production.

2 Making luxuries: the image and reality of luxury workshops in 18th-century London

by Helen Clifford

Introduction

In this contribution I want to present an overview of the different contexts in which the manufacture of luxury goods have been considered, both in the 18th century and by historians. That we can do this suggests that the study of luxury manufactures has come of age, and that we need to stand back and take stock of the different models of practice that have been revealed. I hope that it will raise a series of questions that will contribute to our understanding of vernacular workshops and the frameworks we use to think about them. If we address issues of space, site, labour and its divisions, and authorship, then the apparent gap between the vernacular and the polite workshop closes, and common points of debate emerge. It is a *leitmotif* of this paper that further study in this area demands the crossing of disciplinary and material-based subject boundaries.

The impact of sub-contracting and specialisation

> Different operations may be distributed with economy to different hands, whose age, strength or ability are proportioned to what their task requires (Rouquet 1755, 33)

One of the most important contributions to our knowledge about manufacturing in the 18th century has been the acknowledgement of sub-contracting and specialisation within the urban luxury trades. Yet, as a form of divided labour, it has been overlooked by historians until quite recently. Adam Smith's idea of the division of labour (espoused in his *Wealth of Nations* (Smith 1776)) had been applied to more mundane products, for example pins (the manufacture of which took eighteen separate operations) and buttons. Smith stressed, as an 18th-century economist, that as a result of this division of labour things cost less and could be produced in greater quantity. It is perhaps the emphasis on cheapness and quantity that encouraged a certain, what I would call 'consumer blindness', on the part of 18th-century customers and 20th-century historians to the application of this type of production to more expensive luxury goods.

The virtues of specialisation were well known in the 18th century. Campbell writing an advice book to parents concerned with apprenticing their children in 1747, claimed specialisation was the key to success in manufacture, giving England 'an advantage over many Foreign Nations as they are obliged to employ the same hand in every branch of the trade, and it is impossible to expect that a man employed in such an infinite variety can finish his work to any perfection, at least, not so much as he who is constantly employed in one thing' (Campbell 1747, 142).

Jean André Rouquet the critical Swiss commentator on *The Present State of the Arts in England* published in 1755, admired the facility of organisation demonstrated by the English, characterised by the steel trade, whereby 'different operations may be distributed with economy to different hands, whose age, strength or ability are proportioned to what their task requires' (Rouquet 1755, 33). Such was the success of this method of manufacture that, in a gratifying reversal of the usual state of affairs, the French attempted to imitate the English, sending over spies to try and work out how the system of sub-contracting worked. Le Turc reported back from England to his masters in Paris that 'There is no country where the labour is so divided as here. No country, consequently, where the whole of trade is so difficult to get hold of'. However he was frustrated that 'No worker can explain to you the chain of operations, being perpetually occupied only with a small part, listen to him on anything outside that and you will be burdened with error. However it is this little understood division which results in the cheapness of labour, the perfection of the work and the greater security of the property of the manufacturer' (Harris 1992, 170).

Baron Angerstein, the Swedish spy, 'had to use many tricks and much effort' before he could gain admitance to the many factories he had come from Sweden to see. Once inside the buckle factory in Wednesbury he noted 'each worker had his individual and specialised work to do, some were occupied with filing, others with punching, polishing, grinding, final cleaning and so on' (Angerstein 1753–55, 41).

Each trade had its own range of specialists. The production of a coach for example relied on the skills of quite separate carcase builders, carvers, gilders, painters, lacemen, chasers, harness makers, mercers, bitt makers, milliners, saddlers, woollen drapers, and cover makers (Snodin 1990, 33). *The Book of Trades or Library of Useful Arts* published in the 1760s explained that the craft of the coach maker was 'divided into several parts, whose wages are in proportion to the nicety of their work – the body makers recieved £2 to £3 per week, the carriage makers between £1 and £2, the trimmers 2 guineas, the painters from 20s to 30s, the body painters about 40s, the herald painters from £3 to £4, the smiths 30s'. Different trades relied upon different material and skill-based divisions, which had their own hierarchies. The business accounts of London tradesmen reveal in the lists of their creditors names of countless specialist suppliers, creating complex webs of association. Businesses relied on increasingly large networks of specialist providers. Adam Smith reckoned that 3,000 people in different trades were dependent on the Adam brothers for their work (Uglow 2002, 146). As architects and interior designers to the nobility the number and range of sub-contractors they used was immense, from plasterers to mirror-frame makers; carpenters to oil-cloth suppliers.

Specialisation reflected a more widely held belief in the virtues of a commercial society, which enjoyed a liberty from dependence on particular masters. Smith argued that this independence was achieved through an interlocking social system, so that individuals were truly interdependent. The very interdependency of this world contributed to the maintenance of social order and virtue (Berry 1994, 169). This system was, Smith argued, a result of the evolution of a commercial society, of which England was the prime example. Yet there are a number of key questions which emerge from this history. Was specialisation peculiar and/or precocious in England, and when did it start? Was it only a phenomenon of late 17th- and early 18th-century rationalisation? If specialisation was key to the English triumph over French competition, how was it different from specialisation abroad? Did the distinctive character of the English (as viewed by their competitors the French) – hard working, technically clever, but lacking imaginative flair in design – make them more suited to this form of production (Craske 1999, 199)? Alfred Marshall drew a sharp distinction between French and British social structures, and with this a French consumer market based in luxury and fashion, and a British market based in substantial simple goods and solid comforts (Berg 2001, 519). The difference in consumer markets went with different production processes. 'More and more did her [France's] best artisans specialise themselves on work that called for individual taste and thought as regards form, arrangement and colour: meanwhile English artisans were specialising themselves rather on work that required strength, resolution, judgment, persistence, power to obey and to command, and wherewithal abundant use of capital' (Berg 2001, 520).

As the art historian John Barrell has noted, while 18th-century commentators revealed the good narrative of divided labour, we are more familiar with the idea as it was used by Marx, as a story of alienation, from the unity of the productive process, from social utility, from the self (Barrell 1992, 89). Thorstein Veblen in his *Instinct of Workmanship*, published in 1914, describes the charismatic concept 'of the individual workman as a creative agent standing on his own and as an ultimate, irreducible factor in the community's makeup. He draws on the resources of his own person alone' (Veblen 1914, 235). This personalised view of production is partly an inheritance from the Arts and Crafts Movement, the ideology of which has a complex prehistory based in part on reactions both positive and negative to the facts of life of the machine age, and to urban rather than rural production. Henry Wilson who wrote a textbook for silversmiths in 1902, wrote of the 'clear shining sincerity of the worker and his patient skill . . . the worker's hand travelled lovingly over every part of the work, giving it a kindliness of aspect enduringly attractive' (Wilson 1902, 24). Compare this vision of craftsmanship with evidence from the workbooks of the Vulliamy brothers who specialised in the manufacture of clocks and watches, gilt bronze and ormolu porcelain, furniture, and silver, in late 18th- and early 19th-century London (Clifford 1998, 100). Four cast silver coats of arms supplied by the Vulliamys for mounting on a pair of Lord Brownlow's tureens were the product of the labour of at least seven skilled men. Cramphorn made the model in wax, which was cast as a pattern by Barnet. This was then used to cast the four coats in silver by Cooke which were filed up by Culmore, chased by Caney and Barker and burnished by Seagrave. How then are we to locate and understand authorship? (Clifford 1998, 96).

The evidence of individual trades

Largely the product of a vigorous *trade* rather than the talented *individual* (Culme 1987, xxxvi)

The first publication that began to unpack the system of manufacturing luxury goods is Joy's 1955 MA thesis 'Some Aspects of the London Furniture Industry in the 18th Century' (Joy 1955). However his work remains unpublished, and the implications of his suggestion that single items of furniture emerging from the furniture workshops of London were made collaboratively, went unpursued. The same can be said of Kirkham's 1969 article on the London cabinet maker Samuel Norman, in which she revealed his system of organisation which depended on specialised paper-hangers, carvers, gilders, upholsterers and appraisers in the 1750s (Kirkham 1969, 501–13). Research into sub-contracting has continued to be dominated by trade-specific studies with little communication across disciplinary boundaries. They are also largely metropolitan focussed. The patterns of sub-contracting that had been revealed in 18th-century London furniture manufacture were found to apply to the goldsmiths too, through the research of Culme (1987). Mitchell's (1995) edited collection of essays took the discussion of the precious metal trades beyond England and into Europe, and back into the 17th century. Morrison-Low has tackled subcontracting in the production of scientific instruments

(Morrison-Low 1995). In his work on Cheere and Roubiliac, Baker suggested areas of sub-contracting in the London sculpture trade of the 1730s and 1740s (Baker 1995). In one of Scheemaker's sale catalogues, for example, Baker notes that work and materials are organised under the headings 'modelling room', 'carver's shop', and 'mason's shop'; this not only indicates unsurprisingly that different materials were worked in different rooms but also hints at a division of labour and even a certain hierarchy of activities, with the modelling room apparently adjacent to the parlour. All these trades – furniture, goldsmithing, scientific instruments, and sculpture – had their own customised systems of specialisation.

The metropolitan area was by far the largest manufacturing centre in the country and as Phillips noted it was distinguished by a disproportionately large luxury sector (Styles 1993, 147). Pastor Wendeborn was assured that over a quarter of all English manufactories were in London (Wendeborn 1791, I, 162). Manufacturing had to adapt to the advantages and drawbacks of operating in the nation's capital. There were three large drawbacks, land cost more, so rents were higher than elsewhere; labour cost more; and fuel cost more than it did on or near coalfields. To balance these disadvantages were the factors of London's proximity to the largest and most concentrated market in the country; low transport costs for finished products; and its prime position for the observation of consumer taste. Labour cost more; but there was a great deal of it, and it came in almost any degree of skill required. As William Hazlitt noted, in London 'you are within two or three miles reach of persons, that' outside the capital, 'would be some hundreds apart' (Hazlitt 1902, 272). Manufacturing in the capital adapted to these particular circumstances, with systems of production that favoured smaller scale outfits which were quick to adapt to changing fashions. So, instead of factories, production was shared amongst specialists. In Peter Hall's words the assembly line ran through the street, where the material in its different stages of completion, was carried from one manufacturer to another (Schwarz 1992, 33). It has been argued by Fox that because the processes of production in London were largely hidden from public view in small workshops, they were thus unlikely to be the subject of a spur of the moment sketch, let alone a finished work (Fox 1987, 357). As a result we have very few depictions of workshops in London, and the small core of primary evidence is dominated by printed advertising material.

What we need to track is not only the similarities of sub-contracting between trades, but also how they differed across and even within them. What were the common denominators, and what were not? For example specialisation in the 18th-century silver trade took place within different models of workshop organisation. The Birmingham entrepreneur Matthew Boulton drew his skilled hands together under one roof, often importing them from London. Parker and Wakelin, a partnership of London goldsmiths (1760–76) whose accounts have survived, relied on a complex network of 75 makers, divided between those who had specialist skills, like engravers, raisers and casters, and those who specialised in making particular products, like tureen, cutlery or plates. They were all based in their own workshops, which meant that Parker and Wakelin had to organise the smooth passage of materials and wares between workshops (Clifford 1990). There was another model of manufacture whereby the retailing goldsmith both operated a workshop and contracted out. Thomas Heming, appointed royal goldsmith in 1760, explained that not only did he 'bring up both my sons to the Business', but was also 'contracted with a number of the best hands for a constancy whether there was work or not' (Harcourt 1938, 131).

The discovery of sub-contracting in the luxury trades sent ripples beyond the waters of academe, and impacted on the curator and dealer, connecting abstract learning with the market. These collaborative systems of manufacture challenged the way decorative arts-histories were written. Such histories usually took the form of biographical accounts of individuals, based on the attributed authorship of objects. A classic is Shure's biography of the 18th- and early 19th-century London goldsmith Hester Bateman (Shure 1959). To write about individuals in this way necessarily involves the effacement of collaborative activities, commercial strategies, and workshop organisation. The marginalisation of the mechanical, artisanal elements in making was already evident in later 18th-century writing on the crafts. It was encouraged by those craftsmen and entrepreneurs keen to be regarded as artists and to have their own works valued and discussed in terms of an emerging language of art appreciation, which itself is a significant aspect of the marketing of art in the commercial society of 18th-century Britain.

The challenge now is how to write the histories of these trades; what structure to follow now that the biographical seems misleading. As Culme explained as recently as 1987, 'the study of English silver and the understanding of it as largely the product of a vigorous *trade* rather than the talented *individual*, has been hampered by the temptation to overestimate the value of the so-called maker's mark' (Culme 1987, xxxvi).

The maker's point of view

> I find that one Trade may borrow many Eminent Helps in Work of another Trade (Moxon 1678)

If makers were aware of the collaborative nature of manufacture, then does this knowledge emerge in the literature either written for them or by them? There is a three-stage evolution of writing which focuses first on elite makers, then gentlemen, and

20 The vernacular workshop

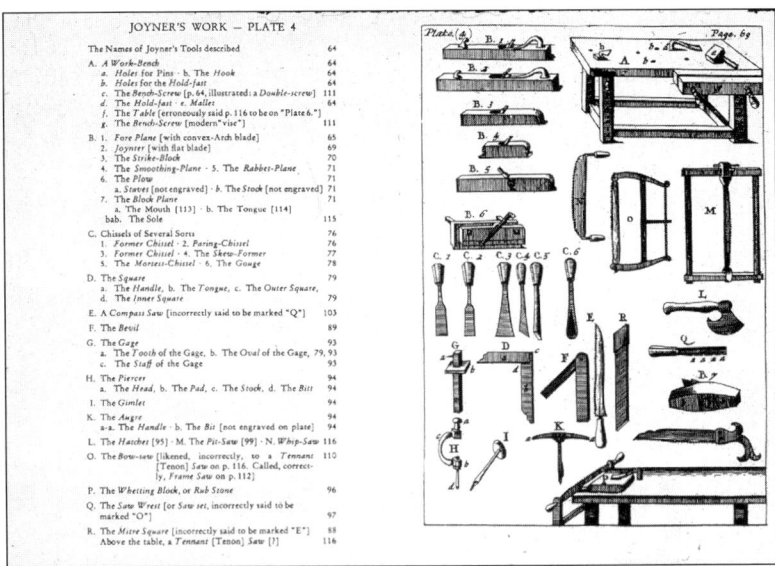

Figure 2.1 'Joyner's Work', from Moxon's Mechanick Exercises or Doctrine of Handyworks, *1678. (© Bodleian Library, Oxford)*

finally common workmen. From the language they employ it is clear that early texts like Biringuccio's 16th-century *Pirotechnia*, and Cellini's *Trattati* were addressed to fellow initiates, or to impress the client with their ancient law and skill. Discussion of the 'mystery' was more about advertising strategy, than revealing the true secrets of the trade which were protected by guild rules (Vitali 2000, 10–13).

This was to change in the 17th century after Sir Francis Bacon stressed the value of studying the crafts and their technical (and tacit) processes of knowledge. He criticised the contempt of philosophers for manual labour and therefore the study of the mechanical (Healey 1963, 837). There was an increasing interest in artisanal skills and labour amongst learned men which is evident in several contemporary publications (Bennet 1986, 22). John Evelyn in his *Silva*, reminded his readers that he 'did not altogether compile this Work for the Sake of our Ordinary Rusticks (meer Forestors and Woodmen), but for the more Ingenious, the benefit and diversion of Gentlemen, the Persons of Quality' (Bennet 1986, 22). André Felibien's 1676 *Dictionary of Architecture, Sculpture and Painting and other Arts Dependent on Them*, strove to do away with what he called 'craft secrets and mysteries', and was written to demonstrate the principles of the *beaux arts* to those gentlemen who might want to know about them but 'who do not wish to apply them in depth'. Here lie larger issues concerning the divide between the professional and amateur.

Joseph Moxon's *Mechanick Exercises or the Doctrine of Handyworks*, first published in 1678, represents a change in direction in that it was written not for the gentleman, but for the workman. It was published in serial form, at 6d per book and aimed to explain the arts of blacksmithing, joinery, carpentry and turning arts, 'in workmens' phrases and their terms explained'. He recognised the importance of shared skills across trades and the virtues of specialisation. 'Besides' he writes 'I find that one Trade may borrow many Eminent Helps in Work of another Trade', thereby challenging the control of the 'mysteries' of each craft by the guilds. It may be no coincidence that it is from this period, that the power of the guilds began to decline, and the forces of innovation (as applied to organisation, methods of manufacture, and product types) began to be felt.

Moxon was not the first in publishing how-to-do-it manuals aimed at the workman. Jacques Aleame's *La Perspective Speculative et Practique* was published in Paris in 1643, and was addressed not only to painters and architects but chasers, engravers, and weavers. John Darling published his *Carpenter's Rule Made Easie*, in 1658. Moxon however was the most thorough. One of the most important features of his *Exercises* is its illustrations, borrowed from Felibien, which depict tools and equipment, like bellows, vices, and drills, but not the workshop or the act of making (Fig 2.1). Earlier works, like the several manuscript versions of the *Goldsmythes Storehouse* (1604–7), also fail to illustrate either site or process of work (Jenstad 1998, 40–3). Incidentally the *Storehouse* of 1607 provides early evidence for sub-contracting in the trade, as it refers to the 'great decay' of the 'art and mystery' of the craft, because so 'few workmen are able to finish and perfect a piece of plate *singularly* with all the garnishings and parts thereof without the help of many and *several* hands'. There is no English equivalent of the late 15th-century engraving of St Eligius (the continental patron saint of goldsmiths) by the Master of Balaam, or Etienne Delaune's two engravings of a silversmith's workshop in Augsburg of 1576 (Fig 2.2) which depict the interiors of workshops in detail, with work in progress.

In England, illustrations of workshops, and men and women at work, are largely restricted to guild invitations and only appear in the later 17th century. One of the earliest is the frontispiece to William Badcock's *New Touch-Stone of Gold and Silver Wares, or a Manual for Goldsmiths* first published in 1677 (Southwick 1997, 584) which depicts the patron

Figure 2.2 A version of Etienne Delaune's 1576 engraving of a goldsmith's workshop in Augsburg (© Worshipful Company of Goldsmiths, London)

saint of English goldsmiths, St Dunstan, at the top, seated on a plinth within a retail shop (Fig 2.3). The shopkeeper is on his right, with his scales to weigh the silver, the glass fronted cases packed with silver, and to his left are small workers, filing and engraving smaller items beneath the large shop window. This presents a 'realistic view' of a retail premises. The numbered scene below depicts the various stages, not of making silver, but of assaying or testing the silver for its sterling quality, appropriate to a book that was aimed at 'Discovering the Rules belonging to that Mystery, and the Way and Means how to know Adulterated wares from those made of the True Standard'. A 1701/2 invitation from the Goldsmiths' Company shows a panorama of craft operations set in one place that would in reality have more often been divided between specialised workshops (Fig 2.4). The gentleman seated at the anvil to the left is raising a beaker, to his left a turner works at his lathe, at the bottom left a chaser is picking out decorative detail, while at the centre another silversmith draws out wire on a bench. The audience for these invitations were the goldsmiths themselves, and their creators were the engravers who worked with and for them, so we can assume a level of accuracy that might not be the case for other types of illustration (Heine 1996, 20–7).

This visual drawing together of divided skills is repeated in another invitation to Goldsmiths' Hall engraved forty years later (Fig 2.5). In the same way the illustrations within the *Encyclopedie*, published in Paris in the mid-18th century show several craft activities or different sequential steps in the assembly process in a single image, as if they were occurring simultaneously. Potentially misleading for the modern viewer, this was a conventional graphic device used for the sake of economy, a standard practice readily understood by most contemporary makers (Fairbanks 1984, 315–30). The art historian John Barrell has argued that the practice of reading these images of divided labour (with reference to Pyne's *Picturesque Delineation of the Arts, Agriculture, Manufactures of Great Britain* (Pyne 1808)) required an abstract viewing position, the philosophic eye, to draw them together. The problem was defining the place from which the social coherence could be perceived. It was argued by the new theorists of craft (like the Encyclopedists) that the required focus could not be achieved by 'pedestrian mechanics', but by those, who defined the 'invisible quality of mind, not visible agility of hand' (Stafford 1994, 134), thus distancing tacit from academic knowledge.

The consumer's point of view

To behold the secrets of Chymistry, & the Mechanick powers, so employ'd & exerted (Elizabeth Montagu to Matthew Boulton, 1770s, Boulton Papers, Birmingham Central Library)

22 *The vernacular workshop*

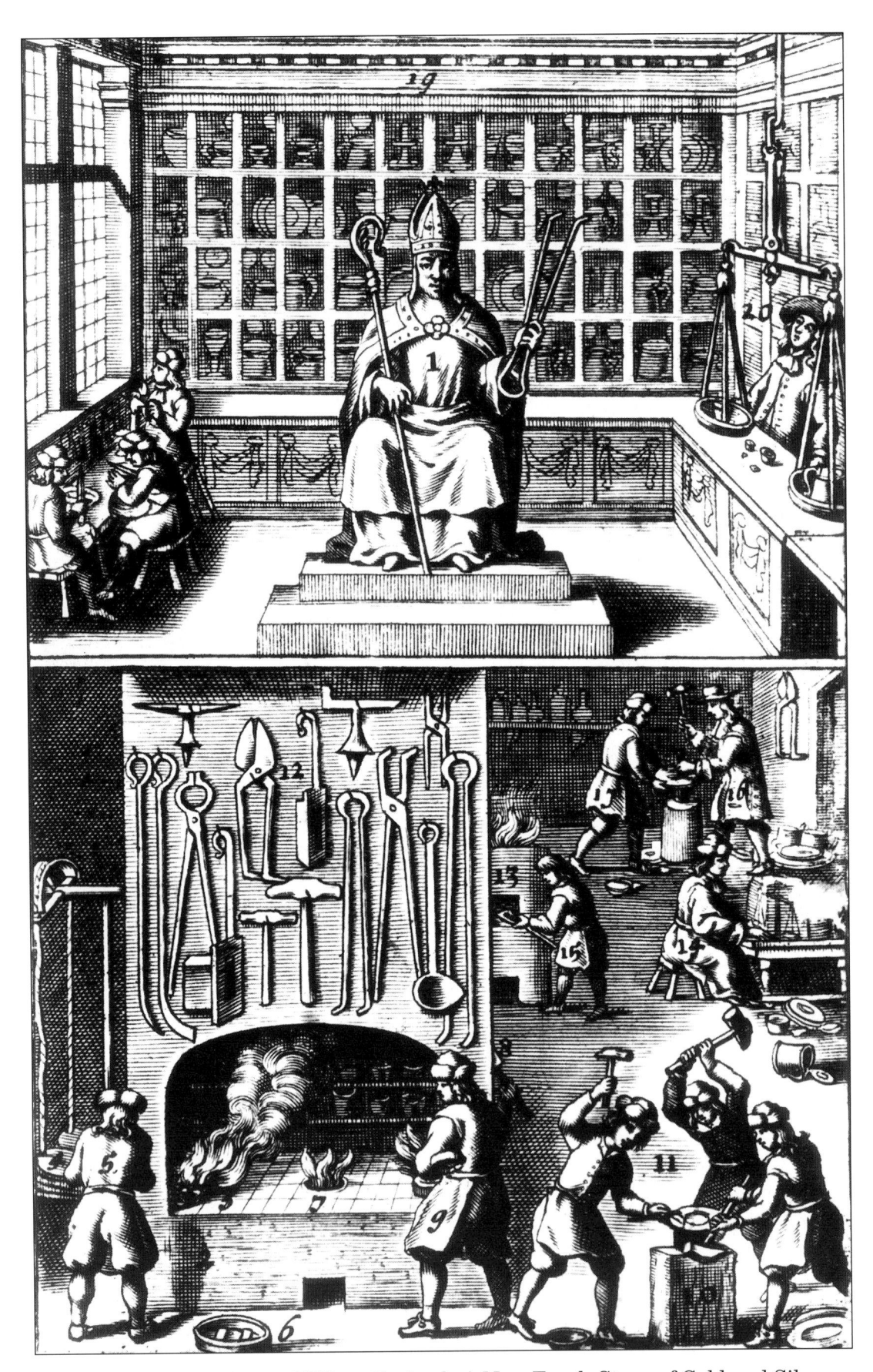

Figure 2.3 Frontispiece to William Badcock, A New Touch-Stone of Gold and Silver Wares, *1677 (© Worshipful Company of Goldsmiths, London)*

Figure 2.4 Invitation from the Goldsmiths' Company, 1701/2 (© Worshipful Company of Goldsmiths, London)

24 *The vernacular workshop*

It is now time to ask how much the consumer understood of the process of manufacture and the organisation of the workshop. According to the celebrated 18th-century blue-stocking Elizabeth Montagu, most were aware of the different value systems, the cost of materials and of worksmanship, which applied when purchasing artistic goods. While the former was subject to standardised and guaranteeable rates, the latter was more difficult to judge. In a letter to Lord Kames of 1767 she explained that 'In every country where there is any degree of civilisation the favourite objects of luxury and pride will be adorned with some cost and pains', but

> As the value and reward of the manufacturer, who makes these decorations depends on the fancy & caprice of a private Patron . . . he depends much on the fineness of the materials in which he works, gold, silver, silk & many other things have a standard value – the workman knows the price at which they will be purchased, but he does not know at what his intention will be estimated . . . the subject the artificer has chosen may displease, then the labour is lost (Warwick University 1999, 319).

During the 18th century we can see a shift in the relationship between those who were willing to pay extra for workmanship, and the growing market for the ready-made in which the cost of making and materials were both fixed for the consumer. Contemporary commentators on the English social, cultural and artistic scene recognised the difference between those who bought ready-made goods over the counter, and those who commissioned. They acknowledged that the power of the patron was important for not only ensuring, but also stimulating the quality of art, design and manufactures, and that it was under pressure from a growing demand for ready-made luxuries. Quality needed to be maintained, as well as quantity increased, and a language of discrimination that favoured the former needed to be encouraged. Robert Dossie, in his *Handmaid to the Arts*, published in London in 1758, believed that 'it particularly behoves us to exert in cultivating those of a more refined nature, where skill and taste (in which we are by no means wanting) are required to give a higher value to the work'. Dossie was defending the importance of quality over quantity production, an expensive commodity that only the rich could afford to promote. Rouquet saw this contrast between quantity and quality production in terms of the differing demands and expectations of the retailer versus the private patron, ready-made versus commissioned goods. He explained that the shopkeeper.

> who employs an artist with a view of profit, . . . requires only a certain degree of perfection, so much as he knows is necessary to the success and reputation of his trade. As soon as the man he employs has finished his work for common sale, every step beyond that is so much out of pocket,

Figure 2.5 Invitation from the Goldsmiths' Company, 1741 (© Trustees of the Ashmolean Museum, Oxford)

> and consequently becomes a superfluity that hurts him: then he stops the artist's hand, and at the same time the progress of the art. But he is right to do so, since his motive is not to enjoy the productions of his ingenuity, but render them subservient to his gain (Rouquet 1755, 43).

The private customer, argued Rouquet, 'acts upon a different footing'. He 'consults only his own taste which inclines him to have the work perfectly executed; hence he is afraid to beat the artist down in his price, lest he should be disappointed: as he has but few occasions to employ him, it would be an ill judged economy to require only indifferent work, on the account of its being cheap'. As Lord Chesterfield advised his son, the gentleman, 'employs, even in the meanest Trifle, none but the ablest and most ingenious Workmen, that his Judgment and Fancy may as evidently appear in the least things that belong to him, as his Wealth and Quality are manifested in those of greater Value' (Chesterfield 1984, 171).

Defoe in 1726 divided tradesmen into three different groups: 'those who do not actually manufacture the goods they sell, those who only make goods for others to sell, and those who make the goods they sell though they keep shops' (Defoe 1726, 34). There is evidence to show that there was increasing confusion from the consumer's point of view of who did what. Thomas Mortimer in 1763 produced his *Universal Director or the Nobleman and Gentleman's True Guide to the Masters and Professors of the*

Figure 2.6 Trade card of Henry Morris, jeweller, goldsmith and toyman, c1760 (Courtesy of the Banks and Heal Collection, © The British Museum)

Liberal and Polite Arts and Sciences, and of the Mechanic Arts, Manufactures and Trades Established in London and Westminster and their Environs. It was intended to help the purchaser go direct to the maker. His entry on hatmakers advises, 'It may not, perhaps, be thought material for the private Gentleman to apply to the manufacturers for a single Hat, but the Merchant and Country Shopkeeper must be very accurate in finding out the real Makers, for the difference is very considerable between prices of the Haberdasher and Maker. The following list contains none but the real Manufacturers'. It should be be noted however that despite this comment the names of solely retailing businesses do appear in the *Director*.

It is clear that some makers resented the power of the skilled retailer in distancing the customer from them. Thomas Bewick in his autobiography recalls his days as an apprentice engraver in the 1760s, when Isaac Hymen:

> had got gathered together a great collection of impressions of well cut Seals, & being a Man of good address & a good singer, he introduced himself into Coffee Rooms frequented by Gentlemen & respectable tradesmen & there he exhibited his Impressions as the work of his own hands & by his own good management (for he knew nothing whatever of engraving of any kind) he got his orders – and somehow or other it was well propagated through the Town that his Seals surpassed, by far any thing we ever did or could do, & though we had done the whole of his orders (Bewick 1762, 49).

Bewick blamed the state of affairs on his customers, for 'this must continue to be the case so long as Gentlemen will not be at the pains to encourage merit & to go themselves to the fountain head for their nice jobs'. It may be for these reasons that retailers were keen to give the idea, if not live up to the fact, that they made the goods they sold. Advertising provided the opportunity to stress the process of making, and a number of trade cards of the 1750s and 1760s include allusions in both text and image to manufacture as much as to product. Henry Morris, for example, a jeweller, goldsmith and toyman in Norris Street in the Haymarket stresses that he 'Manufactures and Sells' jewellery and silver, and includes a scene of gentlemanly manufacture at the base of his trade card (Fig 2.6). The goldsmith Phillips Garden who had a shop in St Paul's Churchyard in the 1750s was keen to state on his trade card that he was a 'working goldsmith and jeweller', and that 'Work' was 'perform'd in my own house', giving the impression that behind a fashionable gothic screen in the retail shop silver was being made on site. Yet we know that Garden bought in the work of others, and that his was a largely retail rather than manufacturing concern. Edward Webb's 1750s trade card gentrifies the act of making by giving cherubs the task of annealing (to the left), and forging (to the right) (Fig 2.7). There

Figure 2.7 Trade card of Edward Webb, goldsmith, clock and watchmaker, Bristol, c1750 (Courtesy of the Banks and Heal Collection, © The British Museum)

are many other examples of trade cards that stress the manufacturing nature of the businesses, which of course may, or may not be true. Like most advertising it aims to create an image that the retailer wanted to sell, and which he thought his customers desired to see.

This interest in the manufacturing process may in part explain the popularity of 'factory visits' in the second half of the 18th century, an opportunity to see the spectacle and benefits of rationalised labour, either by tourists eager to come away with souvenirs, or by those seeking to break the secrets of the English manufacturing process. Between 1781 and 1794 John Byng, later 5th Viscount Torrington made regular tours of England and Wales, and called in on factories as well as gothic ruins, country houses and picturesque parks. In Worcester he 'went to the china manufactory, of which we took an accurate survey, from the first handling to the last removal from the furnace' (Byng [1794], I, 45). In 1792 he went to Mr Roe's great copper works at Macclesfield 'which required purchase on an advance ticket from the banking house in town'. At Etruria he 'was shown about the several workshops of this great pottery, wherein are employed 300 men'. Byng, was not impressed, because 'this is a dull observation for any person who has seen China manufactures [and] I did not find that any persons had attempted to carry off any secrets of the art' (Byng [1794], II, 127). At Boulton's Soho works in Birmingham Elizabeth

Montagu was enchanted 'To behold the secrets of Chymistry, & the Mechanick powers, so employ'd & exerted'. It could be argued that as consumers moved further from the experience of manufacture, viewing the process of making became more attractive, and the 'mystery' of making had changed its nature. It is precisely at this time that the number of illustrations of workshops increases.

In concluding this paper I want to pursue this idea of the distance between maker and consumer, and how production was viewed. The design historian Forty has argued that some manufacturers were keen to hide from their customers how extensive their reliance on divided labour was (Forty 1986). He takes Josiah Wedgwood's pottery at Etruria as an example and notes that although his success lay in the rationalisation of production methods in his factory, his imaginative marketing techniques, and his attention to his products; he used 'antique designs', that is neo-classicism, to clothe technical innovation. If we take one example from his letters, concerning the production of two friezes of 'Apollo and the Nine Muses', it appears that he had a very clear idea of what his customers felt about his production techniques. He wrote to his business partner in London, Thomas Bentley, 'I know they are much cheaper at that price than marble & every way better, but people will not compare things which they conceive to be made out of moulds, or perhaps stamp'd at a blow like the Birmingham articles, with carving and natural stones where they are certain no moulding, casting, or stamping can be done (Wedgwood 1903, 458). For these reasons the image of Etruria as a classic idyll served more than one purpose.

3 The archaeology of the late and post-medieval workshop – a review and proposal for a research agenda *by Jane Grenville*

The purpose of this chapter is to review the current state of knowledge regarding the late medieval and post-medieval workshop as a location for craft and industrial production, as opposed to the technology of craft production, which is a subject that has received much attention from scholars whose work will be heavily plundered here. The aim is to identify, as far as possible, the social relations of production and to propose a research agenda for future work to further elucidate from archaeological and documentary evidence this less thoroughly studied angle. The preparation of the paper for the Oxford conference in November 2002 involved the creation of a database of 164 sites culled mainly from the pages of *Medieval Archaeology* and *Post-Medieval Archaeology* and from the principal syntheses on 15th- to 17th-century industry (Crossley 1990; Blair & Ramsay 1991; Newman 2001). A fairly wide spectrum of industrial activity is included in the database but most of the sites fell into a few major groupings: metal working, pottery, food and drink trades, brick and tile production, tanning and leather working, textiles, and glass manufacture. The database was prepared by Holly Gourley, and my warmest thanks go to her. Space precludes a full examination of the database in a short paper: the material presented here covers metals, pottery, and glass. It is hoped to be able to develop the project at a later date to include a wider range of industries.

Research questions

As noted above, the development of technologies has received much interest in the literature; my particular concern at the outset of the investigation was to consider the relationship between space, production and social organisation. Subsequent discussion and comment at the conference in Oxford extended the range of questions further.

The first issue was that of the definition of the workshop. At the conference, Palmer defined the workshop as: 'a physically defined space in which manufacture is carried out in such a way that the workforce controls the speed, intensity, and rhythm of the work'. This is helpful but there remain problems in identifying such spaces in the period in question, both in surviving buildings and in excavated evidence. As will be seen below when individual crafts are looked at in more detail, archaeological visibility of workspace is often very low indeed. We can find evidence for *craft* in the form of the product, but unless the *process* required heat or water power or deep pits, it is often difficult to 'see' the activity in excavation. Even then, the emphasis has been on the consideration of technologies and relatively little space is given in site reports to the elucidation of the social relations involved in operating that technology. Where it is, the evidence consulted has been documentary only and the potential information contained in the relative disposition and layout of the buildings on site has not been considered. In standing buildings the problem is possibly greater since any workshop spaces that might survive will have had their evidence obscured or stripped by subsequent use. A combination of historical research and careful observation of the spatial relationships within and between both excavated and surviving buildings will be suggested as a way forward here.

A second issue over the definition of the workshop is that often it seems to have been conflated with a shop, in its retail sense. This is one area in which this investigation suggests that a poorly supported generalisation has been taken up into the literature and repeated despite the fact that convincing evidence, based on current knowledge, may be rather flimsy. It may be the case that production and retail were closely associated in physical terms, but at the moment the weight of evidence, or at least its interpretation, does not actually support this view generally, and in any case the situation may vary from industry to industry and craft to craft, depending on the peculiarities of production and the exigencies of markets and sales. It will be shown in the industries considered here that while the craftmaster might take responsibility for sales, these were often made away from the point of manufacture, as records of transport costs and of breakages show.

A third issue arises from the survival and visibility of the evidence and the research imperatives of the archaeological community. Evidence for urban workshops is difficult to come by. Backland areas have remained in intensive use throughout the post-medieval period and even where they have been excavated, there has been a tendency to give more weight to the medieval and earlier evidence, rather than to the post-medieval. Generally speaking, surviving buildings have, as noted above, lost all evidence for former uses or their evidence has passed unobserved. Much of the detailed site evidence used here is inevitably drawn from rural locations where targeted projects have been carried out. The question of how much urban evidence languishes unrecognised in contract archaeology archives deserves closer attention than it has been possible to give it here. Rather, this chapter seeks to consider the potential for further study by revisiting some of the better published sites, and by considering the trends illustrated by the broader sample of sites recorded in the database sites and the potential that their further study would release. The need for a major research project to investigate the survival of evidence for urban workshops is clearly demonstrated by the results of this initial survey of published material.

All of these issues arise to some extent from the nature of previous investigation. Workshops have not been a central focus of archaeological inquiry. Most of what we know has come almost as an aside from researchers investigating other matters. Historians concern themselves with social and economic conditions in the past; industrial and historical archaeologists pursue an interest in artefacts, their production and distribution; contract archaeologists come across such buildings or their sub-surface remains in the course of pre-development investigations and tend to be most interested in answering broad questions about the development of the site itself and the wider area within which they are working. All of these, in the process of answering their own more specific questions, have shed light upon workshops, but it is often a rather oblique light. Buildings archaeologists such as myself, have been primarily concerned with the development of buildings and the social use of space – any type of building is a fair target for research, but to my knowledge the late and post medieval workshop has not been investigated in detail. The aim of this paper, in shifting the focus to this neglected building type, is to try to frame a research agenda for the study of 15th- to 17th-century craft and industry that will encompass both technical and social questions. Because these questions have not been specifically asked, workshops have not received the sort of primary research needed. The result is a total lack of synthesis of material across Britain and generally speaking a lack of synthesis on the smaller city or regional levels as well. This last, geographical, issue is compounded by the fact that, in compiling our database, we discovered a strong bias towards southern sites.

Principal among those questions is that of the social organisation of craft and industry in the period between the breakdown of feudal modes of production and social organisation and the establishment of factory-based large-scale manufacture. Within the feudal mode of production, 'ownership' lay ultimately with the lord of the manor and the rights to production derived from him. In rural crafts the relationship was relatively straightforward, with lords controlling the operation of crafts, even if the craftsman had access to an open market in terms of selling to his neighbours (Dyer 2002, 169–70). In towns, the rights to production were often ceded by the Crown to the town authorities, as their claims to self-determination became ever more successful, and the power of authorising the creation of craft guilds then lay with the city fathers (Ramsay 1991, xxii). By the time of the early manufactures, such as Matthew Boulton's great enterprise at Soho in Birmingham or Josiah Wedgewood's at Burslem, social relations had changed radically (see Uglow 2002, 212–17 for a discussion of paternalistic discipline in the new factories; also McKendrick 1961). What, in the intervening period, was the social make-up of the independent workshop, and how far can the buildings reveal this? Were workshops predominantly domestic in location and scale? What were the social relations within the workshop and how did the workplace operate? What were the household relations? Were these reflected in the way that space was used in the workshop? Could we approach that issue using interdisciplinary approaches? By which I mean going beyond poaching the historians' data for things that would back up an archaeological case and vice versa.

In terms of economic organisation, how far does the evidence from workshops inform us about markets for incoming raw materials and for the finished products? Did the agglomeration of trades in specific districts suggest cooperative purchasing and selling by individuals, or did it simply reflect more functional access to raw materials, sources of power, and transport routes? Common sense indicates that, for instance, horners and tanners might have shared raw material from butchers and that this shared interest might express itself in terms of locations of workshops but the unequivocal identification of these relationships archaeologically remains to be undertaken. Can we substantiate the view that rural industries tended to move into the towns around 1400 and back out again around 1600?

Methodology

Our approach, influenced by the availability of time and funds, was not to comb the county sites and monuments records for information, but rather to review the existing published evidence. We found that there are a few very well known sites and they make repeated appearances in all the syntheses. I shall argue below that this is because of the lack of sustained research in the field except by a limited number of individuals, whose approach, sensibly enough, has been to conduct intensive research campaigns on specific sites. These, then, become the standard sources of information and little impetus exists to investigate more widely. Nevertheless, additional material does exist in the form of notes and short reports from the annual reports on fieldwork in the end sections of *Medieval Archaeology* and *Post-Medieval Archaeology* where short notes of archaeological activity around the country are reported. These reports are often limited to a paragraph or two in which a summary of what was uncovered is provided. One of the first difficulties encountered was that mention of material of interest to us (workshops from 1400 to 1650) may have been summarised in a sentence or two or even less. It seems likely that there may have been more excavation and building recording of post-medieval workshops than there are full published reports of the results. In some cases, it may be hoped that fuller publication will follow or further published information can be tracked down in county journals. However, many of the sites found through this research project were excavated as a result of development work and therefore it seems likely that access to fuller publication will not be forthcoming in many cases.

In deciding upon the kinds of information required, it was assumed that since the paper was to be about workshops specifically, rather than industry more generally, excavated evidence and standing buildings would form the bulk of the material. Nonetheless, there are problems here of the quality of evidence since there is a need for relatively large areas to be excavated to be able to interpret material accurately. The example of baking is offered by Schofield and Vince (1994, 122). We know from documentary sources that baking was carried out on a professional level from at least the early 13th century, but how can one interpret finds of ovens as commercial or domestic? To do this we would need to have excavated sufficient numbers in close proximity to be able to see if they are commonly found, but in a dispersed pattern (maybe indicating household ovens) or that they come in a range of sizes (thus saying something about production levels).

Surviving attested workshops from the first half of the 17th century and earlier are rare in the synthetic literature and the production of the database did not throw up significant numbers that had not previously been considered. This remains, then, a class of building which has either largely disappeared or is not recognised and targeted research to try to find such buildings is one of the recommendations for further work.

Noting these caveats and constraints, the initial trawl, upon which the results presented here are based, was undertaken industry by industry in an attempt to synthesise what is known. Of the 164 sites on the database, 131 are in the south, and only 33 in the north (as defined by the course of the River Trent, for ease of reference). These represented a fairly wide spectrum of industrial activity but with the majority of sites falling into the following categories:

1. Metalworking (including specialist sites producing bells, armour, guns etc)
2. Pottery
3. Brick and tile production
4. Food and drink related industry (including brewing/malting; baking; salt production; corn-mills; and butchers)
5. Leather and animal by-product related industry (tanning, horn working etc)
6. Textile production
7. Glass production

The constraints of space within this chapter prohibit the exploration of all of these categories, although it is hoped that they will be considered in later publications. For present purposes only metalworking, pottery, and glassmaking are discussed.

Metalworking

Metalworking is probably one of the best understood of all the craft industries for several reasons. First and most importantly, the remains of this industry survive much better than those of most others, making the analysis easier to carry out. Secondly, this area of study has benefited from the sustained interest of industrial archaeologists and historical metallurgists (for broad yet detailed syntheses see Tylecote 1986, 142–222; Crossley 1990, 152–203; Cranstone 2001,186–203). Although the focus of previous study has tended to be on process and product, rather than the organisation of the workplace, sufficient plans and discussions of workshops have been published to enable a preliminary consideration of the research issues with which we are concerned here.

The winning of ores is known archaeologically from the Bronze Age onwards but it is difficult to suggest certain dates for many of the simpler forms of extraction. Few examples survive which match the dramatic appearance of the famous Bentley Grange iron pits (Beresford & St Joseph 1979), but Crossley suggests that such simple methods of extraction persisted beyond the medieval period wherever shallow seams were found (Crossley 1990, 204). Outcrops on hillsides were extracted by means of digging drifts into the slope but the dating of such features is difficult indeed and there seem to be no surviving workshops to accompany them dating from before the 18th century (Davies 2002).

Metalworking is a craft which undergoes several important technological changes within our period of interest as a result of an increasing level of financial investment. Before the Black Death iron was smelted in many small bloomeries each having a limited output (Crossley 1990, 153–6) and this form of purifying iron continued well into the 17th century where small-scale production was adequate, such as at Muncaster Head, Cumbria (Tylecote & Cherry 1970). How far did such domestic-scale practices reflect social resistance to the loss of autonomy that a bigger operation implied? Regular operation would provide an output of about 20 or 30 tonnes a year and there was no need to keep the facility in continuous use – it could easily be worked as a sideline for a family with other interests such as farming. Indeed, smelting does seem to be a largely rural occupation throughout most of the period: the well-known site at Rockley in Yorkshire (Fig 3.1), excavated by Crossley and Ashurst in the 1960s, dates from the 16th century and was operated by water power (Crossley & Ashurst 1968). Indeed, the first major technological development to the process of metalworking was

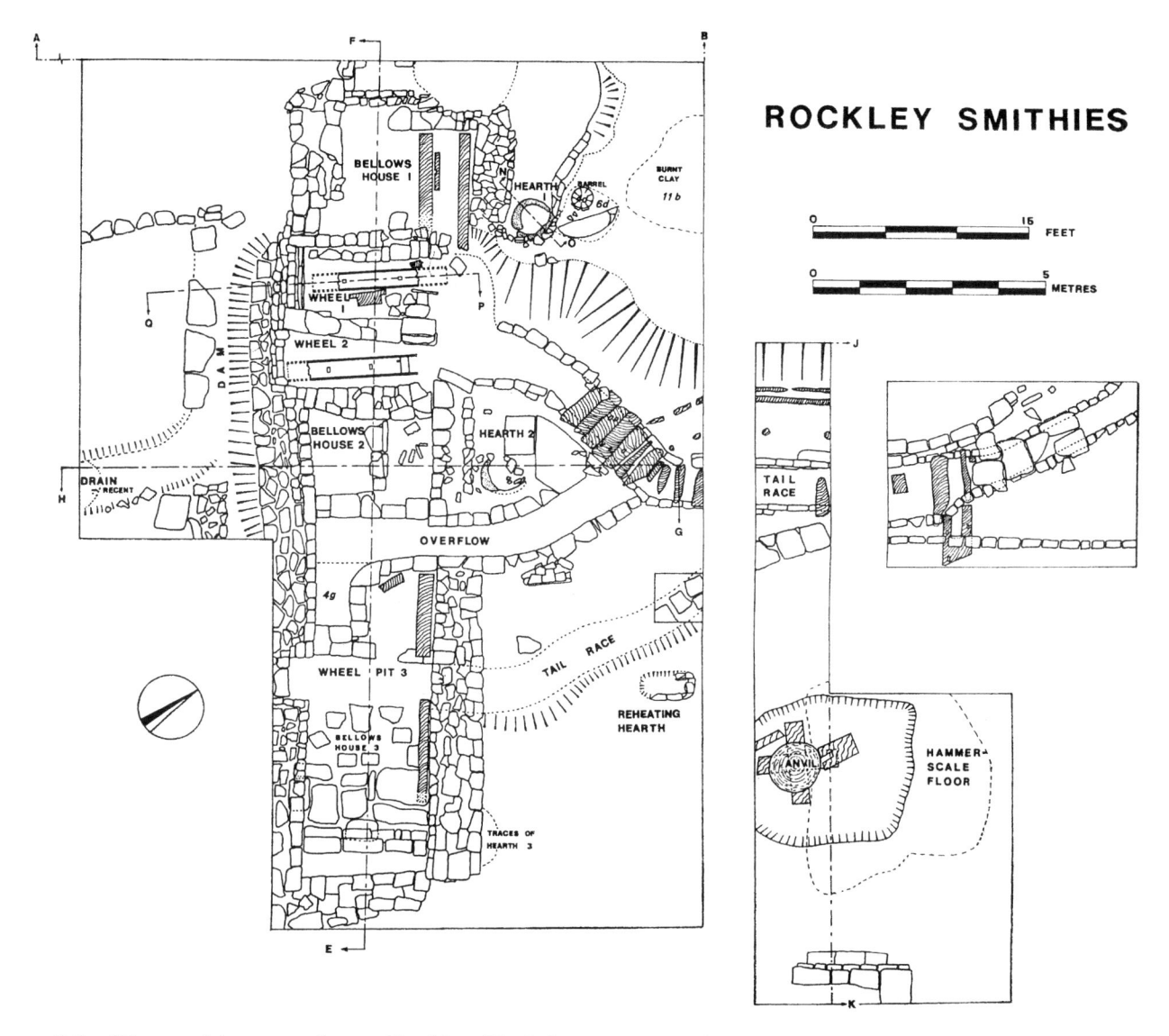

Figure 3.1 The smelting complex at Rockley, Yorkshire, in period 2, showing the importance of the complex water system. (By permission of the Society for Post-Medieval Archaeology)

the introduction of water power, which increased output from about 3 tonnes a year in a furnace with hand-powered bellows to about 25 tonnes where there was water power. The earliest known water-powered forge at Chingley in Kent dates from the early 14th century (Crossley 1975). The use of water to power hammers as well as bellows increased production still further, up to about 45 tonnes (44.25 tons) a year, as illustrated by Agricola in his *De re metallica* (Agricola 1556). There is little here to help us to understand the social relations of production, but it is clear that increased output could be achieved without a commensurate increase in labour. One small insight comes from Byrkenott in Weardale, County Durham (Geddes 1991, 170) where a water-powered furnace was producing 18 tonnes (17.75 tons) of forged iron in less than a year in 1408–09; this seems to have been an intermittent operation if a reference to a casual payment made to the woman who operated the bellows is to be taken at face value. As I noted earlier, the evidence is more about the industry than about the workshops specifically associated with it, but interesting aspects of technological change and social relations are already beginning to emerge.

The next big development was the blast furnace, the first imported from Europe in 1496 at Newbridge in Sussex (Crossley 1990, 156). Here iron ore in a tall, narrow shaft furnace remained in contact with the charcoal fuel and resultant carbon monoxide for a longer time than in a bloomery and had a lower melting point. An early example was excavated at Chingley, Kent (Crossley 1975). The resultant cast iron then had to be converted into malleable wrought iron by oxidising it in a finery. Geddes (1991, 174) has suggested that 'the introduction of cast iron and the indirect process of making it wrought iron marked the end of the Middle Ages and the start of the modern era in the English iron industry'. The continuous operation demanded a greater investment of both time and money and the requirement for charcoal and water ensured that this remained a rural industry. Indeed, as Crossley (1990, 153) has pointed out, the impact of the iron industry on wooded areas such as the Weald and the Forest of Dean was profound, as indeed was its demise on those landscapes.

Technological advances were adopted over long periods of time across the whole of the country so that old-fashioned operations were still in production after the introduction of newer technologies. It would be interesting to know whether installations using different technologies continued to operate in close proximity, or whether technological levels were firmly regionalised – the evidence we have been able to gather does not allow an answer to this question, but given the issue raised at the conference on which this book is based, concerning the degree to which social factors, as well as functional and economic ones, acted as prime movers in decision-making about modes of production, the subject is worth further exploration.

Cranstone (2001, 186–7) notes that in Britain, water-powered bloomeries seem to be largely associated with monastic estates such as Rievaulx (Vernon *et al* 1998) while secular landholders and the Crown were more likely to control the innovative blast furnaces, capable of producing cast iron for use in cannon making. The teams and organisation of labour have been little investigated and perhaps future excavation might seek to elucidate the working conditions of the furnace operators, in much the same way that Money's excavations of the medieval site in Minepit Wood revealed the timber-framed shelter used by the bloomery ironworkers there (Money 1971) (Fig 3.2). More work has been undertaken on the continent into the organisation of the iron industry which seems to have been operated by peasant ironmasters on a small scale of production, but one that was technically innovative, with the introduction of small blast furnaces (Magnusson 1995).

If iron production and forging was predominantly a rural occupation, and apparently one that doubled up with agricultural activity, then the working of metals in specialised ways was clearly urban. Geddes (1991, 182) documents the complexity of the guild system operating within the towns that identified as many as fourteen ironworking guilds by the late medieval period: ironmongers, cutlers, smiths, armourers, clockmakers, lorimers, spurriers, wiredrawers, pinners, nail-makers, lockyers, furbours, ferrours and blacksmiths. According to Dyer (2002, 320) 'the unit of production remained the workshop based on the household, which normally consisted of a handful of workers: the master, his wife, a child or two if they were of working age, and one or two servants or apprentices' but he notes that the metal trades tended to employ a larger workforce, citing Thomas Dounton's pewter workshop in London which boasted eighteen servants and apprentices in 1457. Homer (1991, 71) uses the same evidence of Dounton's establishment to illustrate a rather different picture, namely that of 56 pewterers' 'shops' (*sic*)

Figure 3.2 Reconstruction of iron-working structures at Minepit Wood, Sussex. (By permission of the editor of Medieval Archaeology*)*

in London, 79% consisted of the master working without paid underlings at all, or with only one or two apprentices. Dounton's large establishment was exceptional rather than typical, supporting the argument that the household unit formed the basis of the industrial team within the metals trades as well as in other crafts. Indeed it may be worth noting that small workshop operations, if not household based, continue to this day within the Birmingham Jewellery Quarter, as highlighted by English Heritage in its recent study (Cattell *et al* 2002).

The database compiled for this paper contains 37 metal working sites, 30 of which are southern and 7 are northern. Unsurprisingly, the eight blast furnaces, two bloomeries, and two sites more generally attributed to an association with iron production, are all rural. Two sites specifically associated with bronze are also rural as is the one gun-casting site identified. Urban sites include an armour maker, three bell makers, a pinner and a number of non-specified metal working sites. The Pennington Brass Foundry in Paul Street, Exeter (*PMA* 1983,

199–201) provides one of the few thoroughly excavated urban metal-working sites we were able to track down. Its location on the rear of a burgage plot hard against the city wall is indicative of early concerns about health and safety and environmental control. Cranstone (2001, 190, quoting Rowlands 1975) notes that the metal manufacturing trades tended to operate in a semi-domestic context, with an organised 'putting-out' system, similar to that operating in the textile industry, being developed and run by ironmongers, but also comments that 'the smithies and workshops, and their operatives, of the 16th to 18th centuries have received little attention relative to the blast-furnace and the major ironmaster.' This absence of extensive synthesis of archaeological or documentary evidence for the physical location and layout of the workshop impedes our understanding of the spatial relations of production. Was it attached to the main house or detached within the plot or set at a distance from the master's dwelling?

In total, 14 of the recorded metal working sites are urban and 23 rural. Specialist metal workers tend to be based in the towns. The balance between access to materials and power sources and access to markets is likely to be significant here and one might expect specialist smiths of finished metals to be producing nearer to their markets than to the source of the refined materials, easily transportable to town. Evidence for the point of sale of the finished products in relation to the point of production, is, however, difficult to come by and more work needs to be undertaken on the coincidence of 'workshop' and 'retail shop' in these urban trades. Refining activities, blast furnaces and bloomeries, were all rural, probably reflecting the requirement to be near to raw materials and power sources. The anti-social nature of the work, with its requirement for large spaces, access to fuel, creation of heat, smoke, smells, and pollutants may also be significant here.

Problems exist with exact dating, but of sites where dates are provided 7 were definitely operating in the 15th century, 24 in the 16th century and 20 in the 17th century, indicating better survival for the middle and later part of our period of interest. Interestingly, all of our earliest examples (except one at Trelech, *PMA* 2000, 255) seem to come from urban contexts Norwich (*Med Arch* 1995, 233), Edinburgh (*PMA* 2001, 218), Bath (*PMA* 2000, 215–16) Hounslow (*PMA* 2000, 255), Hedon (*Med Arch* 1997, 300). In the 16th century, nine sites are urban and fifteen rural, which may indicate a shift coinciding with the new technological developments. In the 17th century seven are urban and thirteen rural. Here the urban examples exclusively represent specific types of metal working (for instance, bell casting) and the great number of the rural examples are of blast furnaces and bloomeries. Our database indicates a slight trend for a move to the countryside by the metal working industries between the 15th and the 17th centuries, but whether this generally can be sustained on investigation of a larger set of evidence, and one that runs into the later periods when Sheffield and Birmingham began to be identifiable centres of metal production, requires further research. What we are seeing are relatively small-scale, family-based but entrepreneurial operations – the removal of exclusive ownership rights on the part of the feudal lord of the manor, as well as technological change, seem to be contributing to a change in the industrial base and this may have been contributory to the major changes in the later 18th century. Can these preconditions for changed relations of production be seen elsewhere in the archaeological and historical record for post-medieval industry?

Pottery

Turning to the pottery industry we find some more concrete examples for the relationship between household and craft workshops. Ceramics, the most plentiful component of the medieval and post-medieval archaeological record, are often identified as the signals of major change. The period 1450–1550 saw a dramatic increase in pottery types on the English market, both home-produced and imported, and in the amount of pottery in use. Gaimster and Nenk have suggested that this changing ceramic profile represents 'the division between the respective disciplines of medieval and post-medieval archaeology in this country' (Gaimster & Nenk 1997, 171). Barker, too, looking at the second part of our period, sees the changes in pottery distribution as pivotal, though perhaps more in terms of economic changes in the path than as a marker of disciplinary divides in the late 20th century (Barker 1999). To some extent, one has to agree that the ubiquity of pottery in the record, its usefulness for dating purposes and for identifying trading networks and the consequent expenditure of archaeological resources in terms of both time and money, tends to skew its importance. Nevertheless, it is a useful indicator of standards of living and there is a huge amount of literature on the subject, the synthesis of which only the brave or foolhardy would attempt. Studies deal with typologies, fabrics, production methods, pottery as a dating indicator or as evidence of long-distance trade. Rarely tackled, however, are the social relations of production with which we are concerned here and this is a major area for further investigation.

In his chapter on ceramics, Crossley alludes to the local nature of coarse pottery production in the 16th century. He suggests that specialist potters producing day-to-day earthenwares tended to aggregate in particular localities where access to suitable clays and fuel was convenient and where agricultural incomes were low, as for instance in the area around Wakefield (Crossley 1990, 245–6). Here a concentration of kilns has been found and even some of the placenames (Potovens, Potterton) support his view that pottery production was specialised and localised. This was scarcely new; the same situation

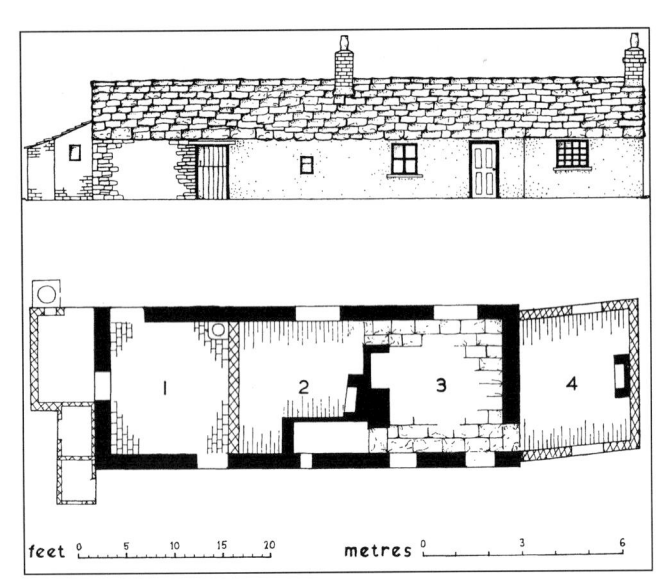

Figure 3.3 Potter's House at Rodger Lane, Potovens, Wakefield. (By permission of the Society for Post-Medieval Archaeology)

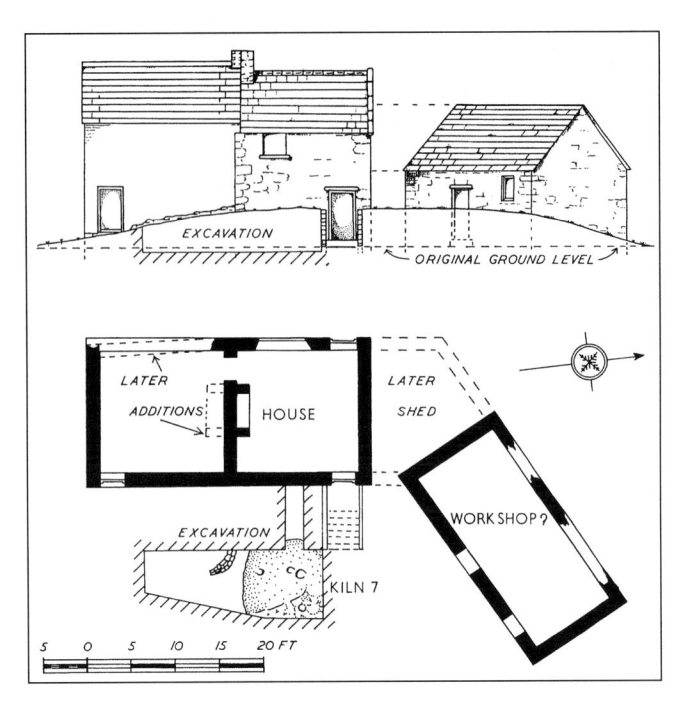

Figure 3.4 Robert Glover's house of 1679, Potovens, Wakefield. (By permission of the Society for Post-Medieval Archaeology)

pertained through the medieval period and indeed the distinctive placenames make their early appearances in documents of the 12th to the 14th centuries (Ekwall 1960, 372). Such centres of production are identified across Britain from central Scotland to Surrey and the south coast, where rural potteries are seen to supply local urban markets (Crossley 1990, 243–53). Crossley argues that increasing specialisation enabled more people to work as full-time potters, rather than using the industry as a supplement to an agricultural living and that at the end of the period covered here, the manufacture of finewares, based on imported prototypes of tin-glazed and stoneware pottery, moved to the towns, while coarseware production remained largely rural. This tendency was amplified in the 18th century when specialist mass-produced finewares began to emanate from the Staffordshire potteries.

If we have some sense, then, of the specialist rural potter, what of his working conditions? Again, the evidence is sparse, but work by Brears and Bartlett at Potovens in West Yorkshire has been particularly helpful, because not only the kilns but also the cottages of the potters have been recorded, and documentary research has revealed something of the social relations of production (Brears 1967; Bartlett 1971). Brears notes that unlike their medieval predecessors, the Potovens potters appear to have worked full-time, rather than engaging in agriculture as well, and supplied a wide area. Although the lord of the manor still controlled access to the raw material, clay, the organisation of the industry was based around small operations (a workshop and a cottage on a small parcel of land) with a master and his apprentice operating a full-time kiln. Brears suggests that the industy was at its height in the second half of the 17th century when there were over a dozen full-time potteries working (Brears 1967, 5–6). Remarkably, a number of the cottages survived to be recorded by Brears, including one that was identified from an initialled datestone with a known potter, Joseph Willans. The surviving mid-17th-century cottages were typical of artisans' dwellings of the period and area, ranging from single-cell units to a three-cell in-line plan and end entry (Fig 3.3). What is interesting in the Rodger Lane example is the pair of external doorways at the southern end, giving access to a waste dump and a heated additional cell, but the absence of direct access to the kilns at the north end – one would have to walk around the gable end to reach these. By the later 17th century, Robert Glover was able to build himself a relatively large stone house with an upper storey, but here the access to the kiln is very direct, as it sits almost directly outside the front door (Fig 3.4). At other sites, settling tanks, sandpits and mixing floors have been identified, but a full articulation of the entire pottery site is so far lacking (Crossley 1990, 274). Nevertheless, a strong sense of household-scale full-time production is gained from the study of the surviving buildings, the excavated evidence for kilns and dumps and the documentary evidence.

Specialisation at particular sites implies that marketing involved travel and Caldwell and Dean (1992) suggest that by the early 17th century, at least, family members were acting as travelling salesmen as well as sales being made from static shops. Certainly, in the absence of a second source of income, it is likely that whole families would be involved in the production and marketing of the wares. Notwithstanding the mass production of earthenwares in the Potteries from the 18th century onwards, Crossley suggests that these rural enterprises survived well into the 19th century to supply the needs of a relatively wide local market (Crossley 1990, 254).

The database compiled for this chapter produced a total of 25 sites, of which 21 were in the south and only four in the north. Of these, only three are conceivably urban (Richmond, Bristol and Boston), but the proximity of Potovens to Wakefield (2.4km (1.5 miles) to the north-west of the town) suggests that a location near to markets and transport was advantageous. In terms of chronological developments, seven of the sites were certainly in use in the 15th century, fifteen were operating in the 16th century and fourteen in the 17th century. From the sites on the database it is hard to draw any conclusions about changes regarding urban and rural locations over our time period. For the whole of our period of interest the industry as represented by our sample is overwhelmingly rural, but the few urban examples seem to have remained in operation over the whole of the period.

Glass production

The frequency of vessel and window glass within medieval assemblages is testimony to its production but evidence is thin in the period up to the middle of the 16th century. Throughout the middle ages, glass sold in Britain mostly came from abroad, (France, Germany, Italy) and English glass producers occupied the lower end of the market both in terms of cost and quality. Crossley (1990, 226) notes three critical technological innovations in post-medieval glass-making. The first, of crucial importance in terms of the social relations of production as well as the physical means, was the introduction of technological innovations by continental immigrants from 1567 onwards, who brought with them more efficient furnaces to make glass of better quality. We will return to the significance of this immigrant population below. At the beginning of the 17th century furnaces began to be fired with fossil fuels rather than wood and this too caused a major shift in the location of production. Finally, by the end of the 17th and the beginning of the 18th century the complexity of furnaces increased, but this development lies outside the time period of this chapter.

The use of wood as the principal fuel for medieval furnaces required their location, like the bloomeries discussed above, in a rural setting. For instance at Knole in Kent a four-pot glasshouse has been calculated to have used about four acres of fifteen-year-old coppice wood a month (Charleston 1991, 244). Furnaces were probably fairly temporary structures of stone, clay and some brickwork and leave little archaeological trace. Only in the 16th century do they seem to have become more permanently built (Charleston 1991, 246). The importance of a good source of timber, along with a coincidence of suitable

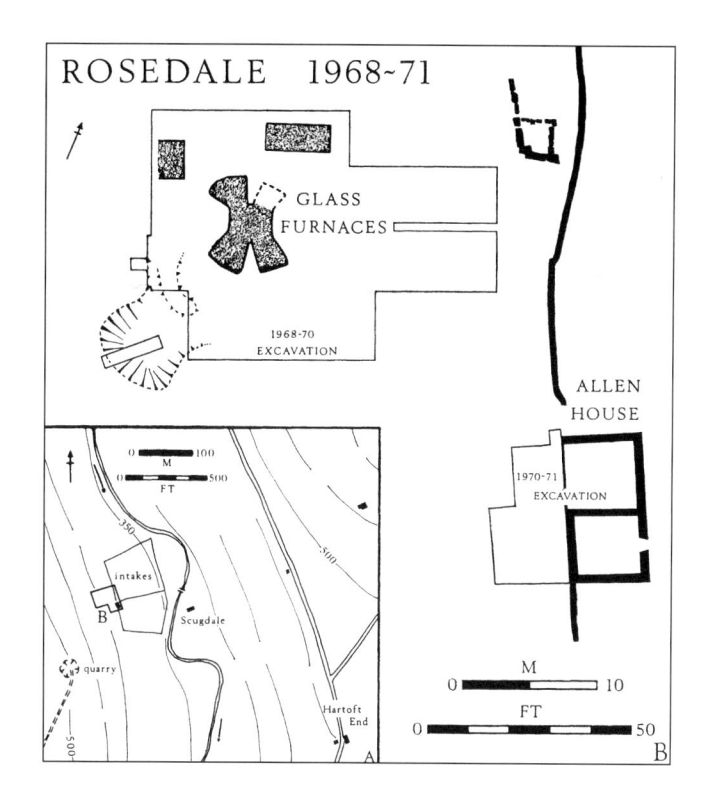

Figure 3.5 Allen House, Rosedale, Yorkshire. The inset (A) shows the relationship of the house to the intakes. The main illustration (B) shows the same area at a larger scale to illustrate the relationship of the house and the furnaces. (By permission of the Society for Post-Medieval Archaeology)

sands, clays and building stone, is reflected in the rural locations of glass furnaces: the sites of Bagot's Park in Staffordshire and Hutton-le-Hole and Rosedale in Yorkshire which we will examine in more detail typify this.

At all of these sites the more elaborate and solidly built furnaces are associated with the immigration of French glassmakers after 1567 when John Carré won the patent to regulate the glass industry (Crossley 1990, 229). In his interesting discussion of the workforce at Bagot's Park near Abbots Bromley in Staffordshire, Crossley (1967, 44–7, 64–7) identifies the importance of family ties in the glassmaking industry and comments on the advent of the French in the documentary record of the later 16th century. For Rosedale and Hutton-le-Hole, the written evidence for immigrant workers is absent, but Crossley postulates a continental origin for the glassmakers, based on the form of the furnaces and interestingly speculates on a possible link between the name of the cottage adjacent to the Rosedale site (Allen House) and a corruption of the word 'Allemain', by which the French from the border province of Lorraine, who dominated the glass trade at this time, might have been known. It is a long shot, but an attractive theory if true.

Allen House (Fig 3.5) provides us with a rare glimpse of the possible domestic arrangements of the glassmakers. Here a two-roomed cottage is associ-

36 *The vernacular workshop*

BOLSTERSTONE GLASSHOUSE

(Pothouse Farm)

STOCKSBRIDGE

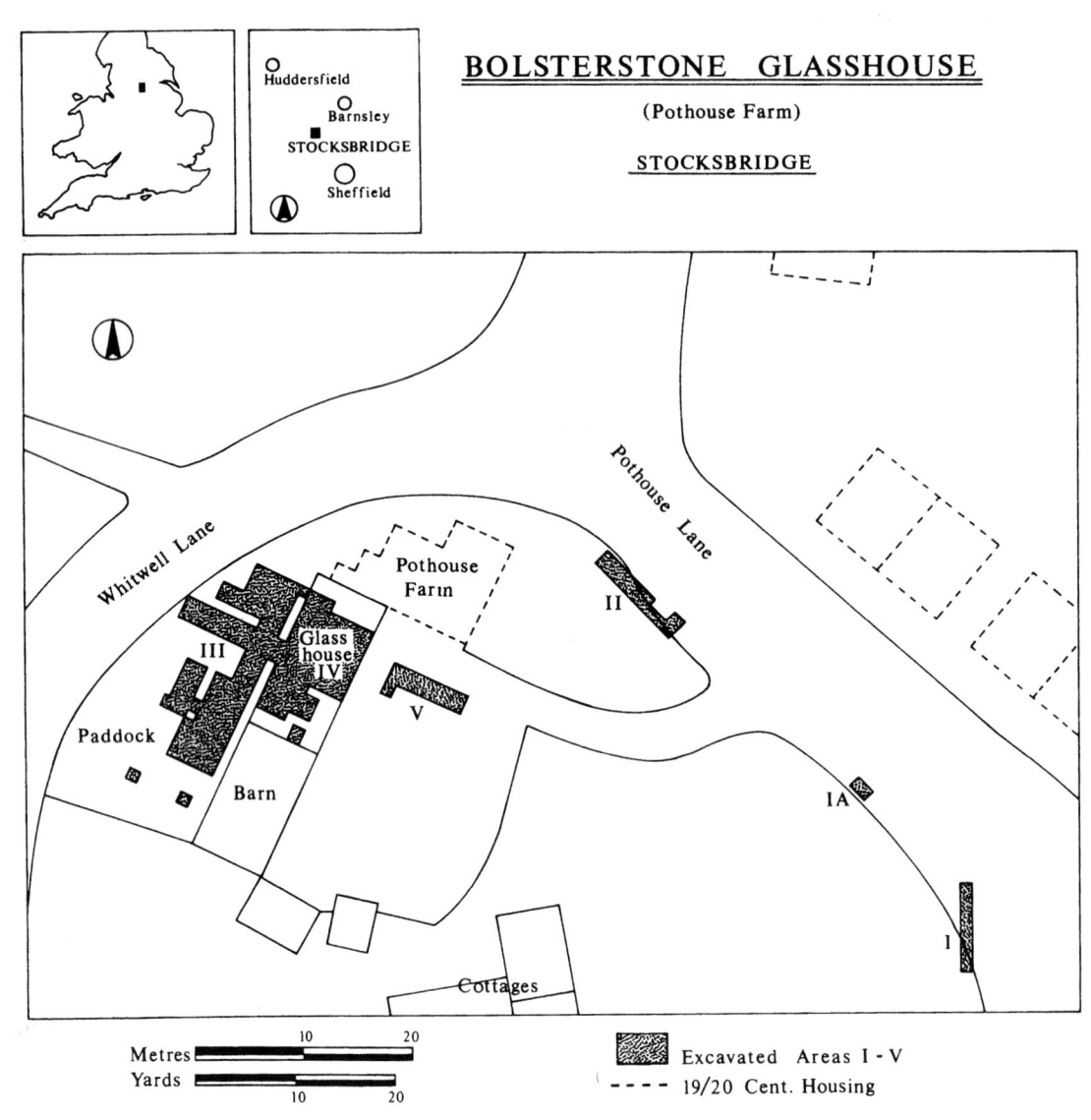

Figure 3.6 Bolsterstone Glasshouse, Stocksbridge, Yorkshire. Location map and plan of excavated areas. (By permission of the Society for Post-Medieval Archaeology)

ated with two intake paddocks and the lower cell is a byre with a central drain running across its width. It is dated on the basis of pottery and clay pipe finds to the early 17th century. Crossley is very cautious about assigning the occupancy of the house to the glassmakers, but its proximity to the furnaces and the absence of other dwellings in the vicinity must surely make a strong argument. The arrangement of the house, with its relationship to the intakes and its byre indicate that farming formed at least part, if not all, of the income of the occupant and it seems reasonable to suggest that glass making was therefore a part-time occupation here in the early 17th century. Documentary evidence from Bagot's Park supports the contention that glass making was not, in the early 17th century, a single and continuous occupation.

The strength of family ties and the consequences of their sundering are explored by Dennis Ashurst in his consideration of the glassmakers of Bolsterstone to the north of Sheffield. This is a somewhat later site, its principal phases dating from the mid-17th to the mid-18th century, after Sir Robert Mansell was granted a patent authorising the licensing of coal-fired furnaces (Crossley 1990, 233), a development which resulted in the abandonment of the wood-burning furnaces such as Rosedale. At Bolsterstone a local family, the Foxes, controlled the furnaces and their monopoly was so jealously guarded that a will was changed in the mid-18th century, effectively to cut out a sub-branch of the family that threatened competition (Ashurst 1987, 149–53). This particular incident occurred later than the time period under investigation here, yet this highly focused and protectionist 'family business' aspect of glassmaking seems to have pertained from the late 16th century. Indeed, the layout of the buildings at Bolsterstone, close to the furnaces (Fig 3.6), reinforces this sense of a domestic level of production, albeit one that, according to Crossley (1967, 65) engaged a team with a master 'but the number of other men varied, with at least one other skilled founder, a batch maker and labourers for stoking, cartage and case-making'. Crossley also notes the 'notorious status-consciousness of the immigrant *gentilhommes verriers*'. An interesting exercise would be to identify more of the houses and workshops of this highly self-identified and exclusive group to see the extent to which their domestic use of space can be seen to reflect their business ethic. Within the broader context of Johnson's 'middling sort' of the 17th century, notable for the enclosure of their houses, the peculiarities of this group would repay closer attention.

The database compiled for the present research project identified eleven sites in total, of which four were urban (three of them associated with London) and seven rural. The north/south divide was less marked than in the other categories of industry explored here, with six southern and four northern sites, but this may reflect a bias in research, given the activities of Crossley and Ashurst in the later 20th century. Unsurprisingly, given the nature of the development of the industry, the 16th and 17th centuries are better represented than the 15th and the shift from wooded to coalfield areas in the 17th century is noticeable.

Conclusions

Our survey has revealed that the evidence for medieval and post-medieval workshops, as opposed to industry and the products of industry, is sketchy in the published literature. Syntheses, such as the excellent work of Crossley, Schofield and Vince and the contributors to Blair and Ramsay's *English Medieval Industries*, have been able to shed some light on technologies and locations. Economic and social historians such as Dyer (2002), Kermode (1998), Goldberg (1992), Swanson (1999), Corfield (1990), Clark and Slack (1976) have discussed the social relations of production and Giles (2000) has situated those social relations within the material context of the guildhalls and parish churches. What we do not have is a detailed consideration of the social relations within the workplace. We have some indications of gender relations from documentary sources but their precise articulation remains obscure, as does the operation of the master/apprentice relationship within the workplace.

One major issue that is inadequately resolved is the relationship of the workshop to the domestic dwelling. Given the oft-repeated statement that medieval workshops were associated with a domestic mode of production, it is perhaps interesting to note that of the 164 sites included in our database, 86% did not provide enough information to be able to say definitively whether or not they were associated with a domestic dwelling. In 5% of cases it was clear that they were not. In this paper, we have highlighted some of the 9% of sites that clearly are associated with a domestic structure, simply because it is this area that we were trying to elucidate. A more systematic interrogation of the unpublished records that lie behind the brief entries in *Medieval Britain* and *Post-Medieval Britain* might produce a more reliable sample.

The matter of craft specialisation was also a central question. It is commonly considered that rural artisans combined their trade with agriculture while their urban counterparts specialised. We are familiar with the idea that post-medieval textile workers operated from workshops at home on a 'putting-out' system and frequently combined their industrial activities with agriculture. Yet the evidence investigated here for the rural and semi-urban industries of metal-working, pottery and glass-making suggests that by the 17th century, a craft workshop was more likely than not to specialise, to the exclusion of agriculture. This tendency towards single-occupation economies may be connected to the fact that these seem to have been *household* economies. The high level of specialised knowledge required seems to have been handed down through families. In the glass industry in particular, the dominance of immigrant families in the 17th century meant that this was a highly self-identified and exclusive group: the strength of family ties can be seen in the history of the Bolsterstone site where the Fox family ran a business that persisted until the 18th century when new technology overtook the capacity of the kiln and it was adapted for pottery firing. There are tantalising glimpses of gender relations in the published material, but a more detailed investigation of both written sources and the houses on the sites of workshops may help to answer critical questions. Did all members of the household participate in the craft or was there some diversification, with junior members working outside the home in other occupations or bringing work in? How was work disposed physically within the house and its plot? How far was access to work areas controlled and restricted?

Finally, how did the changing economic conditions of the early modern world affect craft production and its material expression? The evidence collected for this chapter suggests that craftsmen were working in an increasingly entrepreneurial mode during the 16th and 17th centuries, creating the social, as well as economic, conditions for the acceleration into full industrialisation of the mid-18th and the 19th centuries. The rights of the landlord over the products of industry carried out on his land seem reduced to cash rents only and an increasingly capitalised industrial basis saw the rise of the specialist craftmaster engaged not only in production but in extensive marketing of his wares beyond the immediate vicinity. The extent to which the changes in the post-medieval economy set the preconditions for industrialisation is an area of study that would repay further attention from historical archaeologists, asking questions about the relations of production that are as searching as those they have already asked, and largely successfully answered, about the means of production.

4 Late medieval workshops in East Anglia
by Leigh Alston

Introduction

The market towns and villages of Suffolk and Essex provide a rich source of evidence for the student of medieval and Tudor shops. The combination of the region's economic success during the late 15th and early 16th centuries, based largely upon woollen cloth manufacture, with its subsequent relative poverty, has preserved numerous examples. The towns of central southern Suffolk in particular, of which Lavenham is the best known, retain complete streets of timber-framed houses, often thinly disguised by later veneers of plaster and brick, and a majority of these appear to have contained shops. This degree of survival is a far cry from the very limited urban evidence encountered by colleagues elsewhere in the country, who find that continued commercial affluence has typically caused the modernisation and destruction of early shop fronts.

This chapter describes the principal types of shop encountered in East Anglia, and contends that most were used as workshops rather than retail units in the modern sense; they were areas in which production rather than selling formed the primary activity. Many, and in some towns a large majority, were involved in the manufacture of cloth. Although certain features of appearance and location may be more associated with production than retailing, it is not generally possible or sensible, except in rare instances where documentary evidence may be available, to distinguish shops from workshops in the medieval town.

Documentary evidence

The standard appearance of medieval shops in England has been described elsewhere, most notably by Stenning (1985) and Clark (2000), drawing upon the former's survey of 30 shops located chiefly in Essex, and the latter's national database of 190 examples. Over 100 16th-century or earlier shops have been identified in Suffolk alone by the present author, and many more await discovery. It is to be regretted that few systematic surveys of this most promising region have been undertaken, and the descriptions in the existing List of Buildings of Special Architectural and Historic Significance are based largely upon external evidence. Many important medieval structures in Lavenham and its surrounding parishes remain unlisted or, at best, wrongly described on the basis of Georgian or Victorian façades. The true number of early shops in East Anglia is therefore unknown.

The author's random sample of 60 buildings in Lavenham, dating from the 14th to 16th centuries, has identified 11 complete or fragmentary shop fronts of the type described below. This sample represents approximately half the known total of pre 17th-century houses in the town. Within the sample, only 26 still preserved relevant evidence, so the total of eleven suggests that over 40% of the town's early buildings may have possessed shops. This proportion is compatible with similar archaeological research in other local towns and villages such as Nayland and Woodbridge, and with work in larger towns elsewhere; of 839 houses in Winchester in 1417, for example, 437 were said by Keene (1985, 149, 164) to have 'probably contained either workshops or lock-ups'.

Given the large number of shops in medieval towns we must turn to the written record to understand their precise nature. The term 'shop' is used very loosely in early documents as a place of work or business, and does not imply retail activity. Surviving premises are by no means confined to market places or other commercial sites, or to a single class of property, and are commonly found at the ends of minor side streets or in rear courtyards, attached to houses of both high and low status. Rural shop fronts are rare, although a house that may be isolated today might well have formed part of a small hamlet in the past. The retailing of fresh food and other everyday commodities was probably the concern chiefly of peripatetic traders at the weekly or twice-weekly market rather than a town's permanent shops. The tiny, picturesque village of Kersey in southern Suffolk no longer boasts a single shop, but in 1398 its market contained areas not just for the usual staples such as bread, fish, and meat but for tanners, linen-drapers, spicers, and brass merchants.[1] Larger towns such as Ipswich even maintained timber markets (Malster 2000, 107). This diversity of market trading appears to have declined during the 16th and 17th centuries, as populations and disposable incomes increased and supported permanent retail shops of the modern kind. In 1618 the manorial lord of the thriving town of Haverhill, Suffolk, could lament the contraction of his market and its variety of goods when compared with that recorded in his 15th-century rent rolls.[2]

The evidence of wills and inventories suggests that permanent shops did not seek to compete with the influx of retailers on market day, but concentrated on manufacture. Specialist retail outlets were few, and sold an enormous variety of merchandise that would shame a major 21st-century department store. In 1574 the Council of King's Lynn tried to settle a dispute between the two main types of general retailer in the town by specifying precisely what each could lawfully stock (Parker 1971, 124); both the chandlers on the one hand and grocers on the other were able to sell soap, vinegar, resin, hops, honey, nails, birdlime, wax, bottles, string and ties, flax, shoe horns, trenchers, cord, ink, paper, pins, needles, combs, clothes fastenings, sacking, woolcards, cotton wool, pots, and straw hats, but only the chandlers were permitted to deal in various additional items such as scales, shovels, lanterns, breadgrates, and whetstones, while the grocers also sold food and cloth. Smaller towns were still served by retailers of this kind in the 17th and 18th centuries, and their shelf and box-lined interiors are reminiscent of the one-stop general stores of the American West as depicted in Hollywood movies. The 1692 inventory of a grocer and draper in the Essex market town of Roxwell values the boxes, shelves, scales, and weights in the shop at £2 (just 3 shillings less than the entire contents of his well furnished hall), and reveals a stock ranging from innumerable lengths and types of cloth to finished coats, hose, pepper, gunpowder and balls, tobacco, raisins, mops, bed cords, sugar, tar, indigo, candles, bellows, mouse traps, and 'some odd things' (Steer 1969, 213).

If general retailing was confined to a few medieval shops, what was the purpose of the majority? Inventories are rare survivals before the mid-17th century, but numerous 15th- and 16th-century wills suggest an answer. Elizabeth Braunche, for example, a wealthy Lavenham widow who made her will in 1501, left the two looms in her shop, while in 1537 clothier Roger Critoft of Prentice Street bequeathed the looms, trendles, and instruments in his, and in 1542 John Browne, a sherman, mentioned six pairs of shears and other equipment 'belonging to his occupation' in his shop. The exact locations of these workshops within houses are rarely specified, although in 1498 John Smyth of Long Melford, some 4.8 km (3 miles) distant from Lavenham, specified the looms, slays, and trendles in his shop next to the street, and John Berner of the same town referred to the shop 'on the corner' in 1454.[3] Elizabeth Braunche's shop was on the ground floor as her chantry priest lived in the chamber above it.

Late medieval Suffolk, and in particular its central southern area around Lavenham, was dominated by the manufacture of woollen cloth. A taxation survey of the wealth and occupations of Lavenham's residents in 1522, when most of its surviving shop fronts were relatively new, reveals the trade as almost the only source of affluence in the town (Pound 1986). Over 70% of all individuals whose occupations were recorded worked in the industry, and of the 47 with savings of £5 or more (a substantial sum, when a skilled artisan would earn only 6d per day on piece work) only five were not engaged in the industry. Not a single carpenter lived in the town, despite the high proportion of existing buildings that date from precisely this period, and its economy seems to have been highly distorted. A very similar picture is found nearby in Nayland, but other neighbouring towns such as Long Melford and Sudbury have more broadly based patterns of occupation, with no more than half related to woollen production, and totals of five and seven carpenters respectively. Documentary sources prove that weaving and finishing took place in small workshops with relatively few looms in comparison with the large weaving sheds of later centuries. The weavers in the large Suffolk town of Bury St Edmunds were bound by a statute of 1477 that prohibited the possession of more than four looms at any one time (Betterton & Dymond 1989), and wills suggest the presence of numerous shops containing only one or two looms. According to contemporary descriptions, the clothiers who controlled the industry could employ as many as 500 weavers and other outworkers based in their own homes. Given this overwhelming documentary evidence, it is difficult to avoid the conclusion that a high proportion of the surviving shops in Lavenham and other East Anglian towns were designed as cloth workshops. While local sale was more common in the 13th and 14th centuries, most Suffolk cloth was destined for export in the later Middle Ages and these shops would have seen little or no direct retailing.

This is not to say, of course, that many workshops were not occupied by other trades. A barber surgeon in the small town of Bures St Mary on the Essex-Suffolk border possessed a shop and an operating chamber ('camera operationis') in 1474, and a glover in the same parish left 'oone hundred of lether redy tannyd owt of my shoppe' in his will of 1551.[4] His neighbour, George Simpson, was fined in 1543 for emptying 'le Bevyr domus officius sue vocatur le woad hous' into the street, that is, discharging the foul-smelling 'beaver' residue of his woad fermenting vats from his workshop called the woad house.[5] Dyehouses of this kind are common in the documentary record, but archaeologically elusive. They are not usually described as shops, and, given their need for hearths and large vats, cannot have been contained in the standard shop units described below. Cloth production declined sharply in the mid-16th century as religious conflict removed its vital export markets, and many cloth towns were plunged into a relative poverty from which many emerged only in the late 20th century. Lavenham's extreme dependence on the industry caused its fall from the fourteenth most wealthy town in England in 1524 to the rank of only seventh in central southern Suffolk alone a generation later in 1568.[6] This economic collapse was the direct cause of the area's high survival rate of early buildings and shop fronts.

Although cloth workshops had dwindled by the 17th century, with many converted into living accommodation, primary retail outlets continued in the minority. Of the 25 17th-century Essex shop

40 *The vernacular workshop*

inventories recorded by Steer (1969), only four can be recognised as those of retailers of the modern type as opposed to manufacturing workshops. A Roxwell weaver who died in 1638 had 'three old Loomes with all the other ymplements belonging to them', while a variety of other trades possessed working tools in their 'shops'. Gamaliell Rathbane of Writtle was described as a gentleman, but still had a shop in his townhouse that contained turning tools and was perhaps let accordingly. Several houses contain shop chambers or other rooms named with reference to shops but lack inventories of the shops themselves, as might be expected if shops were often let to third parties. The 1665 shop inventory of Thomas Poultar, a Writtle glover, was probably typical of a workshop with a retail counter that would have been recognised throughout the Middle Ages: 'one shopp-board, one stake and withe, one pairing knife, Severall Plankes and boards, one Beame knife with some other implements, 10s; one Bullock hyde drest, 5s; one dozon of Sheepe skins & one dozen of lambe skins, 8s; Tenn calve-skins drest, 7s 6d; twelve pair of Gloves, 6s; fower broken Hydes, 16s; Seaven Broken Calve skins, 4s.'

Shops in domestic houses

The great majority of medieval and Tudor shops in East Anglia formed part of domestic houses. They are recognised on the basis of their distinctive windows; as Stenning (1985) puts it, 'the shop front, of two or more relatively wide, arch-topped openings, is the crucial identifying feature', although single openings are occasionally found. The most typical arrangement can be seen in the Market Place of Lavenham (Figs 4.1 and 4.2). This much published early 16th-century shop is perfectly authentic, although one arch has been renewed and its external hinged shutters are 18th or 19th-century replacements of earlier internal examples. The shop extended to 3.65 × 2.4 m (12 × 8 ft), and was lit by two wide openings with solid arched heads that lacked either glazing or mullions. Rebates and pintles for internal, vertically hinged shutters are preserved behind the arches; these single shutters would have been hooked to the ceiling by day, clear of the working area, and lowered at night. A narrow door opened directly into the shop to the right of its windows, and another from inside the house. It is generally assumed that shops of this type were used in the manner of modern market stalls, with merchandise displayed on counters set up either inside or outside the windows (or both). In only one example of the author's acquaintance is there evidence of a fixed counter attached by external mortices (Saffron Walden Youth Hostel, Essex) but inventories sometimes include shop boards and trestles. Customers were not expected to enter the premises, and the openings operated as serving hatches. Similar hatches can be found in the kitchens of large medieval houses such as Badly Hall

Figure 4.1 26 Market Place, Lavenham (Lavenham Guildhall Restaurant). A good example of the standard East Anglian shop façade, with later external shutters. Early 16th century. (© David Clark)

in Suffolk and Gainsborough Old Hall in Lincolnshire, where food was collected for delivery to the table. In some instances, such as the Woolpack Inn, Coggeshall, Essex, evidence remains of framed canopies or awnings that projected above the windows to protect them from rain and direct sunlight.

The large windows of medieval shops would certainly have been ideally suited to the display of merchandise, and the often narrow proportions of their doors are sensibly explained by the desire to maximise space for this purpose (it is not necessary to interpret them as security measures against shop-lifting, as have other students of the subject). Where the shop windows fail to fill the available space, leaving a solid panel as shown to the left in Figure 4.1, it is possible to suggest the presence of shelving inside the shop that would otherwise have intruded upon the opening. It is normal to find evidence of large pegs in horizontal rows within former shops that once projected to support shelves and perhaps other fixtures such as benches (medieval furniture was often attached to timber-framed walls in this way). If it is accepted, as documentary

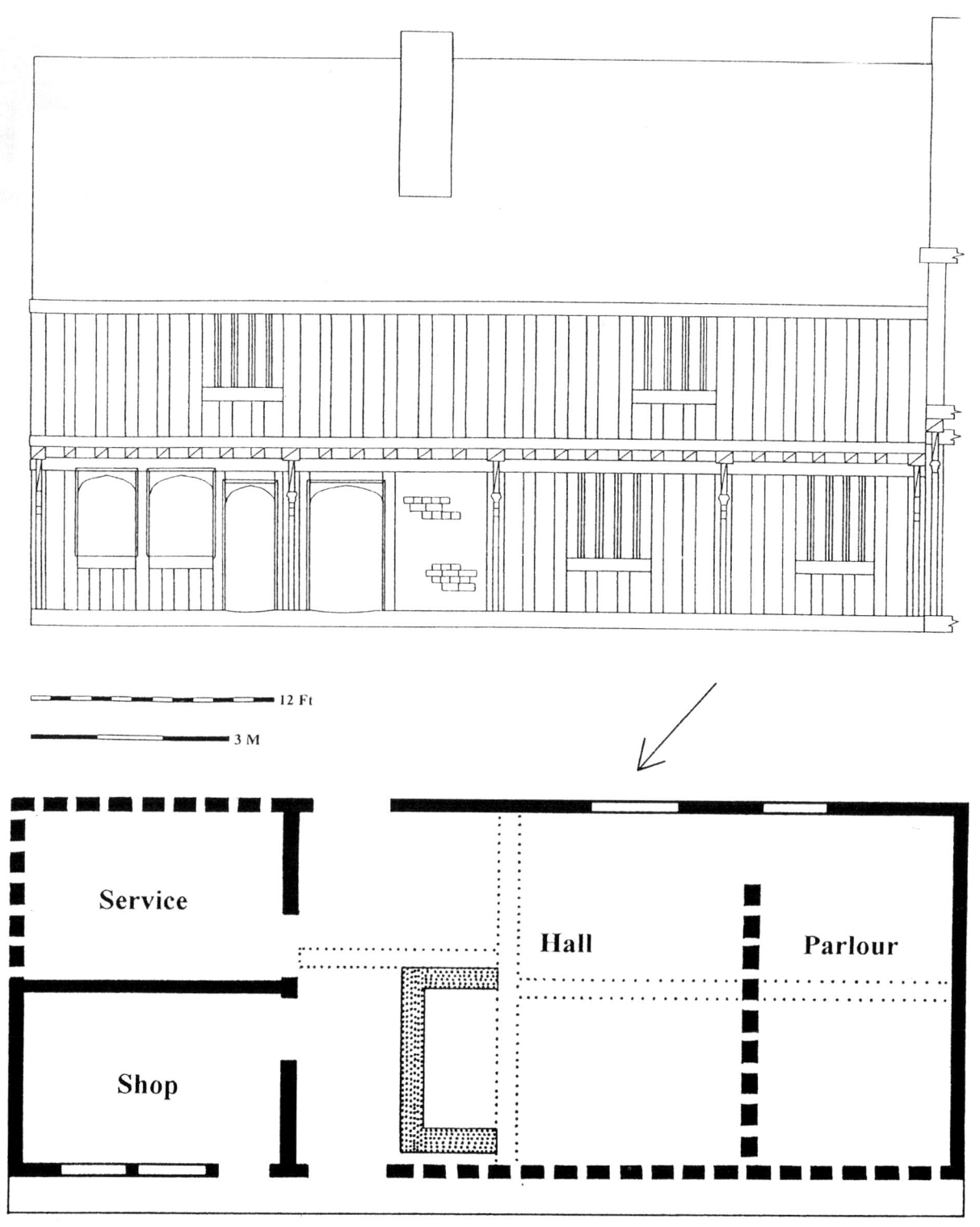

Figure 4.2 26 Market Place, Lavenham. Reconstruction of original façade and ground plan. (© Leigh Alston)

evidence insists, that retail activity played a relatively minor role in the activity of most early shops, the large windows can also be interpreted as the means of admitting as much light to the working area as possible. In the absence of adequate artificial lighting this must have been of vital concern in a workshop. The inconveniently high sills of certain windows are no longer problematic if it is appreciated that retail sale and display was not their sole purpose.

Shops are encountered most frequently in the front service rooms of domestic houses, and in many Suffolk cloth towns it is almost a surprise not to find evidence of them, however subtle, where the relevant wall has escaped destruction or an inconvenient coat of plaster. The room plan shown in Figure 4.2 was ubiquitous in medieval and Tudor East Anglia, as in much of the country, and was reflected to one degree or another in houses across the social scale.[7] A central hall, open to its roof and heated by an open hearth until the gradual introduction of chimneys during the late-15th and early–16th centuries, was flanked on one side by a pair of service (storage) rooms and on the other by a single chamber often termed a parlour and used as the principal sleeping area. The medieval parlour and service rooms were usually floored over, in contrast to the central hall, but wills and inventories indicate that the unheated upper rooms were used chiefly for storage rather than living (despite exceptions such as Elizabeth Braunche's chantry priest) and raw wool, grain, or finished cloth are commonly recorded here. The hall was divided by a cross-passage from the two service rooms, known collectively in contemporary sources as 'spences' (from dispensary, i.e. rooms from which items were dispensed into the hall), or individually as butteries (for wet goods) and pantries (for dry). The front service room was usually the larger of the two, as the stair to the chamber above typically intruded into its counterpart to the rear, and was the natural choice for a shop; it left the parlour free for sleeping and the private affairs of the household, while the smoky hall, even where space permitted, would not have been suitable for the manufacture or sale of anything that needed to be kept clean and free of smuts. The size of the service room was limited nonetheless, and explains the rarity of more than two looms in documented weaving shops.

It should be emphasised that a lack of shop fenestration by no means excludes the possibility of either retail or manufacturing activity in a given context. Shop fronts are not common in rural communities, although isolated examples do exist, yet large numbers of widows in such areas are known to have brewed and sold ale from their houses (Bennett, 1996) and many weavers and other cloth workers were also active in the countryside. We must assume that individual looms were set up in service rooms or parlours lit by normal windows barred with mullions. It may be that arched windows carried additional significance, regarded perhaps as a badge of commercial probity and permanence; announcing a place of business to passers-by and neighbours alike in a manner less necessary if neighbours and passers-by were few and far between. The display of expensive, ostentatious close-studding is also confined largely to urban or semi-urban locations in Suffolk, with even high-status rural manor houses content with plastered exteriors. The proximity of the small number of otherwise isolated rural shop fronts to major road junctions may support such an interpretation.[8]

While the service façade of twin arched windows with a narrow entrance beside a cross-passage is the most common shop type in East Anglian cloth towns, there is, inevitably, considerable variation on the theme, both in terms of fenestration, access, and location within the house. Figure 4.3 shows a mid-

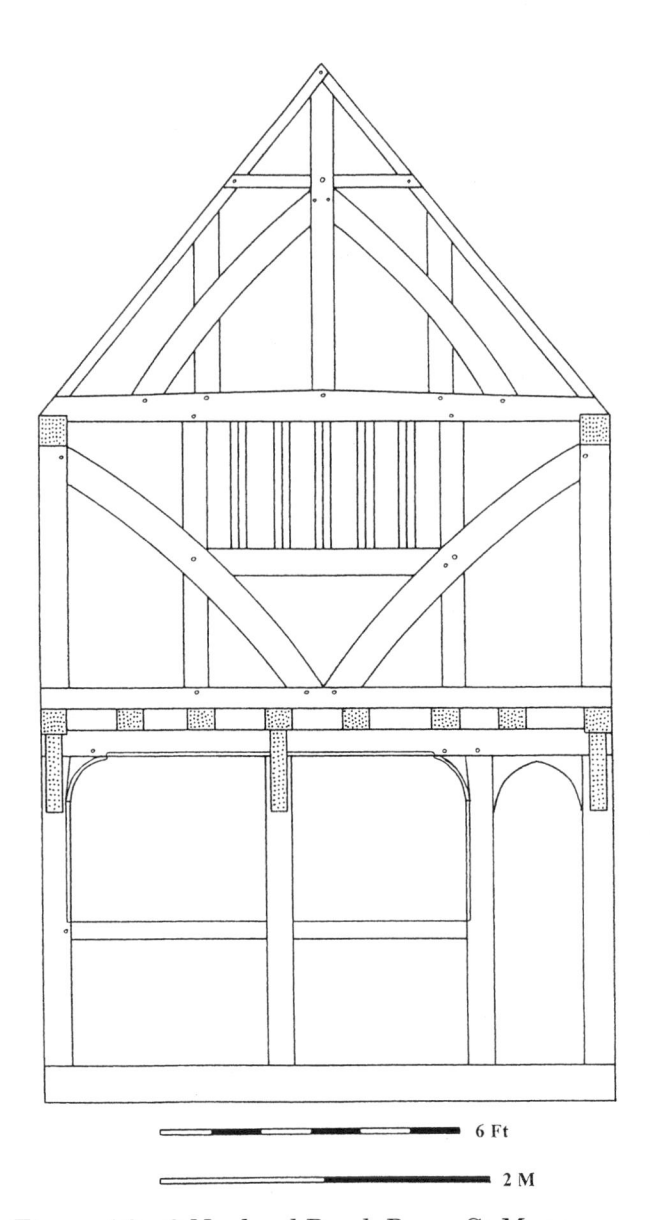

Figure 4.3 2 Nayland Road, Bures St Mary, Suffolk. Mid 14th-century service gable (reconstruction) showing a typical earlier pattern of shop front in the region. (© Leigh Alston)

14th-century example of a service cross-wing where the sense of an arch is conveyed by a pair of corner brackets; this represents a relatively early survival for the region, and is essentially a single, wide aperture supported by its brackets and a post that is slightly off-centre (thanks to the distribution of jetty joists to which it could be braced, rather than any desire for asymmetry). The use of brackets in this manner is typical of 14th- and early 15th-century shops in the region, with the solid arch more usual in the late 15th and 16th centuries, although there is a distinct regional variation in Suffolk with bracket openings persisting far later in the central and northern area of the county. The widely spaced gable timbers in Figure 4.3 pre-date the fashion of subsequent centuries for close-studding. There are surprisingly few significant departures from this standard pattern, although three windows instead of two can

Figure 4.4 Antrim House, Haughley, Suffolk. Internal elevation of a service bay shop front with a unique pattern, incorporating a central door and small hatch. (© Leigh Alston)

sometimes be found (famously at 10–11 Lady Street, Lavenham), and the occasional unique variation such as that at Antrim House, Haughley, Suffolk (Fig 4.4) seems only to emphasise the general uniformity. There is no obvious explanation for the central door and small hatch in the service bay at Haughley, which faces the market place; perhaps the hatch was used for retail display while the artisan worked by the light of his arched windows.

The uniformity of shops in East Anglian market towns probably owes much to the lack of pressure on building space that produced greater variety of plan and façade in larger cities. It is relatively rare, for example, to encounter the rows of shops with domestic accommodation either behind or above that are often discussed as urban norms in the literature (eg Grenville 1997, 165–171). In attempting to interpret the purpose of these shops, and link layout with function, we should probably not be too precise. Whether the windows were used to display retail goods or light a workshop, or which of the entrances was used by the customer or the owner, were probably matters of usage rather than design. The standard shop was probably a multi-purpose unit that could function in several different ways as the owner's needs changed over time. Just as the standard layout of domestic houses was fixed by custom, so was that of the shop; in many cases the question faced by the builder of a new property, when asked by his carpenter, was simply whether or not he wanted a shop. The carpenter would provide the standard type, as copied from the numerous models in the region. Contracts for new medieval houses in Suffolk were drawn up in this manner, with the owner's input restricted to a choice of carved decoration or general shape as specified with reference to a neighbouring building. In the 1460s, for example, Laurence Smith's new town house in Bury St Edmunds was to be 'tymberyd after Edmund Ampes hall' (Dymond 1998). The standard shop, accessible from both inside the house and from the street, offered great flexibility and could serve equally well as a retail outlet or workshop operated by the occupant of the house or let as a 'lock-up' to a third party who could gain access from the street without disturbing the owner. Where modern shop fronts rarely seem to endure more than a few months, their medieval predecessors were designed to meet the changing needs of several generations.

A significant proportion of shops in front service rooms were provided with narrow entrances both from the street and the hall, as at 40–43 Prentice Street in Lavenham (Fig 4.5). The internal service door to the 14th-century shop in Figure 4.3 is also just 0.45 m (18 in) in width. This is somewhat surprising given the usual insistence on symmetry in medieval interiors, and indicates the need to maximise wall space within the shop both for shelving and machinery. A minority of shops could not be entered from the street. This lack of any external entrance is usually associated with narrow bays or cross-wings that could not readily have accommodated even narrow doors in their frontages without restricting working or display space. Figure 4.6 reconstructs the façade of Bildeston Hall, Bildeston, Suffolk, which originally comprised a row of at least four early 16th-century tenements on the market place. Only the two central tenements now survive, each containing a hall separated by a cross-passage from a narrow shop that was lit by twin arched windows. The absence of an external shop door is scarcely surprising given the narrow shop bay (2.4 m or 8 ft) and is unlikely to indicate any dramatic difference of function. These shops could only be entered via the cross-passage, and while the internal partition in this instance has unfortunately been removed, similar examples elsewhere were sometimes provided with doors against their front walls rather than in the usual central position. In other instances, such as the Tendring Estate Office in Stoke-by-Nayland, Suffolk, the shop entrance is central but distinguished from the adjacent service door by size or

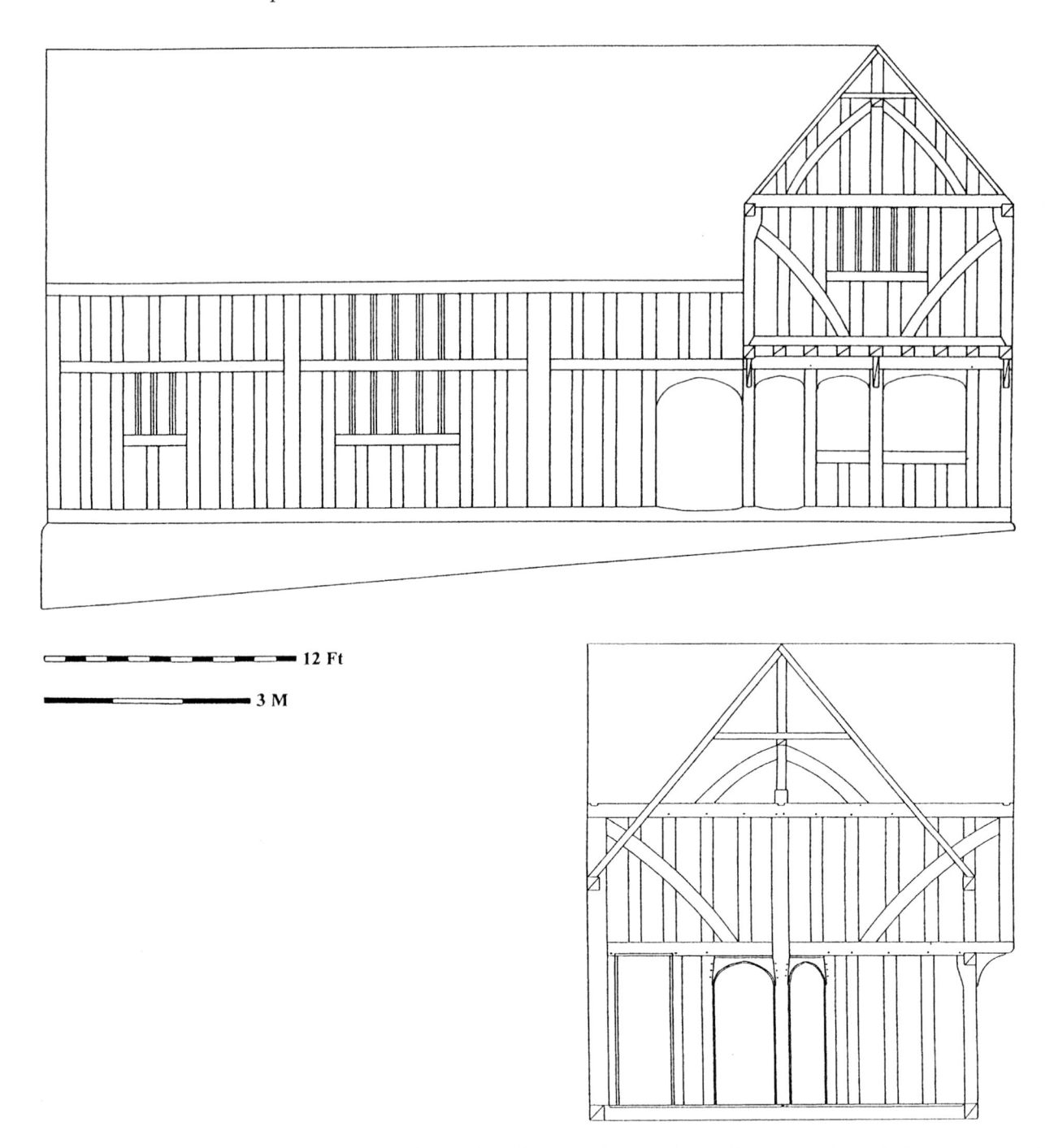

Figure 4.5 40–43 Prenctice Street, Lavenham, Suffolk. Reconstructions of the façade and the service end of the open hall. A service room shop with narrow entrances from both hall and street, intended to maximise storage and working space. (© Leigh Alston)

shape; the shop door at Stoke is somewhat taller that its neighbour, while at 70 Bear Street in nearby Nayland the shop is indicated by a segmental arch and the service room by a two-centred arch.

Considerable numbers of small, 'two-cell' medieval houses remain in East Anglia, where space or money was insufficient to accommodate all three elements of the usual domestic plan. In some cases, as at Bildeston Hall and 27 Cumberland Street, Woodbridge (Fig 4.7) they contain service bays and halls without parlours, but others sacrifice their service rooms and place shops in their parlours. Figure 4.8 shows a well-preserved 15th-century example at 16 Fen Street, Nayland, where one of a pair of semi-detached tenements contains a standard shop front in the front half of a subdivided parlour. The shop was entered both from the street and the high end of the hall, despite a clash of doors, and the small room behind the shop presumably combined the function of parlour and service area. The surviving evidence for this shop front, as shown in Figure 4.9, is typical of the region; although both window arches have been removed to accommodate modern casements,

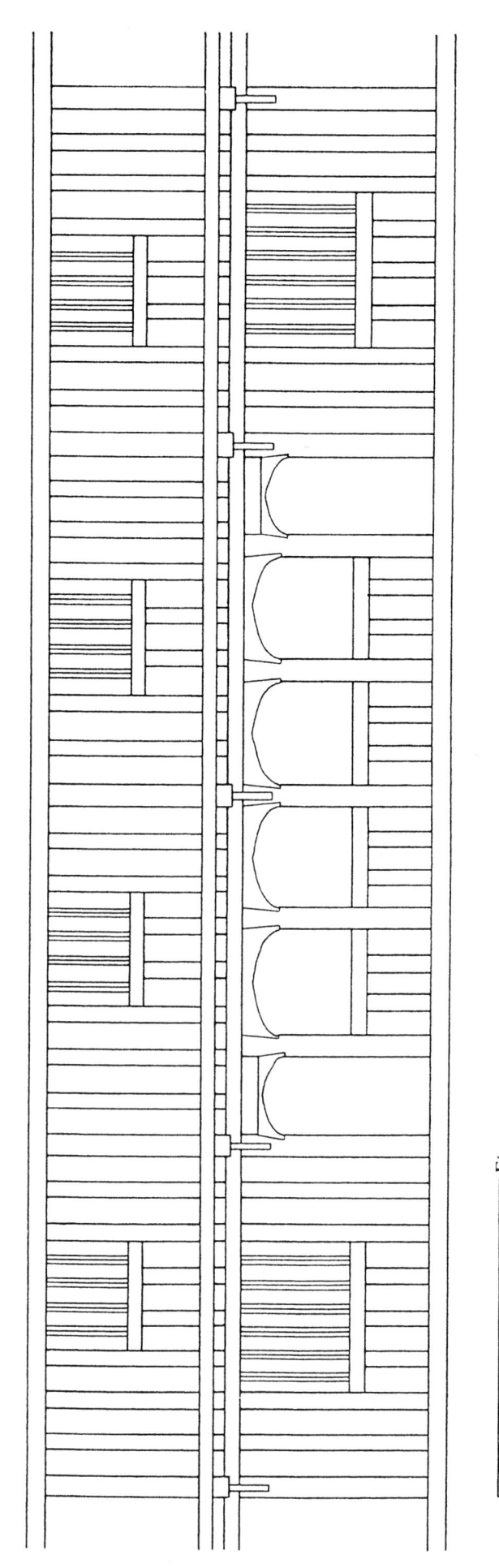

Figure 4.6 Bildeston Hall, Bildeston, Suffolk. The central two properties of a row that once contained at least four two-roomed tenements, each with a hall, cross-passage and workshop. Reconstruction of original façade. (© Leigh Alston)

Figure 4.7 27 Cumberland Street, Woodbridge, Suffolk. An early 16th-century semi-detached pair of 'two-cell' tenements, with a shop in each front service room. Reconstruction of original façade and ground plan. (© Leigh Alston)

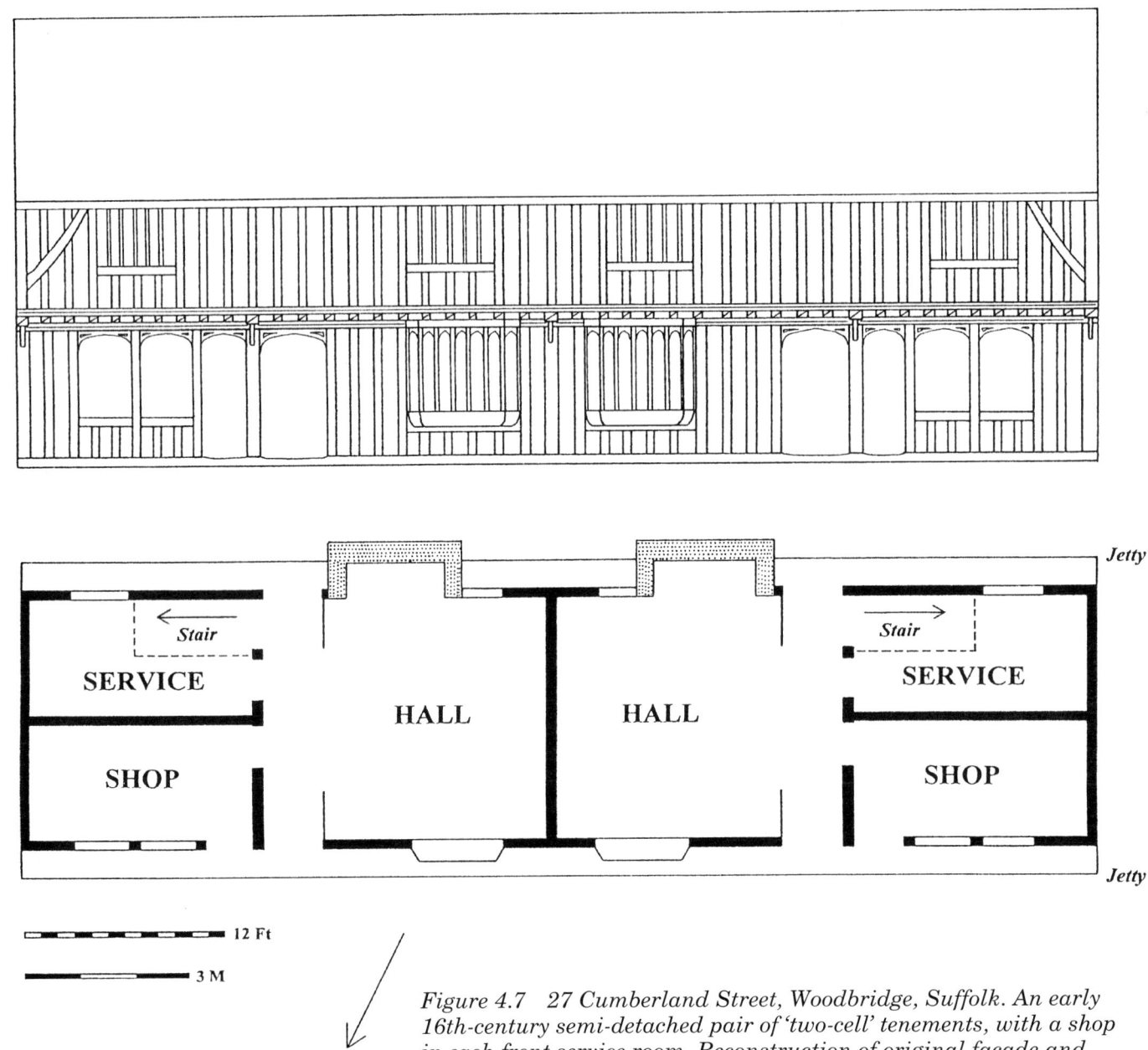

leaving only tell-tale angled mortices, the narrow arch of the blocked shop door remains intact to the right. Nos 31–39 Chapel Street in Bildeston faced, like Bildeston Hall, the medieval market place of a thriving cloth town (Fig 4.10). This remarkable row of early 16th-century renters, as leased tenements were termed, contains four identical houses of tripartite plan, with paired service rooms, halls, and parlours, and extends to 43 m (140 ft) in length. Each house is unusual in that its parlour is lit by two arched 'shop' windows, but is not sub-divided and is entered only from the hall. This row may perhaps have been built by a wealthy clothier as 'tied-cottages' for his weavers, who would certainly have found their well-lit parlours ideal workshops; retail customers were clearly not encouraged, as they would have been obliged to enter by the cross-passage and cross the hall to enter the parlour/workshop. In some cases there is no obvious evidence that service bays with shops were sub-divided, despite the presence of twin doors (eg, 31–35 High Street, Debenham, Suffolk). Where the usual fully-framed partition is lacking, a moveable screen may have existed to enlarge a shop when necessary, but other explanations are possible. Permanent partitions were not necessarily tenoned to the ceiling joists, for example, and others stopped short to admit borrowed light from one service room to another.

A more dramatic variation on the standard theme survives at Woodbine Cottage, opposite the parish church in Kersey (Fig 4.11). This mid-15th-century cross-wing house of considerable quality contains a sub-divided parlour with a façade that consisted of three arched openings without sills. Shops are occasionally found at the parlour rather than service

Late medieval workshops in East Anglia 47

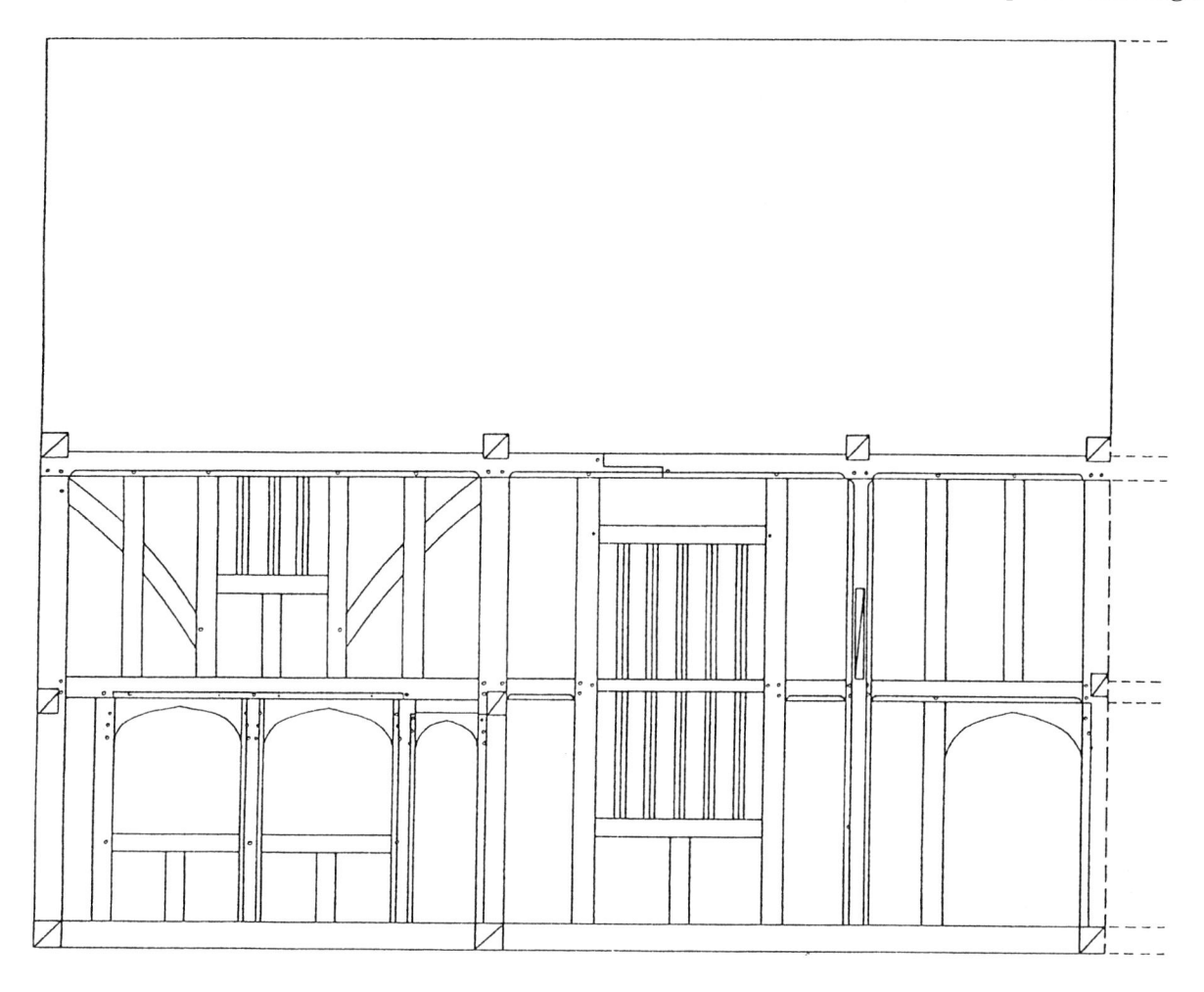

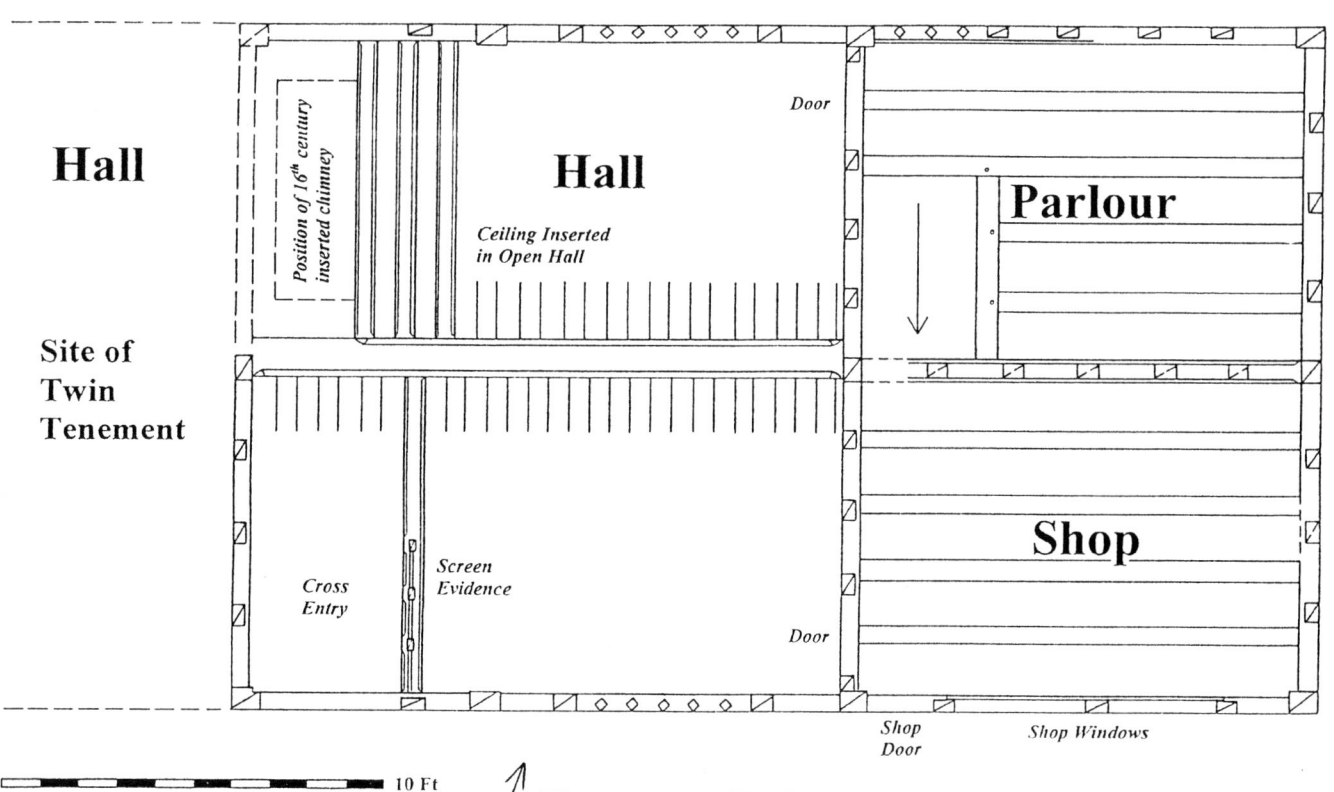

Figure 4.8 16 Fen Street, Nayland, Suffolk. One of an identical pair of tenements in a side street, each containing an open hall with a shop in the front half of a subdivided parlour bay. Original ground plan and internal elevation of façade. (© Leigh Alston)

48 *The vernacular workshop*

Figure 4.9   16 Fen Street, Nayland, Suffolk. Typical evidence of a medieval shop front, seen from within. The two window arches have been removed, leaving tell-tale mortises in their jambs, but the arch of the blocked narrow doorway remains. (© Leigh Alston)

Figure 4.10   31–39 Chapel Street, Bildeston, Suffolk. Facing the medieval market place, this row of four identical tenements contains parlours lit by arched windows without external access. The right-hand tenement is now rendered. (© Leigh Alston)

Figure 4.11   Woodbine Cottage, Kersey, Suffolk. A rare open shop front in a parlour cross-wing with three arched openings that lack sills. The central arch has been removed, and the vertical studs are later insertions. (© Leigh Alston)

ends of larger houses, and more rarely still at both, but open arcades are highly unusual. Close to the market place, this area may have been let to stall-holders in the manner of a market hall, but the high-end doorway linking it to the domestic hall suggests otherwise. Similar examples are known elsewhere, as at 'Bonners' in central Colchester, Essex, and the type may represent the late survival

Figure 4.12 Cordell Cottages, High Street, Long Melford. A rear courtyard, looking towards the hall on the street. These yards are typically lined with small lock-ups. (© Leigh Alston)

of an older tradition usually associated with stone undercrofts of the early Middle Ages. The 12th-century first-floor hall at Moyses Hall in Bury St Edmunds appears to have possessed an arcaded ground-floor undercroft, and numerous similar examples survive in well-preserved French cities such as Provins. The timber-framed shop fronts of the 14th, 15th, and 16th centuries may well have evolved from this source. Subterranean undercrofts that were used primarily as warehousing are found in the larger towns of the region, notably Bury St Edmunds and Norwich, although a fine 14th-century example survives in the small market town of Clare, Suffolk.

Shops in merchants' courtyards

A remarkable number of larger 15th- and 16th-century urban merchants' houses retain rear courtyards with extensive evidence for shops and other industrial activity. Most of these yards, often formed by extending the ubiquitous parlour and service cross wings by several bays behind the central hall, are now fragmentary, but some complete examples survive. A pictorial map of Long Melford dating from 1613 indicates that every other house in the main street possessed a rear courtyard enclosed on at least three if not all four sides, and this seems to have been typical of the region. It would appear that while the merchants of East Anglian market towns competed to occupy prime commercial sites, they built their domestic accommodation on the street, often, as already seen, with a shop in their front service room, but provided warehouses, workshops and stables to the rear. These courtyard structures were largely redundant with the collapse of the cloth industry in the mid-16th century, and were prone to demolition and domestic conversion; invisible from the street and ignored by list descriptions, many, sadly, continue to suffer the same fate.

Figure 4.12 shows a typical late 15th-century courtyard in Long Melford, looking towards the hall that adjoins the street. Courtyard wings are usually jettied in this way, and can either be formed in a single phase of construction or, as here, by extending the original cross-wings of the house. While no two are identical, the ground-floor rooms beneath the jetties normally consist of a number of lock-ups, each containing one or sometimes two bays and entered only from the yard with no internal communication. The upper storeys are usually large, undivided spaces, open to their roofs and reached either from the main house or, more often, by a separate stair rising from the yard. The first-floor arrangement of the early 16th-century wing behind the parlour of 'Shangri-La', Hall Street, Long Melford, consists of six bays of which four are undivided to create a chamber 11 m long by 5 m wide (36 × 16 ft). The separate stairs that serve these large upper spaces can be of exceptional height and width; the chamber behind the street-side parlour chamber at 18–20 Stonham Street, Coggeshall, Essex, rose through an arched opening 2.75 m (9 ft) in height by 1.5 m (5 ft) in width that interrupted the jetty. Most courtyards were reached through the hall cross-passage, often 4 or 5 ft (1.2 or 1.5 m) wide (although an extreme case in East Street, Coggeshall, extends to eight feet), but some were provided with separate street gateways, often gabled and jettied, forming imposing entrances. Six such gateways survive, more or less intact, in Lavenham, and most retain evidence for stabilising ground braces that would have prevented wheeled vehicles from passing through. Transport at this period was primarily by pack animal.

What then was the precise purpose of the numerous small 'lock-up' rooms in these rear courtyards, and the vast open spaces reached by wide stairs above them? The arrangement is similar to a number of London houses surveyed in the late 16th century by Ralph Treswell, where ground-floor rooms in rear yards, entered only from the yard, are often labelled as warehouses (Schofield 1987). East Anglian clothiers certainly required ample storage space for the numerous bulky packs of wool, bales of woad, and finished cloth they left in their wills (wool was imported from Essex, Lincolnshire and elsewhere in preference to the poor quality Suffolk variety). A Suffolk broadcloth measured 1.6 m (1¾ yards) in width by over 8.5 m (28 ft) in length, and represented a considerable weight. In those rare instances where the locations of such items are specified in early documents they are usually on an upper storey, where they were presumably less likely to suffer from damp. While some ground-floor rooms in courtyards may have served as warehouses, the large spaces above them seem more probable candidates for this purpose. Their wide stairs seem ideally suited for the passage of large items, and if these great, draughty chambers were not used for

50 *The vernacular workshop*

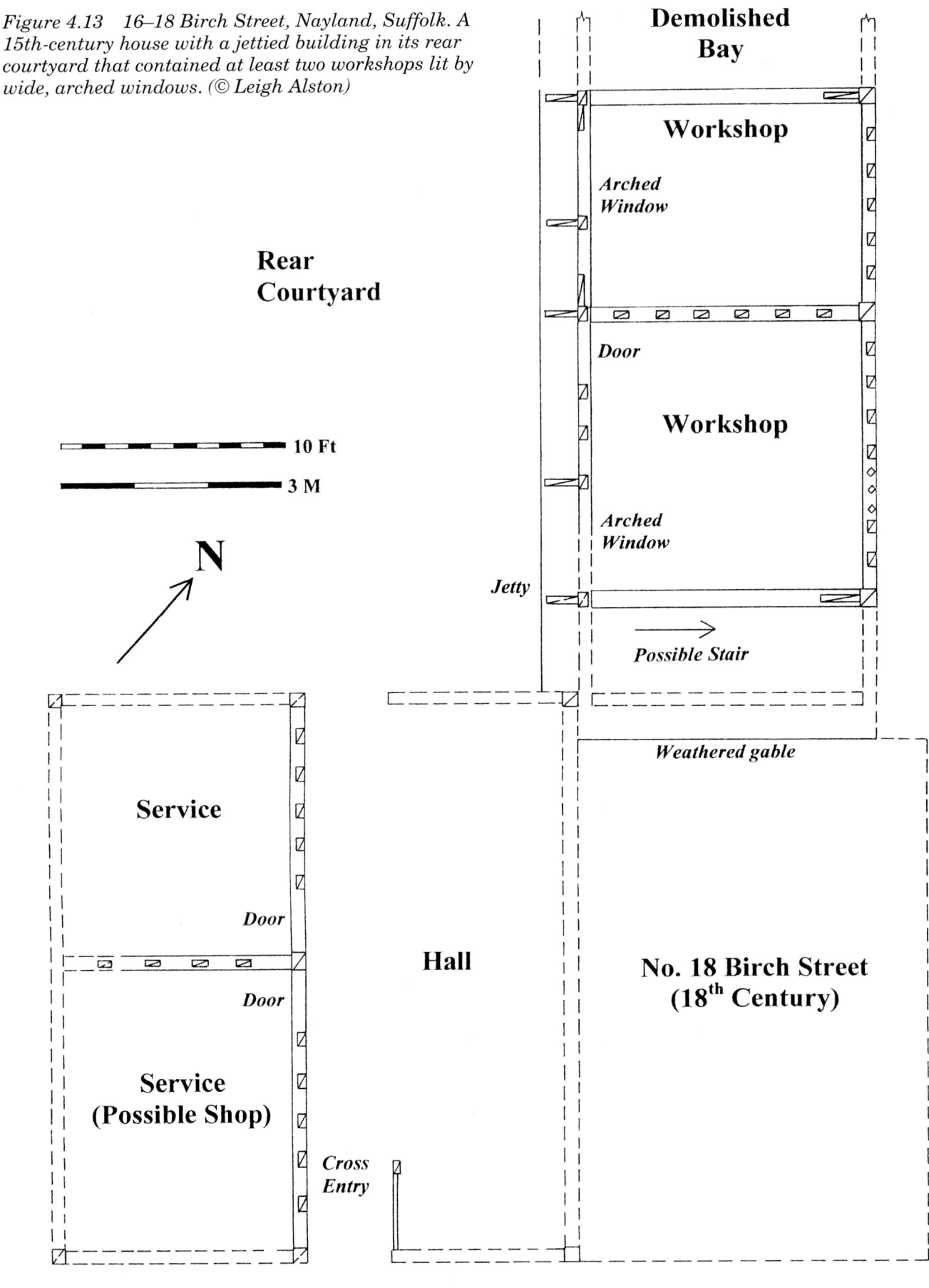

Figure 4.13 16–18 Birch Street, Nayland, Suffolk. A 15th-century house with a jettied building in its rear courtyard that contained at least two workshops lit by wide, arched windows. (© Leigh Alston)

Late medieval workshops in East Anglia 51

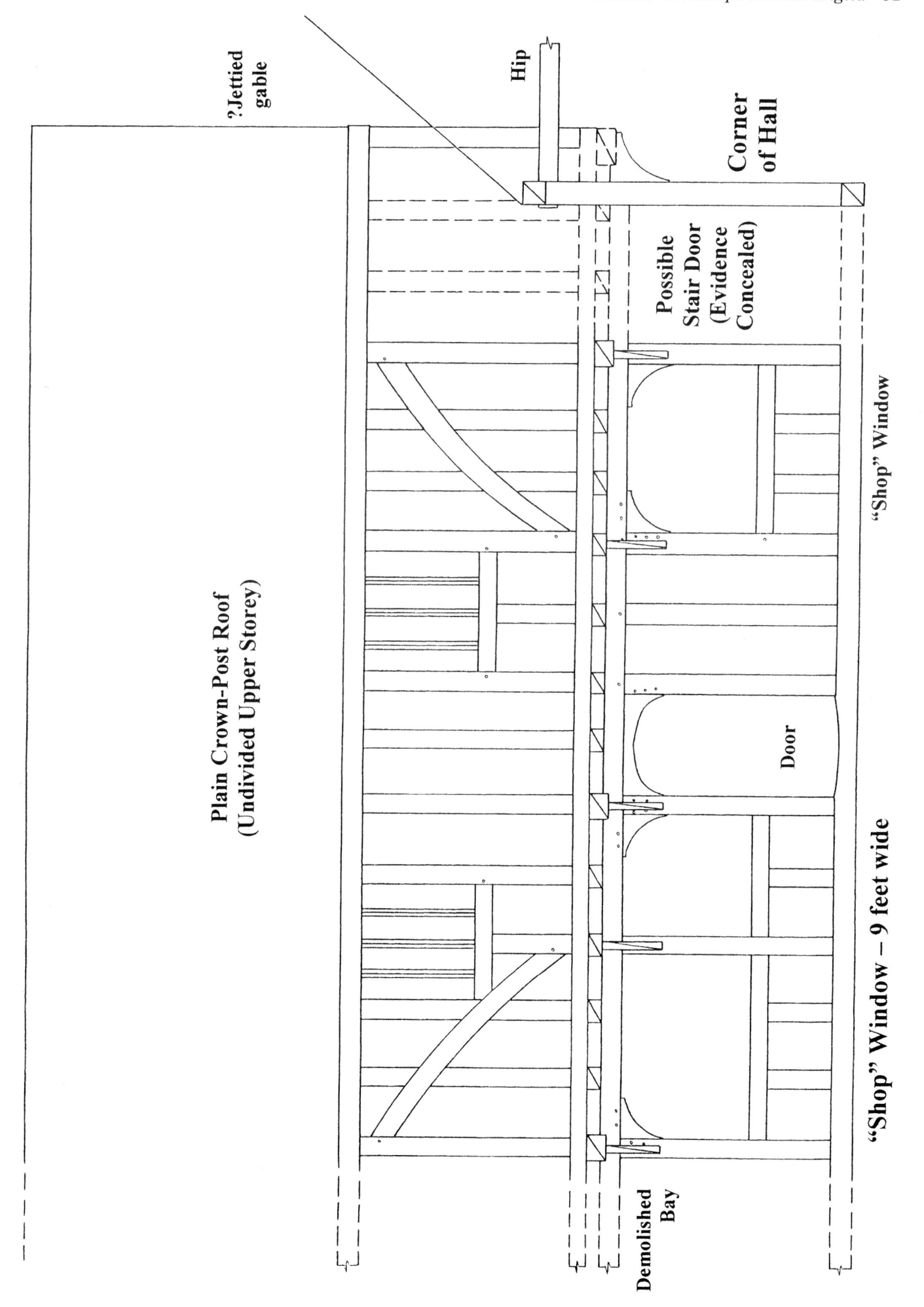

Figure 4.14 6 High Street, Lavenham, Suffolk. The rear gable of a two-cell early 16th-century tenement, whose upper chamber was lit by an arcade of arched windows and presumably used as a workshop. The chamber was ventilated by a hooded open gablet. (© Leigh Alston)

storage it is difficult to find alternative explanations. The upper storeys of smaller urban houses of the 16th century that lack courtyards are frequently undivided, that is, they lack first-floor partitions above their parlour, hall, and service rooms, creating similar spaces to those which their wealthier neighbours were able to confine to their yards.

Although most courtyard rooms were lit by ordinary mullioned windows, many contain wide arched openings and were undoubtedly used as workshops. Space was at less of a premium away from the street, and the dictates of fashion were less forceful; in consequence, the façades of courtyard shops display far greater variety than their more public counterparts, and do not, for example, feature narrow entrances. Figure 4.13 shows the plan and façade of an early to mid-15th-century courtyard building that contained at least two workshops lit by wide, arched windows beneath a large, undivided upper chamber (16–18 Birch Street, Nayland). The shop to the rear has been truncated by the demolition of one or more bays, but retains an impressive window of 2.75 m (9 ft) in width, albeit interrupted by a supporting post; its neighbour still extends to a relatively spacious 3.6 m (12 ft) square, and is also lit by a normal mullioned window in its rear wall. The building plots along this section of street are uniformly narrow at 7.6 m or 1½ perches (25 ft), and the rear wing was apparently built behind the neighbouring tenement, corner to corner with the unusually wide two-cell hall. The Bell and Steelyard Public House in New Street, Woodbridge, preserves an exceptional single-storeyed rear workshop adjoining a service bay that contains a standard shop; this example, just 2.75 m (9 ft) wide, was entered from the corner of the courtyard and lit by an arcade of three arched windows. Nearby, at 13 Market Place, Woodbridge, a free-standing two-storeyed rear building of similar width appears to have contained a shop front. Small, independent structures of this kind may once have been common in domestic courtyards, as they undoubtedly were in market places, but are unlikely to have survived.

Documentary evidence for courtyard shops, and for merchants with more than one shop, can be found in contemporary wills: John Smyth of Long Melford specifies the looms, slays and trendles in his shop next to the street in 1498, together with additional looms standing 'within', while Robert Trippe, a Lavenham clothier, leaves his tenter yard with a shop and access through the house in 1549.[9] Tenter yards are often mentioned in such sources, with tenter fields confined to the most wealthy, and many rear courtyards must have contained long easel-like tenter frames to which broadcloth was secured by tenter hooks to be stretched and dried after fulling. Now quiet retreats behind busy streets, these surviving East Anglian yards must once have hummed with noise and activity. Remarkably, in many instances where the external timber-framing remains exposed, evidence of cloister-like pentice roofs can be found, extending from the jetties to form dry passages between the various courtyard doors.

In some cases arched, shop-type windows can be found on upper storeys, where retail explanations are improbable. Figure 4.14 shows the rear gable of a small mid-16th-century tenement at 6 High Street in

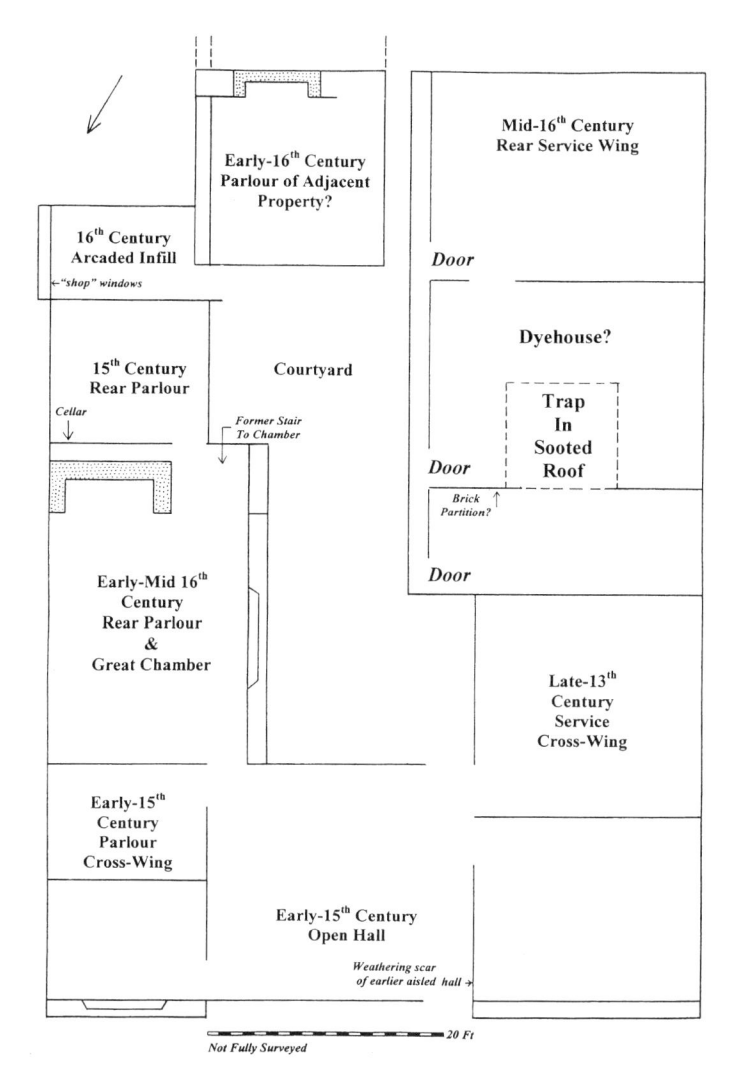

Figure 4.15 Alston Court, Nayland, Suffolk. The ground plan of a rear courtyard of complex evolution, containing a possible dyehouse. (© Leigh Alston)

Lavenham where the undivided upper storey of three bays (above a hall and twin service rooms) was lit by an arcade of three such windows in its west-facing gable. Looms may perhaps have operated on upper storeys at this early date but alternative activities such as wool combing may also be suggested. The preparation of yarn for export to Essex manufacturers of new draperies increased in importance during the late 16th century, as the traditional broadcloth industry failed, and combing workshops are known from 17th-century contexts. The gablet of the hipped roof was left open, and protected from rain by a hood, perhaps in order to ventilate the workshop in summer (there is no evidence of sooting). Hooded open gablets of this kind are, however, very common in East Anglia, and its presence may not relate to the purpose of this particular chamber. A commercial explanation of a different kind must be sought for the exceptionally small windows sometimes found lighting upper rooms. The most extreme instance in Lavenham is the narrow example, 0.45 m (18 in) wide, that provides the only light in the early 16th-century hall chamber of the Old Grammar School in Barn Street, which was built as a merchant's house of high status. The chamber was reached only by a wide stair from the courtyard, and was presumably a warehouse for the storage of dyed wool and other fabric that might fade in sunlight (Shackle & Alston 1998).

Rise Farm in the rural parish of Preston St Mary near Lavenham consists of a jettied early 16th-century structure with an arcade of four arched windows on its upper storey. The timber frame bears two sequences of carpenter's numerals, and was evidently dismantled and transported from its original site in the 17th century to form the core of a new farmhouse. The unusual layout of the 16th-century building strongly suggests that it was designed as a courtyard wing, and a number of other 17th-century houses in the area, including Lavenham Hall itself, appear to have recycled industrial structures in the same way. As early as the late 16th century a poverty-stricken Lavenham was being mined by local builders as a source of cheap, ready-made timber frames to form fashionable new farmhouses funded by the agricultural boom of the period. The lord of the manor in Lavenham took his tenants to court in 1613 in order to prevent the demolition, claiming that not a single house would be left standing in the town if it continued.[10] His tenants claimed they were unable to maintain the great houses built by their grandfathers, and were obliged to sell their timbers for what they would fetch. Many redundant courtyard buildings were probably the first to disappear, and it is indeed remarkable that we are now able to retrieve evidence of their appearance from surrounding farmhouses.

In addition to workshops and warehousing, merchants' courtyards would have accommodated stabling and kitchens, and in some instances brewhouses and dyehouses. Stables may be difficult to recognise, as animals could have been housed in lock-up rooms similar to those used as warehouses or workshops, but kitchens are common survivals that are usually characterised by small rooms heated by large brick chimneys or smoke-bays. The kitchen is often found immediately behind the service rooms, with a separate entrance from the corner of the yard adjacent to the cross-passage. A number of rear courtyards in market towns contain small open halls heated by open hearths, which are sometimes interpreted as kitchens. Like their more common rural counterparts, non-domestic open halls of this kind were more probably designed primarily for brewing and baking, although they would no doubt have served a number of purposes. Brewhouses were often fitted with platforms or galleries lit by windows at irregular heights, upon which a series of brewing vessels could be tended and supported at different heights. Kentwell Hall, Long Melford, possesses a particularly impressive early 16th-century example.

The construction of a brewhouse might have been justified by the master of a large mercantile estab-

54 *The vernacular workshop*

lishment in order to provide his employees with their necessary ale, but its presence would support the interpretation of the house in question as an inn. In two known instances, however, similar arrangements in courtyards probably operated as dyehouses. Dyehouses were very necessary to the East Anglian cloth trade, and are frequently mentioned in wills and other sources. Most were shared by two or more clothiers, with many wills referring to half or quarter parts of dyehouses, but larger merchants possessed their own. Figure 4.15 shows the ground plan of a particularly complex courtyard house at Alston Court, Nayland, that evolved by adding to, and replacing, various elements of a late 13th-century house. This arrangement is not typical of local courtyards in its possession of a high-status rear parlour. In the 16th century a jettied wing was added to the rear gable of the medieval service cross-wing, containing three separate ground-floor rooms entered from the courtyard; the central room contained a very large trap in its ceiling, immediately beneath a sooted roof that also contained a framed trap that may in turn have contained a louver. A very similar pattern can be discerned in a particularly expensive, brick-built courtyard wing at 111 High Street, Needham Market, Suffolk, which is known to have been owned by a wealthy clothier. The 'hole' in the heavily framed ceiling here extends to 2.75 m by 4.39 m (9 × 14 ft). Neither example is an open hall, as might be expected of a brewhouse, and both were probably associated with furnaces and dyeing vats.

Shops in non-domestic buildings

Documentary evidence demonstrates that medieval towns, both large and small, contained many purpose-built shops that were as likely as those in domestic houses to be manufacturing workshops rather than retail outlets. Structures of this kind were not able to survive the centuries as desirable residences, and are now very rare even in the otherwise well-preserved streets of East Anglia. The region is far more fortunate in its surviving public buildings such as guildhalls, with which shops were also often associated. Approximately 30 halls built by religious guilds are known to remain in Suffolk, with a further twenty in Essex, and the number of market halls and court halls is probably similar. Many such buildings were placed in the commercial centres of their respective towns, and their owners were inevitably keen to recoup their outlay, and raise as much money as possible, by placing their meeting halls on upper storeys and leasing shop units in prime locations on the lower.

Thaxted Guildhall in Essex, constructed probably as a market house in the mid-15th century (contrary to popular opinion, which links it with a spurious cutlers' guild) shows a typical arrangement (Fig 4.16). Like many buildings of its type, it is generally assumed that retail stalls were set up beneath the arcade on market day. Given the importance of the site, this restriction of income to one day in the week would not have been a sensible arrangement on the part of the building's owners. Medieval court and account rolls reveal that the ground floor of a similar building (which does not survive) in the market place of Clare, Suffolk, was leased on a permanent basis; in 1386 two bays of the 'chamber beneath the Moot Hall' were let for nine years to John Cardemakere, who presumably made and sold carding combs there for straightening the fibres of wool. No rent was collected in 1429 as the tenant of the 'shope' beneath the hall had decamped by night, but by 1482 the area was let as a commercial stable to two individuals who annoyed the manorial court held upstairs, and perhaps its victims, by making dunghills against the adjacent pillory. Thaxted Guildhall's open arcade is not quite as it seems, with evidence of removed sills in all but two arches; its first-floor arcade of arched windows is unique in the region, and may well have lit a second commercial tier with occasional public business confined to the upper storey.

Many surviving public buildings contain ground-floor shops that resemble the standard pattern of twin windows and narrow doors, although more variations are found than in domestic contexts. Nayland guildhall is unusual in containing a first-floor meeting hall with a complete domestic house beneath, albeit with shops in both parlour and service bays (the parlour shop with internal and external doors, the service accessed only via the cross-passage). With this exception, shops in public buildings are lock-up units that would have been rented by tenants living elsewhere, although some may have been kept in-hand for the sale of ale and other fund-raising items produced by the guilds. Lock-ups are, in contrast, rare in domestic buildings, where access is normally possible from within the house even though, as argued above, they may sometimes have been let to third parties as lock-ups. The Bull Inn, Needham Market, contains one of the few genuine examples in the region, with a standard shop in its front service room and an additional narrow lock-up beyond with a single arched window and external entrance from the street. The Bull is known to have been built as an inn in the early 16th century.

Figure 4.17 shows the original ground plan and façade of a rare pair of 15th-century semi-detached lock-up shops at 1 Church Street, Coggeshall (Argentum Antiques). These purpose-built commercial units had no heating or any link with domestic accommodation, although a street survey of 1575, which describes them as 'two freehold shops', has the left-hand part in the same ownership as the (demolished) house that adjoined it, while the other belonged to a resident on the opposite side of the street.[11] At 3 m wide by 3.3 m deep (10 × 11 ft) each shop was considerably larger than its standard domestic counterpart, particularly given the storage area on its jettied upper floor, and would have been ideally suited as a workshop. With less pressure on

Figure 4.16 The Guildhall, Thaxted, Essex. A mid-15th-century public building with open-arcaded ground storey. (© Leigh Alston)

space, the two doors are respectably wide (0.78 m or 31 in), and each window is an impressive 2.1 m (7 ft), although curiously, only the right-hand example is sub-divided by a stud; the left-hand window is accordingly the widest example on record in the region. Perhaps this single difference between the units can be combined with the evidence of the survey to suggest that the left-hand unit was built to the specification of its owner, living next door, while the other more standard example was designed to be let or sold to fund the project. Independent lock-ups of this kind were probably more common in the sophisticated economies of larger towns, where they are sadly less likely to survive. During recent alterations to a modern shop front at 33–34 Abbeygate Street, Bury St Edmunds, still the main shopping area of the town, a larger but apparently similar pair of lock-ups was partly and briefly uncovered. More examples would almost certainly be unearthed if such restorations were adequately monitored.

The most remarkable evidence of a purpose-built shop in East Anglia, representing the sole known survivor of a large class of medieval buildings, was temporarily revealed during the refitting of commercial premises in the old market place of Debenham, Suffolk. Figure 4.18 shows a reconstruction of what may be regarded as a permanent early 16th-century market stall with an open-arcaded ground storey extending to just 2 m (6 ft 6 in) in overall width, increasing to 3 m (10 ft) on its upper storey due to front and rear jetties. The entire structure was 5.8 m (19 ft) long and contained two units of 2.75 m (9 ft) that were described in a survey of 1621 as two small shops with solars above, measuring 5.5 m by 2.75 m (18 × 9 ft).[12] Access to the upper storey was by means of a ladder that passed between the widely spaced joists. An unexplained mortice in the gable may have held a shop sign, and a bar between the posts of the same gable suggests that access was not encouraged at this point. Counters were presumably set up in the open sides of the structure on market day, and stored with any unperishable merchandise in the upper chamber until the following week, although permanent occupation as a workshop can by no means be ruled out. A narrow alley stills runs behind the stalls, and larger markets were characterised by labyrinths that would have been well sheltered by jetties to form a relatively comfortable working environment.

Market stalls with solars above were a common feature of medieval market places, and Thaxted Guildhall may well have been surrounded by diminutive versions of itself. References to similar structures occur in the borough court records of Colchester as early as the 1380s, and an account of building five new stalls (stallagia) in Bury St

56 *The vernacular workshop*

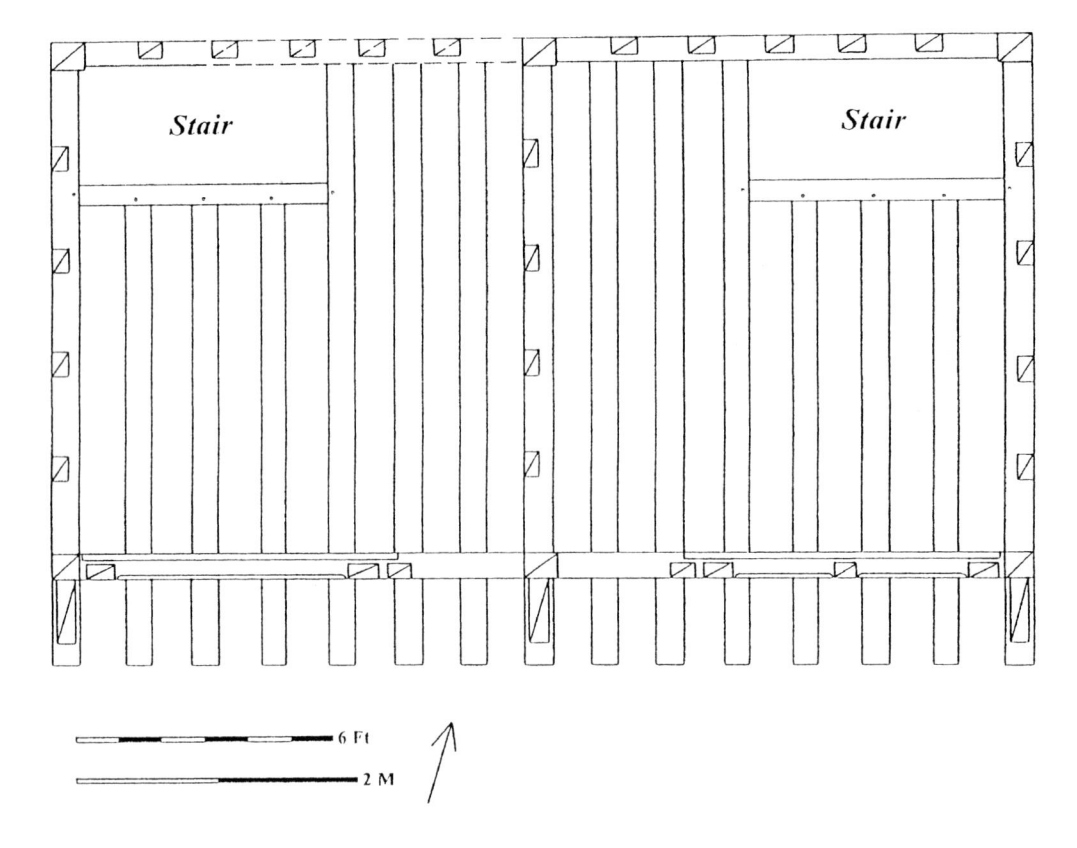

Figure 4.17 1 Church Street, Coggeshall, Essex. The ground plan and shop fronts of a rare pair of purpose-built 15th-century lock-up shops. (© Leigh Alston)

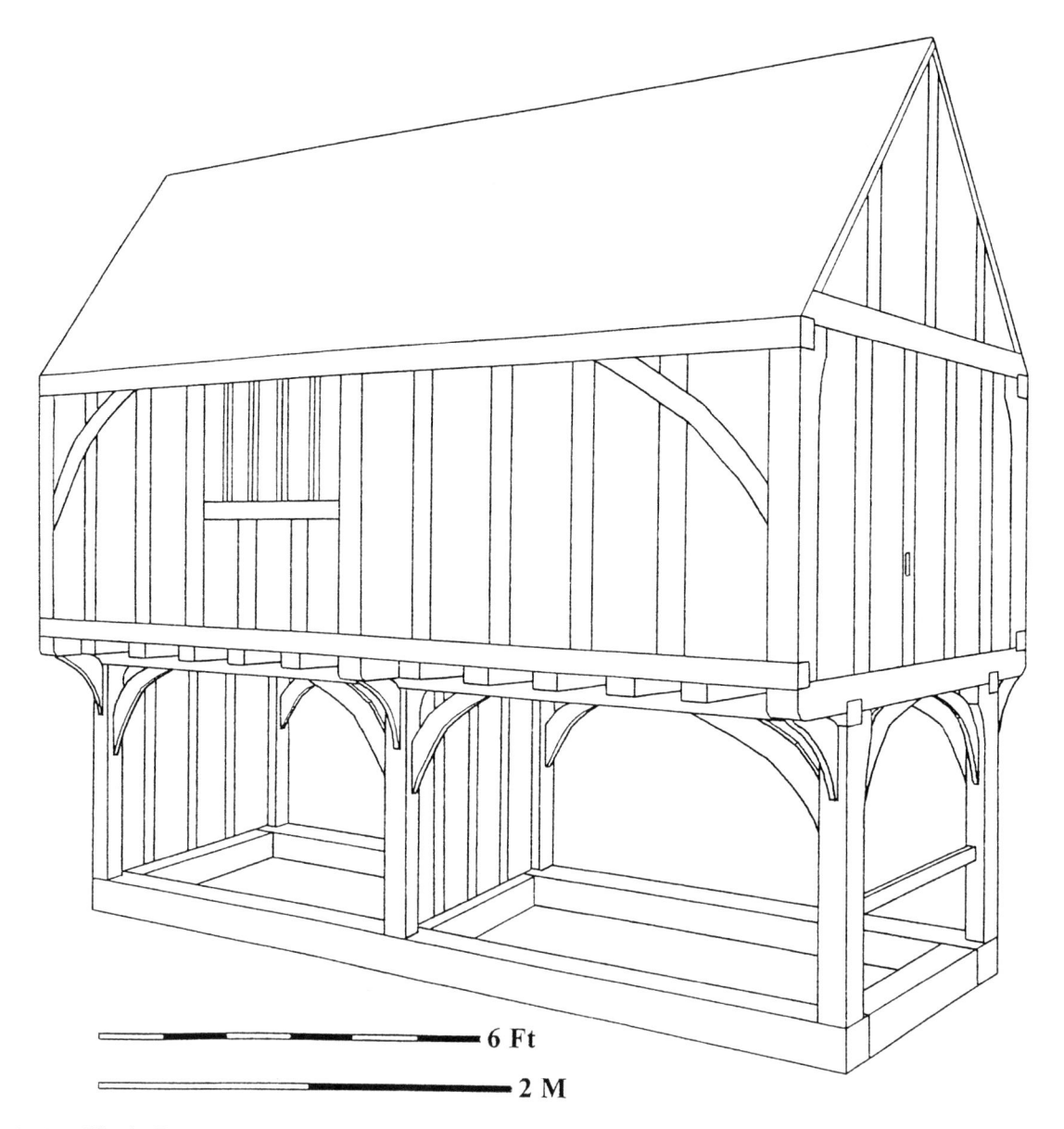

Figure 4.18 Cleo's Restaurant, Market Place, Debenham (Reconstruction). A rare 'permanent market stall' of the early 16th century, measuring just 2 m (6 ft 6 in.) in width. (© Leigh Alston)

Edmunds in 1388 portrays them as timber-framed and boarded with thatched roofs, rather than the temporary arrangements with which we are familiar today.[13] The market of Kersey possessed two distinct types of stall in 1398: moveable stalls measuring 1.5 m by 2.1 m (5 × 7 ft) and permanent stalls of varying sizes that were typically long and narrow. A similar situation is found in most medieval market records, such as the new 'shop' of 7 ft by 22 ft (2.1 × 6.7 m) in Haverhill for which permission was granted in 1447 (almost exactly the same proportions, and possibly appearance, as the Debenham example). This new shop in Haverhill adjoined what must represent one of the earliest named establishments on record, 'a shopp in the Markett thear called Palmers of Kedyngton', Kedington being a neighbouring village.[14] Unusually specific permission for a new shop of 14 by 9 statutory feet (4.25 × 2.75 m) excepting only 'le evesdrepe' was granted in 1553 to a Bures St Mary speculator (a clothier) who promptly sold the new building to a butcher.[15] In this relatively small town the new buyer may be presumed to have occupied his new shop on a permanent basis, rather than once a week, and the trouble and expense of constructing these 'permanent stalls' would surely be difficult to justify if many were not workshops rather than market retail outlets.

The interpretation of the long, narrow market place shops of the Middle Ages as something more than shelters for use on market day is supported by the further end of the Debenham example. Figure 4.19 shows a row of three fully enclosed shops, each measuring 3 m (10 ft) square, built against its gable in the early 17th century. Two units were lit by a pair of windows without arches, closed by vertically hinged internal shutters, while the third had a single window (the fenestration of the rear wall is uncertain). The small chambers above were lit by

58 *The vernacular workshop*

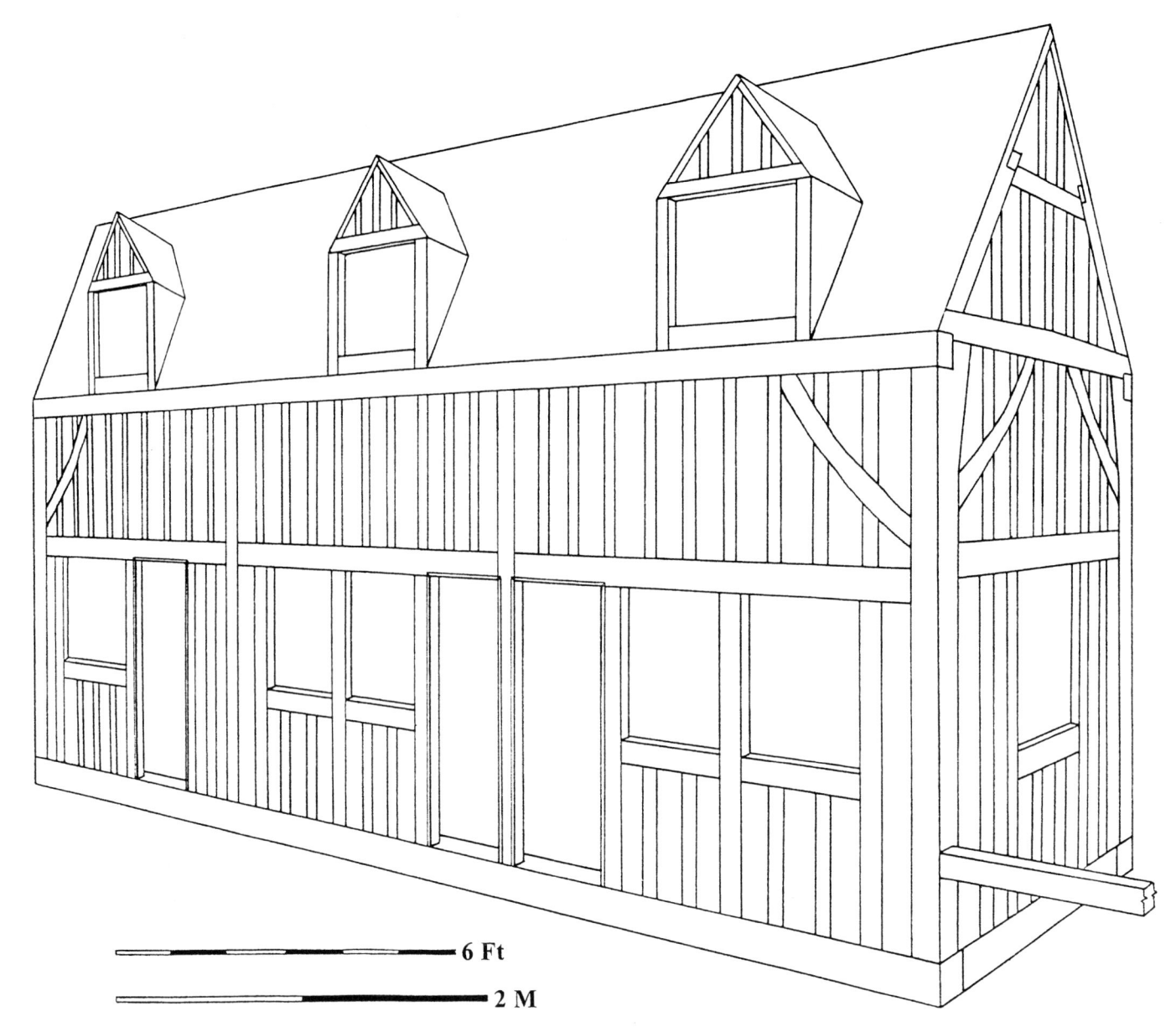

Figure 4.19 Cleo's Restaurant, Market Place, Debenham (Reconstruction). A row of three early 17th-century lock-up shops, each 3 m (10 ft) square, built against the gable of the open-arcaded stall shown in Figure 4.18. (© Leigh Alston)

dormers and, like those of its open-arcaded neighbour, reached by ladders, while an empty mortice in the foreground corner post may, according to the 1621 survey, have related to an animal pen. The survey specifies the building's dimensions at 32 by 9 feet (9.75 × 2.75 m), and refers to at least one other similar structure measuring 18½ by 10 ft (5.6 × 3 m). These well-framed lock-ups in the market row were surely intended as permanent workshops in the same manner as their domestic counterparts, which they closely resemble. A number of later partitions in the building consisted of recycled timbers from much flimsier single-storied structures, albeit fully framed, that were probably salvaged from less substantial, fixed stalls that might indeed have been occupied only on market day. It is difficult to believe that more fascinating buildings of this distinctive kind do not await discovery, albeit in fragmentary form, on the sites of market encroachment elsewhere.

Conclusion

Documentary evidence reveals that medieval and Tudor buildings that have generally been interpreted as shops were in fact workshops involved primarily or exclusively with production rather than retailing. It is not possible on the basis of physical evidence such as the arrangement of 'shop windows' to determine the craft or business of the original occupant, or to distinguish between retail and manufacturing activity. Early shops were clearly built to a standard, multi-purpose pattern, particularly when visible from the street, that simply declared 'business' rather than 'domestic' to passers-by. Shop fronts were not renewed frequently, as they are today, to advertise individual concerns, but served many different trades and crafts over several centuries. Successful entrepreneurs invested in domestic and commercial property, with Lavenham's cloth merchants sometimes owning more than a dozen buildings in the town in addition to their own residence or 'head house', and we can rarely be sure that a given shop was occupied by its documented owner. As the great majority of early shops were involved in production to one degree or another, whether or not retail goods were available on the premises, it is not sensible to impose the modern distinction between shops and workshops when interpreting the past. Early documents refer to shops and stalls but not workshops, and 'stalls' are often substantial lock-ups of a kind that we would not describe as such. Latin words such as 'opellam' and 'officinam' that historians now confusingly render as 'workshop' were intended by the scribes to translate only 'shop', and while this term is common in medieval sources the first occurrence of 'workshop' cited by the Oxford English Dictionary does not occur until the late 16th century. One of the Debenham stalls described above was recorded in 1621 as an 'officinam Anglice a shop', that is 'a workshop called in English a shop'. In a modern world where the difference between factories and High Street shops is taken for granted, we would probably be better advised to refer to all medieval shops as workshops if we are to convey their true nature to a 21st-century audience. In East Anglia at least, those workshops were small, cramped spaces attached either to domestic houses, both on the street and in rear yards, or lock-ups positioned chiefly in and around market places. Even in the thriving woollen cloth industry there is no indication of large, multi-loomed sheds before the 17th and 18th centuries, and certainly nothing resembling the large, long room containing 200 looms that the famous west-country clothier Jack of Newbury is said to have possessed in the 16th century.[16] There is, of course, an exception to prove every good historical rule.

Notes

1. Kersey Bailiff's Account, PRO SC6 1001/3.
2. Haverhill Court Book, SRO (Bury) E7/26/4(c).
3. Probate Court of Canterbury (Braunche, Critoft and Smyth) and Archdeaconry of Sudbury (Berner), PRO and SRO (Bury) respectively. Transcripts kindly provided by Peter Northeast
4. Archdeaconry of Sudbury wills, SRO (Bury), John Resshey senior and Thomas Bartelott respectively.
5. Bures St Mary Manorial Court Roll, ERO (Chelmsford) D/DB M206.
6. Figures from Hoskins, W G, 1972 *Local History in England*, quoted in Betterton & Dymond (1989, 41), and *Suffolk in 1568*, Suffolk Green Books XII, n.d. Central southern Suffolk is equated with the medieval administrative area of Babergh Hundred for this purpose
7. See Grenville (1997) for a wider discussion of the nature of medieval housing than is appropriate here.
8. Primrose Farm, South Lopham, Norfolk is a much-cited example of an ostensibly isolated shop front that faces a major junction and would have been a conspicuous landmark.
9. Probate Court of Canterbury wills. Transcripts kindly provided by Peter Northeast
10. British Library, Harl. 597/104. I am grateful to Lyn Boothman for bringing this material to my attention.
11. Survey of the manor of Coggeshall, PRO Rentals and Surveys 43/2/14.
12. Survey of the manors of Debenham, SRO (Ipswich) S1/2/31.6. I am grateful to Timothy Easton for drawing this building to my attention, and to Ian McKechnie for identifying the documentary references. 'Solar' is a standard medieval term for any upper room.
13. Receiver's account of the manor of Clare, PRO SC6 1111/27.
14. Haverhill Court Book, SRO (Bury) E7/26/4(c).
15. Bures Manorial Court Roll, ERO (Chelmsford) D/DB M207.
16. In a poem by Thomas Deloney (1543–1600) The Pleasant History of John Winchcombe in F.O. Mann (ed.), 1912, *The Works of Thomas Deloney*, 20, quoted in Betterton and Dymond (1989).

5 Transformations in Georgian London's silk-weaving workshop homes, with a comparative detour to Lyons *by Peter Guillery*

Among the weavers of Spitalfields a man has a loom in his room and sleeps in it with all his family. A report of 1817 by the Society for Preventing Contagious Fever (as quoted in George 1925, 192)

London

London is often overlooked in discussions both of vernacular architecture and of industrialisation.[1] In a collection of conference papers dedicated to English vernacular workshops, London permits, indeed demands, a perspective on the shift from craft to industry that emphasises neither the urbanising nor the rural, but rather the already urban. As there were not early modern urban industrial centres of remotely comparable scale elsewhere in Britain, London's vernacular workshops also beg comparison with those of places elsewhere in Europe. Silk weavers' workshop homes in Spitalfields are presented here as a case study, looking at architectural developments from the late 17th century to the early 19th. Following this, the housing of the weavers of France's silk industry in Lyons are introduced, raising questions of comparability and difference with regard to the way industrialisation brought change.[2]

Whether it is called craft or industry, it is well known that manufacturing in London in the early modern period was essentially domestic. It is important to revisit some basics about London in the 'long 18th century' to drive home the importance and scale of metropolitan domestic industry in this already urban context. In contemporary terms 18th-century London was vast. There had been enormous growth through immigration, the number of Londoners all but trebling in the 17th century, from about 200,000 in 1600 to about 575,000 in 1700, making London western Europe's largest city, for the first time more populous than less rapidly growing Paris. England's next biggest towns c1670 were Norwich and Bristol with about 20,000 people each, that is each then about 4% the size of London. London's rate of growth slowed, but population did increase substantially to close to 1,000,000 by 1800, when Manchester, Liverpool and Birmingham all remained less than a tenth the size of London (Wrigley 1990, 41–7; Boulton 2000, 316; Schwarz 2000, 642).

Around 75% of London's population was made up of the 'working' classes, a highly disparate group, though – with a very few exceptions, these people did not work in factories. Through this workforce London in the 18th century, and into the 19th, was Europe's, if not the world's, biggest centre of industrial output. Despite its overall scale the components of London's manufacturing remained structurally small, diverse, and specialised, with production increasingly concentrated in the finishing trades where skilled labour was most important. The highly developed 'putting-out' sub-contracting system used the household as the unit and locus of production wherever possible. In such a densely populated city with plentiful labour, expensive land, and high rents this arrangement made sense in a way that factories could not have done. For many manufacturers keeping production in London was advantageous because it meant proximity to a vast, concentrated, and fickle market, as well as to the country's largest port. Around 1700 the biggest industry, clothing, employed perhaps 40,000 to 50,000 people. As much as about half of these people were engaged in the silk trade. Industrialisation elsewhere did, of course, have an impact on London, but it was limited. Labour costs caused framework knitting to move to Nottingham, with some shoe and hat making also leaving. Yet, despite similarly high labour costs, silk weaving, watch making, ship building, and other manufacturing trades all endured in London well into the 19th century, concentrated in suburbs to the east, south and north. Furthest out, where land was cheaper, were the industries that could not be run on a purely domestic basis – tanning in Bermondsey, and ship building on both sides of the Thames to the east, the latter in yards which could represent notable concentrations of labour, but were not, in conventional terms, factories (Schwarz 1992, 34, 197, 206–7; Beier 1986; Berg 1994, 219–20, 244).

Spitalfields

In the late 17th and early 18th centuries the silk district grew outwards to the east and north from its heart in Spitalfields, just north-east of the City of London. Weavers were far and away the largest group in the industry, but there were related trades, notably silk throwsters (those who twisted raw silk into thread, often women), silk winders, and dyers. Imported raw silk was thrown, wound, then dyed, bought by a master weaver, and 'put out' to journeymen for weaving in houses. The masters sold the

Figure 5.1 Nos 113 and 115 Bethnal Green Road, perspective reconstruction of the one-room-deep houses as built c1735, showing part of a front winder staircase, and full-width workshop windows in a timber-framed back wall. (© English Heritage. NMR)

woven silk to mercers, much of it as elaborate brocaded taffetas, satins, and damasks. Made up and sold on, a silk dress might easily have cost twice what a weaver could earn in a year. While the industry's capitalistic structure tended towards concentration there remained numerous masters paying wages to very much more numerous artisan weavers, mostly journeymen. By and large those calling themselves weavers were men; women who were not widows were not permitted to use looms under Weavers' Company ordinances, though this typical artisan defence against the undermining of pay rates and the loss of control over the property of skill did break down in the later Georgian period. The weaving was carried out in houses, in areas that were first built up in association with the growth of the industry, on crude timber looms, cheaply built and rented (George 1925, 176–95; Rothstein 1961; Sheppard 1957; VCH 1998, 178–82). Pay was poor and the living conditions were not good. In 1743 it was said that journeymen weavers 'by hard Labour and Industry can scarcely, in the most frugal Way of Life, maintain themselves and Families' (Anon 1742/3). Men, women and children all worked, the last quilling, that is filling quills for the shuttles, or as drawboys, drawing threads in the looms, but only when there was work; the trade was subject to huge fluctuations, being easily affected by both fashion and war, dependent as it was on imports. Along with poverty the industry was characterised by religious nonconformity, embracing many Huguenot immigrants, high rates of literacy and social unrest. Weavers starved of work and income were not slow to riot or to resort to machine breaking. There were several outbursts in the late 17th century, including riots against the use of machinery in 1675. Spitalfields weavers led the calico riots of 1719–20, and successfully gained protective legislation. Newly immigrant Irish weavers working for low pay provoked further riots in 1736 (George 1925, 180, 193; Baker 1998, 18, 94–5, 177).

Silk throwing and winding had largely gone from Spitalfields by the middle of the 18th century. The successful pirating into England of Italian water-powered silk-throwing and winding-machine technology had led to the building of Lombe's Mill in Derby in 1721. Thereafter the silk-throwing industry was taken up in mechanised mills in Macclesfield, Congleton, Leek and Stockport in well-chronicled early developments of a factory system (Calladine & Fricker 1993; Berg 1994, 211). The relatively unskilled work of silk throwing thus departed London, but the capital's silk weavers remained a major presence.

Early buildings

Recent investigation in Bethnal Green, in what were the northern parts of London's 18th-century silk district, where it is known that large numbers of the journeymen to whom silk masters put out the weaving lived, has shown that a number of humble 18th-century buildings survive, invariably very much altered (Fig 5.1). Survivals can be related to drawn and photographed views of other local late 17th- and early 18th-century buildings now demolished (Fig 5.2). The distinctive characteristics of these buildings can be summarised as upper-storey long light and small entrance-bay windows, and one-room or single-pile depth, making the buildings proportionally tall or vertical. These features can all be related to industrial use; they indicate that the buildings were designed to incorporate weaving workshops.

Good light was especially crucial for the intricate skill of silk weaving, for the joining of fine threads, and for precise colour matching. The maximisation of light in rooms used for weaving was an absolute architectural priority. However, in the brick walls that London's post-1707 Building Acts required, full-width windows were structurally difficult except just below the eaves. The Building Acts were notoriously poorly enforced, so this effectively only applied to front walls. Illegal but inconspicuous timber back walls were widespread. Trabeated timber construction being free from the constraints that came with arched window heads in brick walls, full-width fenestration was more readily achieved to the rear. This may have influenced the placement of stair-

Figure 5.2 Nos 71–79 Sclater Street, one-room-deep houses in the silk district, first built c1719. Small windows for front staircases and large workshop windows are indicative of origins as weavers' tenements. Photographed in the early 20th century and showing the locality's then famous bird market. Demolished (© Tower Hamlets Local History Library)

cases. Stairs at the back, as was usual in London's better speculatively built 18th-century houses, would have blocked out light. Here they were generally placed at the front, where full-width fenestration was anyway compromised (Fig 5.3).

The front-stair position was the only alternative to a rearwards position because most of the buildings were only one room deep; there was no middle option. The one-room layout and consequent proportional verticality were also, of course, functions of design for through light. In any two-room or double-pile layout on a narrow urban plot the inner parts of the rooms lack good natural light. The staircase was thus best placed immediately inside the front door, where it could be framed into the brick front and side walls. This explains the peculiar small entrance-bay windows that are so out of keeping with the classical proportionality that we tend to associate with houses from 18th-century London. Even though these were humble buildings it would have been important to light the staircases, if only because silk, a valuable commodity that needed to be kept clean, was carried up and down them. These were industrial buildings; it is worth noting in passing that front staircases were also used in 18th-century dock warehouses in both London and Liverpool (Porter 1994, 284–6; Giles & Hawkins forthcoming 2004).

Multiple occupation

Such industrial considerations could be sufficient explanation for this staircase feature, but there is reason to believe that they are not, especially given that the front staircase is not characteristic of domestic industry elsewhere in Britain. There is another, non-industrial, reason why this stair position may have been favoured. Front stairs are rare in multi-storey homes, where circulation between the levels is generally mediated internally, to control access and provide differing degrees of privacy, but they are suited to multiple occupation, as they allow upper-storey tenants to come and go without intruding into the ground-floor tenant's space. There is good evidence from a range of contexts that front-staircase layouts can often be associated with design for multiple occupation, without necessary reference to industrial use. This applies across late 17th-century London, from Southwark and Wapping to Westminster, and across various 17th- and

Georgian London's silk-weaving workshop homes 63

TWO HOUSES AT
21 CHESHIRE STREET
FIRST FLOOR
late 17th century (dem.)

46 CHESHIRE STREET
SECOND FLOOR
1670s

97-99 SCLATER STREET
FIRST FLOOR
c.1720

70-76 SCLATER STREET
GROUND FLOOR
c.1719

7-9 GRANBY STREET
GROUND FLOOR
c.1725 (dem.)

3-4 HARE COURT
BETHNAL GREEN
GROUND FLOOR
c.1725 (dem.)

113-115 BETHNAL GREEN ROAD
FIRST FLOOR
c.1735

S = FORMER STAIR POSITION

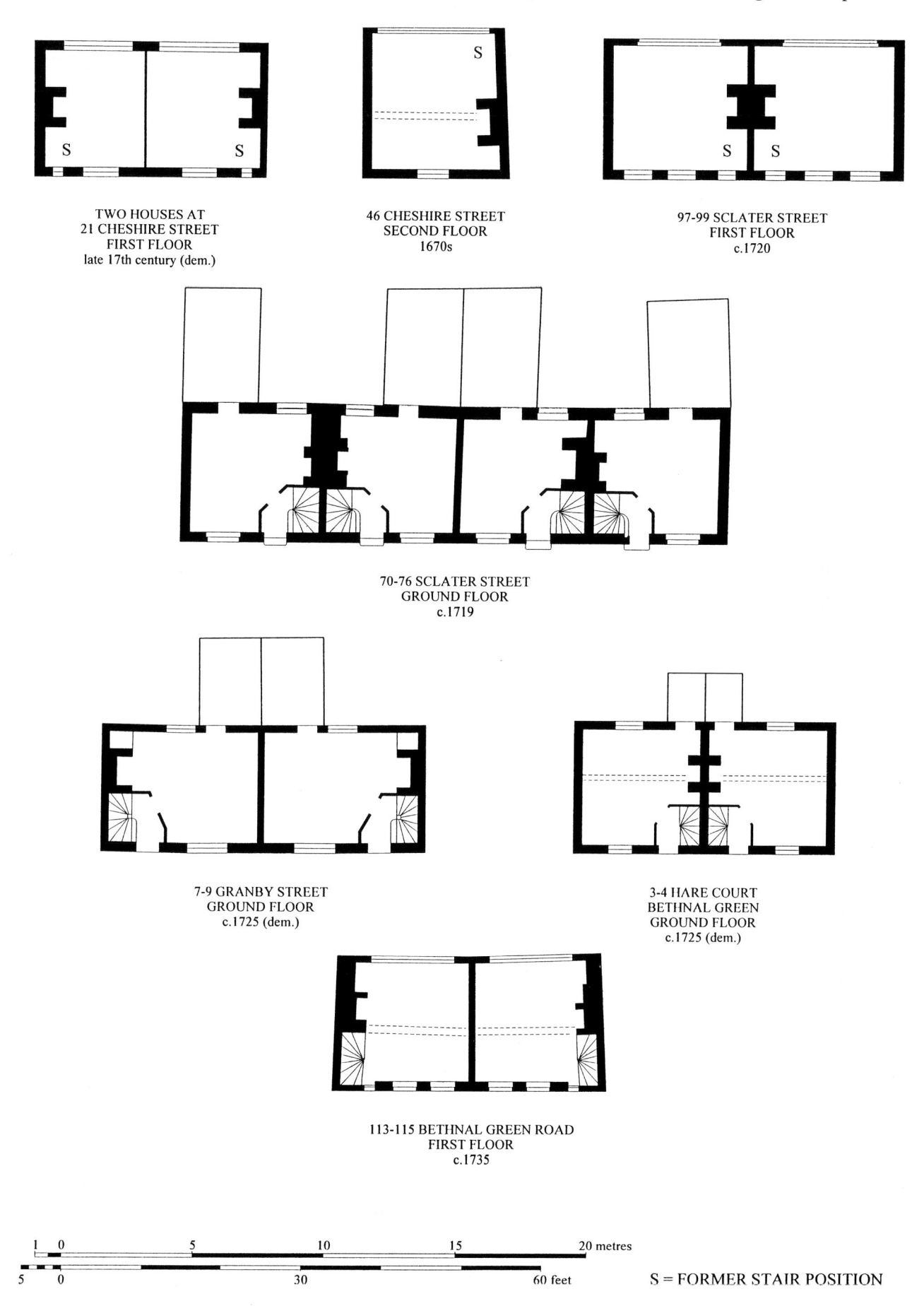

Figure 5.3 Reconstructed plans of late 17th- and early 18th-century houses in the Bethnal Green part of the Spitalfields silk district. (© English Heritage. NMR)

18th-century building types, from almshouses to the blocks of chambers in the Inns of Court, and up and down Britain from Great Yarmouth to Edinburgh, though not, it seems, across the Channel in Paris or Lyons (Guillery forthcoming). In the Spitalfields silk district, industrial use may have been a leading determinant of architectural form. However, domestic use would not have been a minor consideration for speculative builders and landlords. It was fundamental to economic equations, as it influenced rent. There would have been no sense in developing expensive town plots for anything other than weaving and living combined. So, poor though the inhabitants were, these buildings do perhaps also speak of the journeymen who lived in them, though evidence as to what 18th-century weavers' rooms were like as homes is elusive. In the absence of contemporary pictorial representations probate inventories can be evocative, but they tend to exclude the poor and disguise multiple occupation.

There is, however, straightforward evidence of multiple occupation, not least in a petition of 1743 that tells us that 'by far the greatest Part of the Houses in the said Hamlet are lett at Ten Pounds per Annum, and under; and are mostly lett out by the Owners of such Houses, in Two or Three distinct Parts or Tenements, by reason of the Great Poverty of the Inhabitants, who are unable to take a whole House upon themselves' (Anon 1742/3). The area already had many more households than houses by 1700. With this as the *status quo* about 200 new houses were built in the years following 1719, in the face of what would have been obvious and intensifying local poverty. So these houses were designed with sure knowledge that many were destined for multiple occupation. A typical room rental of £2 or £3 a year can be deduced, this being within reach of typical journeymen weavers, whose household incomes were often £20 a year or less. Two rooms would have been affordable only for prospering fully employed artisans or those families with substantial supplementary incomes (George 1925, 179–85; Schwarz 1992, 87–100; Guillery 2004). The early 18th-century rooms are generally about 5.1 m (17ft) square, enough space for a loom or two, a fireplace, a bed or two (perhaps folded away), a family, and little else. This would have been how most weavers lived. Demographic and topographic logic, architectural design, contemporary testimony, and other documentary evidence all point to multiple occupation and single-room tenancies as being the rule.

The late 18th century

As Georgian London's greatest social historian put it in describing Spitalfields: 'The work was done in small, crowded rooms in horribly insanitary dwellings, and the air was carefully excluded by paper pasted over the cracks of the windows, to prevent the silk from losing weight and so making the weaver liable to deductions from his earnings' (George 1925, 194). Here a caution is necessary. This evocation and many others relating to the living conditions of Spitalfields weavers derive principally from the documentation of a period of decline in the first half of the 19th century (see below). There was always great poverty, but against images of squalor should be set an awareness that cleanliness was of paramount importance in the production of silk. There was also great variability of status within the trade. At the top there were highly skilled artisans, literate and self improving, patient with intricate work, and with strong traditions of horticulture and bird fancying, as it was said, 'to cheer their quiet hours when at the loom' (Edward Church, a Spitalfields solicitor, as quoted in Clapham 1916, 466). This prompts a counter caution. This side of weavers' culture has been romanticised. There undoubtedly was artisan respectability, but there were also many who were less skilled and illiterate, out of work and vagrant. There was much criss-crossing between trades. Many weavers were other things as well.

In the 1760s there was a serious downturn in the silk trade, the workforce being reduced by 50%, bringing impoverishment that took people to the point of starvation. Riots and sabotage achieved a prohibition on the importation of French silks in 1766, reducing competition. However, there followed further confrontation and 'combination', the word generally used in the 18th century, before trade unions, to describe trade association for mutual benefit. Journeymen organised themselves with unparalleled rigour and carried out further sabotage, of both cloth and machines, reacting against the breakdown of established piece-work rates, and alarming government. An alliance of weavers with coal heavers working nearby on the Thames pushed for lower food prices, bringing affairs closer to a revolutionary edge, and to a denouement through the passage of the first Spitalfields Act in 1773. This introduced wage regulation, through a system for negotiating agreed piece rates for silk weaving in London. The Spitalfields Act and subsequent consolidating Acts were long recognised as a monument to the power the weavers had managed to wield, though they did also outlaw combination (Clapham 1916; George 1925, 192–5; Linebaugh 1991, 270–83; Baker 1998, 95, 178).

It may then be supposed, given that silk throwing had largely moved out of London and into factories by this time, and that wage regulation and stroppy weavers were not advantageous to employers, that silk weaving would have moved quickly out of London and out of reach of the restrictive Acts. To understand why it did not it must first be recalled that the production of higher-class silks involved developed skills that could not be simply relocated. Further, low transport costs arising from proximity to the landing place of the raw material in the Port of London and to the consumer market did matter, though they were perhaps not a major factor, silk being a high-value low-bulk commodity. More significant, perhaps, was a clause in the Act of 1773 that stipulated that masters resident in London could not employ persons resident outside. These masters did perhaps feel it important that they themselves should remain close to what was a famously fickle market: if so they were legally bound to employ Londoners.

Nor was there much scope for substantial reorganisation of the industry within London to apply economies of scale through factory working. The Acts worked against the introduction of any available mechanical improvement, as masters had to pay the same piece rates whether labour-saving appliances were used or not, a provision that, had it been applied to the cotton trade, would have done for Arkwright. It should be remembered that, at this stage, there had not in any case been significant technological advances in weaving; Jacquard exhibited his innovative loom in Paris only in 1801, and it was not applied in England until much later (see below). Further, it remained the case that factories that could have been used for weaving only during daylight hours, and which would thus have stood empty at night, made no economic sense in a densely populated city with expensive land. It was better to continue to build weaving space that also provided 24-hour housing for a captive market of workers who needed homes for which they had to pay rent as much as they needed work to enable them to pay that rent.

The Spitalfields Acts did bring a period of relative stability to the silk district, though there was not prosperity, and multiple occupation, three or four families in each house, remained the rule. The industrial-domestic vernacular architecture of the district did not, however, continue unchanging. While a largely homogenous building type has been described as typical of the early 18th century, intriguing and complex shifts in local architectural practice can be tracked from the 1760s (Fig 5.4). A growing concentration of property in the hands of a local oligarchy, weavers and labourers who had risen up by means of pawnbroking and the building trades to become big landlords, seems to be linked with the building of even larger tenement blocks in the 1760s and 1770s, just when the area was in political uproar (Fig 5.5). These buildings appear to have been up-scale tenement speculations, not in any meaningful sense proto-factories. Many variations in form were explored in the 1770s and 1780s, but the old front-staircase type did also endure into the 1790s. Faced with this heterogeneity it is worth remembering that this was late 18th-century London, the archetypal home of market-driven standardisation in speculatively built housing (Summerson 1945).

Standardisation was not only market driven. It also arose from legislation. The London Building Act of 1774 was the capital's first rigorously enforced building control, and a major factor in the decline of metropolitan vernacular architecture generally. Builders could no longer get away with timber construction behind brick fronts. In the silk district this meant that full-width windows were no longer possible to the rear other than on the upper storey. This would have meant less good light than heretofore on the intermediate levels of buildings of three or more storeys, as well as that stair placement would no longer have been influenced by lighting considerations. The Building Act is significant, but what is more remarkable is that after 1774 there was no more than a gradual and tentative move away from traditional building practices in the silk district.

The early 19th century

Yet by 1800 tall tenement blocks and front staircases were no longer being built, and by 1815 a new standard house form was being established in a building boom that can be interpreted either as adaptation for a still thriving domestic weaving industry, or alternatively, as new infrastructure intended to prop up an industry threatened with extinction. This new form was the two-storey weavers' 'cottage', manifest in rows and rows of two- or three-room homes, with amply fenestrated workshops over separate living space, the latter sometimes divided into two rooms (Figs 5.6 & 5.7). There were rear-staircase layouts, but many of these houses had only ladders and trap-doors to the workshops, to maximise the floor space for looms. These buildings were numerous and were clearly designed as single-occupation houses, not as divided tenement houses. The better examples undoubtedly represented an improvement in the area's housing stock when new, but many others were only two rooms, each about 3–3.6 m (10–12 ft) square, totalling 18–26 m^2 (200–88 sq ft), and therefore together not more spacious than a single room of 5.1m (17 ft) square (ie 26 sq m or 289 sq ft).

While the eradication of timber construction that followed from the Building Act of 1774 and its consequences for the lighting of workshops may have been a factor in the shift from tall blocks to low cottages, the more thoroughgoing standardisation of the building type after 1800 needs also to be understood as part of a general shift in London housebuilding at the bottom end of the market after financial collapses in and following 1793. Housebuilding moved away from local and building trade roots, becoming, markedly more than previously, an industry wherein houses were simply another 'industrialised' commodity, the large-scale, standardised and often poor-quality production of which could generate profits for an entrepreneur from whatever background (Clarke 1992).

The architectural transformation might also be considered in relation to some of the social and political ramifications of housing the poor. As has been argued in the context of 18th-century Paris, the density and permeability of tenement living denied privacy and built solidarity, feeding a revolutionary climate (Garrioch 1986, 16–55, 205–60; Farge 1993, 9–20; see also Hervier and Ferault 1998). In closely packed dwellings without substantial separating walls there was no alternative to collective identity. Distinctions between private and public space were

66 *The vernacular workshop*

3-5 CLUB ROW
GROUND FLOOR
1764-1766

125-127 BRICK LANE
SECOND FLOOR
1778

190-192 BRICK LANE
SECOND FLOOR
1778-1779

9 GRANBY ROW
FIRST FLOOR
c.1780 (dem.)

4a-6a PADBURY COURT
GROUND FLOOR
c.1790

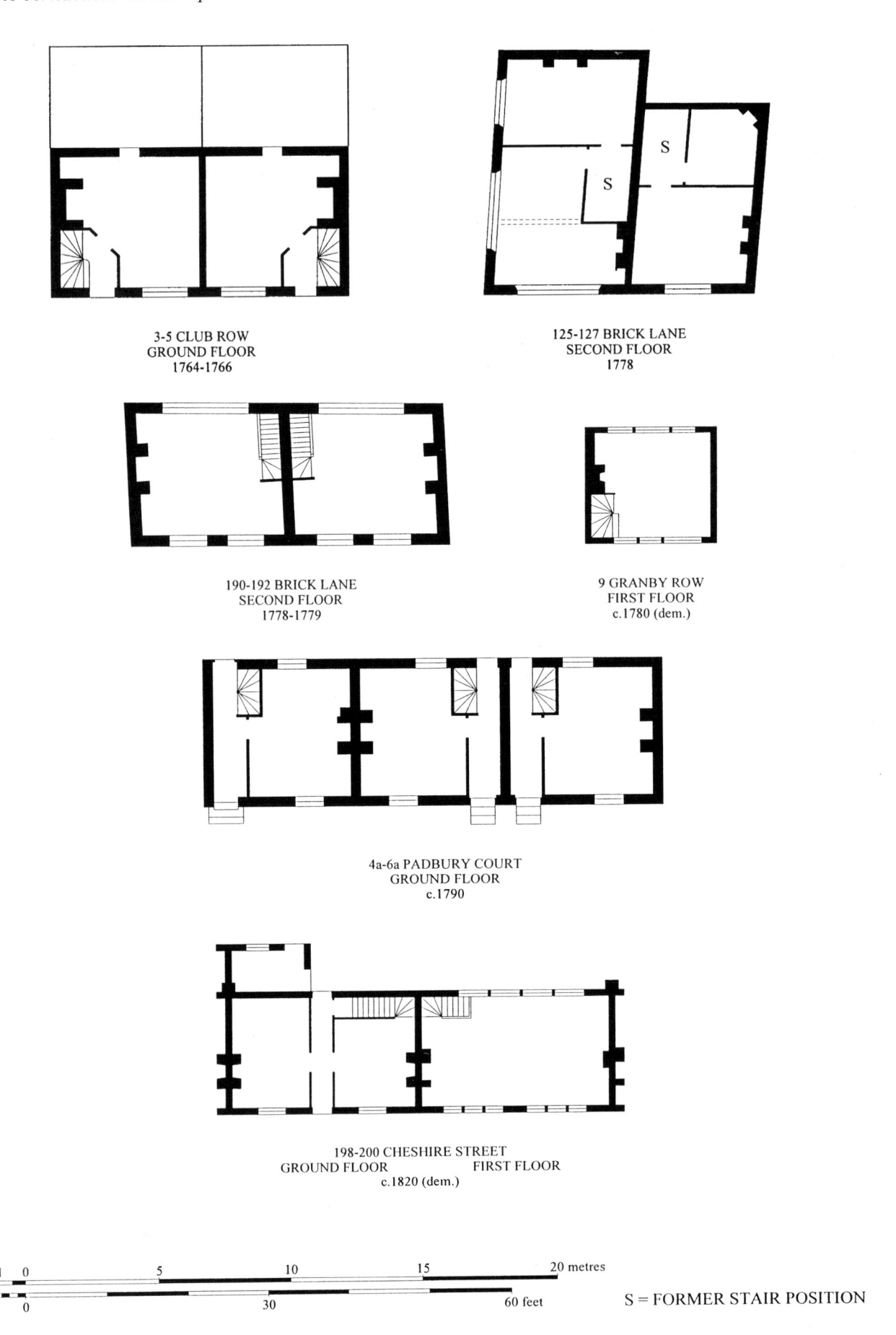

198-200 CHESHIRE STREET
GROUND FLOOR   FIRST FLOOR
c.1820 (dem.)

S = FORMER STAIR POSITION

Figure 5.4 Reconstructed plans of late 18th- and early 19th-century houses in the Bethnal Green part of the Spitalfields silk district. (© English Heritage. NMR)

Figure 5.5 No. 125 Brick Lane, a building of 1778 that probably incorporated a ground-level shop and upper-storey loomshop tenements. Watercolour by E A Phipson in 1914. (© London Metropolitan Archives, SC/PZ/BG/01/005)

impossible, and the intimidating fact of neighbourhood life was omnipresent. The Spitalfields silk district's dense and tenemental living conditions can only have reinforced the unusually strong tendency to 'combination' that characterised and empowered the weavers. In the late Georgian period the architecture of the area's housing shifted gradually from tenement blocks to single-family cottages. These

68 *The vernacular workshop*

Figure 5.6   Nos 34 and 36 Florida Street, Bethnal Green, weavers' 'cottages' of c1815 with two-room rear-staircase layouts on the ground floor and workshops on the upper storey. Demolished. Drawn for the London County Council in 1935–36. (© English Heritage, Greater London Council Drawings Collection 96/2095)

cottages, firmly separated by brick party walls, might have loosened some of the bonds of weaver identity and helped to bring the riot-prone area a measure of calm. This was not a premeditated or concerted programme of housing reform, though it does seem to reflect an imposition from outside of an essentially 'middling sort' concern for privacy and social separation (Heyl 2002). The move away from the purpose-built tenements that had typified local domestic architecture up to the 1770s coincided with the Act that brought relative peace to the silk industry, both changes offering better living conditions and undermining 'combination'. In both cases short-term improvement led to extreme hardship in the longer run.

Streatham

The Spitalfields Acts eventually brought decline to London's silk industry, the regulated wages tending to drive production out of London, increasingly so after 1800 when weaving was done in small towns where labour was cheaper, in Essex, Suffolk, and Berkshire, and further away in Norwich, Macclesfield, Coventry, Manchester, and Paisley. The clause preventing London manufacturers from putting work out beyond London was evaded and seldom prosecuted. Stephen Wilson, a London silk master and a key figure in the history of the English silk industry, found that concerted lobbying against the Acts and legal action to reduce wage rates was getting him nowhere. In 1820 he conducted a significant experiment, building a large silk factory in Streatham. What is now a suburb on the South Circular was then just outside London and beyond the reach of the Acts. Wilson was able significantly to reduce labour costs there through the first introduction to England of the Jacquard loom, the principal advantage of which was that it needed no drawboys. It was too tall to be installed in the

Figure 5.7 Early 19th-century weavers' 'cottages', in the 'Old Nichol' or 'Jago' in Bethnal Green (latterly the site of the Boundary Street Estate). Designed as two-room houses, there were workshops over living space. Photographed c1890. Demolished. (© London Metropolitan Archives 76/5903)

houses of the silk district (Clapham 1916, 464–9; Rothstein 1977; Saint 1987; Berg 1994, 228).

The view that the Acts were damaging spread. In evidence to Parliament in 1818 Wilson had said that they encouraged a 'spirit of combination' among the journeymen, who were, he also said 'after a little talking to, very tractable' (as quoted by Clapham 1916, 469). To David Ricardo and other liberal reformers the Spitalfields Acts were a disgrace, limiting as they did free and open competition and the exploitation of tractability. Theirs was the day, and the Acts were repealed in 1824. The import of foreign silks, again legal from 1826, further harmed the Spitalfields industry, and incidentally also finished off Wilson's Streatham factory (Clapham 1916; Saint 1987). The removal of legislative protection had a more immediately negative impact on Spitalfields than did the re-mechanisation of weaving in factories, which did not spread widely until the 1840s. By then poverty was rampant, dissent had resurfaced, and the 'distress' of the Spitalfields' weavers caught the nation's attention, becoming a focus for investigating reformers who published descriptions and depictions of unending filth and misery. The two-room early 19th-century buildings had been quickly subdivided as London's population boomed. They rapidly became much worse housing than that which was still available in the taller and roomier 18th-century buildings. The worst problems identified by Chadwick, Mayhew and other early Victorian reformers were in the newer early 19th-century houses, now all gone, not in the 18th-century districts, where there are still a few survivors (Gavin 1848; Yeo and Thompson 1971, 104–15; Anon 1853a; VCH 1998, 124–5, 178–9).

London's silk industry thus died away, though it was not finally extinguished for some time (Kean & Wheeler 2003). No more vernacular workshop tenements or houses were built, though many continued to be used for tailoring, as new waves of immigration filled the area's buildings. Artisan housing came to be a matter of middle-class beneficence, as through the Metropolitan Association for Improving the Dwellings of the Industrious Classes, founded in 1841, or the Improved Industrial Dwellings Company, providers from the 1860s of four-storey tenement blocks laid out with front staircases, in Bethnal Green and beyond.

Lyons

France's second city, Lyons, provides intriguing parallels for transformations in the architecture of urban silk-weaving workshop homes in the years around 1800. The silk industry was established in Lyons in the 1530s, quickly growing to employ thousands. There was industrial diversification, and decline in the industry after the exiling of Protestants in 1685, but through the 18th century silk,

Figure 5.8 Rue Major Martin on the Presqu'île in Lyons, showing tenement buildings that are typical of 17th- and 18th-century developments in the area – tall, shallow, and amply fenestrated. These would have accommodated silk weavers and others. (© Peter Guillery)

Figure 5.9 Modest houses on the Grande Rue de la Guillotière, the main road linking Lyons to Italy, in the 18th century when the Guillotière district on the left (east) bank of the Rhône was an outlying area in which numerous silk weavers lived. (© Peter Guillery)

controlled by Colbert's 'Grand Fabrique', was dominant in Lyons, employing up to 40% of the city's workforce. There were about 18,000 looms in Lyons in the 1780s spread through the whole urban area, there being no specialised district comparable to Spitalfields in what was a smaller city. Housing varied, and, with occupations thoroughly mixed, there is no evidence that any houses were designed especially for silk weavers, as opposed to cotton weavers, hat makers, goldsmiths or even non-industrial inhabitants. As in Spitalfields, silk weavers in Lyons were generally literate and well capable of organising themselves in defence of their collective interests, resisting reforms and mechanising inventions introduced by Jacques de Vaucanson in 1744, and rioting again in 1786.

In the Presqu'île between the Saône and the Rhône, and in other central districts, there was by the 18th century a long-established local vernacular architecture of tall tenement blocks, five- or six-storey buildings densely grouped along narrow streets. These are highly varied in form, but often only one room deep and generally characterised by ample, sometimes full-width, fenestration, provision for the good light that workshop use required, whether for weaving or not. The upper storeys are often accessible via external staircases reached through 'traboules', the communal passages under buildings that are one of the most distinctive features of Lyons (Fig 5.8). Landlords and tenants mixed in the same buildings, weavers and their families probably occupied a single room for all domestic and work purposes, as in Spitalfields. Silk weavers were also to be found on the urban fringe, as on the left (east) bank of the Rhône along the Grande Rue de la Guillotière, the main road to and from Italy, perhaps living in humbler two-storey houses, the few that survive not speaking clearly of industrial use (Fig 5.9). By the 1780s weavers' habitations were beginning to be concentrated on the northern margins of Lyons, north of the Presqu'île in the Grande-Côte and St Vincent districts, areas that were then only sparsely built up below the steep and open slopes of the Croix Rousse (Garden 1970, 275–353, 405–22; Cayez 1978, 316; Barre 2001, 34–6; Chalabi *et al* 2000).

The looms of Lyons were said to have all but stopped working in the revolutionary years of 1789 to 1793. Following Lyons' short-lived Royalist counter-revolution in 1793, disorder in the trade continued through the 1790s. It was against this background that Joseph-Marie Jacquard (1752–1834), born and bred a Lyonnais weaver, rose to fame. From 1778 he had begun to experiment with mechanical improvements to weaving looms. In 1801 his inventions were exhibited in Paris and given an award. With encouragement and subsidy from the Emperor Napoleon and civic authorities in Lyons, both keen to revive the city's silk industry, in part in response to English competition, Jacquard refined and enhanced his invention up to 1804, when he perfected mechanisms that definitively removed the need for a second person drawing threads. There was, of course, resistance from weavers to the introduction of the Jacquard loom, but in a post-revolutionary climate this had little sway. The new technology was, however, problematic in practical terms as the 3.9 m (13 ft) tall Jacquard loom could not be accommodated in existing houses. The concerted revival of silk production in Lyons brought in new weavers and encouraged the extensive development of new housing. As the industry once again boomed from c1810 the slopes of the Croix Rousse began to be built over, religious lands having been expropriated and sold off. Many new streets were laid out, but they were not lined with single-family two-storey weavers' cottages like those that were being built in London. Rather the local tenement building tradition was intensified, in blocks that were substantially bigger and more regular than their forerunners. About two thirds of the new buildings on the hill, most built from c1816 up to the early 1830s, are of a distinctive type, purpose-built weavers' housing, designed with workshop habitation in mind. These early 19th-century tenements are tall, typically six storeys, to maximise site value, as had always been the practice, and often depend on traditional traboule access to external rear staircases. They have simple and unembellished façades, premises that were intended to house weavers being built at minimum cost. Tall windows maximise light in highly repetitive façades, some of massive extent (Fig 5.10). Height is all the more pronounced as each storey has the 3.9 m (13 ft) clearances necessary to accommodate Jacquard looms. Within there were one- or two-room dwellings in which there were generally as many looms as windows, the looms being framed into the floors and ceilings, with mezzanine platforms for beds and other domestic furnishings being common (Barre 2001, 67–80). Lyons' silk industry was revived and expanding, but it was anything but stable. The weavers were more than ever organised and politicised, mounting revolts in 1831 and 1834 that led to pitched battles in the Croix Rousse district that have become the stuff of legend (Barre 2001, 97, 106–08). There were further confrontations in 1848–49, but the industry continued to prosper and grow, decline not coming until the 1870s.

Conclusions

Transformations in the nature of vernacular workshop homes for the silk industries of London and Lyons thus followed very different paths. In both places housing for silk weaving changed utterly in the years around 1820. In London change came in a way that had roots in 18th-century 'combination', that is the locally concentrated strength of the weavers and related legislation, the sheer size of the metropolis and building control being among other factors. This change could not and did not accommodate Jacquard looms or any other shift towards factory production, moving from workshop tenements to workshop cottages. In Lyons renewal in a climate of post-revolutionary recovery was designedly industrialising, though no more factory oriented, accommodating Jacquard looms while intensifying and even ghettoising tenement living in a place where the industry had previously been more diffuse. In the face of subsequent threats to the livelihoods of weavers it was in Lyons that resistance was most vigorous and effective. In London earlier success in securing continuity had perhaps helped to bring about a situation where the trade could be reduced to fragmented impoverishment. In both places workshop production endured well into the 19th century, but differently displaced into distinct kinds of 'industrialised' as opposed to vernacular workshops.

In the absence of a detailed study of the Lyons buildings these comparisons can only be tentatively made. But it is clear enough that silk weaving in London and Lyons illustrates ways in which industrialisation took different courses along which architectural developments were correspondingly different. Even with the benefit of more detailed study it would, of course, remain endlessly debatable as to whether, and to what degree, the differing social consequences of these transformations might have been related to, and affected by, changes in the nature of the built environment, but that is no reason not to broach the possibilities.

Finally, and facing the other direction from Lyons, another question arises over the relationship, if there is any, between, the architecture of the late 17th- and 18th-century industrial tenements or vernacular workshops of London's silk district, with that of other vernacular workshops familiar from elsewhere in England, and elsewhere in this volume. Are the late 18th- and early 19th-century domestic loomshops that tend to be associated with the north of England and the industrial revolution, whether in Cheshire, Lancashire, or Yorkshire, outwardly similar to what existed in Spitalfields simply because of comparable functional dictates? Or did London's earlier vernacular workshop architecture provide a model? The former may well hold more than the latter, similarities perhaps being to some large degree an instance of convergent vernacular evolution. However, the question warrants exploration, if only because difference can be as instructive

Figure 5.10 La Maison des Canuts (the weavers' house), on the rue d'Ivry, Lyons, laid out from 1825. This building is typical, and by no means the largest, of the tenement blocks built in the Croix Rousse district of Lyons in the early 19th century to house silk weavers and tall Jacquard looms. It now holds a museum devoted to the history of the Lyons silk industry. (© Peter Guillery)

74 *The vernacular workshop*

as similarity. In the study of English vernacular architecture and industrialisation neither London nor the rest of Europe should be overlooked.

Notes

1. I am grateful to colleagues in English Heritage who, alongside others outside the organisation, notably Andrew Byrne, Bernard Herman, Natalie Rothstein and the owners and occupiers of the buildings surveyed, are more amply acknowledged in the survey report mentioned in note 2. For the simple overview of Lyons' weavers' housing I am grateful to Maryannick Chalabi and Nadine Halitim-Dubois, at the Inventaire Général (Rhône-Alpes), and to Olivier Zeller, at the Université Lumière Lyons, for sharing information and research findings. Figs 5.1, 5.3 & 5.4 are © English Heritage, NMR. Fig 5.6 is © Crown Copyright, NMR. Fig 5.2 is reproduced by permission of the London Borough of Tower Hamlets and Figs 5.5 & 5.7 by permission of London Metropolitan Archives.

2. The paper given at the conference in November 2002 was devoted entirely to Spitalfields, and derived largely from material since published elsewhere (Guillery, 2004). Discussion following the paper homed in on comparisons with Lyons, about which I then knew very little. Spurred on principally by Marilyn Palmer, limited investigations into the housing of silkweavers in Lyons since have led me and the editors of this volume to decide to pursue here questions arising from discussion at the conference. So this essay is proceedings from as well as the proceedings of the vernacular workshops conference. For detailed accounts, fuller references (including primary sources) and bibliography regarding the Spitalfields silk industry and the recently investigated buildings associated with it see Guillery 2000 and Guillery 2004. The former may be consulted through the National Monuments Record.

6 The Yorkshire textile loomshop: from weaver's cottage to the factory *by Colum Giles*

Introduction

Recent years have produced an extensive literature on the transformation of Britain's economy between 1700 and 1850. For many sectors, historians now place emphasis on continuity and evolution, and only 'shock' industries like cotton are now seen as approximating to older views of an Industrial Revolution. Research has suggested different stages in the process, and the concept of proto-industrialisation has been advanced as a way of explaining the transformation from a largely craft-based rural economy to an industrial, machine-based economy (Hudson 1986, 57–84; Berg 1994, 67–8).

The role of the textile industry in the study of industrialisation has been prominent. The cotton industry, along with iron production, offered one model for industrial change, but other branches demonstrate different experiences. The diversity of the industry – its many branches, its almost ubiquitous distribution across England – has been established, as have the varying fortunes experienced within the different branches. Taking the wool textiles branch, it has been shown that some long-established regional industries, for example that of East Anglia, largely fell by the wayside in this period; that in other areas, for example the South West, the woollen industry remained important throughout the period; and that one area, Yorkshire, built on ancient foundations to dominate the nation's output of woollen and worsted cloth (Jenkins & Ponting 1982).

Historians have examined the process of industrialisation largely through documentary sources; they have used buildings – mills, warehouses and so on – mainly to illustrate conclusions drawn from the records of official bodies and from private papers. But more recently architectural evidence has been seen as a valuable additional source, for much that remained undocumented is still expressed in surviving buildings. Buildings represent investment in an industrial system, and their location, numbers, dates, and forms can provide an insight into how the textile industry changed under the pressure of powerful influences such as the development of mechanised working.

Many stages of wool textiles production were undertaken outside what we think of as factories. Spinning was, before 1780, a domestic occupation; until the mid-19th century thousands were employed in worsted combing shops; and cloth finishing was undertaken in workshops, often in the major market towns. But the best architectural evidence for workshop-based industrial activity relates to weaving, and this paper explores the evidence for hand-loom domestic weaving in the Yorkshire woollen and worsted branches.[1]

The Yorkshire wool textile industry before 1780

Woollen cloth production was a vital part of the West Riding's economy from at least the 15th century, and some diversification was provided in the 18th century with the development of worsted or 'stuff' manufacture. Although never absolutely segregated geographically, the two branches became seated in different areas: 'white' and 'coloured' woollen broadcloth production was concentrated to the west and south of Leeds, the main market centre for the whole branch, and 'narrow' woollen cloth production dominated the hills and valleys around Huddersfield. Worsted manufacturing was first important in the upper Calder Valley, where Halifax provided the main market centre, but later the Bradford area came to dominate production (Wilson 1971, 53–5) (Fig 6.1).

Historians have identified a broad distinction between the two branches in the way in which production was organised (Jenkins & Ponting 1982, 8–10; Berg 1994, 215–17). In the woollen branch, the typical figure was the small independent clothier, buying his own wool and, in his home and with his own labour and that of his family and perhaps of a very few employees, working it through the different stages. He used the public mills for fulling and sold his cloth directly in the cloth halls. This method of production is frequently termed the domestic system. A vivid picture of the rhythm of work is glimpsed in the diary of Cornelius Ashworth, a small-scale clothier working in the Calder Valley in the 1780s, doubtless in ways familiar a century earlier. Ashworth frequently recorded how much he had woven on particular days. Time on the loom varied with the seasons, for he combined weaving with farming: on a good day for weaving he might work up nine yards of a piece, but on other days he might do less at the loom and spend time instead in the fields. This division was a common one, and in 1799 it was reported that 'in harvest the manufacturers generally leave their looms and assist in reaping the crop' (Atkinson 1956, 27–32; Gregory 1982, 82–4). This must have been a continuation of a long-established custom of dual occupation.

In contrast to the woollen trade, the worsted

76 *The vernacular workshop*

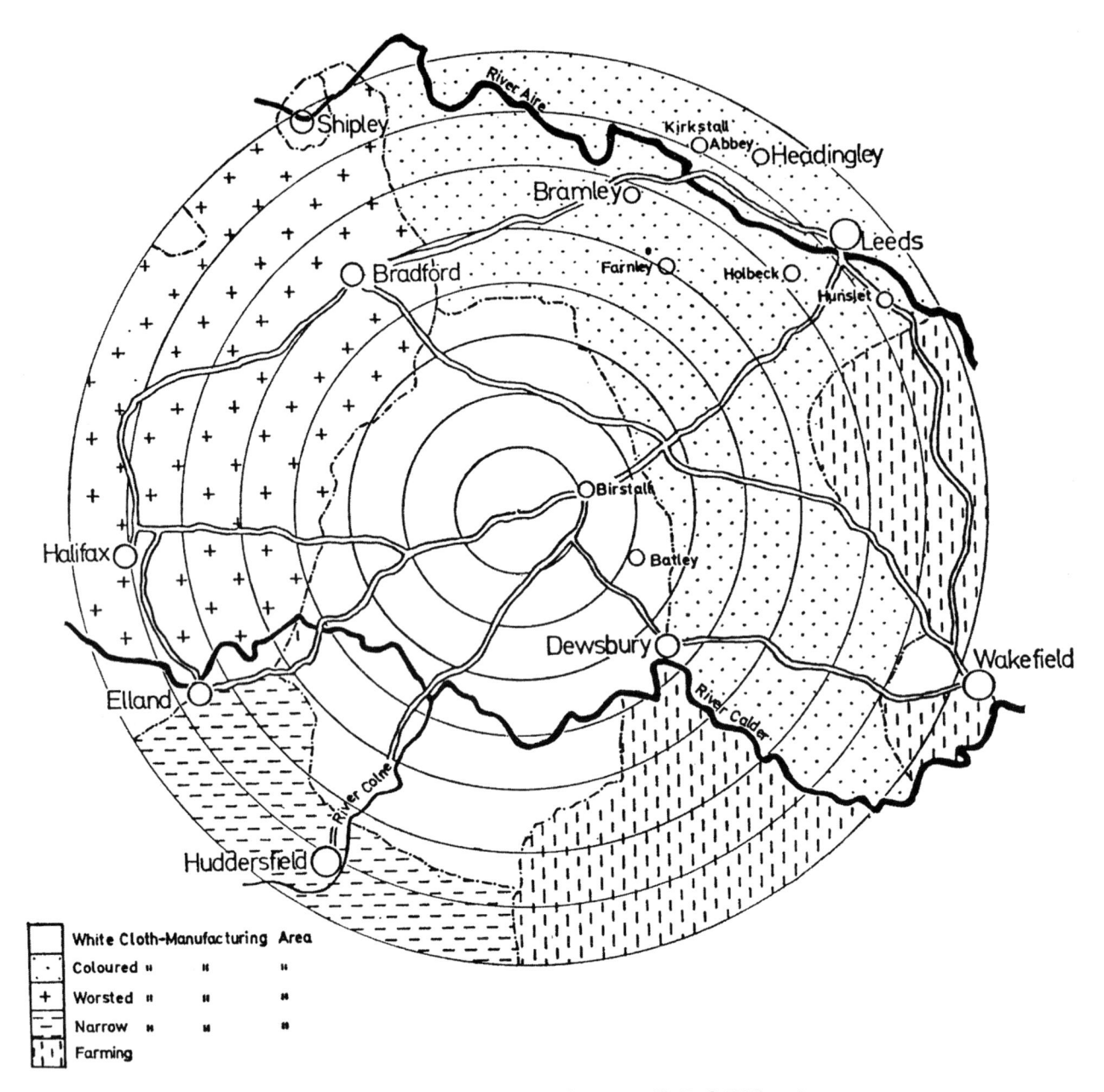

Figure 6.1 Schematic map of the West Riding wool textile area. (© R G Wilson)

branch was organised on the putting-out system, in which the typical figure was the large coordinating manufacturer, buying wool and sending it out to wage-earning domestic combers, spinners and weavers before selling in the piece halls of Halifax and Bradford or, in the case of very large operators like Samuel Hill of Soyland, shipping to order. Hill, in fact a coordinating manufacturer of both woollen and worsted cloth, must have employed hundreds of outworkers to fulfil the huge orders which he is recorded as dispatching (Atkinson 1956, 1–18). Thomas Crosley, a Bradford worsted manufacturer, had 'spinning done in Lancashire, as far as Ormskirk, in Craven, and at Kirkby Lonsdale. In Wensleydale, Swaledale and other parts of north Yorkshire' (Firth 1990, 152). At a more modest scale, Robert Heaton, a worsted manufacturer from Stanbury, near Haworth, working between 1762 and 1783, employed two agents to take wool and yarn to outworkers, and had forty spinners in Haworth and in adjacent Lancashire (Sigsworth 1958, 13–14; Firth 1990, 147–8). The different forms of organisation are reflected in the exchange buildings serving the two branches: in Leeds, the markets for woollen cloth, the Mixed Cloth Hall of 1756–58 and the White Cloth Hall of 1775–76, provided 1770 stands and 1210 stands respectively, but the Piece Halls of Bradford (1773) and Halifax (1775–78) had, respectively, only 258 and 315 rooms (Grady 1989, 85–7, 153, 157, 162–3). The distinction between the two branches influenced the way in which each adopted mechanised working after 1780, and is reflected in the provision made for domestic production after that date.

The importance of the textile industry before 1780 is directly demonstrated by the form of much of the

Figure 6.2   Greenwood Lee, Heptonstall, built by the Sutcliffe family, wealthy clothiers in the 17th and 18th centuries: the workshop lies at the left-hand end of the elevation. (© Crown Copyright. NMR)

housing found in one particular valley, that of the River Calder, flowing east from the Pennine watershed and skirting Halifax. For centuries the valley had been a major centre of woollen production, and in the 18th century it added worsted manufacturing to its economy. Defoe famously described the landscape of the valley: 'almost at every house there was a tenter, and almost on every tenter a piece of cloth, or kersey, or shalloon'. Seeking to explain the lack of people in this landscape, he stated that if he 'knocked at the door of any of the master manufacturers, we presently saw a house full of lusty fellows, some at the dye-fat, some dressing the cloths, some in the loom, some one thing, some another, all hard at work and full employed upon the manufacture' (Defoe 1724–26, 490–7). Surviving in the valley today are large numbers of these master manufacturers' houses, significantly larger and more elaborate than the houses of other Yorkshire valleys, and very often demonstrating a clear distinction between a living area and, separated by a passage, a workshop (Fig 6.2). Inventories of Defoe's period allow us to furnish these rooms: Daniel Greene of Soyland, high in the hills, a yeoman, died in 1696, and in his shop he had a press and papers, three pairs of shears, a shearboard, a raising board, and a pair of looms, and in the chamber over he had 30 kersey cloths worth £50 and wool worth £24.[2]

The architectural evidence of the vernacular houses of the upper Calder Valley raises a number of questions about the organisation of the textile industry in this early period. Accepted views are challenged by the evidence of the numerous fine houses of 17th-century woollen manufacturers, who were clearly far higher in status than the conventional image of the small independent clothier, supposedly characteristic of this branch, would suggest. By the 18th century, many manufacturers were involved in both woollen and worsted production, with no sharp distinction between the branches, both of which operated a putting-out system (RCHME 1986, 125–30; Jennings 1992, 82–5).

What is incontestable is that the Yorkshire wool textiles industry was already by 1780 carried out on a considerable scale and formed the backbone of the region's economy. But where did the manufacturing take place? Defoe identifies the houses of the master manufacturers as the centre of production, but the scale of the industry and the small size of the shops which formed part of the typical Calder Valley yeoman house together suggest that workers toiled

78 *The vernacular workshop*

Figure 6.3 Three-storeyed houses in Heptonstall village, possibly early examples of the 'weavers' cottage' form. (© English Heritage. NMR)

elsewhere. Spinning, we have seen, was conducted in the cottages of the workers, often over a wide area. Weaving, too, was probably undertaken largely in the homes of workers, but there is very little evidence that purpose-built accommodation was provided for or built by weavers before 1780. In Heptonstall there is a very small number of proto-type weavers' cottages, by their style dating from the 17th century (Fig 6.3), so perhaps in a few cases substantial houses of a form reflecting their intended industrial use were provided for outworkers.

Documents throw some light on where weaving was undertaken and how weavers were accommodated. Probate inventories show that looms were present in what seem to be small houses or the houses of relatively poor families, and Defoe noted 'an infinite number of cottages or small dwellings, in which dwell the workmen which are employed' in the industry (Defoe 1724–26, 493). He does not, however, clearly state that they worked in their houses, but we may assume that this was the case. That these cottages have not survived suggests that they were insubstantial, perhaps timber-framed and cruck-built, and incapable of adaptation to changing standards of living. In 1725 a Pudsey clothier, Richard Farrer, paid 2s 6d for a single-roomed cottage built on the waste, and in 1809 Joseph Rogerson, a miller of Bramley, near Leeds, described a 'little straw Thatche'd house situate at the corner of our croft of that Villain called Jsh Pickles; it was occupied by a poor Man who had lived in it for 50 years back his name was Jerh Proctor a stuff weaver; it was the only straw thatched house remaining in Bramley' (Strong 1999, 68; Hargave & Crump 1931, 96–7). What is not clear is whether the cottages occupied by the army of domestic clothiers and weavers before 1780 were in any way distinct from other cottages, nor is it evident how they compared to the later type which is recognisable as representing purpose-built accommodation for domestic weaving.

The Yorkshire textile industry 1780–1850

The many improvements and inventions in textile machinery made in the decades after 1750 led, by the late 18th century, to a sharp rise in the output of the Yorkshire wool textile industry. Apart from the flying shuttle, all the advances accelerated production at the preparatory and spinning stages of manufacture. Some machines, particularly the jenny, could be worked by hand, but most demanded power, and in both the woollen and worsted branches scores or hundreds of new water- and steam-powered mills were built to accommodate the new machines. In 1787 the first worsted mill was built and by 1822 over 100 were in operation: in 1797 alone 43 woollen mills are first recorded as being in use (Jenkins 1975, 10–25). The result was steadily increased production, and Yorkshire broadcloth production increased four-fold between 1780 and 1815 (Berg 1994, 41).

The new mills produced yarn, and for some firms, particularly in the worsted branch, this was the end product, shipped out of the area for use in Norfolk and elsewhere (Firth 1981, 9). For most businesses in the Yorkshire industry, however, cloth manufacture remained the principal focus, and the yarn was worked up locally into a variety of woollen and worsted cloths. The industry had always coped with bottlenecks at one or other stage of production: after 1780 the bottleneck settled firmly in the weaving stage, still dependent on handlooms. Not until the 1820s were power looms successfully introduced to the worsted branch, and only in the 1830s were they adopted on a large scale; and the woollen branch operated almost exclusively with the hand-loom until after 1850 (Jenkins & Ponting 1982, 110–17). Between 1780 and the second quarter of the 19th century, therefore, the fate of the Yorkshire industry pivoted on the ability of the hand-loom weaver to respond to the new potential for increased production.

The adoption of the flying shuttle allowed one man to operate a loom where previously assistance had been required, at least for some types of cloth, but the shuttle cannot, on its own, explain how the Yorkshire industry raised its levels of production. More significant in the industry's response was probably a rapid and large-scale expansion in the numbers of handloom weavers, the key workers in the industry. By the 1830s there were estimated to be 20,000 woollen weavers in the Huddersfield area, 10,000 in the Leeds area, and 14,000 in the worsted district (Brooke 1993, 8; Gregory 1982, 246; Sigsworth 1958, 35). Major manufacturers in both branches might employ many hundreds of cotttage-based weavers. In the worsted branch, Willett and Co of Bradford employed 500 handloom weavers in 1838, and J and J Craven of Keighley, despite introducing power looms in 1834, had 'the far greater part of their goods . . . woven by hand: at that time they delivered work out to handloom weavers at Silsden, Sutton, Icornshaw, Cowling and several other places' (Sigsworth 1958, 35; Hodgson 1879, 30). In the 1830s, John Wrigley, woollen manufacturer at Cocking Steps Mill in Honley near Huddersfield, undertook scribbling, carding, slubbing, fulling, and finishing in his mill, but 'all our spinning, weaving, burling and wool picking [is] worked at our servants' own houses, in the neighbourhood . . . from three to four hundred of them are in our employ' (Giles & Goodall 1992, 288). Alongside these large employing manufacturers there were still, before 1850, many hundreds of independent small clothiers in the woollen branch, working much as their predecessors had done a century earlier. In 1830, nearly 500 woollen manufacturers attended the Cloth Hall in Huddersfield, over 100 from a single township, Golcar; and in 1851 nearly 5000 people in Yorkshire described themselves for the Census as clothiers, indicating that they operated on a scale that would have been recognisable centuries earlier (Crump & Ghorbal 1935, 106; Parson & White 1830; Jenkins & Ponting 1982, 10).

The weaver's cottage 1780–1850

The architectural response to the demand for more hand-loom weavers dominates the landscape of one particular part of the Yorkshire textile region. This area encompasses the Colne and Holme Valleys, which meet in Huddersfield, the centre of the narrow woollen-cloth trade. The architectural evidence for hand-loom weaving here provides a great deal of information about the location of the industry, about when and how provision was made for domestic and factory-based weaving, and about the scale of operation typical in this branch of the trade. The absence of similar evidence elsewhere, in other parts

80 *The vernacular workshop*

Figure 6.4   Lumb, Almondbury, near Huddersfield. The industrial use of the cottages is indicated by the provision of long 'weavers' windows'. (© English Heritage. NMR)

of the woollen-cloth producing area and in the worsted area, raises questions about whether the industry in the Colne and Holme Valleys enjoyed particular conditions which led to this abundant construction of hand-loom weaving accommodation.

The architectural expression of industrial occupation takes the form of the provision of generous fenestration in cottages and loomshops (Fig 6.4). The presence of large windows, typically of multi-light mullioned form, may be taken to indicate, if not the certain use of the internal space for weaving, then at least a probable intention on the part of the builder that the space should be set to this purpose. In support of this assumption, it is possible to point to other contemporary forms of workers' housing which lack large windows. Clearly choice was available: where domestic weaving was not likely to be practised, windows could be of conventional size, and it may, therefore, be concluded that builders were not slavishly following traditional forms in the provision of large windows. Where these occur, it is fair to assume that deliberate efforts were made to provide good accommodation for weaving.

If this is accepted, then the evidence for domestic weaving is found at every turn in the Colne and Holme Valleys, for two and three-storeyed weavers' cottages are here very numerous. A survey of the Colne Valley recorded 199 such cottages, and the Huddersfield area as a whole may have perhaps twice that number (Barke 1979, 51). Allowing for loss since, say, 1850, there may have been as many as 500 weavers' cottages here, and a generous number elsewhere in the wool textiles belt.

The type of house represented by the weaver's cottage seems, on surviving evidence, to have sprung almost out of nothing in the late 18th century. There are, it is true, very few examples of cottages of the same general form which might date to the 17th century, and it must be admitted that, in the absence of large numbers of surviving pre-1780 workers' houses, we know very little about the characteristics of earlier domestic forms at this level of society. The impression created by the abundance of weavers' cottages dating from after 1780 is, however, that these cottages, and the very particular forms that they took, were a direct response to new circumstances, the need to house a growing population, upon the fruits of whose labour depended the prosperity of the regional economy.

If this is the case, then the architectural evidence suggests that the response took some time to develop. Few weavers' cottages have reliable date-

Figure 6.5 Cliffe Ash, Golcar: the top-floor loomshop in this cottage built in 1845. (© Crown Copyright. NMR)

stones or are securely dated from documents, but available evidence points to little activity in the first decades of the period. A short terrace of cottages near Holmfirth is dated 1790, but this is a rare example of an 18th-century date, and datestones of the 1820s and 1830s seem more common, an impression confirmed by limited documentary searches. It appears probable that, in the Colne and Holme Valleys, the peak of building activity was the second quarter of the 19th century, a logical outcome of the construction of more and bigger mills in the early 19th century. One short row at Junction Hill, Golcar, is dated as late as 1860, surely a last gasp for domestic weaving or an indication that 'weavers' windows' had at last become an architectural convention.

There is no single type of weaver's cottage. The most common form is that of a two-storeyed dwelling, with one or two living rooms on the ground floor and, on the first floor, chambers for sleeping and weaving, the loom or looms being set up against the window. In 1849 it was observed of cottages at Paddock, near Huddersfield, that the looms 'invariably occupied the first floor. In some cases one and two uncurtained beds ... were placed in the corners' (Reach 1849b, 9). Many cottages have three storeys, and here it is possible that the ground floor was used for living, the first floor for sleeping and weaving, and the top floor entirely for weaving (Fig 6.5).

Cottages are found in a wide variety of situations. Some stand alone, sometimes with an attached or detached farm building, evidence for the late persistence of dual occupation in this area. Others are grouped as semi-detached dwellings, as back-to-backs, and as terraces, either built in one phase or developing in many stages. Well House Fold, in Golcar, began as a cottage and barn, occupied in 1841 by Joseph Cock, clothier, but developed in three further stages into a terrace of six houses (1841 Census Returns) (Fig 6.6). Piecemeal development of individual houses and small terraces produced settlements of chaotic form, strikingly different to the planned model villages of the same era (Fig 6.7). The settlement of Oldfield, in Honley, is made up of perhaps a dozen weavers' cottages, further housing of conventional form, agricultural buildings, and what appears to have been a combined agricultural building and loomshop (Caffyn 1986, 9–10) (Fig 6.8). In 1841, the settlement sheltered 32 woollen weavers and 8 woollen manufacturers, all or most at this date probably working from their houses. Some families appear to have taken in weavers as lodgers: Joseph Sykes, his wife and two sons were all woollen weavers, and Jonathan Cross, another weaver, completed the household: and George Heap was a beer seller but took in two woollen-weavers as lodgers (1841 Census Returns). Together the evi-

82 *The vernacular workshop*

Figure 6.6 Well House Fold, Golcar: the original house and detached barn were incorporated into a terrace by the addition of five cottages. (© Crown Copyright. NMR)

Figure 6.7 Upper Well House, Golcar, a small group of weavers' cottages developed in a number of stages. (© English Heritage. NMR)

Figure 6.8 Oldfield, Honley: a weaving village in the Holme Valley. (© English Heritage. NMR)

dence of Oldfield's buildings – weavers' cottages, loomshop, barns (or laithes in the local vernacular), and even a diminutive Church of England national school house of 1838 – and of the 1841 Census – which shows, alongside the weavers and manufacturers, four farmers, a joiner, a stone mason, and the ale house keeper – provides a vivid illustration of how local communities developed in this period of great social and ecomomic change.

Not enough is known about who was responsible for the construction of weavers' cottages, in the Colne and Holme Valleys and elsewhere. Landowners, especially those with estates on the fringes of the region's towns, were certainly attracted by the large returns to be gained from investment in housing. In the 1790s, James Graham split his farms near Leeds into plots of 2–4 ha (5–10 acres) and built a house suitable for a clothier on each, and his venture was rewarded by instant take-up 'at almost any price I chose to fix' (Thornes 1981, 19–20; Caffyn 1986, 21–2). Most of the wretched urban cottages described by Angus Bethune Reach for the *Morning Chronicle* in 1849 in Huddersfield, Bradford, and Leeds were rented by the occupiers and were probably built and owned by property developers, exploiting a rising market (Reach 1849b). More modest speculation was also evident. A pair of cottages at Gully, above Holmfirth, was built by Joseph Beaumont, a Holmfirth shoemaker, to provide an income for his daughters, and it is likely that many of the smaller developments were built for this sort of purpose (Thornes 1981, 20).

There is some evidence for the construction of weavers' cottages by employing manufacturers. Reach described a recently erected row of cottages in Leeds, with cellar loomshops, built by an employer who let out one loom with each cottage and took the weekly rent out of the wages of his employees (Reach 1849b, 30). Small-scale manufacturers might make more modest provision, for themselves and perhaps for an associated workforce. Cliffe Ash, in Golcar, was built in 1845 by a family of small independent clothiers, in all probability among the hundred from the township who attended the Huddersfield Cloth Hall (Thornes 1981, 19). Spring Grove, across the valley in Linthwaite, was built in 1824 by the Crowther family, clothiers, and the substantial house served as the centre of their business (Fig 6.9). Soon after, with the business prospering, the family built an adjoining terrace of back-to-back weavers' cottages, perhaps with the intention of filling them with weavers working for the business. Where cottages within a terrace or in a small block are reported to have interconnecting loomshops, the hand of an employing manufacturer may be assumed to be responsible for their construction, for one may infer that weaving was undertaken for a single manufacturing concern (Caffyn 1986, 14).

Confirmation of the generally modest wealth of those responsible for building weavers' cottages is provided by the buildings themselves. Most cottages were built singly or in pairs, like those at Gully, Holmfirth, built by the shoemaker Joseph Beaumont. Many 'terraces', like Scar House and Well House Fold, both in Golcar (see Fig 6.6), result from a number of phases of construction, each again involving only one

Figure 6.9 Spring Grove, Linthwaite: the large double-fronted house, home of the Crowther family, has some architectural pretension, but the added short row of back-to-back weavers' cottages are plain and functional. (© English Heritage. NMR)

or two houses. Single-phase blocks of four or more houses are rare: six back-to-backs were built at Thongsbridge, near Holmfirth, in 1790 (Caffyn 1986, 51), and a substantial block of four houses at Well Hill, Honley, is of one build. The picture is one of modest, piecemeal, accumulative investment, a picture that is entirely consistent with the structure of the local woollen-cloth manufacturing industry. It provides a telling contrast with the large-scale philanthropic or employer provision of workers' housing found, albeit always somewhat exceptionally, in other branches of the textile industry and, locally, among a very few of the largest woollen manufacturing firms such as the Brookes at Armitage Bridge Mills. The contrast is one between an organic, evolutionary, responsive, and self-generating process and an imposed, controlling provision.

There was probably some broad correspondence between the size of weavers' cottages and the status of the occupiers. Larger houses, that is, those of three storeys and double-fronted two-storeyed houses, were substantial enough in their workshop accommodation to house a number of looms, and this implies that the occupiers were running their own business and were independent clothiers. New Hagg, Honley, a double-fronted three-storeyed house with impressive industrial fenestration, was occupied in 1851 by John Heap, a woollen cloth manufacturer and farmer of 31 acres (12.5 ha) (Census Returns, 1851) (Fig 6.10). If in 1806 it was true that not 'one domestic clothier in twenty . . . has above four looms in his house', the architectural evidence suggests that, two or three decades later, this larger scale of operation was rather more common, for the more substantial houses were capable of holding more than this number. The smaller, two-storey cottages are likely to have been built for and occupied by the employed outworker and the smallest independent operators. Scar House, in Golcar, is largely made up to two-storey cottages, but in 1841 there were, making up the neighbourhood, not only five woollen-cloth weavers but also thirteen cloth manufacturers. Exact correlation between house type and trade description cannot be made, but it is quite possible that the small, two-storey 'weaver's cottage' could accommodate the most modest level of independent clothier, producing a piece for sale each week in the Huddersfield Cloth Hall.

Figure 6.10 The dual economy: New Hagg, Oldfield, Honley, was built by a farmer and woollen manufacturer and was later extended to give an attached weaver's cottage. (© English Heritage. NMR)

The loomshop 1800–50

As early as the first years of the 19th century, the threat to traditional ways of working was recognised by contemporaries. In 1806, attempts were made to restrict to six the number of looms operated under one roof, but this was a rearguard action, against the tide of the day, when 'many who were masters are brought to be workmen' (Gregory 1982, 90–4). The protests of small independent manufacturers focused on the development of loomshop working, distinct from domestic operation. In loomshops, larger numbers of weavers were employed in businesses which worked on a greater scale. These businesses therefore benefited from some economies and enjoyed greater control than did the clothiers, who foresaw ruin.

The architectural evidence of this intermediate stage of development, between small-scale cottage industry and large, factory-based manufacturing, takes two forms: the non-factory loomshop and the factory loomshop. It is likely that a few loomshops were built in the late 18th century, but most surviving examples date from the early decades of the 19th century. The architectural evidence allows two strands of development to be identified. On the one hand are the efforts of modestly prosperous manufacturers, often probably rising away from the domestic origin of their businesses. Their means, although perhaps not their ambitions, were limited, and what they built may have represented either a scaling-up of their operation two, three, four, or perhaps as much as ten-fold, or a drawing-in of previously dispersed outworking weavers (such as, it has been argued, probably occupied many of the smallest weavers' cottages) into a single building, where their production and habits could be more closely controlled. A three-storey loomshop in Honley may have been able to house six or more looms (Fig 6.11); an agricultural building at Oldfield had an upper-floor loomshop which could accommodate rather more than this; a loomshop at Ramsden Mill Lane, Golcar, had looms on two floors, above domestic accommodation (Giles & Goodall 1992, 83, 86); and Coffin Row, Linthwaite, occupied from 1840 by a fancy woollen manufacturer, had space for as many

Figure 6.11 A loomshop in Meltham Road, Honley, built in the early 19th century next to what was probably the manufacturer's house. (© English Heritage. NMR)

as 40 looms (Bodey 1971, 388). The advantages of the loomshop for the manufacturer rested in control, and they must have been significant enough to have warranted the investment in not only a substantial building but also all the tools of the trade required by the workforce. It would be interesting to learn whether these loomshops acted for the woollen manufacturer as a springboard to the next stage of industrial production, that is, fully mechanised operation from a mill.

The example of mill-based operation was provided in the same period by some of the largest woollen manufacturers of the age. These were mill owners: like John Wrigley of Cocking Steps Mill, Honley (see above), they ran their mills as private concerns rather than as 'public' mills to provide mechanised services (scribbling, carding, fulling) for the domestic manufacturers. But, unlike Wrigley, they did not use outworkers for spinning and weaving but instead provided workshops within the mill complex to house these hand-powered processes (Fig 6.12).[4] At Benjamin Gott's Park Mill in Leeds there were, by 1806, two weaving shops, one over one hundred metres long and both with the characteristic narrow plan which ensured good illumination throughout the interior (Jenkins 1975, 57). In the Huddersfield area, the best example of workshops for hand processes is found within Armitage Bridge Mills, on the River Holme just south of the town. Here in 1819 the Brooke family, for centuries manufacturers and merchants on a considerable scale, built a large water-powered factory, with mechanised scribbling, carding, and fulling housed in a substantial mill; and hand-powered processes – spinning and weaving – accommodated in an extensive four-storey workshop, narrow in plan and very well lit from one wall. In *c*1830 a new loomshop, on five floors, increased the mill's hand-loom weaving capacity. A few years later, the first power looms were introduced to the mill, signalling the beginning of the end for the hand-loom weaver.

The regional distribution of weavers' cottages

If it is accepted that the particular form of the weaver's cottage, especially its provision of large

Figure 6.12 Sowerby Bridge Mills: the huge loomshop may have accommodated over 100 hand looms. (© Crown Copyright. NMR)

windows and often a third storey, implies the intention on the part of the builder to facilitate the use of part of the dwelling for hand-loom weaving, then the geographical distribution of these cottages may have some significance. More research is required before this significance is fully understood. First, it is necessary to demonstrate that the present pattern of survival reflects earlier distribution. The architectural evidence, for now, might only be able to highlight some previously obscure patterns and perhaps to act as a starting point for inquiry. The evidence of the buildings must be seen in the light of differences between and within the branches of the wool textiles sector. The picture is complex and at present incomplete: further research might seek to study the relationship between the distribution of architectural forms and, for example, sub-regional specialisation in certain forms of cloth production.

Some large questions arise out of the study of the distribution of the 'classic' weaver's cottage described earlier. Before 1830, the power loom was virtually unknown in all branches of the textile industry: the hand loom and domestic operation were everywhere dominant. But the weaver's cottage is not found uniformly throughout the West Riding textile belt. It is ubiquitous in the Huddersfield woollen manufacturing area, which has provided virtually all the examples illustrated in this article, and the Calder Valley, in this period an area of mixed cotton, silk, woollen and worsted production, also has many surviving specimens. Outside these areas, weavers' cottages of conventional form, that is, with large windows, certainly exist, but the impression gained from unsystematic study suggests in much smaller numbers. This is the case in the worsted producing area in and around Bradford and most interestingly, in other parts of the woollen manufacturing area between Leeds and, to the west, Bradford and, to the south, Huddersfield.

The contrast between the Huddersfield woollen-manufacturing area and the worsted area of Bradford is the less surprising, for this might be explained by the accepted wisdom which holds that the two branches had very different structures, the woollen branch characterised by small independent manufacturers, the worsted branch by larger-scale operators who moved rapidly from the putting-out system to mill production of yarn. The question arises of why weaving on the putting-out system failed to inspire speculators to provide the type of housing enjoyed by the Huddersfield woollen weaver. Two possible explanations merit further investigation.

First, around Huddersfield, it might be suggested, there was sufficient confidence in the industry and in the demand for suitable accommodation from the small-scale manufacturers to encourage speculators to make provision, and, once provided, a constant demonstration of the success of the investment. In the Bradford area, in contrast, the demand may not have existed, nor was it generated. For the speculator, it might have appeared that the waged outworker could not in such numbers afford a similar level of accommodation. More generic types of housing were instead provided, which if it could be demonstrated that they were occupied by worsted hand-loom weavers, may at least prove that the generous fenestration of the Huddersfield weaver's cottage was not essential to worsted weaving.

The second possible explanation for the different pattern of distribution concerns the date at which the majority of weavers' cottages were constructed. It was suggested above that the peak period of building activity around Huddersfield was the second quarter of the 19th century, and there is some evidence to suggest that much activity took place in the 1840s rather than earlier. In the woollen branch, this chronology – somewhat intermittent activity before, say, 1830, and more intense investment later – is understandable as a response to the state of the industry, which saw slowly increasing production of yarn but the very late adoption of the power loom. In the 1830s and 1840s the demand for domestic hand-loom weaving accommodation was still a powerful incentive for speculative building of weavers' cottages around Huddersfield, and produced the bulk of our surviving examples. In the worsted branch, in contrast, no such demand existed, for in this branch the power loom was adopted on a large scale in the 1830s. Here, just when so many cottages were being built in the Huddersfield area, the extinction of domestic occupation was clearly in prospect, and housing for workers took forms which made no provision for domestic industrial occupation.

Less clearly explicable is the pattern of distribution of weavers' cottages within the woollen-manufacturing area as a whole, for, as noted above, the northern and eastern parts of the area, in the hinterland of Leeds, lack the abundance of weavers' cottages found around Huddersfield. The contrast cannot be explained by the absence of domestic weaving around Leeds. It was said of Pudsey that 'there was not a house... but what had workrooms in the upper storeys for looms, warping, spinning, etc' (Strong 2000, 19), and in the small village of Thackley, to the west of Leeds, in 1841 there were 87 clothiers and eleven cloth manufacturers as well as fulling millers, slubbers. and other tradespeople working within the woollen industry (1841 Census Returns). There are, in Thackley and in the wider area, some weavers' cottages but nothing commensurate with the scale of the industry or matching the provision made around Huddersfield. There is some evidence that the rise of the larger woollen manufacturer may have been evident first around Leeds: if this was the case, then incentive to build for the domestic clothier may have been weakened. A number of Leeds woollen mills – Gott's Park Mills, Stonebridge Mills, Wortley, and Winker Green Mills, Armley – had large loomshops by the 1820s, and this too might have discouraged provision of weavers' cottages. The Leeds industry furthermore, specialised in broadcloth using larger looms, and from an early date it might have been apparent that this favoured production in loomshops and in mills rather than in the houses of outworkers or small independent manufacturers. If so, the exceptional provision of weavers' cottages around Huddersfield might be seen as closely linked to the structure of the system which specialised in narrow-cloth production and to the persistence in this trade, alongside larger manufacturers, of the small independent manufacturer.

Conclusion

This study of the domestic textile industry in the West Riding has sought to relate architectural evidence to the development of wool textiles manufacture between the 17th century and the mid-19th century. The period before 1780 was one characterised by a 'proto-industrial' stage of production: a regional industry, rural 'peasant' handicraft production for the market, international markets, specialised agriculture, and urban marketing, finishing, and mercantile activity (Berg 1994, 67). What the evidence of the buildings demonstrates is that the historians' neat distinction between the domestic system of the woollen branch and the putting-out system of the worsted branch needs to be treated with caution, for it has been shown that the large vernacular houses of the upper Calder Valley were built not by worsted manufacturers, as the orthodoxy might suggest, but by woollen manufacturers, behaving out of 'type' as coordinating agents. The study has also shown that, although deeply entrenched before 1780, the textile industry has left very little evidence for the system of domestic production which prevailed: the 'weaver's cottage' which we recognise in the 19th century has very few early counterparts.

The great age of the weaver's cottage dawned in the late 18th century, when the textile industry in the West Riding began to move from its proto-industrial phase towards full factory production, attained in the woollen branch only after 1850. In this period, mill production at the preparatory stages of manufacture was balanced by a large increase in the number of hand-loom weavers working from home. Domestic weaving was almost universal throughout the region, in both woollen and worsted areas, but in only one part – the woollen-cloth producing around Huddersfield (and to a lesser extent in the Calder Valley) – did it lead to the construction of large numbers of purpose-built weavers' cottages. There is some evidence that, around Huddersfield, the response to the need for more domestic accommodation for weaving was gradual rather than immediate, slowly growing from the 1790s to a peak perhaps in the second quarter of the 19th century, when the amount of mill-produced yarn was far larger than in earlier decades.

Although built in large numbers, weavers' cottages were typically built in small units of two, three, or four houses, giving a pleasing symmetry with the scale of the typical woollen-manufacturing concern. The inference is that the builders were people of small capital, but their cumulative effort demonstrates that domestic weaving was not a peripheral aspect of industrial production but rather an integral part of the local woollen manufacturing system, a full-scale complement to the development of mill-based yarn production.

The highly unbalanced distribution of weavers' cottages in the wool textiles belt raises important questions. An explanation has been offered for why the worsted industry failed to make large-scale provision: if a high proportion of the weavers' cottages in the Huddersfield area were indeed built after say 1835, then the clear success of the worsted power loom by that date would have made the construction of domestic loomshops for worsted weaving redundant. But no clear reason has emerged for the clear differences in the provision of weavers' cottages within the woollen-cloth producing area: the architectural evidence might, one hopes, act as a spur to further research into ways in which different sub-branches – narrow cloth, broadcloth – reacted to the transition from the proto-industrial stage of manufacture to full factory production.

This study has also examined the architectural expression of the demise of the domestic hand-loom weaver in the woollen branch. There is some evidence, in the form of large domestic loomshops, for the grouping of weavers working under supervision: these buildings demonstrate not only the loss of the outworking weaver's way of life, but also the way in which some successful independent manufacturers maintained a role in the woollen industry, raising levels of production and imposing greater control but using traditional methods and providing employment. This partial but important evidence for a rise in the scale of production was matched by two further developments. First, private woollen-mill owners began to draw their hand-loom weavers inside the factory to work in large loomshops. Second, after 1850, the power loom began to replace the hand loom in the woollen branch.

All these circumstances began to erode the place of domestic weaving within the woollen sector. But in a period of transition, from 1780 to 1850, domestic weaving was an essential part of the system which allowed the wool textile industry to maintain and develop its international importance. Around Huddersfield, the contribution of the domestic weaver finds striking architectural expression and has produced a highly distinctive historic landscape.

Notes

1. For discussions of the architectural evidence for domestic hand-loom weaving in other parts of the country, see Palmer & Neaverson 2003, and Timmins 1977.
2. Inventory of Daniel Greene of Soyland, Pontefract Deanery, September 1697 (Borthwick Institute of Historical Research, University of York).
3. Linthwaite Tithe Map and Award, 1847, West Yorkshire Archives Service, Kirklees.
4. See Giles & Goodall 1992, 84–90 for a discussion of mill loomshops and the reasons for their construction.

7 Domestic weaving premises in Lancashire: a contextual analysis *by Geoffrey Timmins*

Introduction

Research into the physical remains of Lancashire's handloom weaving industry has been particularly concerned with the design characteristics of the cottages in which it largely took place (Fig 7.1). A major finding has been the preponderance of cottages equipped with cellar or ground-floor loomshops – sometimes both – a reflection of the need to weave at least the finer grades of cotton and linen fabric in humid conditions. Discussion has also taken place on the settlements to which rows of hand-loom weavers' cottages commonly gave rise, in rural and urban areas alike, and on the link between the construction of these cottages and the development of the early building society movement.

Through revisiting these issues, opportunity arises both to draw together the main findings that have been reported and to review the conclusions that have been reached. In doing so, however, there is scope to extend analysis in two main ways. One is to adduce further evidence in relation to the county's hand-weaving premises, the investigation of which, though continuing to progress, remains far from complete. And this is so with regard to documentary as well as field investigation. The other is to contextualise more fully the Lancashire findings, in part by comparison with those relating to other localities and in part by considering the ways in which they can be used to shed light on matters of more general concern to historians. The essays in this volume do much to facilitate the former process, demonstrating the high potential that field investigation of redundant weavers' cottages has to offer. As to the latter process, the crucial matter is the way in which the study of domestic weaving premises can be used to aid understanding of industrialisation. A key point here is the comparative neglect of physical evidence in the analysis of regional industrialisation, especially with regard to the nature and degree of change that took place.

With these considerations in mind, discussion in this chapter centres on two themes that feature strongly in the literature on the Industrial Revolution period. The first relates to the growth of settlement that accompanied the rise in population and the expansion of industry and commerce. The line is taken that, in Lancashire, the impact of hand-loom weavers' colonisation on the development of both urban and rural settlement, though little considered, was profound, both in quantitative and qualitative terms. The second theme contributes to discussion on accommodation standards, a key element in the long-standing debate on working-class living standards. The argument put forward is that, as was the case more generally, considerable variation occurred in the accommodation standards experienced by hand-loom weaving families, with much depending on the way in which the available space in their cottages was distributed amongst working and domestic functions.

Settlement growth

The only detailed study so far undertaken into the impact of hand-loom weavers' colonisation on settlement growth is that by Morgan (1990). Relating to Preston, the study makes particular use of the 1840s 5 Foot Ordnance Survey maps to identify cottages that were likely to have contained cellar loomshops. The cottages are revealed by the flights of steps that were required to reach the living accommodation and the cellars projecting above ground level to improve natural lighting (Fig 7.2). Most were built before

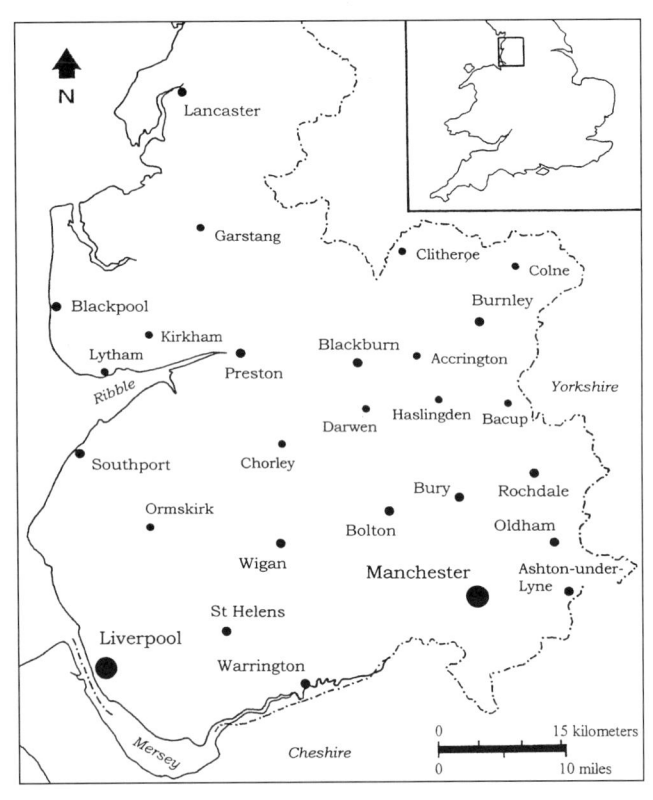

Figure 7.1 Location of Lancashire towns. (© G Timmins)

Figure 7.2 Handloom weavers' cottages with cellar loomshops in Mount Pleasant, Preston. The cellar windows were raised a considerable height above ground level to create good lighting, but at the expense of providing high flights of steps to the front doors. (Courtesy of Harris Library, Preston)

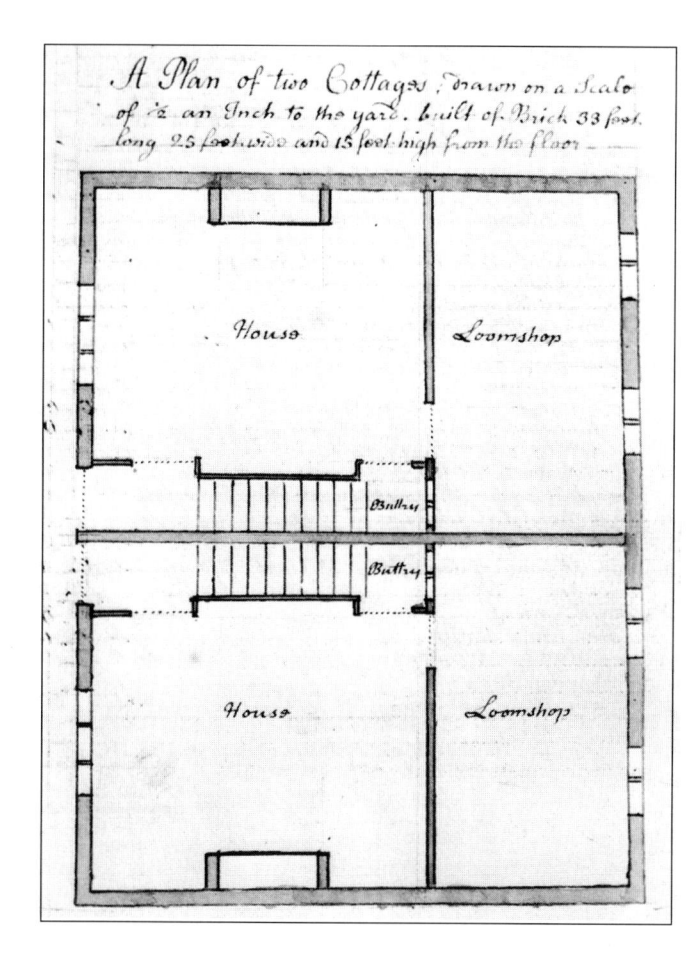

1825 and were concentrated on the north-western and south-eastern fringes of the town. It seems probable that over 1000 were built, comprising over a quarter of the town's housing stock in the early 19th century.

A number of considerations arise in relation to the Preston findings. The first concerns the reliability of the map evidence used. Morgan cautions that not all cellar loomshops might be discernible from the large-scale Ordnance Survey maps, though he is able to adduce additional evidence in identifying Preston examples from the town's sewer maps. He notes, too, that not all domestic loomshops were located in cellars (Morgan 1990, 40–7). Of particular concern in this respect are the two-up two-down terraced dwellings in which the back downstairs room was used as a small loomshop, normally housing two looms (Fig 7.3). Such cottages are undifferentiated on large-scale maps from the more usual two-up two downs of the period, in which the rear downstairs room comprised a back kitchen. How frequently this type of hand-loom weavers' cottage would have been built in Preston is unknown. Evidence from Black-

Figure 7.3 (left) Plan of two handloom weavers' cottages, each with a rear downstairs loomshop. Source: James Brandwood Account Book, 1795. (Courtesy of Turton Tower Museum)

92 *The vernacular workshop*

Table 7.1 Bridegroom weaver proportions in selected Lancashire parishes, 1818–22

Parish	Weaver proportion
Manchester	18
Preston	23
Wigan	32
Bury	40
Bolton	47
Oldham	47
Rochdale	50
Blackburn	55

Source: Timmins 1993a, 44.

burn and Manchester however, indicates that domestic loomshops accommodating two looms were the next most common after those with space for four looms (Timmins 1979, 246–8). Also of concern are upper-storey loomshops, some of which may also have been designed to accommodate two looms, though these were largely confined to east Lancashire. Probably, therefore, large-scale map evidence is likely to understate the numbers of handloom weavers' cottages that were built in Lancashire towns and hence the importance of handloom weavers' colonisation.

The second consideration concerns how representative the Preston findings are likely to be of Lancashire's textile towns in general. In the absence of detailed analysis of the type undertaken for Preston, the best insights that can be offered are derived from early 19th-century occupational data. Drawn from parish registers and expressed as annual averages for the period 1818–22, they give the proportions of bridegrooms that were recorded as hand-loom weavers in Lancashire parishes (Table 7.1).

The data must be used with caution for the purpose in hand, especially since they combine the populations of towns and adjoining rural districts. This could matter if there were marked variations between parishes in the proportion of rural to urban dwellers and of rural to urban hand-loom weavers. Even so, the differences from district to district shown in the table are appreciable. Amongst the labour forces of Lancashire's major textile towns, those at Preston

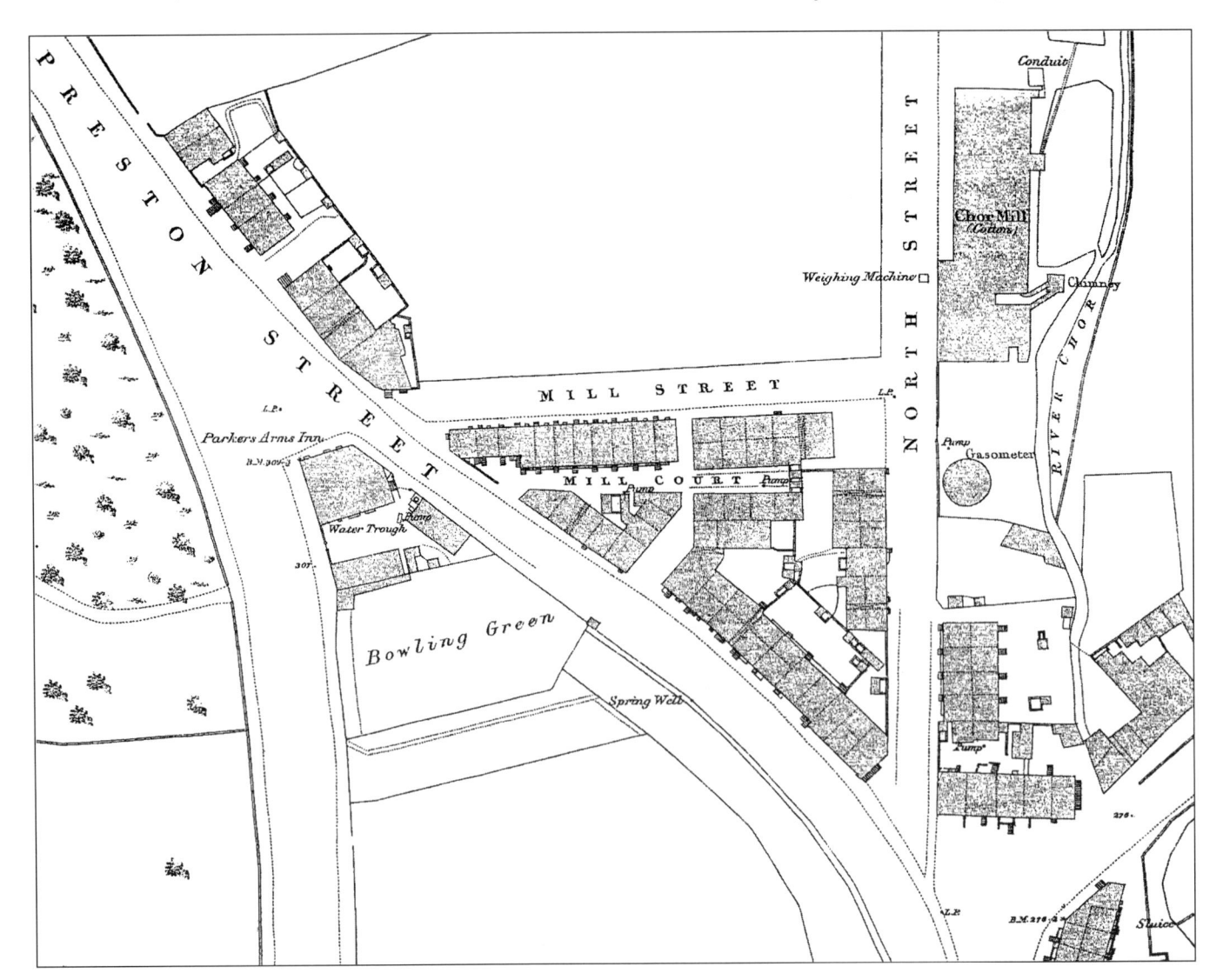

Figure 7.4 Hand-loom weavers' colonisation at Chorley. 1848 5 Foot Ordnance Survey map. (Ordnance Survey)

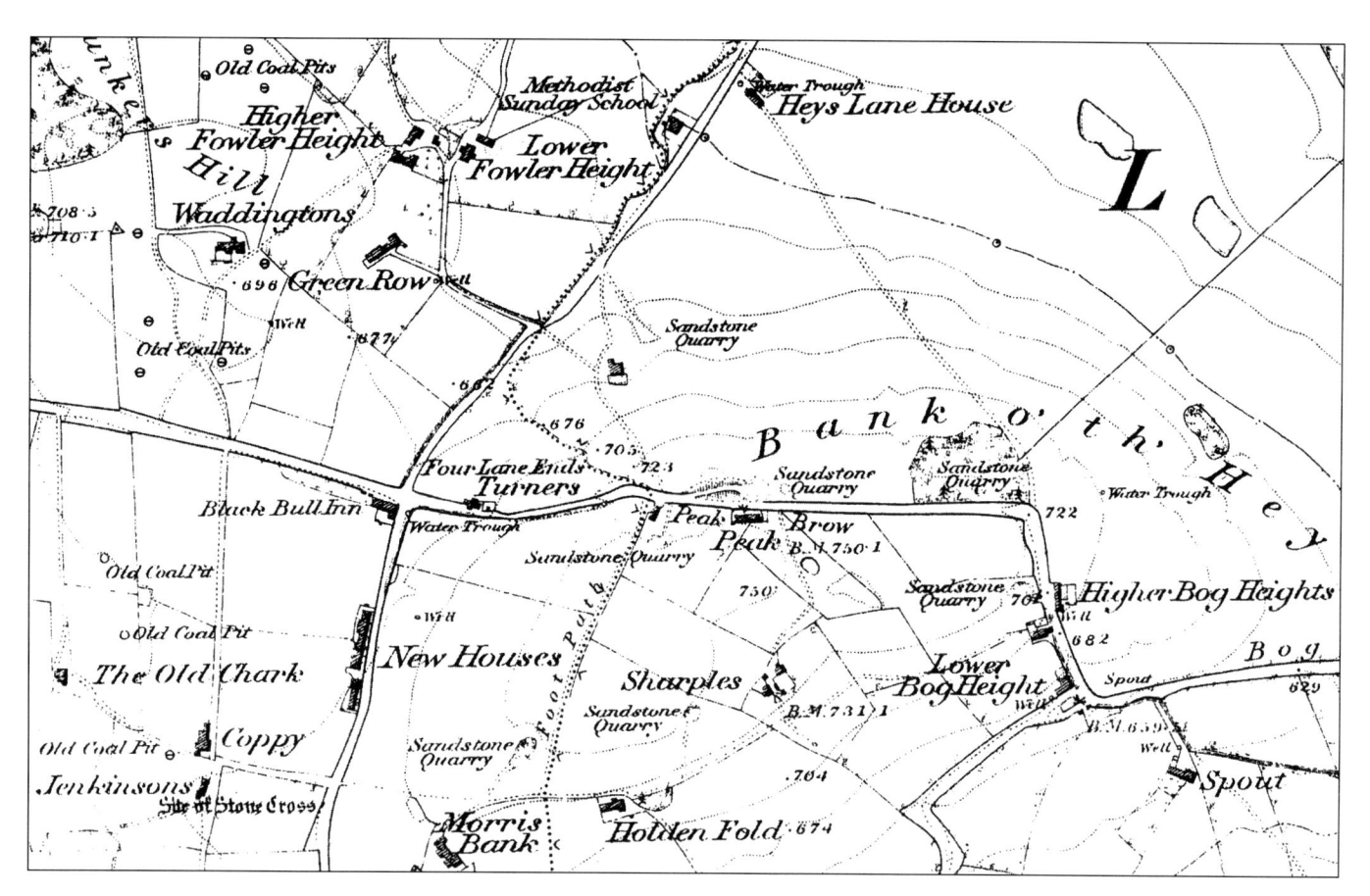

Figure 7.5 Handloom weavers' settlement at Livesey. 1848 5 Foot Ordnance Survey map. (Ordnance Survey)

and Manchester probably contained unusually small proportions of hand-loom weavers, implying that, in both places, handloom weavers' cottages formed comparatively small proportions of the total housing stock. If this was the case, the growth of most major textile towns in Lancashire during the late 18th and early 19th centuries owed a great deal to the formation of hand-loom weavers' colonies.

The third consideration relates to the location of hand-loom weavers' colonies in urban areas. Evidence from large-scale Ordnance Survey maps indicates that, as at Preston, these colonies were mostly built on urban fringes occupying green-field sites. Whilst expanding commercial interests consolidated their hold on the central areas of towns, making ever-growing demands on the space available, hand-loom weavers' colonies added to, and were intermixed with, the range of industrial premises that grew up on town outskirts. These colonies formed a significant element in the creation of industrial zones that were characterised by concentrations of manufacturing, domestic, and social buildings. The area to the north of Chorley gives some idea of this type of development (Fig 7.4). As can be seen, hand-loom weavers' cottages with cellar loomshops, some of them back-to-backs, were juxtaposed with dwellings that may have been built solely to provide domestic accommodation, especially for factory workers. The public house and bowling green demonstrate the type of social facilities that emerged and there were an infants' school and two non-conformist chapels close by.

Turning to the importance of hand-loom weavers' colonisation in rural areas, analysis is facilitated for several reasons. Firstly, survival rates of former handloom weavers' cottages are far higher than in towns, though alteration has commonly obscured the obvious features by which these cottages can be identified. Secondly, as early- and mid-Victorian census schedules reveal, hand-loom weaving tended to persist more strongly in rural than in urban areas, the evidence provided by the schedules helping to identify the cottages in which hand-weaving took place. Thirdly, although 5 Foot Ordnance Survey maps are not available for rural districts, the general pattern of rural settlement can nonetheless be discerned by reference to the first edition 6 Inch Ordnance Survey series, which was also published during the 1840s.

Systematic investigation of rural hand-loom weavers' colonies using these sources has yet to be undertaken, but the insights they offer can be illustrated by considering part of the settlement at Livesey, to the south-west of Blackburn. As can be seen from the 1840s map extract (Fig 7.5), the housing there was fairly scattered, though several short terraces had been built, an indication that industrial workers were being accommodated. In fact, the 1851 census schedule evidence for the district, summarised in Table 7.2, reveals that hand-loom weavers were to be found in most of the houses. Probably their numbers had declined somewhat by this time, but they still averaged more than two per household, a figure that suggests the cottages in which they lived were equipped with loomshops. And in many instances, field evidence supports this view. Figure 7.6 shows one of the cottages at New Houses, which had a ground-floor loomshop lit by a row of three windows.

Not all rural districts in textile Lancashire showed such a preponderance of weavers' cottages, of course. Numerous factory colonies were also to be found in country areas, along with settlement spawned by the rise of extractive industry and the expansion of agriculture. Even so, hand-loom weavers' colonisation frequently accounted for the bulk of rural settlement, with farming families commonly earning part of their livelihood from domestic weaving. This was the situation, for example, in parts of the Ribble Valley, as further evidence derived from 1851 census schedules demonstrates. The evidence, set out in Table 3, relates to several neighbouring districts, showing, for each one, the number and proportion of households containing hand-loom weavers.

As the table reveals, the relative importance of hand-loom weaving settlement varied from district to district. In every case, however, domestic weaving took place in a clear majority of households, often

Table 7.2 Hand-loom weaving settlement at Livesey, 1851

Location	Number of households	Number of hand weavers
Fowler Height	1	2
Green Row	3	9
Bull Inn Row	1	1
New Houses	11	24
Coppice (Coppy)	1	3
Jenkinsons	1	5
Holden Fold	1	2
Higher Bog Height	3	7
Lower Bog Height	1	1
Peak	3	9
Total	26	63

giving employment to several family members. Both sets of figures recorded in the table would probably have been even higher had they related to the early 19th century when the cotton hand weaving trade was at its height. The implications are that settlement in the selected districts largely comprised hand-loom weavers' cottages and that the loomshops they contained were often of sufficient capacity to permit all the family income, or most of it, to be earned from weaving.

The final point to be addressed in this section concerns the qualitative impact that hand-loom

Figure 7.6 Former hand-loom weaver's cottage at the New Houses settlement, Livesey. The cottage is double fronted, the loomshop formerly having a row of three windows in its front wall, the two outer ones of which have been blocked. Their sills and lintels survive, however, as does one of the mullions by which two of the windows were separated. (© G Timmins)

Figure 7.7 Former handloom weavers' cottages near Littleborough. The cottages were fitted with rows of windows in the upper storeys, one having a blocked taking-in door. Each was double-fronted, probably having a living room/kitchen and a back kitchen. (© Copyrignt G Timmins)

advantage in minimising obstruction to natural lighting, cellar or ground-floor loomshops helped to provide the humid conditions favoured by cotton and linen weavers (Timmins 1977, 20–3). Neither fenestration nor size clearly distinguished every type of hand-loom weavers' cottage, as in the case of the two-up two-down dwelling in which a small loomshop in the rear downstairs room was lit by a pair of separated windows rather than a row of windows. Figure 7.3 illustrates the ground-floor layout of such a cottage. Even so, handloom weavers' cottages with distinctive loomshop windows played a crucial part in transforming the appearance of Lancashire's built environment, even if they excited less in the way of contemporary interest and comment in this respect than textile factories.

Why rows of windows were provided in some of Lancashire's domestic loomshops and not others is unclear. It seems that the window tax did not act as a deterrent, since, as W J Smith points out, two or more lights in one opening were charged as a single window as long as the division between them was less than a foot wide, as was normally the case (Smith 1971, 253; Timmins, 1977, 19–20). Thus, as Palmer and Neaverson observe, window tax encouraged the use of fewer but larger windows (Palmer & Neaverson, 2003, 133), so that, in the context of Lancashire examples, a pair of separated windows in a loomshop would have incurred a greater window tax liability than an elongated window divided by mullions. Plainly, rows of windows would have provided the fullest natural lighting, particularly when they were incorporated into both front and rear walls, though perhaps more than some loomshop designers thought was necessary. The argument here may have been that adequate lighting for the weaver could be achieved by ensuring each loom was placed alongside a single window. Perhaps, too, fewer windows may have been seen to bring advantage in allowing more even loomshop temperatures to be maintained, lessening the impact of excessive heat in summer and extreme cold in winter. The desire to use space flexibly in hand-loom weavers' cottages may also enter into the account, a point that is given detailed consideration in the following section. It may be noted here, however, that since less natural light was required for domestic activities than for weaving, and that household circumstances would change with time, the argument in

weavers' colonisation had on Lancashire's built environment. At issue here is the construction of cottages that commonly stood out from others, including those built prior to the late 18th century, because they had loomshops usually fitted with rows of windows in order to maximise natural lighting (Fig 7.7). Moreover, to provide the space required for loomshops, the cottages were often bigger than usual, in some cases being double-fronted and in others rising to more than two storeys. They might also have rear extensions that contained loomshops. The loomshops could be located at any level in the cottages and whilst upper-storey loomshops had

Table 7.3 Hand-loom weavers' settlement in Ribble Valley districts, 1851

District	Number of houses	Number of houses with hand weavers	Percentage of houses with hand weavers
Balderstone	122	70	57
Osbaldeston	49	37	76
Clayton-le-dale	80	45	56
Ramsgreave	76	51	67
Salesbury	67	55	82
Dinckley	25	19	76
Dutton	88	51	58

96 The vernacular workshop

favour of having rows of windows in rooms may not always have seemed compelling. Finally, there is the view expressed by Taylor that long mullioned windows in cotton weavers' cottages were superseded by pairs of smaller windows (Taylor, 1966, 253). Yet he does not cite supportive evidence and it is known that late examples of cotton hand-loom weavers' cottages were still being fitted with rows of windows, including those at the Mile End colony, near Blackburn, which was started in 1818 (Timmins 1988, 22, 24).

The emergence of cottages with dedicated loomshops reflected the differing rates at which technological change was taking place in the textile industry. As is well known, effective mechanised spinning was developed from the late 1760s, with the result that far more plentiful supplies of yarn became available than had been possible using hand-spinning wheels. Yet weaving remained largely a handicraft trade until well into the 19th century, its expansion adding greatly to the demand for weavers and providing increasingly opportunities for females who could no longer find employment in domestic spinning (Timmins 1993a, 118–24). In these circumstances, families came to require greater numbers of looms – a single loom in a household would commonly have sufficed prior to the late 18th century – creating a demand for cottages equipped with rooms that could be designated as specialist loomshops. Moreover, in weaving the finer grades of cotton, which was made possible by the availability of mule-spun yarn from the late 1770s, specialised loomshops were also provided because the humid atmosphere that was required could be more easily created and maintained within them than in other parts of the house. Cellar locations helped in this respect, as did rooms with non-opening windows and rooms which could not be entered directly from the outside (Timmins 1977, 22–3, 45). In some cases, as is clear from examples at Delph and Uppermill, villages to the east of Oldham, the loomshops were created within existing premises, perhaps by partial rebuilding (Smith 1971, 250–4), a practice that has been noted elsewhere (Caffyn 1986, 9–10; Smith 1965, 34–5; Palmer & Neaverson 1992, 14). For the most part, however, Lancashire's hand-loom weavers' cottages were purpose built.

It is clear from the evidence presented in this section that, both in quantitative and qualitative terms, hand-loom weavers' colonies constituted a highly significant element in the development of both rural and urban settlement in Lancashire during the Industrial Revolution period. For the most part, these colonies comprised rows of vernacular cottages, which, in rural districts, tended to occur singly and were built directly alongside roadways to facilitate the delivery of warp and weft for weaving and the dispatch of woven cloth to warehouses. In towns, the colonies were generally far more substantial, consisting of several rows of cottages clustered together on the outskirts and contributing substantially to the formation of more general industrial settlement associated particularly with factory industry. The cottages within these colonies might differ appreciably in both size and design, a reflection of the varying needs and preferences of their inhabitants, but they nonetheless added a new and distinctive element to the built environment.

Accommodation standards

If analysis of working-class accommodation standards during the Industrial Revolution period has offered a generally pessimistic interpretation, it has also recognised that standards varied enormously. At one extreme were the cellar and back-to-back dwellings, which were characterised by high-density development and provision of a limited range of facilities, and at the other were the model houses built by factory and estate owners, which, for the period, were often spacious and well appointed. In between, quality could still vary markedly, according to such key characteristics as constructional standards, provision of water and heating facilities, sanitation, number and size of rooms, internal layout, and location. Quite commonly, houses that might be seen to score well in terms of some of these characteristics might be found wanting in terms of others, making the assessment of accommodation standards a complex business (Burnett 1986, chs 2 and 3).

But what of the accommodation standards offered by hand-loom weavers' cottages at this time? The first point to make is that, as is evident from the Chorley and Livesey examples noted in the previous section (Figs 7.4 and 7.5), a high degree of variation occurred; the stock of weavers' cottages comprised cramped back-to-backs with limited facilities, as well as sizeable, well-appointed through houses (with access at the back as well as the front). But with hand-loom weavers' cottages of all types, an additional complication arises. It relates to the allocation of space for weaving as opposed to domestic purposes. Of concern here is that the demands for loomshop provision might require the sacrifice of domestic space and facilities that added appreciably to the comfort and convenience of everyday living. Whether or not this was the case depended partly on the size and design of the cottage, but also on the amount of the available space that domestic weaving required and how far this space could be used in a flexible manner. These are matters to which discussion now turns, drawing on examples of different types of hand-loom weavers' cottage for illustrative purposes.

To begin with, the ground-floor plans of the cottages shown in Figure 7.3 may be further considered. As can be seen, domestic living space was centred in the house, which contained the one downstairs fireplace and thus functioned as a living room/kitchen. The house occupied almost two thirds of the ground-floor area, though the effective living space it provided was reduced somewhat because it contained the stairs, a buttery, and a vestibule. The loomshop was designed to take two looms and, in order to maintain humidity levels, it was entered via the house rather than directly from outside. An earth floor may also have been provided, though the house floor would probably have been flagged.

Had a loomshop not been provided in each of these cottages, several advantages could have arisen. They may be summarised as follows:

- The stairs and buttery could have been accommodated in the rear room to give a more spacious front room. This practice was common during the period, the stairs taking a dog-leg form (Brunskill 1971, 165).
- A back door could have been fitted to give access to outside facilities and to provide better ventilation. Indeed, it is far from clear with hand-loom weavers' cottages built to this design where toilet and storage provision, along with facilities for the disposal of household waste, principally ashes, were located.
- The rear downstairs room could have been equipped with a slop stone and drain to facilitate washing. Better quality cottages in Lancashire certainly benefited from such provision by the 1830s, if not earlier (Timmins 2000, 23–9).
- A more equal division of floor space would have enabled a fireplace to be incorporated in the rear downstairs room. As a result, two downstairs rooms capable of being heated would have been available, the one at the rear becoming a kitchen. In this case, the stairs might be relocated between the two rooms (Timmins 1993b, 113–14).

Quite clearly, the inclusion of a ground-floor loomshop in a cottage with only two ground-floor rooms was disadvantageous with regard to both the space available for domestic activity and the domestic facilities that could be provided. Had a greater degree of specialisation been achieved in room function by substituting the loomshop for a kitchen or a back kitchen (that is, a kitchen without a fireplace) domestic comfort and convenience would have been enhanced to a considerable degree.

Unfortunately, plans for the upper storeys of the cottages shown in Figure 7.3 were not drawn. Quite possibly though, the plans relate to two-up two-down dwellings with the upstairs rooms being used as bedrooms. If so, then less than a quarter of the space within the cottages was intended for loomshop purposes and the extent of bedroom provision would have been equal to that commonly provided in terraced cottages of the period. However, Smith has reported examples of two-up two-down cottages at Middleton in which *both* of the rear rooms were designed as loomshops. These rooms occupied about half of the ground-floor area at each level and were fitted with rows of windows that stretched across the entire width of the room (Smith 1971, 264–6). It seems likely that each loomshop would have been capable of taking two looms.

How living and working space was distributed in such cottages would have depended largely on household size and structure. A household comprising, say, hand-loom weaving parents and two very young children could assign specialist functions to each room with no great difficulty. On the other hand, if loomshop capacity was used to the full, giving employment to four living-in weavers, and if there were other household members besides, some flexibility would have been required in the way rooms were used. Evidence on this matter in relation to the Middleton cottages is lacking, though Smith suggests that the rear upstairs room could have been used as both bedroom and loomshop, with 'the beds being placed between the looms'. And it may be that, as occasion demanded, beds replaced looms, the loomshop capacity being adjusted to accord with the size of the domestic labour force available.

The notion of rooms designed as loomshops being used for domestic as well as working purposes finds support in relation to cottages built for woollen weavers in the Rochdale area, Lancashire's main centre for woollen cloth manufacturing. Writing about such cottages in the 1840s, an example of which is shown in Figure 7.6, Samuel Bamford observed that the downstairs – the house – occupied a space of about seven yards by eight and that the:

> chambers above, of two heights, were the same size as the house; and it should be remarked, that flannel weavers require capacious, open rooms, on account of the space necessary for their jennies, their working mills, looms, and other implements of manufacture. At the head of the stairs, in the first chamber, was a good bed in an old-fashioned black oaken bedstead. Near that was a loom, at which the weaver sat, tying in his work. Beyond the loom was another decent-looking bed in an old bedstead, next to that was a warping mill, taking up much room; then a stove, with a fire burning, – and then another loom . . .
>
> In the upper room two other jennies, of seventy spindles each, a loom, a stove, a bed, and other matters. Overhead the naked timbers of the roof and the cold, unlofted slates.

Bamford maintained that most of the flannel weavers' cottages in the Rochdale area conformed to his description, though the evidence on which he based his view is not stated (Bamford 1844, 276). Nor does his description record all the main design characteristics of the cottages, especially the window arrangements. Even so, his comments enable the crucial point to be made that the upper room, or rooms, in woollen weavers' cottages could be used as both bedroom and workshop rather than as workshop alone, a practice that also occurred in Yorkshire (Caffyn 1986, 48).

Several issues arise from this observation in terms of assessing accommodation standards. The first is the extent to which *downstairs* rooms in woollen weavers' cottages might also have been seen to have more than one function. Certainly Bamford refers to a small parlour being used as a bedroom in the cottage he describes. But the question arises as to whether or not the downstairs room (or rooms) might have provided further space for the spinning and weaving processes, including carding and winding, as was reported to have occurred in Gloucestershire during the 1840s (Palmer & Neaverson, 2003, 139–40). With regard to Lancashire examples, it may have been the case that sufficient space was available in the upper storey (or storeys), especially if household numbers were small. However, that ground-floor space may have been utilised for domestic production could help to explain why, in many instances, woollen hand-loom weavers' cottages in the county display rows of windows at ground-floor level which are little shorter than those in upper storeys. Such windows would seem to have provided more natural light than was required for domestic purposes alone and would have impacted both on insulation and household privacy. Furthermore, that they were not always provided suggests that differing ideas prevailed as to the use of ground-floor space in woollen weavers' cottages, those with single rather than rows of windows being seen to offer a higher degree of specialisation in terms of room function.

The second issue is how far rooms doubled as loomshops in cottages other than those intended for woollen weaving. The likelihood is that they would commonly have done so in small cottages, including those occupied by cotton weavers in north-east Lancashire, an example of which is shown in Figure 7.8. Pairs of windows lit the upstairs rooms (or room) in these cottages, whereas single windows – which might be somewhat larger than those upstairs – were provided at ground-floor level. Seemingly, therefore, the upstairs rooms could have given both working and bedroom space, with allocations between them being made according to the varying circumstances in which families found themselves. In larger cottages, however, the pressure to find sleeping space in loomshops would have been less intense. The type of cotton hand-loom weaver's cottage shown in Figure 7.6, for example, was twice as big as normal two-up two-down cottages – the loomshop, which could accommodate four looms, taking up no more than a quarter of the total floor area; there would certainly have been space in it for at least three quite sizeable bedrooms, as was the case with similar cottages built at Middleton (Smith 1971, 262–3) and at Calverton, near Nottingham (Campion, 1996, 848–52). The same sort of reasoning might be applied as far as to two-up two-down cottages with either cellar or attic loomshops are concerned. In the case of the former, which were very frequently built in the Lancashire cotton districts, the loomshops generally took four looms and it seems likely that, if families living in them required additional sleeping space beyond that available in the bedrooms, it would have been found in the downstairs living rooms rather than in the damp cellars with earth floors (see Fig 7.9). In the case of the latter, which may have been built in some numbers at Manchester, but which are more particularly associated with the Macclesfield

Figure 7.8 Former hand-loom weavers' cottages, Hill Top, Barrowford, near Colne. The cottages have a pair of windows in their upper storeys at both front and rear. (© G Timmins)

silk industry, upper-storey loomshops would have provided a more appealing location for additional bedroom space than cellars. However, on his visit to Macclesfield in 1849, Angus Bethune Reach discounted such an idea. He wrote:

> The houses inhabited by the Macclesfield hand-loom weavers are very generally similar in construction, having been mostly all built with an eye to the staple manufacture of the place. They consist, in nine cases out of ten, of five rooms: two on the ground floor, one serving as sitting room and kitchen, and the other as a scullery. On the first floor are generally a couple of bedrooms – those into which I peeped were clean and neat – and then, ascending a ladder and making your way through a trap door, you reach the loomshop, which is always located in the garret, and which is exclusively devoted to the operation of weaving (Reach 1849a, 93).

It may be that Reach's statement should be viewed in terms of normal rather than universal practice,

Figure 7.9 Former hand-loom weavers' cottages in Wolfenden Street, Bolton. Blocked cellar windows can be seen, smaller flights of steps giving access to the front doors than in the case of the examples shown in Figure 7.2. In order to provide adequate lighting in the loomshop, therefore, cellar wells would have been provided. (© G Timmins)

however, not least because some upper-storey loomshops in Macclesfield were equipped with rows of windows at front and back and others with windows in one wall only. The cottages in Paradise Street illustrate the former and those in Newton Street the latter (fig 7.7).

The third issue is how far the use of loomshops as bedrooms accords with contemporary views about what constituted desirable sleeping arrangements for families. One strand of thought urged by paternalist factory owners in Lancashire was that a minimum number of three bedrooms should be available in order to avoid having older children of each sex sleeping in the same bedroom (Chadwick 1842, 194: Royston Pike 1966, 57). In the bigger weavers' cottages, this goal might well have proved to be attainable, but it would plainly have been far more difficult to achieve in the smaller cottages. Besides, questions arise as to whether the lack of private sleeping arrangements mattered as much to the inhabitants of hand-loom weavers' cottages as it did to their social superiors. No doubt, too, any ambitions hand-loom weaving families might have had concerning the availability of private sleeping arrangements were commonly thwarted by the need to take in kin and/or lodgers, if only temporarily (Timmins 2000, 33–5).

Even on the basis of the limited amount of evidence that has been presented in this section, it is clear that the accommodation standards experienced by hand-loom weaving families showed marked variation. At one end of the spectrum were large families living in properties with a few small rooms that had to provide space for both domestic and workshop activity. At the other were spacious and well-appointed cottages that gave a good deal of privacy to their inhabitants, even if the numbers living in them were not particularly small. In terms of providing the most space that could be set aside for domestic purposes, the cottages similar to that at Livesey (Fig 7.6) were to the fore. It seems likely too, that the space available in weavers' cottages, at least where ground-floor and upper-storey loomshops were provided, might often have to be used flexibly, with loomshops doubling as bedrooms. The extent to which this happened would have depended on the amount of manufacturing equipment that was needed; the size of the household; and the amount of expenditure on housing that could be afforded or preferred. And such considerations would have been strongly influenced by the life-cycle stage of those living in the cottages, as well as by the short- and long-term fluctuations in economic activity over which they had no control.

Conclusion

Whilst a number of general conclusions can be drawn from the work already undertaken on the premises in which domestic textile production took place in Lancashire, especially their importance in promoting settlement growth and the marked variation they offered in accommodation standards, much more research is needed to provide fuller and more informed insights. Detailed local studies have much to offer in this respect, with the high survival rates of former hand-loom weavers' cottages in rural areas offering a great deal of scope for further investigation. And even in urban areas, where demolition of these cottages has taken a very heavy toll, piecing together the evidence relating to them that can be derived from various types of documentary source, especially large-scale Ordnance Survey maps and photographs, can still prove highly instructive. Indeed, given the importance of hand-loom weavers' colonisation, the process of urban growth in textile Lancashire cannot be understood without research of this type.

In terms of investigating the physical remains of Lancashire's domestic textile production, there is much to be derived from more detailed recording of both internal and external features. Such activity will enhance understanding of the design characteristics of hand-loom weavers' cottages, especially in relation to sub-regional differences, which are not entirely explained by variation in the type of fabric being woven, and to the recognition of less familiar types, including those formed from house and outbuilding conversions. But it will also shed further light on how people lived in these cottages. The fundamental point here is that, with the marked expansion of textile production during the Industrial Revolution period, cottages were increasingly erected for Lancashire's hand-loom weavers that were characterised by separating living space from working space. However, the extent to which this division was achieved varied considerably. As census schedule evidence reveals, large families frequently lived in small weavers' cottages, so that, in all probability, rooms primarily intended as loomshops would often have been used for domestic purposes as well. At the same time, many hand-loom weaving families did live in relatively spacious cottages and were able to experience a degree of privacy with regard to their domestic arrangements that was unlikely to have been common amongst working-class families throughout the Industrial Revolution period.

8 Outworking dynamism and stasis: Nottinghamshire's 19th-century machine-made lace and framework knitting industries *by Garry Campion*

Introduction

The East Midlands machine-made lace and framework knitting industries reflected striking contrasts during the 19th century despite their common origins and close proximity.[1] The lace industry evolved rapidly into a factory-based system by mid-century, yet framework knitting outworking continued into the 1890s and beyond, despite factory production.

This chapter has three aims: firstly, to show that lace outworking on machines derived from the stocking-frame was short-lived; secondly, to demonstrate that framework knitting continued at least into the 1880s in four production centres; and finally, to discuss the buildings in these centres: lace in Nottingham, and framework-knitting in Ruddington, Calverton, and Hucknall (Fig 8.1). Census returns and trade directories are used to reflect knitting and lace outworking employment. Campion (1996, 1999, 2001) and Palmer (1989, 1990, 1994) discuss the buildings and processes of outworking, and its regional context.

Machine-made lace

Machine-made lace evolved from framework knitting during the late 18th century, surpassing it technologically, with factory centralisation from the 1840s. The industry reflected a low intensity involvement during the early 19th century. The first major divergence from the stocking-frame was Heathcoat's 1808 bobbin-net machine, whose numbers increased from 1000 in 1820 to 5000 in 1833, where Nottingham prospered in the 'twist-net boom'. In addition, by 1810 there were 15,000 outworkers hand-embroidering net for curtains, antimacassars, drapes, clothing, and other lace goods. Point-net, warp, bobbin-net, jacquard looms, and finishing work was undertaken in houses and workshops, but most worked on bobbin-net machines and associated outworking during the 1820s and 1830s. Production had become fully mechanised by 1850, but by 1855 manufacturing had contracted. Most was centred upon Nottingham and Long Eaton, with finishing and merchanting in Nottingham's Lace Market. The industry declined permanently towards world war in 1914. For overviews see Campion (1999, 2001), Chapman (1963), Halls (1973), Mason (1994), and Palmer (1994).

Mansfield Road area, Nottingham

Much has been written about the socio-economic history of Nottingham and the slum development resulting from the failure to enclose land in the early 19th century, including Beckett (1997), Campion (1999, 2001), Chapman (1963), Halls (1973), and Mason (1994). The sample discussed here is a rare assemblage of early 19th century, pre-enclosure lace-workers' buildings; much elsewhere was demolished during 20th-century slum clearances.

The 1801 Jalland map[2] shows the sample area: the Nottingham City Corporation owned the thin sliver of land as one of potentially few housing sites, and the map's land survey book provides occupancy data.[3] A *c*1820[4] plan suggests impending plot sales and Wood's 1825 map[5] shows some in-filling of the northernmost end of the sample area; Staveley and Wood's 1831 map[6] records in-filling of these former plots along Mansfield Road, and parallel North Sherwood Street (Fig 8.2). The sample (hereafter 'Nottingham') comprised three elements: Bluecoat Street forming the southern-most boundary, Forest Road East its northern end, while Babbington and Chatham Streets divide the three main blocks. By 1844 development along Mansfield Road was mature;[7] and by 1880 surrounded by housing.[8]

Workrooms on the top-floor were usually to the rear of houses (Fig 8.3). Largely extant along Mansfield Road, these are of fine quality brick, terraced Georgian style, with sash and casement windows, and varying decorative lintels and mouldings. The number of storeys varies from two to four. Some two-storey workshops remain in the area enclosed between Mansfield Road and North Sherwood Street, and others survive of up to five storeys.

Mansfield Road is substantially complete, providing an insight into outworking (Table 8.1), but many of North Sherwood's street's buildings have been lost (Table 8.2). Losses for both streets identified through fieldwork using the 1880 25 Inch Ordnance Survey map, suggests that of all 438 buildings extant then, only 165 survive – a loss of 273, or 62.4% (Fig 8.4).

The largely complete nature of Mansfield Road makes it possible to identify the usage of individual buildings. Although houses were originally dwellings, some were converted into shops on their ground floors, certainly by the 1850s. Of 96 houses identified in 1880, only 22 can positively and five possibly be identified as having workrooms.

102 *The vernacular workshop*

Figure 8.1 Details from Sanderson map of 1836. Top-left: Nottingham city, the Mansfield Road sample to upper-centre; top-right: Ruddington; bottom-left: Hucknall; bottom-right: Calverton. (NAO)

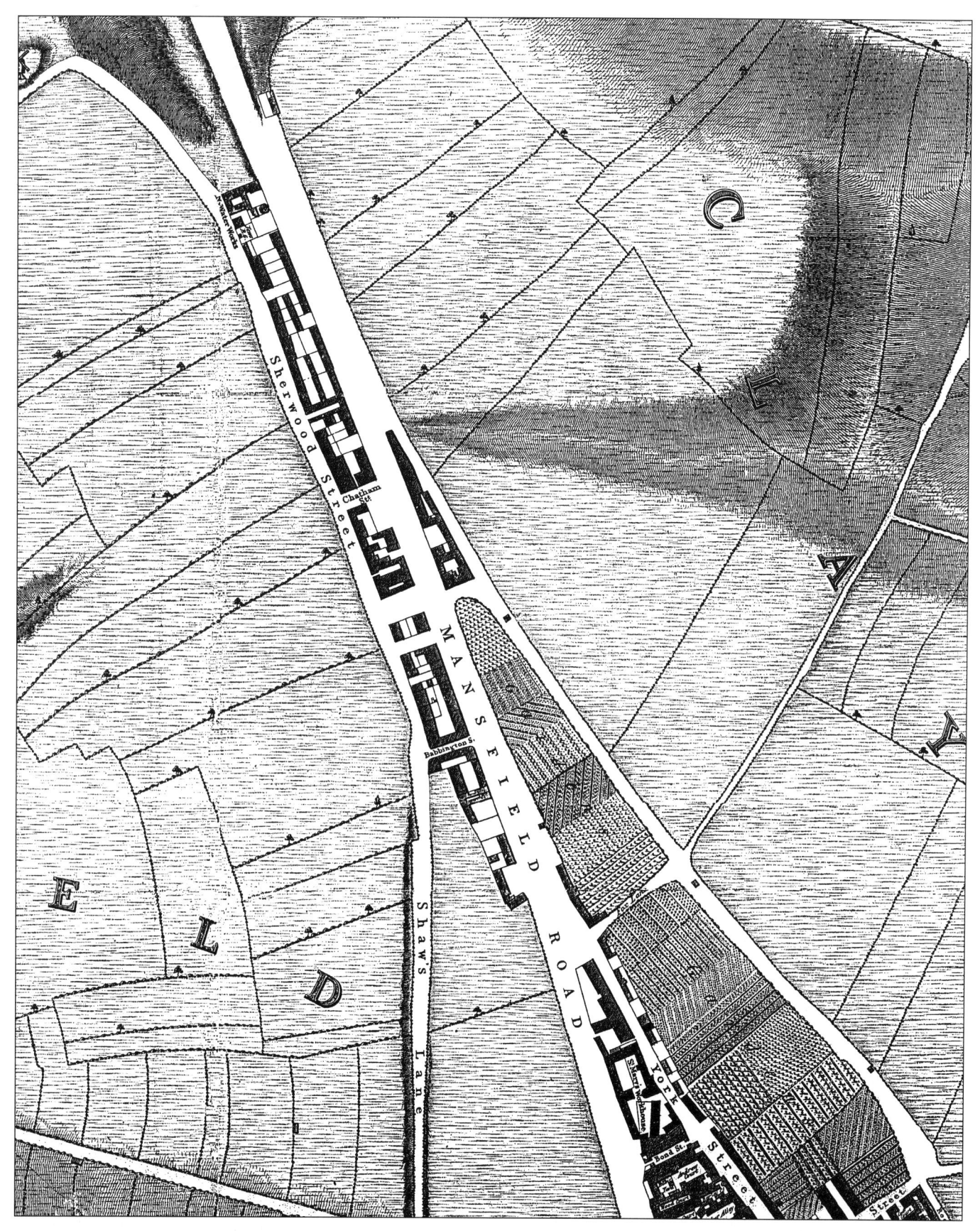

Figure 8.2 Staveley and Wood map detail of Nottingham, 1831, showing area of Mansfield Road and North Sherwood Street. (NAO)

104 The vernacular workshop

Table 8.1 Identified or possible extant outworking buildings –
Mansfield Road, Nottingham (Figure 3 shows building locations)

No.	Street No.	Description	Comments
1	–	Wild & Balm's workshop	Large lace complex 1824
2	113–121	5 houses	3rd flr workrooms to rear
3	123–125	2 houses	Rear workrooms?
4	127	1 house	4th flr workroom to rear?
5	187–189	2 houses	Rear workrooms
6	197	1 house	Rear workrooms
7	205	1 house	Rear workrooms
8	223–229	4 houses	Rear workrooms
9	231–233	2 houses	Rear workrooms?
10	235–241	4 houses	Rear workrooms
11	247–249	2 houses	Rear workrooms
12	253–255	2 houses	Rear workrooms
13	5 Forest Rd East	4 houses	Three storeys + top wksps
14	160–90	Houses	Not lace; earliest houses

Table 8.2 Identified or possible outworking buildings –
North Sherwood Street, Nottingham (Figure 3 shows building locations)

No.	Street No.	Description	Extant/source	Comments
15	248–254	Originally 8 houses	Yes – altered	Back-to-backs
16	–	Workshops × 3	2 of 3: NCL47460*	Lace workshops?
17	182–184	Originally 4 houses	Yes	Back-to-backs
18	144–154	Originally 12 houses	No: NCL41694	Back-to-backs
19	138–142	Large workshop	Yes	Four storeys
20	116–124	Originally 8 houses	No: NCL41685	Back-to-backs

* NCL: Nottingham Central Library

Table 8.3 1841 census data for Mansfield Road and (North) Sherwood Street [9]

	1	2	3	4	5	6	7	8	9	10	11
Mansfield Rd	7	44	22	7	–	1/3h	1	1	–	5	91
Sherwood St	13	68	30	8	1	–	4/1s	3	1	5	134
Babbington St	–	4	–	–	–	–	–	–	–	–	4
Chatham St	1		–	–	–	–	–	–	–	–	1
(total: 230)	21	116	52	15	1	4	6	4	1	10	230
(percentages)	(9.1)	(50.4)	(22.6)	(6.5)	(0.4)	(1.7)	(2.6)	(1.7)	(0.4)	(4.3)	

Key:
1 – Framework knitters   2 – Lace makers   3 – Lace menders
4 – Lace dressers   5 – Lace embroiderers   6 – Lace agents or hosiers (h)
7 – Cheveners or seamers (s)   8 – Winders   9 – Needlemakers
10 – Framesmiths   11 – Totals

In an advanced state of development by 1830, census and directory evidence confirms the primacy of lace manufacture as providing income for residents. Table 8.3 summarises census data but no attempt has been made to reconcile these with the 1880 Ordnance Survey map, or buildings, because of extensive changes between the recording events.

Lace makers are a significant class of outworker, representing 50% of the total workforce, as against 9% for knitters in the sample area. The manufacture of lace required mending and finishing, involving 68 workers. Building evidence suggests there were insufficient houses with purpose-built workrooms to accommodate this workforce, especially along Mansfield Road, so they must have worked in 'normal' houses or workshops.

The above contrasts strikingly with directory data in Table 8.4. With the exception of lace warpers there is no reference to operators of frames or lace machines. Details are recorded for those producing or servicing machines, and others employed as agents or producers. The large numbers producing

Figure 8.3 Rear view of closely packed 1820s lace outworkers' housing and workshops on Mansfield Road, Nottingham. The two house extensions in the centre post-date 1880. View taken in front of site of 19th-century housing on North Sherwood Street (Building nos 8 & 16 on Fig 8.4). (© Garry Campion)

Table 8.4   Nottingham directory evidence 1832–42 [10]

	1	2	3	4	5	6	7	8	9
1832 White's									
Mansfield Road	1	23	5	2	–	–	–	–	31
Sherwood Street	1	13	–	–	–	–	–	–	14
Babbington Street	–	3	–	–	–	–	–	–	3
1834 Dearden's									
Mansfield Road	–	–	–	–	201	–	–	21
1842 Pigot's									
Mansfield Road	–	–	2	2	–	–	1	–	5
Sherwood Street	–	–	–	–	–	–	1	2	3

Key:
1 – lace agents   2 – bobbin and carriage makers   3 – framesmiths
4 – needlemakers   5 – lace makers/manufacturers   6 – lace warpers
7 – lace dressers   8 – machine makers   9 – total outworkers

bobbins and carriages for lace machines reflects the impetus behind the twist-net boom. Appendix 8.1 records occupations in 1858 where, despite the concentrated development of housing and workshops between Bluecoat Street to the south and Forest Road to the north, not all occupants are listed for North Sherwood Street, in contrast with Mansfield Road. Overall, for both, little can be identified as actual outworking and many former workrooms perhaps now formed extra, well-lit bedrooms; alternatively, of these, occupants listed as 'private' may have operated machines in such rooms, or undertaken lace mending activities. By 1880, 235 buildings are within the North Sherwood Street area but many have no commercial involvement, unlike shops along Mansfield Road.

Despite the availability of outworking houses and workshops, lace outworking here had largely evaporated by the 1850s. A much needed housing development responding to the twist-net boom of the 1820s had undergone a change to some retailing and non-outworking activities only 30 years later, whereas the framework knitting industry was still operating along traditional 18th-century lines.

Framework knitting

The hand-powered stocking-frame was invented *c*1589, evolving through a series of developments, the most radical being the wide stocking-frame during the later 18th century. This enabled perhaps the production of three or four garments in one knitting episode, as against only one possible on a

106 *The vernacular workshop*

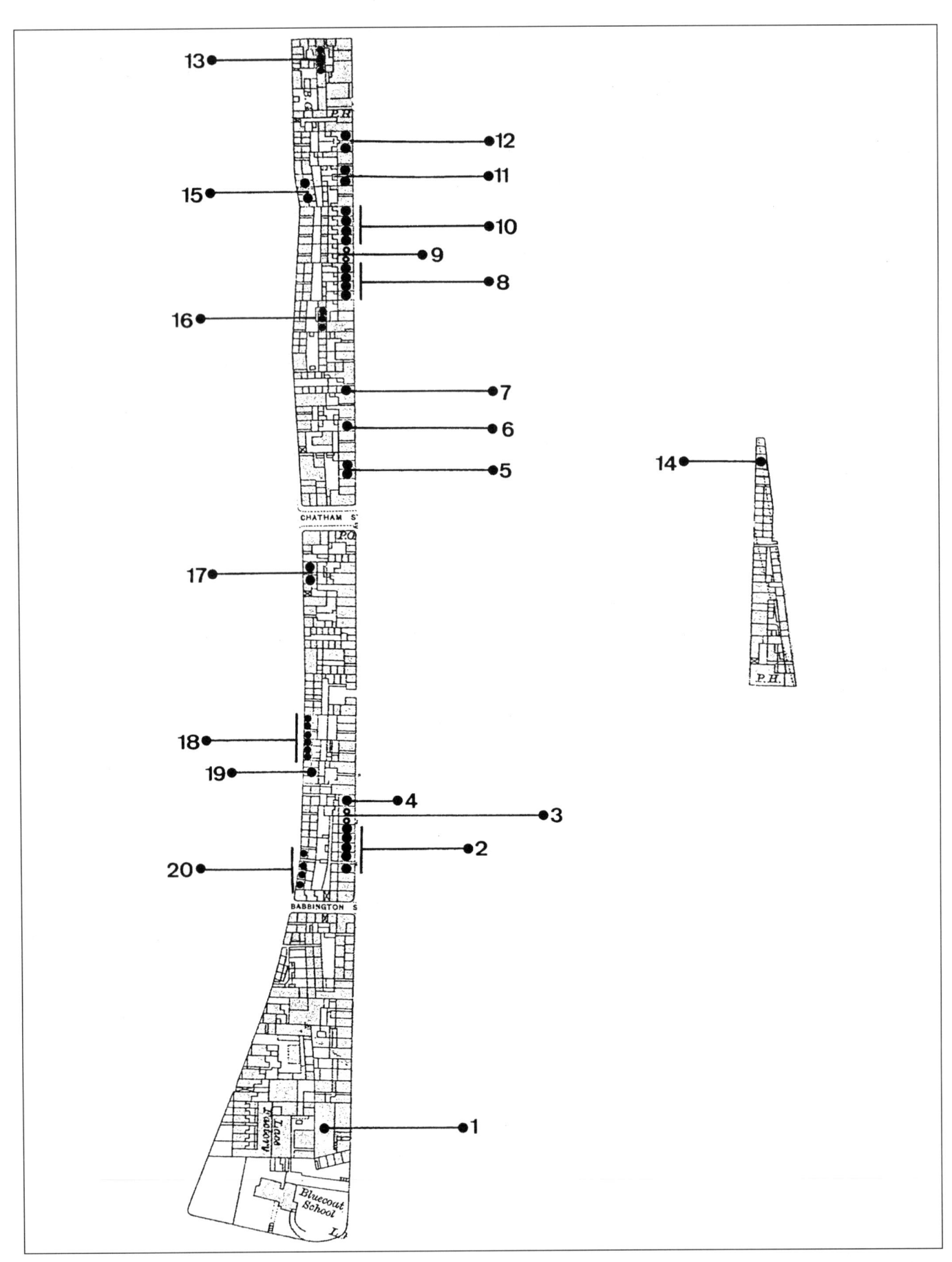

Figure 8.4 1915 25 Inch Ordnance Survey map detail of Mansfield Road and North Sherwood Street, of outworking buildings. Open circles show possible outworking buildings (1915 map of better quality than that for 1880, but same topography). (Ordnance Survey)

Table 8.5 Identified or possible outworking buildings in Calverton
(Figures 4 & 5 shows building locations)

No.	Location	Description	Extant/Source*	Comments
1	Foxwood Terrace	Terraced houses	No: survey	Some FWK+ workrooms
2	211–15 Main St	Group of houses	Yes	Dated 1857
3	'Dovey's'	Workshop	Yes	Sole wksp? No dwelling
4	Main St	Houses	No: NCL 43444	1st flr FWK?
5	Village museum	C18 cottage	Yes	Possible FWK
6	54 The Nook	House	Yes	Possible FWK
7	The Nook	Workshop	Yes	Possible FWK
8	73/75 Main St	Houses	Yes	FWK windows
9	7 The Avenue	House	Yes	FWK window
10	24 Burnor Pool	House	Yes	Used for FWK
11	18 Burnor Pool	House	Yes	Possible FWK
12	Main St	Houses	No: NCL 43453	Possible FWK
13	10/12 Main St	Houses	Yes: NCL 68477	Possible FWK
14	9/11/13 Main St	Houses	Yes	FWK windows
15	5 Main St	House	Yes	FWK window
16	Windles Square	Houses	Partly/survey	c.22 FWK workrooms
17	36/38 Main St	Houses	Yes	FWK

* NCL = Nottingham Central Library   + FWK = framework knitter

Table 8.6 1881 Census figures – outworking activity in Calverton[11]

Occupation	Total	%
Framework-knitters	221	(63.1)
Seamers	123	(35.1)
Framesmith	2	(0.5)
Hosiers	2	(0.5)
Lace manufacturers	1	(0.2)
Bag hosiers	1	(0.2)
Total Workforce	350	(100.0)

narrow-frame, thereby changing the nature of home-based outworking. Wide-frames were unknown before 1776, with 3500 recorded by 1833, and probably twice that number in operation, often requiring a 'team' oriented approach in separate workshops. Nineteenth-century hosiery production occurred within houses, workshops, and hosiers' houses. Framework knitters fashioned spun yarn into mostly finished goods, then to be processed in warehouses and supplied to wholesalers – woollen, cotton, or worsted socks, gloves, stockings, and jackets; cloth caps; shirts and sleeves. Legislation and technological progress within factories (Palmer 1990) led to outworking declining from the 1870s, but widespread family production continued into the 1890s.

Figure 8.5 (left) Windles Square, Calverton. Originally 22 houses built in 1834, only two ranges survive. Typical of village's knitters' dwellings with workrooms to the ground floor, outworking continued in the square into the 1920s (no. 16 on Fig 8.7.) (© Garry Campion)

108 *The vernacular workshop*

Figure 8.6   1889 25 Inch Ordnance Survey map detail of Calverton showing western area, and outworking building locations. (Ordnance Survey)

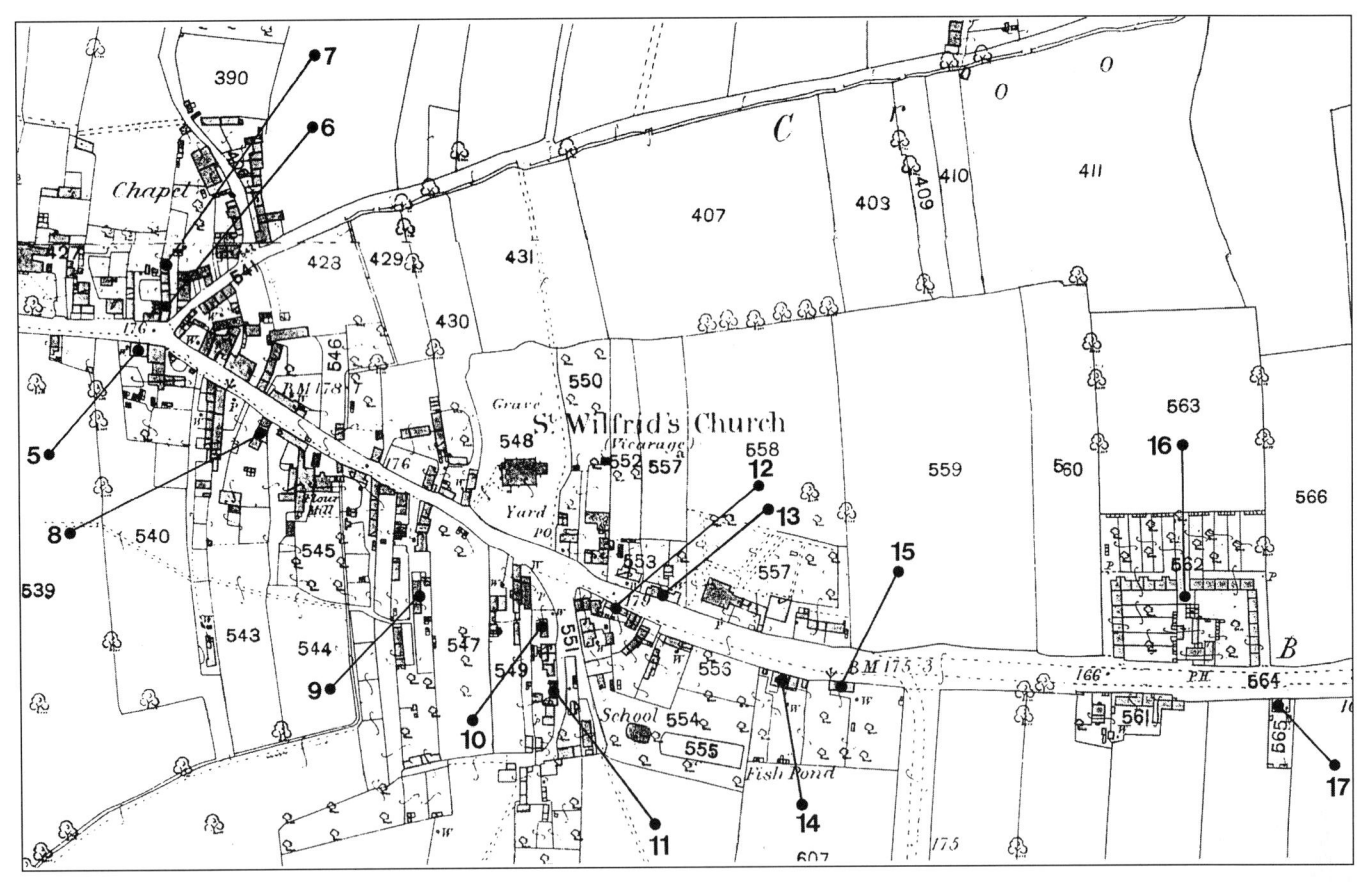

Figure 8.7   1889 25 Inch Ordnance Survey map detail of Calverton showing eastern area, and outworking building locations. (Ordnance Survey)

Table 8.7 Trade directory entries[12]

Year & Directory	1	2	3	4	5	6	7	8	9
1832 White's	2	–	4	–	–	–	–	–	6
1864 White's	2	–	1	–	2	–	–	–	5
1887 Wright's	–	–	1	12	–	–	–	–	13
1891 Wright's	–	–	–	12	–	–	–	–	12
1895 Kelly's	–	–	2	–	2	–	–	–	4
1904 Wright's	–	–	1	4	2	–	–	–	7

1 – framesmiths 2 – needlemakers 3 – hosiers 4 – bag hosiers
5 – framework-knitters 6 – hosiery agents 7 – bobbin-net maker 8 – sinkermaker (frames)
9 – total outworkers

Outworking involved the area denoted by Mansfield and Southwell to the north, Hinckley and Lutterworth to the south, Derby to the west, and Melton Mowbray to the east. Belper, Nottingham, Loughborough and Leicester were major centres. The three sample centres were selected because of their proximity to Nottingham, diverse outworking building styles and survivals, archival materials, and longevity of outworking activity, beginning substantially during the 18th century. Campion (1996, 1999, 2001), Felkin (1844), BPP (1845), and Palmer (1989, 1990, 1994) provide details of the industry.

Calverton

Little has been written about the village's history: Anon (n.d.) is a brief account with some attention to outworking, but Calverton was not included in the 1845 report (BPP 1845). The village is rural in its setting and some 20.8 km (13 miles) to the north-east of Nottingham. Most of the village development occurred along the margins of Main Street or lanes radiating from it. The enclosure award map of 1780[13] suggests little change in field boundaries, but significant building development took place in the 19th century between existing farms.[14] Building plots were also established at the margins of extant arable fields, confirming the willingness of local farmers to sell, but there is little evidence suggesting speculative building by the latter. Calverton has no obvious centre: St Wilfrid's Church lies to its eastern end, but agglomeration here is not obvious. Calverton had no railway link. Population figures in the census returns for the village (1801: 636; 1861: 1372; 1871: 1319; 1881: 1246; 1891: 1199; and in 1901: 1159) indicate a doubling of population in the first half of the 19th century but stagnation and decline thereafter. A total of 409 frames (narrow and wide) were operated in 128 workshops in 1844, a figure of 2.98 frames per shop (Felkin 1844; BPP 1845).

The pattern of outworkers' housing is erratic. To the extreme west and east are Foxwood Terrace and Windles Square, purpose-built knitters' dwellings. Other housing developments are between these two points, little conforming to uniform terraced housing in Ruddington or Hucknall. Calverton's workrooms were on the ground floor, usually visible from the roadside in small brick-built houses of two storeys (Fig 8.5). A large area was devoted to the workroom in purpose-built houses, characterised by wide knitters' windows. However, agricultural labourers may have supplemented their incomes as outworkers, operating in houses with no adaptations to windows, perhaps explaining the few extant knitters' houses. Losses identified through fieldwork using the 1900 25 Inch Ordnance Survey map show that of all 358 buildings extant then, 186 survive – a loss of 172, or 48.1% (Table 8.5; Figs 8.6 and 8.7). Late 18th and early 19th outworking housing may have been demolished towards the end of the latter century, which has proved a problem in all the centres considered.

By 1881, of 1246 inhabitants, 350 worked in outworking – or 28.0%. Table 8.6 records that knitters are the largest group, followed by seamers, with few other participants.

The distribution of outworkers within Calverton, by street, road, or yard, is detailed in Appendix 8.2 that is based upon the 1881 census returns. Each table is arranged hierarchically, those streets with the highest numbers of outworkers towards the top. Many Calverton outworkers are based in traditional zones: Main Street, Jenny Nook, Windles Square, and Foxwood Terrace, but outworking is widespread. Directory evidence records hosiers and bag-hosiers as the most commonly occurring class of practitioner (Table 8.7), at odds with the 1881 census data.

Calverton is believed to be the birthplace of the stocking-frame's inventor and it is fitting that outworking, albeit on a small scale, carried on as a home based activity until the 1920s in Windles Square. It finally ended in 1955 with the closure of 'Dovey's Factory', and its 30 frames (Campion 1996).

Ruddington

Anon (1971) and Shrimpton (1989) discuss aspects of Ruddington's outworking past. The 1845 report included a section on Ruddington (BPP 1845), a minor putting-out centre. It is located 13.5 km (8.4 miles) due south of Nottingham. By the late 19th century, it was affluently urban in nature, housing and public buildings concentrated around two focal points: St Peter's Church to the north and the village

Figure 8.8 Knitters' workshop, Chapel Street, Ruddington. Probably dating from the 1860s, is typical of the 69 wide-frame workshops recorded here in 1844. One of two workshops at framework knitters' museum (no. 8 on Fig 8.9). (© Garry Campion)

green to the south. The village straddled the high street at its centre, from which radiated numerous roads and lanes, not obviously adhering to the field system on the enclosure award map,[15] demonstrating a clear need to maximise potential land.[16] This may reflect its closer proximity to Nottingham and the relative wealth from wide-frame operation, requiring large numbers of local outworkers. The railway link to the north-west of the village at the century's end was advantageous. The population expanded steadily until 1881. Population figures from the census returns for the village (1801: 868; 1861: 2283; 1871: 2436; 1881: 2638; 1891: 2370; and in 1901: 2493) again indicate the growth in the first half of the century.

Outworking was based upon separate workshops, undertaking predominantly wide-frame production, supplemented with narrow-frame working (Fig 8.8). Workshops were of brick, generally large, of two storeys, with typical knitters' casement windows, and often adjacent to a hosier's house; some workshops were built even after 1887. A total of 333 frames (104 narrow and 229 wide) were operated in 69 workshops in 1844, making 4.78 frames per shop (Felkin 1844). Of these 69 workshops, Shrimpton (1989, 12) noted only 38 in 1968–69 from a survey, while around ten survived to the mid-1990s. During

Table 8.8 Identified or possible outworking buildings (Figures 6 & 7 shows building locations)

No.	Location	Description	Extant/source*	Comments
1	Fuller St	Workshop	No: RVM 68.5	One of three, small
2	Fuller St	Workshop	No: RVM 76–132	ditto
3	Fuller St	Workshop	No: RVM 71.199	ditto
4	Fuller St	Workshop	No: RFWKM	Location unclear
5	Fuller St	Workshop	No: RVM	Location unclear
6	Asher Lane	Workshop	Yes	Very altered
7	Distillery St	Workshop	Yes	Built 1887–1900
8	Chapel St	FWK complex/houses	Yes	Museum (2 wksps)
9	41 Church St	Small workshop	Yes	Very altered
10	The Green	Workshop	Yes	Built 1887–1900
11	Parkyns St	Workshop	Yes	Hosier house?
12	6 Shaw St	Workshop/house	Yes: RVM68.470	Altered
13	11 High St	Workshop/house	Yes	Original condition
14	16 Easthorpe St	Workshop	Yes: RVM68.4750	Re-used FWK?
15	Woodley St	Large workshop	No: RVM72.228	Attached house
16	18 Woodley St	Small workshop	No: RVM68.91	Attached house?
17	Wilford Road	Workshop	No: RVM69.22	FWK?
18	Wilford Road	Back-to-backs	No: RVM	Top-floor FWK
19	Woodley St	Workshop	No: RVM71.380	Frameshop
20	84 Wilford Rd	Workshop	Yes: RVM84.300	FWK?
21	Savage's Row	Housing	Yes	FWK housing
22	East Street	Housing	No: RVM68.17	Small houses
23	Easthorpe St	Housing	Yes	Widdowson Row
24	Wilford Road	Housing	No: RVM68.93	Wilson's Row
25	16 Church St	House	Yes	FWK window?
26	1 The Elms	Workshop	Yes	FWK?

* RVM = Ruddington Village Museum; RFWKM = Ruddington Knitters' Museum

Nottinghamshire's lace and framework knitting industries 111

Table 8.9   1881 Census figures – outworking activity[17]

Occupation	Total	%
Framework-knitters	335	(58.2)
Seamers	160	(27.8)
Winders	24	(4.1)
Embroiderers	17	(2.9)
Hosiers	10	(1.7)
Hosiery hands	8	(1.3)
Framesmith	7	(1.2)
Bag hosiers	5	(0.8)
Spinners	4	(0.6)
Lace manufacturers	3	(0.5)
Lace dressers	1	(0.1)
Sinkermakers	1	(0.1)
Total Workforce	575	(100.0)

Table 8.10   Trade directory entries[18]

Year & Directory	1	2	3	4	5	6	7	8	9
1832 White's	1	1	–	–	–	5	10	–	17
1864 White's	2	–	1 (lace)	–	1	–	–	–	4
1887 Wright's	1	–	1 (lace)	22	–	–	–	–	24
1891 Wright's	1	–	16	20	–	–	–	–	37
1895 Kelly's	1	–	–	–	–	–	–	–	1
1904 Wright's	1	–	11	–	–	–	–	–	12

1 – framesmiths   2 – needlemakers   3 – hosiers   4 – bag hosiers   5 – framework-knitters

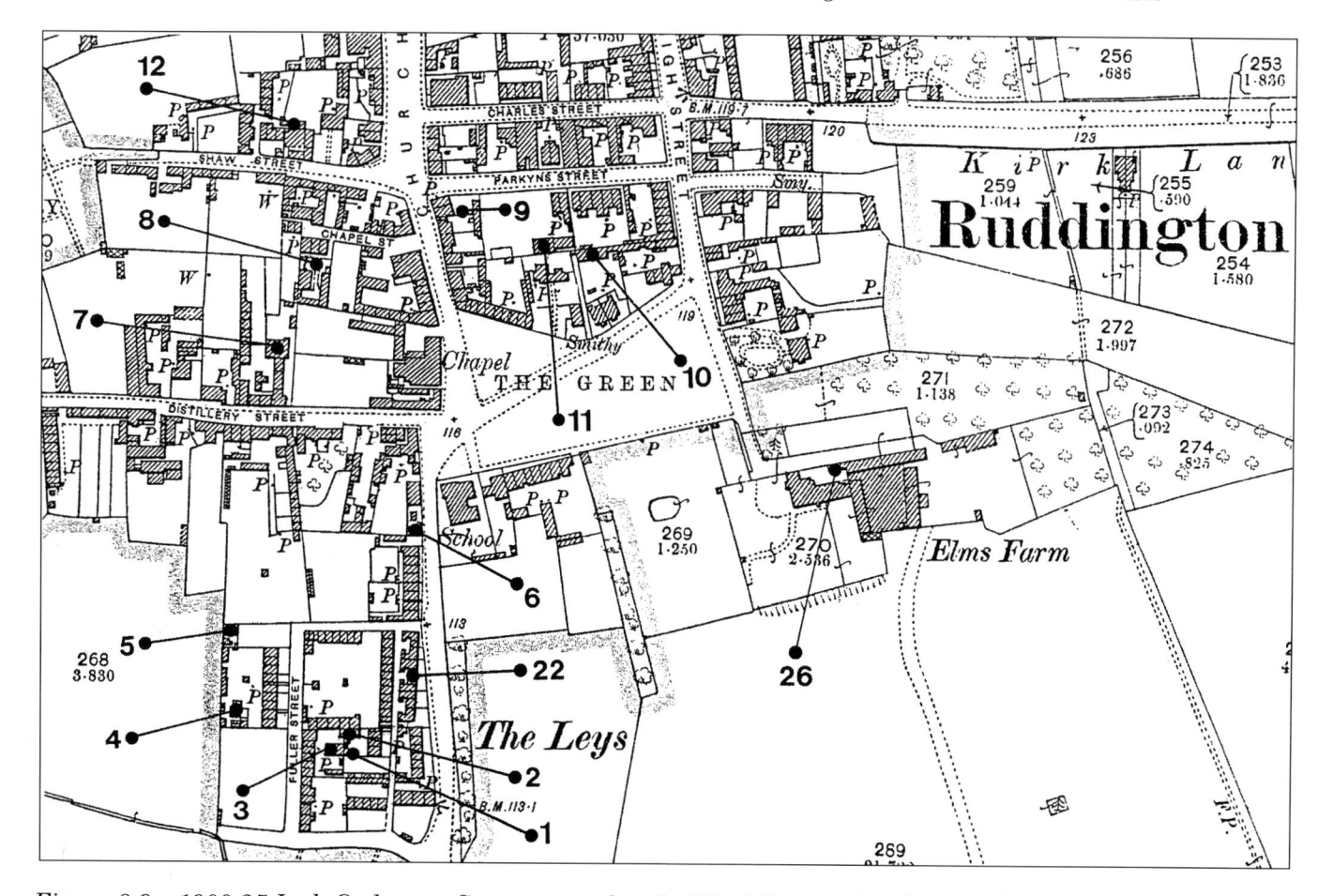

Figure 8.9   1900 25 Inch Ordnance Survey map detail of Ruddington showing southern area, and outworking building locations. (Ordnance Survey)

112 *The vernacular workshop*

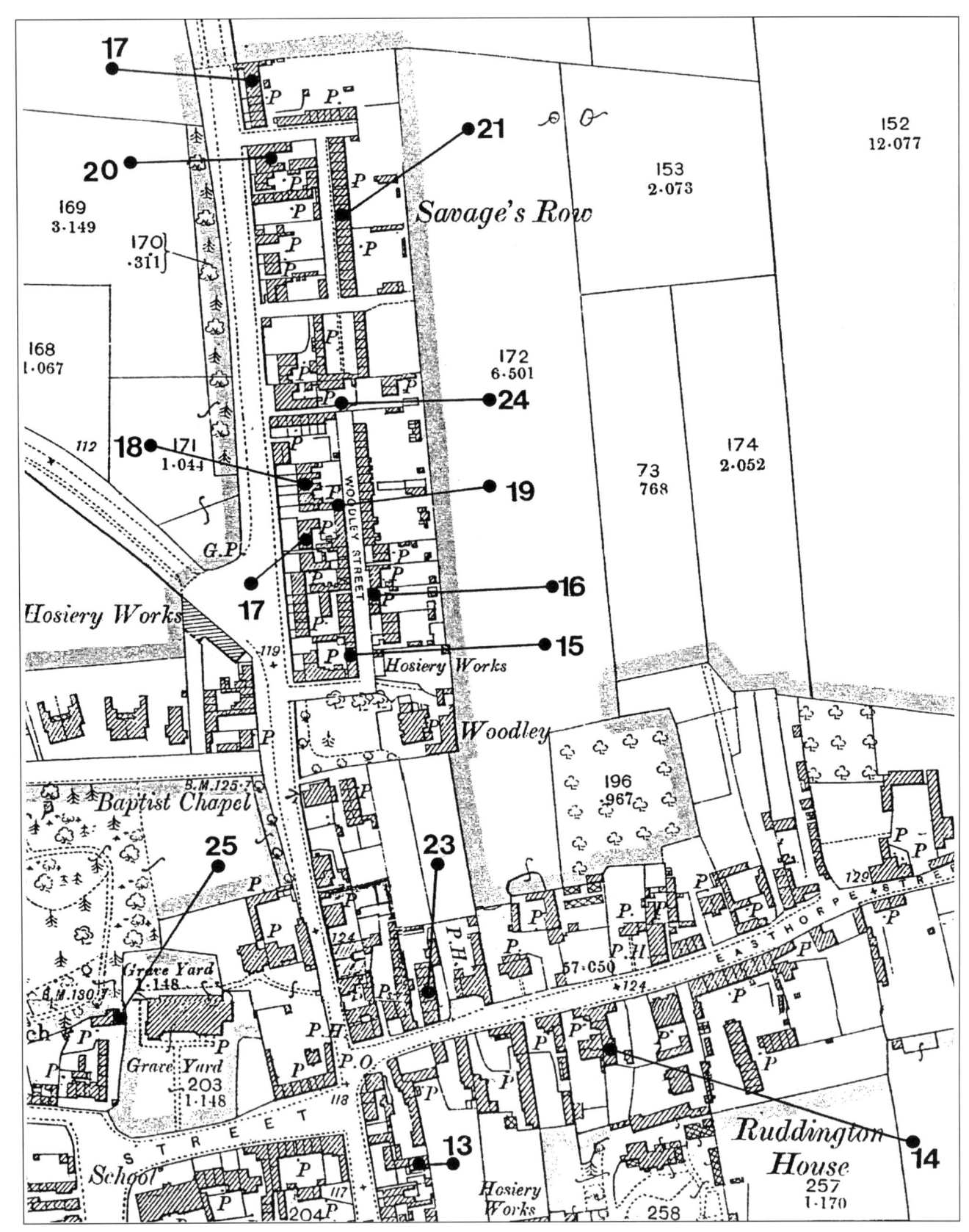

Figure 8.10   1900 25 Inch Ordnance Survey map detail of Ruddington showing northern area, and outworking building locations. (Ordnance Survey)

the 19th century two 'colonies' of knitters' housing evolved, Savage's Row to the north and The Leys to the south. Outworkers lived in bland, small, brick-built terraced housing, usually of two-storeys, interspersed with workshops also within the village centre. There was no obvious pattern, except the use of suitable development plots between existing farms. Losses identified through fieldwork using the

Table 8.11 Identified or possible outworking buildings[19]
(Figures 8.8–8.10 show building locations)

No.	Location	Description	Extant/Image*	Comments
1	Orchard St	Workshops	No: HPL 150	Assumed FWK
2	Watnall Rd	Houses	No: HPL 218	FWK = 3rd floor
3	Orchard St	Houses	No: MN	FWK = 1st floor
4	32 Watnall Rd	House	Yes	FWK = 2nd floor?
5	Gilbert St	Houses	No: NCL 37217	FWK = 2nd floor
6	27/29 High St	House/shop	Yes	FWK = 3rd floor?
7	Market Square	House	No: MN	FWK to r/h side
8	Lambert Hill	House	No: HPL 206	?2 FWK houses
9	79 Annesley Rd	Hosier's house	Yes	Attached workshop
10	Portland Terrace	Houses	No: HPL 018	Uncertain match
11	Northhill Bldgs	Houses	No: HPL 204/5	FWK = 3rd & 4th floors
12	Allen St	Houses	No (various: HPL/NCL)	FWK = 3rd floor
13	Allen St	Houses	No (various: HPL/NCL)	FWK = 3rd floor
14	Allen St	Houses	No (various: HPL/NCL)	FWK = 3rd floor
15	The Connery	Houses	No: HPL 129/155/8	FWK = 1st floor
16	77–85 Albert St	Houses	Yes	FWK = 1st floor
17	67 Albert St	House	Yes	FWK = 1st floor
18	47–49 Albert St	Houses	Yes	?FWK = 1st floor
19	8–18 Albert St	Houses	Yes	FWK = 1st floor
20	34 Albert St	House	Yes	?FWK = 1st floor
21	Albert St	Hosier house?	No: HPL 1973	Aerial photo
22	Portland Road	Houses	No: HPL 016	2 × FWK
23	Mellow's Row	Houses	No: HPL 211–3	Various FWK
24	Portland Road	Workshop	No: NMR/Smith	Rare in Hucknall?
25	Portland Road	Terraced hses	No: HPL 141	?FWK = 1st floor
26	Whyburn Street	Framesmiths	No: MN	Small brick wksp
27	31 Bestwood Rd	Workshop	No: MN	FWK/lace?
28	51 Nottm Rd	House/wksp	Yes	Framesmith?
29	2–10 Nottm Rd	Houses	3 of 5 (6–10)	FWK = 1st floor
30	67–69 Nottm Rd	Houses	Yes	FWK to rear?
–	48 Florence St	Hosier house	Yes	Built after 1880

* HPL = Hucknall Public Library; NMR = National Monuments Record; MN = Mrs Maureen Newton, Hucknall

1900 25 Inch Ordnance Survey map show that of all 873 buildings then extant, only 381 now survive – a loss of 492, or 56.4% (Table 8.8; Figs 8.9 and 8.10).

Of 2638 people in 1881, 575 or 21.7% were employed in outworking (Table 8.9). Appendix 8.3 details the distribution of outworkers. Substantial numbers lived in The Leys, Wilford Street, Distillery Street, and The Green. These figures suggest that all workshops were probably in operation at this stage, housing 335 wide-frame knitters, and other workers. The 1891 data (Table 8.10) highlights hosiers and bag-hosiers, in keeping with census data for this late period, but details few others connected with the trade.

In terms of continuity there was a long period of demise in traditional outworking practices (but not perhaps as protracted as Calverton's) to 1955. The building of some Ruddington workshops after 1887 suggests confidence in framework knitting as a staple, and reliance upon many outworkers with few employment options other than agricultural labouring.

Hucknall

Horriben (?1973) and Beardsmore (1909) provide histories of Hucknall, with some details from the 1845 report (BPP 1845). Hucknall, originally Hucknall Torkard, is located 20.8 km (13 miles) to the north-west of Nottingham. It is the largest knitting centre considered in this study and also indicates rapid development during the latter half of the 19th century due to the opening of two large collieries. Aesthetically, it was the most unattractive of the four centres.[20]

By 1880 the original village had expanded to become a small town, based around earlier farms and housing. It has no single centre, the market square and St Mary Magdalen's Church being its focal point, evident on the 1771 enclosure award map.[21] By 1880 Hucknall had developed along four main arterial routes.[22] In addition to housing within the town's central area there were four other large

114 *The vernacular workshop*

Table 8.12 1881 Outworking activity[23]

Occupation	Total	%
Framework-knitters	337	(49.5)
Seamers	248	(36.4)
Lace dressers	44	(6.4)
Silk mitt makers/stitchers	13	(1.9)
Hosiers	11	(1.6)
Winders	11	(1.6)
Framesmith	9	(1.3)
Shawl manufacturers	5	(0.7)
Needlemakers	2	(0.2)
Total Workforce	680	(100.0)

Table 8.13 Trade directory data[24]

Year & Directory	1	2	3	4	5	6	7	8	9
1832 White's	4	1	12	–	1	–	2	1	21
1864 White's	3	1	36	–	–	–	–	1	41
1887 Wright's	–	–	11	7	–	–	–	–	18
1891 Wright's	–	–	8	5	–	–	–	–	13
1895 Kelly's	1	–	10	–	–	–	–	–	11
1904 Wright's	1	–	13	–	1	–	–	–	15

1 – framesmiths 2 – needlemakers 3 – hosiers 4 – bag hosiers
5 – framework knitters 6 – hosiery agents 7 – bobbin-net maker 8 – sinkermaker (frames)
9 – total outworkers

Figure 8.11 Rear view of 1850–60s outworkers' houses, Albert Street, Hucknall. Workrooms at left, and centre, probably used into the 1880s. A later hosiery factory is visible to the right, background. View taken from rear of master hosier's house (no. 16 on Fig 8.13). (© Garry Campion)

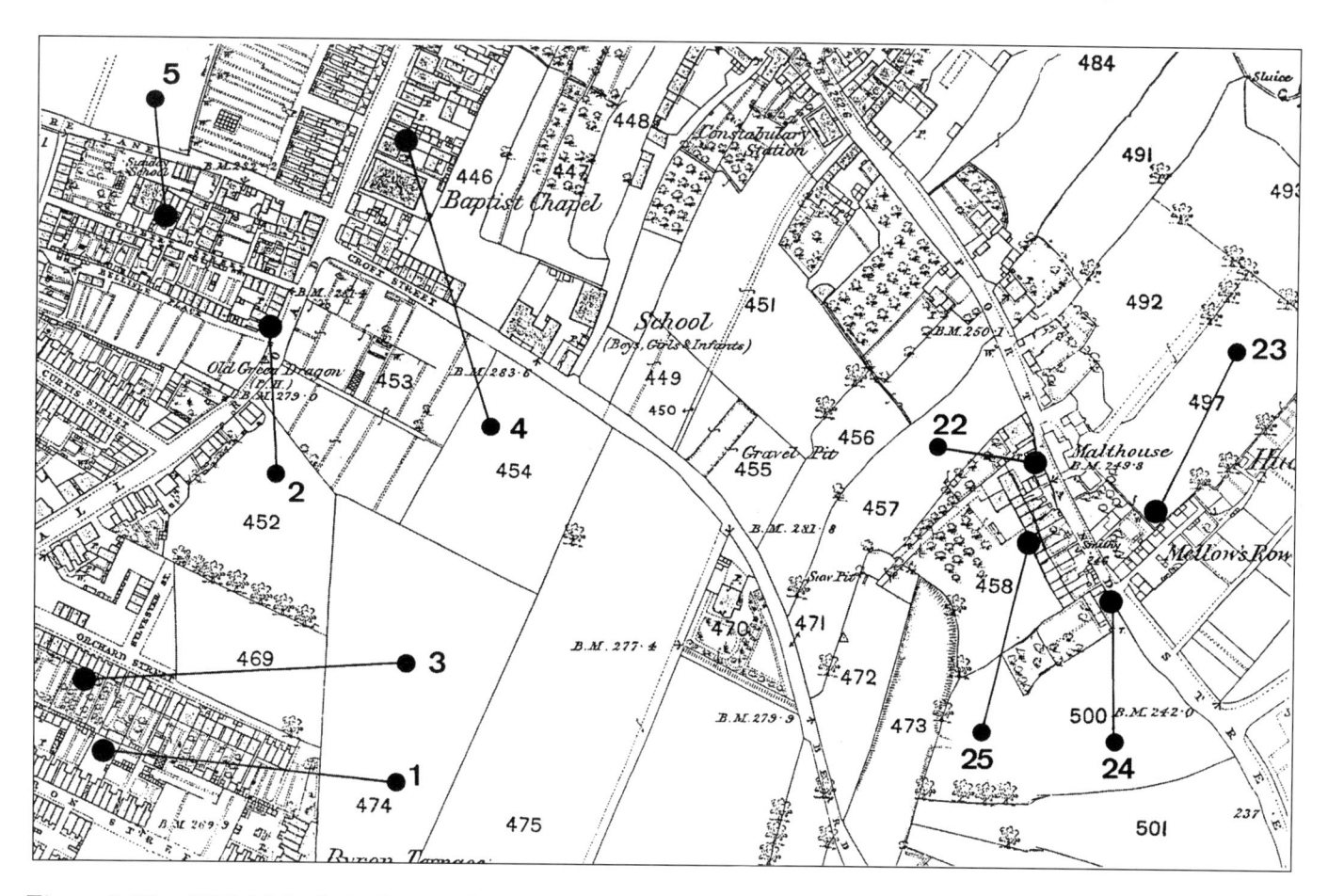

Figure 8.12 1880 25 Inch Ordnance Survey map detail of Hucknall showing central and eastern areas, and outworking building locations. (Ordnance Survey)

developments: Butler's Hill;[25] Broomhill to the south-east; and two large housing areas straddling Watnall Road to the south. A later development occurred at Hazelgrove[26] to the town's south-west. Hucknall had a railway link principally for the collieries. Population figures in the census returns for the village are 1801: 1497; 1851: 2970; 1861: 2836; 1871: 4257; 1881: 10,023; 1891: 13,094; and in 1901: 15,250, indicating a sustained growth, unlike the other centres considered.

Outworkers operated from small, mostly stone-built houses in lengthy terraces of two or three storeys, usually with a middle-floor workroom often facing to the rear (Fig 8.11). Large workshops of the type common in Ruddington were very rare. 842 frames (837 narrow and 5 wide) operated in 69 workshops in 1844, making 2.7 frames per shop (Felkin 1844; BPP 1845). Shetland shawl manufacture from c1865 resulted in a number of purpose-built hosiers' houses, usually with attached workrooms, but it is not clear that smaller garden workshops existed on any scale.

Losses identified through fieldwork using the 1880 25 Inch Ordnance Survey map show that of all 1878 buildings extant then, only 625 survived – a loss of 1253, or 66.8% (Table 8.11; Figs 8.12–8.14).

Hucknall retained a substantial but relatively small outworking population into the 1880s (Table 8.12): of 10,023 people in 1881, 680 or 6.7% were employed in outworking. The large number of seamers and other support workers suggests a still large output from the 337 knitters, but a probably smaller volume overall compared with Ruddington, when assessed in terms of relative hourly productivity.

Appendix 8.4 is a breakdown of all outworkers showing the largest and smallest concentrations. The distribution of buildings is not easy to reconcile with census data, even as late as 1881 where some 'colonies' such as that of Byron Street (7.2% of the town's workforce) are difficult to portray except through demographic data (Appendix 8.4). Buildings survive erratically, many retaining original workrooms, such as those in Albert Street (5.8% of the town's workforce). Note also the lack of focus into outworking enclaves or colonies – some outworkers were living in relatively new areas of miners' housing. Census data is reinforced by trade directory entries (Table 8.13).

After 1865, Shetland shawl manufacture provided some stability to outworking, when decline was otherwise inevitable through factory production and employment in the collieries. Some outworkers carried on their involvement in areas newly built for coal-miners whilst knitters' workrooms elsewhere may have gone unused, except perhaps as bedrooms. Knitters' housing may have been cheaper to rent,

116 *The vernacular workshop*

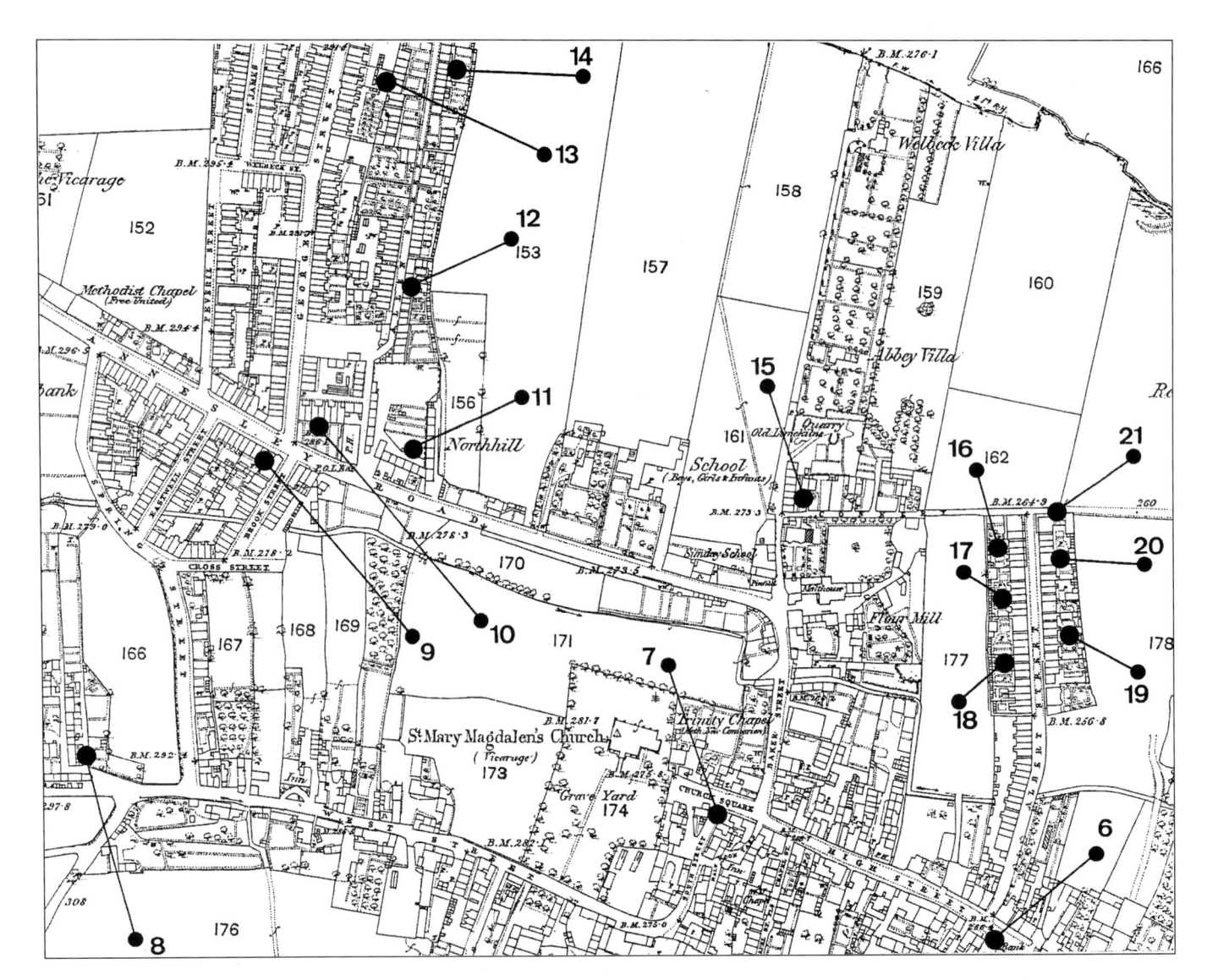

Figure 8.13   1880 25 Inch Ordnance Survey map detail of Hucknall showing central and northern areas, and outworking building locations. (Ordnance Survey)

representing good value for money if a collier's wife worked in outworking and used the workroom. Outworkers may also have moved to Hucknall during the 1860s to benefit from shawl making when knitting was declining elsewhere. Short-lived, the Shetland shawl 'boom' had largely evaporated by the late 1890s leaving only coal and agriculture as staples, with limited outworking continuing into the 20th century.

Discussion

The Nottingham sample considered here was a direct response to housing demands for twist-net outworkers, yet few houses were provided with purpose-built workrooms. Lace outworkers during the 1820s and 30s operated in either purpose-built, or improvised, workrooms and separate workshops. Knitters worked in similar buildings, but the exceptions were the large, unique, four- or more storey lace workshops. These buildings reflected their location, date, economic context, and expected rents. This early economic dynamism led to the demise of lace outworking and the outworkers' housing obsolescence evident within the Nottingham sample by the 1850s.

By contrast, even in 1881, framework knitters, at 893 (55.6%) and seamers at 531 (33.0%), made up the bulk of outworkers in the three centres where the total force was 1606, or 11.5%, out of a combined population of 13,907. This large workforce, predicated on a system maturing a century earlier, had to operate from suitable premises, be they purpose-built or within a home. Solutions varied: Ruddington continued to invest in outworking between 1887 and 1900, constructing large, wide-frame; Hucknall's outworkers sometimes migrated into areas built for miners, reflecting an often female outworking ingress to benefit from the 'last gasp' of Shetland shawl making; and Calverton had no obvious reprieve in the sense of Ruddington's sustainable organisation or Hucknall's new products, yet managed to maintain a substantial level of outworking involvement, perhaps of wider regional significance.

In these knitting centres the diversity of building

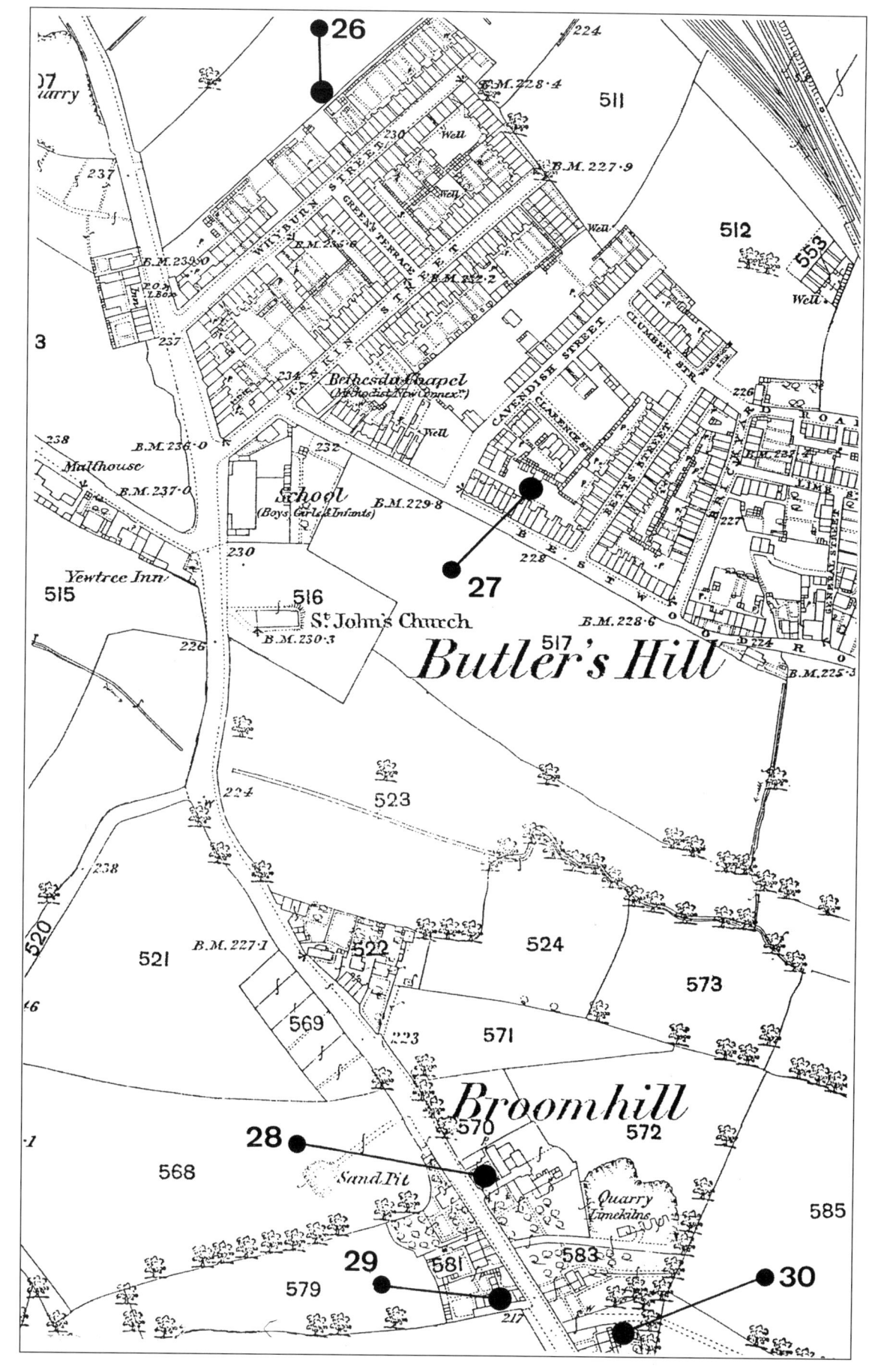

Figure 8.14 1880 25 Inch Ordnance Survey map detail of Hucknall showing the southern and south-eastern areas of Butler's Hill and Broomhill, and outworking building locations. (Ordnance Survey)

styles, despite the similarity of process and close proximity, are striking. Hucknall's middle-floor workrooms contrasted with ground-floor positions in Calverton, both probably eclipsed in productivity terms by Ruddington's wide-frame workshops, the latter a more efficient system for organising and monitoring output along factory lines. In both Hucknall and Calverton, centres based upon knitters' housing, the large-scale change brought about by persuading investors to risk capital on workshops at this stage did not materialise. The potential for greater production was therefore lost at a time when factory competition grew strongly. This was in surprising contrast to Nottingham's very large workshops, producing lace as early as the 1820s, initially operating with machinery not significantly different from that employed in framework knitting, at least in terms of its accommodation within buildings. The lace industry's early expansion into such workshops was arguably central to its economic success, at a time when the framework knitting industry was beset with problems and perhaps lacking the means to do likewise.

In the knitting centres local outworking organisation was also a factor in limiting a rapid transition to factory production, determined by available buildings, produce, and the skills of local outworkers. Modernisation might also be diluted by sources of income such as agricultural labouring. A reluctance to engage with factory production would also be easier to sustain in rural production centres: profiting hosiers and middlemen might accommodate the much-documented resistance until change became irresistible.

The distribution and nature of land within these centres – excluding Nottingham – does not suggest markedly different challenges and possibilities. Hucknall had sufficient land available for workshop construction, but used it for terraced housing. With the exceptions of Windles Square and Foxwood Terrace, Calverton largely eschewed workers' terraces, developing dispersed, small-scale, speculative developments instead. Calverton's knitters must also have operated a frame by a normal window as and when work was available, given the paucity of purpose-built houses, workshops, and other evidence to the contrary. Ruddington was the most forward looking, its workshop-based system already much in evidence by 1844 and continuing strongly into the 1890s.

Conclusion

Very close to Nottingham, the three knitting centres studied here may reflect a regional pattern of stasis, with others clinging to uncertain outworking into the 20th century, a topic worthy of further investigation. The contrast between framework knitting and the burgeoning lace industry of the 1820s and 30s is stark, but the demise of lace into the 20th century is sobering. For all its early dynamism new lace technologies and flexibility were ultimately unable to thwart headlong decline, and despite the 19th century stasis of its knitting forebear, both industries bore comparison as mere regional shadows by the Second World War.

Notes

1. Professor Marilyn Palmer supervised my PhD from 1993 to 1999 – I am very grateful for her support and wise guidance, and for her work in producing the current volume. Dr Paul Barnwell is also thanked for his editing work and support. Grateful thanks to Nottinghamshire Record Office, Local Studies section of Nottingham Central Library, Hucknall Library, Ruddington Framework Knitters Museum, Ruddington Village Museum, and Calverton Social History Society. Mrs Maureen Newton, Hucknall, is thanked for archival materials. I am especially grateful to Suzanne Stenning for her unwavering support, encouragement, and humour during the last three years.
2. NAO, CA 4110
3. NAO, DDTS 16/23
4. NAO, DD 1089/90–1
5. NAO, NO 95
6. NAO, NO 15; cf. Sanderson's 1836 Nottinghamshire map
7. NAO, NO 225 – Dearden's map; Jackson's 1851–61 map of the city
8. 25 Inch Ordnance Survey map 38.14: 1880, 1901, 1915
9. NAO, 1841, City of Nottingham, St Mary's Ward, microfiche 8. 'North' was added c1860 to Sherwood Street
10. Dearden 1834; Pigot 1842; White 1832
11. NAO, microfiche census returns for 1881 Calverton
12. Kelly 1895; White 1832; White 1864; Wright 1887; Wright 1891; Wright 1904
13. NAO, EA 18/2
14. 25 Inch Ordnance Survey maps 33.11: 1889, 1915; 33.12: 1889, 1915; 33.16: 1889, 1915
15. NAO, EA 74/2
16. 25 Inch Ordnance Survey maps 46.2: 1887, 1900, 1914; 46.6: 1887, 1900, 1914
17. NAO, microfiche census returns for 1881 Ruddington
18. Sources as note 11
19. Hucknall's 1930s local authority produced photographs of buildings before demolition but some locations were inaccurate, and it has not been possible to identify them (NCL & HPL)
20. HPL, L90.2HK
21. NAO, EA/00/2/1–2
22. 25 Inch Ordnance Survey maps 32.16: 1880, 1900, 1915; 33.13: 1880, 1900, 1915; 32.12: 1880, 1900, 1916
23. NAO: microfiche census returns for 1881 Hucknall
24. Sources as note 11
25. NAO, DD BW 151/9; auction plan dated 1876
26. NAO, DD 607/30

Appendix 8.1   1858 Wright's directory for Mansfield Road area (nos = house numbers)

(*Blue Coat Street*)
Blue Coat School   Wild & Bradbury's lace factory   Bobbin and carriage makers
27 – pork butcher   28 – private   29 – proprietor
30 – private   31 – private   32 – private
33 – private   34 – brass founders   35 – painter
36 – butcher   37 – milliners   38 – grocer
39 – haberdasher   40 – fishmonger   41 – tobacconist
42 – baker   43 – Golden Fleece

(*Babbington St* intersects – 38 buildings fronting Mansfield Road in 1881 between former and Chatham St)
44 – grocer   45 – private   46 – private
47 – milliner(w)   48 – private(w)   49 – private(w)
50 – private(w)   51 – private(w)   52 – clerk of races(?w)
53 – druggist(?w)   54 – whipthong maker(w)   55 – milliner
56 – private   58 – builder   59 – hosier
60 – shopkeeper   63 – hosier   64 – butcher
65 – hairdresser   66 – confectioner   67 – maltster
68 – warper   69 – seamstress   70 – baker
71 – joiner; chimney sweep   72 – Old Nag's Head   73 – private
74 – private   75 – shoemaker   76 – provision dealer
77 – dress-maker   79 – private   80 – poulterer

(*Chatham Street*)
81 – baker   82 – builder   83 – melicent
84 – private(w)   85 – private(w)   86 – butcher
87 – tailor   88 – private   89 – butcher(w)
90 – private(?w)   91/92 – private   93 – private(w)
94 – victualler, Dog & Gun   95 – private   96 – painter
97 – private   98 – grocer   99 – private
100 – private   101 – private(w)   102 – baker(w)
103 – private(w)   104 – private(w)   105 – reverend(?w)
106 – reverend(?w)   107 – private(w)   108 – coal agent(w)
109 – private(w)   110 – proprieter(w)   111 – proprieter
112 – private   113 – private(w)   114 – private(w)
115 – private   116 – private(w)   118 – painter(w)
119 – Forest Tavern   120 – letter of cabs &c   121 – beerseller and cattle dealer

1858 Wright's Directory – North Sherwood Street

(*Forest Road*)
1 – school staff   Water works   15 – haberdasher
18 – shoemaker   20 – private   28 – painter and glazier
31 – haberdasher   32 – shopkeeper   (Machine Place)
Wright's lace factory   (Packer's Place)   Slater, bobbin and carriage maker
Shopkeeper   Maltster
(*Chatham Street*)
William, lace manufacturer   Sunday School   58 – butcher
59 – shopkeeper   60 – shopkeeper   66 – cowkeeper
Fann & Lamb's hosiery factory   general smiths works   76 – silk and cotton winder
82 – tailor   Grocer
(*Babbington Street*)
85 – bonnet maker

Appendix 8.2 1881 Census breakdown of outworkers for Calverton, by street

Street name	1	2	3	4	5	6
Main Street	66	38	2	1	107	(30.5)
Jenny Nook	26	13	1	1	41	(11.7)
Bottom Buildings (Windles Square)	32	8	–	–	40	(11.4)
Foxwood Terrace	20	12	–	–	32	(9.1)
Burnor Pool	13	8	1	–	22	(6.2)
Mansfield Lane	9	10	–	1	20	(5.7)
Stripes Yard	12	5	–	–	17	(4.8)
Meads Yard	11	5	–	–	16	(4.5)
White's Yard	7	3	–	–	10	(2.8)
George's Lane	5	2	–	–	7	(2.0)
Burton's Yard	6	1	–	–	7	(2.0)
Muse Lane	5	1	–	–	6	(1.7)
South Terrace	3	2	–	–	5	(1.4)
Flatts Lane	2	1	–	–	3	(0.8)
?Stubborn Yard	2	1	–	–	3	(0.8)
Crookdale Lane	1	2	–	–	3	(0.8)
Pottery Lane	–	2	–	–	2	(0.5)
Collyers Yard	1	1	–	–	2	(0.5)
Forest Lane	–	1	–	–	1	(0.2)

1 – framework knitters   2 – seamers   3 – manufacturers (all types)   4 – framesmiths   5 – total for street/road/yard   6 – % of village workforce

Appendix 8.3 1881 Census breakdown of outworkers for Ruddington, by street

Street name	1	2	3	4	5	6	7
The Leys	84	25	1	19	1	130	(22.6)
Wilford Street	70	16	4	5	3	98	(17.0)
Distillery Street	32	20	2	2	–	56	(9.7)
The Green	33	17	1	1	1	53	(9.2)
Church Street	22	17	2	8	1	50	(8.6)
Easthorpe Street	28	9	3	7	–	47	(8.1)
Woodley Street	22	18	–	5	–	45	(7.8)
High Street	13	7	–	3	–	23	(4.0)
Chapel Street	7	9	1	–	–	17	(2.9)
Easthorpe Lodge	10	4	–	1	–	15	(2.6)
Vicarage Lane	3	10	–	1	–	14	(2.4)
Shaw Street	5	5	1	1	–	12	(2.0)
Sanday's Yard	4	2	–	–	–	6	(1.0)
Arnott Hill	–	–	1	2	–	3	(0.5)
Parkyns Street	2	–	–	–	1	3	(0.5)
The Grange	–	–	2	–	–	2	(0.3)
Elizabeth House	–	1	–	–	–	1	(0.1)

1 – framework knitters   2 – seamers   3 – manufacturers (lace and hosiery)   4 – other outworkers   5 – framesmiths   6 – total for street/road/yard   7 – % of village workforce

Appendix 4 1881 Census breakdown of outworkers for Hucknall, by street

Street Name	1	2	3	4	5	6	7
Byron Street	19	27	–	3	–	49	(7.2)
Watnall Road	26	16	1	2	2	47	(6.9)
Orchard Street	23	18	1	3	–	45	(6.6)
Allen Street	24	13	1	3	–	41	(6.0)
Albert Street	14	4	7	14	1 (nm)	40	(5.8)
Whybourn Street	15	15	–	6	1	37	(5.4)
Gilbert Street	18	14	1	–	1 (nm)	34	(5.0)
Curtis Street	12	10	1	1	–	24	(3.5)
Portland Road	9	11	1	1	–	22	(3.2)
Beardall Street	14	4	–	2	–	20	(2.9)
West Street	11	9	–	–	–	20	(2.8)
Wood Lane	5	9	–	3	–	17	(2.5)
Bestwood Road	15	1	–	1	–	17	(2.5)
Hankin Street	1	10	–	3	1	15	(2.2)
Wash Dyke Lane	11	3	–	1	–	15	(2.2)
Moseley Street	8	5	1	–	–	14	(2.0)
Building Street	6	8	–	–	–	14	(2.0)
Broomhill	5	2	–	2	4	13	(1.9)
Croft Street	9	1	3	–	–	13	(1.9)
Betts Street	6	5	–	1	–	12	(1.7)
George Street	8	1	–	3	–	12	(1.7)
Cavendish Street	2	3	–	5	1	11	(1.6)
Annersley Road	8	1	–	2	–	11	(1.6)
Hankin Terrace	1	7	–	2	–	10	(1.4)
Brook Street	5	5	–	–	–	10	(1.4)
James Street	5	3	–	1	–	9	(1.3)
Lambert Hill	5	4	–	–	–	9	(1.3)
Derbyshire Lane	7	1	1	–	–	9	(1.3)
Eastwell Street	2	6	–	1	–	9	(1.3)
West Terrace	3	3	2	–	–	8	(1.1)
Spring Street	3	4	–	–	–	7	(1.0)
Mellors Row	2	3	–	1	–	6	(0.8)
High Street (pub)	1	5	–	–	–	6	(0.8)
High Street	4	1	–	1	–	6	(0.8)
Church Square	4	–	–	1	–	5	(0.7)
Limb Street	1	2	–	2	–	5	(0.7)
Baker Street	2	–	–	2	–	4	(0.5)
Welbeck Street	4	–	–	–	–	4	(0.5)
Brickyard Road	2	2	–	–	–	4	(0.5)
General Street	2	1	–	–	–	3	(0.4)
Station Lane	1	–	2	–	–	3	(0.4)
The Connery	1	2	–	–	–	3	(0.4)
South Street Place	2	1	–	–	–	3	(0.4)
Half Moon Yard	1	1	–	–	–	2	(0.2)
Peverill Street	1	1	–	–	–	2	(0.2)
Willmott's Yard	–	2	–	–	–	2	(0.2)
Cross Street	–	2	–	–	–	2	(0.2)
Hawkin Terrace	–	1	–	–	–	1	(0.1)
North Hill	1	–	–	–	–	1	(0.1)
Portland Terrace	1	–	–	–	–	1	(0.1)
Lynby Terrace	–	–	–	1	–	1	(0.1)
Farley's Lane	–	1	–	–	–	1	(0.1)

1 – framework knitters   2 – seamers   3 – manufacturers   4 – other outworkers   5 – framesmiths and/or needlemakers (nm)   6 – total for street/road/yard   7 – % of town workforce

9 Domesticated factories and industrialised houses: the buildings of the Northamptonshire boot and shoe industry *by Adam Menuge*

Introduction

This paper is based substantially on fieldwork conducted by staff of the Cambridge office of English Heritage in late 1999 and early 2000, which aimed to identify, classify, and begin to understand, the surviving buildings of the Northamptonshire boot and shoe industry (Cooke *et al* 2000). Subsequent recording and research have clarified many of the issues raised by the initial survey (Menuge 2001).[1] The fieldwork was actuated by growing concern for this distinctive building stock, which is proving increasingly prone to demolition or radical conversion, and which lies almost entirely outside the realm of statutory protection, whether through listing or through conservation area designation. During the period over which the initial fieldwork extended, no fewer than 21% of the 450 or so buildings noted (excluding the numerous very small workshops) were either vacant or already undergoing conversion or demolition. Brief discussions of one element of an industry inevitably risk obscuring a wide range of connections and interdependencies. This paper can say little about the ancillary trades – the manufacture of shoe leather, lasts, shoemaking machinery, adhesives, cardboard boxes, and so on – with which the Northamptonshire boot and shoe industry is intermingled. Nor can it range with the same confidence outside Northamptonshire, though there are some other important shoemaking centres, notably in Leicestershire, Norwich and Staffordshire, and these exhibit some different emphases and specialisms. The article will focus primarily on the period from the late 1850s to the early 1900s; specialists in other industries will recognise that this is a late (though not entirely unparalleled) period for the study of both outworking and workshops.

Shoemaking is a craft which, at least until the 19th century, was more or less ubiquitous in England, with firm ties to the countrywide production of leather, which was in turn a by-product of livestock farming. On a small-scale shoemaking catered to essentially local demand. The trade itself, by the second half of the 19th century, made a very clear distinction between shoe *making*, and wholesale shoe *manufacturing*, and it is the latter for which Northamptonshire became noted. Within the county it was concentrated overwhelmingly in a crescent extending from Northampton at the south-western extremity, through Earls Barton, Wellingborough, Rushden, Raunds and Kettering, to Rothwell, and Desborough at its northern tip, taking in a number of smaller settlements in its path. Some production went on elsewhere, however, and there were particular concentrations further west in Daventry and Long Buckby. There was a considerable variety of specialism and technique within the county, but Northamptonshire's core business was men's and boys' shoes, including army boots. This contrasts with Leicestershire, which was more involved with the making of women's shoes. Northamptonshire also exhibits a generally more conservative adherence to craft traditions, whereas Leicestershire exploits the mass-market more successfully.

Collectively, wholesale boot and shoemaking earns the title of an industry, as distinct from a craft, not so much through the emergence of elements of mechanised production – though these hastened its recognition as such by contemporaries for whom machinery was a touchstone – but by virtue of its being enmeshed in a complex, and increasingly compartmentalised, network of production and commercial relationships. By the second half of the 19th century these relationships extended all the way round the globe. Export markets included North America, Australia, and New Zealand; tanned hides were imported from India and South America. Yet the productive heart of the industry was an odd mixture of modern technology and craft practices and organisation.

The origins of the industry

Northamptonshire's rise to prominence is traditionally attributed to the English Civil War, and to the ability of factors, or middlemen, to satisfy large orders for the Parliamentarian forces (VCH, 1906). Military orders, large-scale and often peremptory, but also erratic, continued to shape the emerging industry, making quick profits for some, while periodically ruining others. The system of outworking meant that relatively large-scale production could be coordinated in very small units, multiplied across the towns and villages. In common with many small-scale industries, early images are scarce. While this is disappointing, in itself it tells us something about the place occupied by the industry in the contemporary imagination: with its small scale and retention of traditional craft skills, it did not startle. But also, being located to a very large extent within private space, it did not invite scrutiny

Figure 9.1 Contrasting images of the boot and shoe industry.
a (left): The shoemaker in his own home, emphatically master of his own time – note the insouciant angle of the clock. (Anonymous print, 1866, Northampton Museum and Art Gallery)
*b (below): the strictly regulated, time-conscious regime of an early machine-closing workshop. (*Good Words, *1 November 1869). (Northampton Museum and Art Gallery)*

in the way that some larger industrial enterprises did. Those larger buildings which had a public presence – the warehouses of the factors – were clearly accommodating elements of the manufacturing process, such as clicking, by the second quarter of the 19th century, and may have done so for many years before then. They remain elusive, however, most having disappeared in the 20th-century redevelopment of central Northampton; even if examples survive, their connection with boot and shoe manufacturing may, in individual cases, be difficult to prove.

It is quite clear that, up until the mid-19th century, the greater part of the industry was conducted in a working environment that required no substantial modification of ordinary domestic accommodation. This is in marked contrast to contemporary outworking in the textiles industry. All that was needed was sufficient light to work by, space for a chair, for small hand-tools and for the storage of limited quantities of materials and finished work, and a source of heat for the winter months. A comparison with the textile industry suggests how modest these requirements were: when even the bulky hand-loom did not absolutely demand larger-than-normal windows, it is hardly to be wondered at that the shoemaker's craft was often architecturally invisible. Many outworkers did not even require a bench to work at. It might be desirable to remove this work, with its sharp tools and sometimes noisy operations, out of the everyday living space of the family, but it was certainly not essential. The result, then, is a minimal architectural legacy, and one that would in any case be hard to distinguish from those of other local outwork traditions, notably in textiles. There is currently little evidence that outworking influenced house design before the middle of the 19th century, though it should be acknowledged that the systematic inspection of housing in pursuit of subtle variations in planning and fenestration lay beyond the scope of the present survey.

It is easy, in a discipline which takes material evidence as its starting point, to write off this area as insignificant or unrewarding. But the social significance of the architectural elision of working space is of course rather greater. Even when, as rising living standards permit, work is removed into specialist accommodation either within the house or on the garden plot, the culture of the workplace remains qualitatively distinct through its proximity to the home and its inclusion within a seemingly autonomous domestic regime. The domestic workplace is one where hours can be varied to suit domestic obligations, but also to indulge other appetites, which might include sharing a friend's pipe; where language and behaviour are not subject to the scrutiny and sanctions of a higher authority; where the boundaries between work and domestic life are flexible and where, for example, family members (such as the wife or daughter illustrated in Figure 9.1a) can be drawn informally within the circle of labour. This last is perhaps not merely a pragmatic consideration. The craftsman (and head of household) surrounded by his family feels himself part of a hierarchical continuum of which he is not himself the lowest member. In factory employment – and gender historians have argued, controversially perhaps, that new forms of industrial organisation were perceived as subjugating masculine labour to feminine submissiveness – this dignity may fall away.

In the case of the shoe industry – as with some others – outwork was intimately associated, certainly in the minds of contemporary temperance reformers, with the 'cult' of St Monday and with what some historians have characterised as 'pre-industrial' (or 'proto-industrial') work rhythms (Anon, 1853; Rowe, 1869; Thompson 1967; Mendels 1972; Safley & Rosenband 1993). Is it a coincidence that the clock – one of the powerful symbols of the factory regime – is disregarded and awry in the illustration (Fig 9.1a)? Of course the image is a sentimental one, and the historical authenticity of a near contemporary image of a machine-closing workshop may be equally compromised by propagandist intent (Fig 9.1b). But the clash of cultures that they encapsulate is no less real and historical. Factory work could perpetuate some flexibility in earnings by allowing piece-rates, but otherwise presented a forbidding system of restrictive hours and conditions, which many shoemakers resisted bitterly. In such ways, the buildings which remain for us to study are expressive as much of cultural considerations – what today might be termed 'lifestyle choices' – as they are of ineluctable production needs.

The advent of the factory system and mechanised working

The transition from craft to industry was continuous throughout the second half of the 19th century, and went hand-in-hand with a progressive division and re-division of labour. It is entirely possible for a single craftsman to make a pair of shoes from start to finish, and in a specialist area such as orthopaedic work this practice has continued down to the present day. But the norm by the end of the 19th century was for work to be grouped into a small number of main areas which, in very simple terms, are as follows. The highest-status task, requiring great skill and handling the most expensive materials, was 'clicking' – the cutting by hand of the finer leather used for uppers. This has always been a male preserve. 'Closing' involved stitching together the various parts of the upper. Closing was made more attractive to female labour by the introduction of the sewing machine in the 1850s. The 'bottom stock' or 'rough stuff' cutter meanwhile cut out the coarse, heavy leather used for soles, welts, and heels, a process for which heavy mechanical presses were in widespread use by the end of the 19th century. The 'maker' then stretched the upper over a last, attached the sole, heel and, in welted construction, the welts, and carried out any necessary finishing. These broad

Figure 9.2 Two early shoe factories?
a (above): The earlier portion of the Castle Factory in Long Buckby with the pre-1884 addition to its right.
b (below): A factory behind Havelock St, Kettering, complete in its present form by 1884.
Both probably originate no later than the 1860s. (© English Heritage. NMR)

divisions conceal a potentially huge number of sub-processes, varying with the type and fashion of footwear being made (Swaysland 1905; Anon, 1917; Salaman, 1986).

The earliest factories were built to capitalise on the opportunities presented by the sewing machine, which allowed closing to be brought into the factory environment, but they did not signal the complete mechanisation of the industry. A large amount of space continued to be devoted to warehousing and the associated functions of reception, packing, and despatch. This is reflected in contemporary nomenclature, which more often than not refers to 'warehouses' rather than 'factories' even as late as the early 1880s. The earliest examples were in Northampton, and have all disappeared, some as recently as the 1980s. Outside Northampton the type emerged slightly later, but two examples are set apart typologically, or stylistically, from the numerous survivals of the last three decades of the 19th century. The first is the Castle Factory in Long Buckby (Fig 9.2a). Its early date is confirmed by its relationship with the addition to the right, which was built by 1884. There is quite a marked contrast between the two, particularly in the fenestration and proportions. The wide, cambered, or segmental-headed windows are characteristic of workshops in a number of industries, and frequently date from before the middle of the century. The Long Buckby example may be as late as the 1860s, but it can hardly be later.

A second example (Fig 9.2b) is located in Kettering on a back alley behind Havelock St, which was developed from 1857 onwards – confirming the potentially late occurrence of this window type in Northamptonshire. The right-hand range, built before 1882 on map evidence, is an addition to the left-hand, yet it has the same 'early' window form, so a date for the first phase within a decade of 1857 seems not unreasonable. The limited fenestration on the lower floors of the original range is striking and may indicate that processes were confined to the top storey, an arrangement that conforms to the contemporary denomination of early shoe factories as 'warehouses'. Leather-trades uses for both these buildings are documented at various dates, but not as yet for the crucial earliest period. The problem is that they are situated in settlements where a lingering textile industry conceivably offers an alternative explanation for their origins.

Much more familiar to anyone who knows the Northamptonshire boot and shoe towns are the slightly taller-proportioned factories, with narrower windows, of which the second phase of the Long Buckby factory is an example (Fig 9.2a). Several hundred factories of this type were built between about 1870 and 1900. Although they exhibit some stylistic diversity, ranging from the severely plain to the architecturally quite striking, there is a remarkable uniformity of parts. The great majority are of three storeys, some with a basement in addition; not many reach four and five storeys, and there are also a few two-storeyed examples. Most have a more or less elaborate business entrance and a plainer works entrance, and nearly all distinguish some office accommodation, usually on the first floor, by a variation in fenestration. Sometimes the office is marked out by the presence of an oriel window; more often a transition from cast-iron frames to timber sashes makes the same point. All of these factories have at least one loading door with an iron crane, or evidence for one.

The persistence of outwork

However, before settling into the comfortable notion that these factories indicate a consolidated body of working practices, consistently applied, it is worthwhile considering the place of factory working within the wider production sphere. The first factories, self-evidently, operated in an industry still largely organised around outwork. Mechanisation began with the introduction of the sewing machine in the 1850s, and by 1900 had extended to most parts of the production process, but technical innovations were taken up unevenly. Some 'warehouses' in which a proportion of manufacturing was carried on were certainly un-powered originally; in other buildings power was applied to some processes only. It was some years before more than a handful of processes were successfully mechanised, and in the interim the remainder of the chain of production fell to hand methods. These could be brought within the factory envelope, where there were certain benefits in terms of security, quality control, and other forms of work-discipline, but they often continued to be put out.

There are a variety of reasons for this. Even where the technology of machine processes was proven, outworking might be perpetuated because a manufacturer sought to maintain high production standards through craft practices, or because his profit margins did not justify the capital resources needed to invest in either machinery or the extra factory space needed to accommodate more workers. As in other industries where it competed with powered working in factories, outworking could also be used to satisfy large orders quickly, and then be abandoned when orders were short. For a variety of reasons, therefore, out working remained an important component of the industry up to, and even a little beyond, its official suppression (with the exception of closing) in 1894. The majority of shoe factories within the second half of the 19th century need to be seen as the hubs of a more extensive and intricate system of production. The situation is complicated, not only by outworking, but by the existence of small or medium-sized factories specialising in particular operations, such as heel-making or closing.

A proportion of the space in early factories, moreover, is devoted to the handling of incoming and outgoing components involved in outworking, and with the reception of the outworkers themselves. The

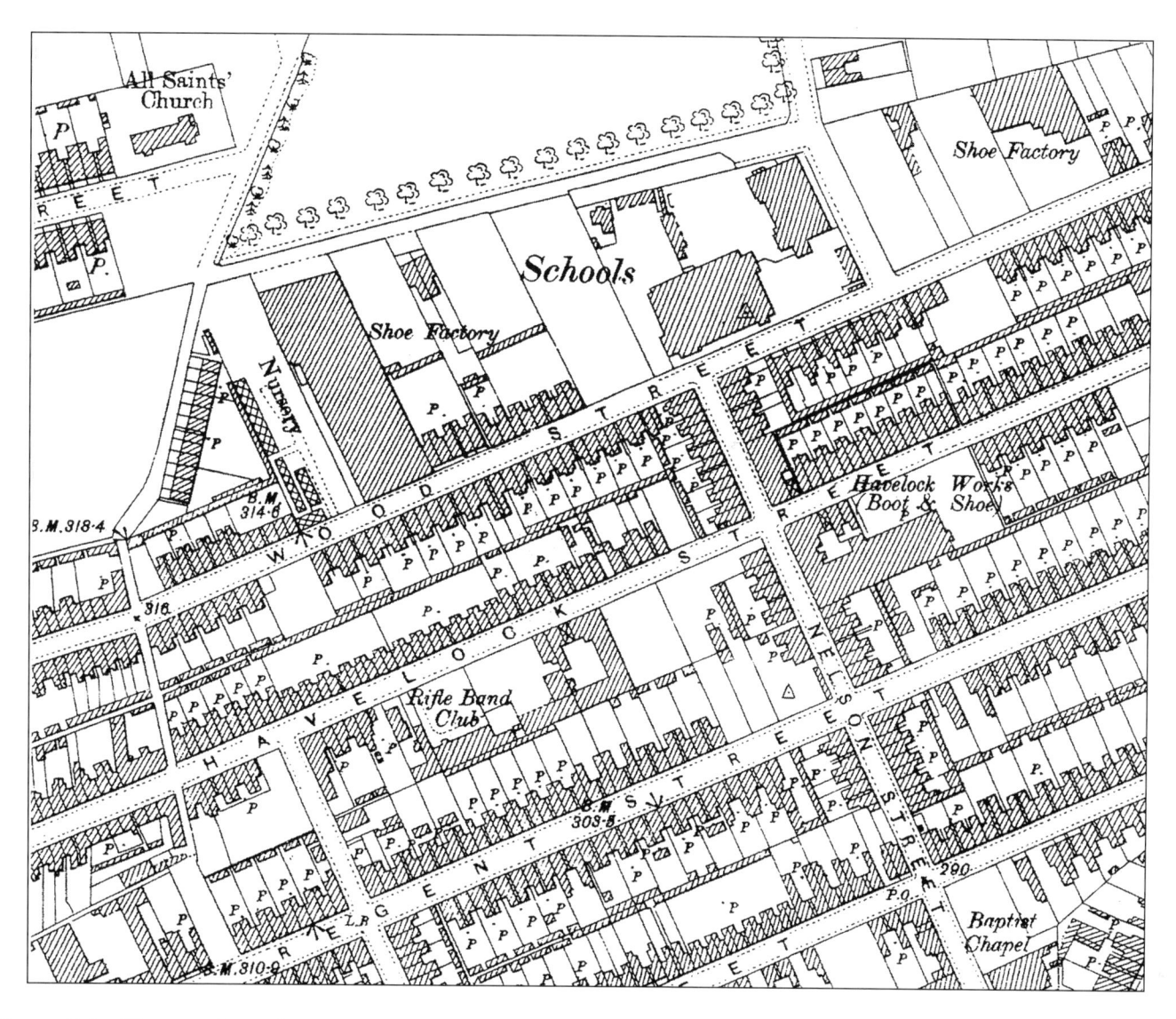

Figure 9.3 Extract from the 1899 25 Inch Ordnance Survey map of Kettering, showing the proximity of shoe factories, houses, and garden workshops in the Wood St, Havelock St, and Regent St area. (Ordnance Survey)

factory at 56 Lorne Road, Northampton, described as 'newly erected' in 1873, was advertised as containing the following accommodation: 'large Rivetting Shop on the basement; rough-stuff shop, taking-in room and waiting room for work people on the ground floor; large clicking room, stock room and counting house on the first floor; packing room and shoe room on the upper floor'.[2] This suggests that while the majority of processes were being carried on within the factory, closing was being put out. In view of the 'waiting room' it is likely that in this case the factory employed outworkers, but others engaged the services of specialist closing firms.

These specialist closing works survive in small numbers. They are normally two-storeyed, and there is thus some overlap between them and the smaller shoe factories. An example of about 1880 at 20 Bailiff Street, Northampton, characteristically forms the upper floor of a range attached to the rear of a house occupying a street-corner plot. George Coles was listed as a machine closer here in 1890, but six years later Alfred Flint was the householder, while Mrs Flint ran the closing business (Kelly 1890: White 1896). These buildings occupy a middle ground, somewhere between factories and workshops. The Goad Insurance Plans of the 1890s describe them as factories, yet most would have had no motive power, relying instead on a series of treadle-operated sewing machines. On the other hand they have a master and hands, so the characteristic productive autonomy of the workshop is very considerably curtailed, with speed, rhythm, and intensity subject to the intervention of an overseer. Similar considerations might apply to other specialist areas, such as the manufacture of boot uppers. Heel-making, on the other hand, as at the c1900 Ernest Chambers heel factory in Raunds, is more unequivocally a factory operation, relying on the use of heavy mechanical presses.

Beyond these specialist suppliers, operating from factories or workshops, lay the outworking sphere. As in other industries, the patchy progress of mecha-

128 *The vernacular workshop*

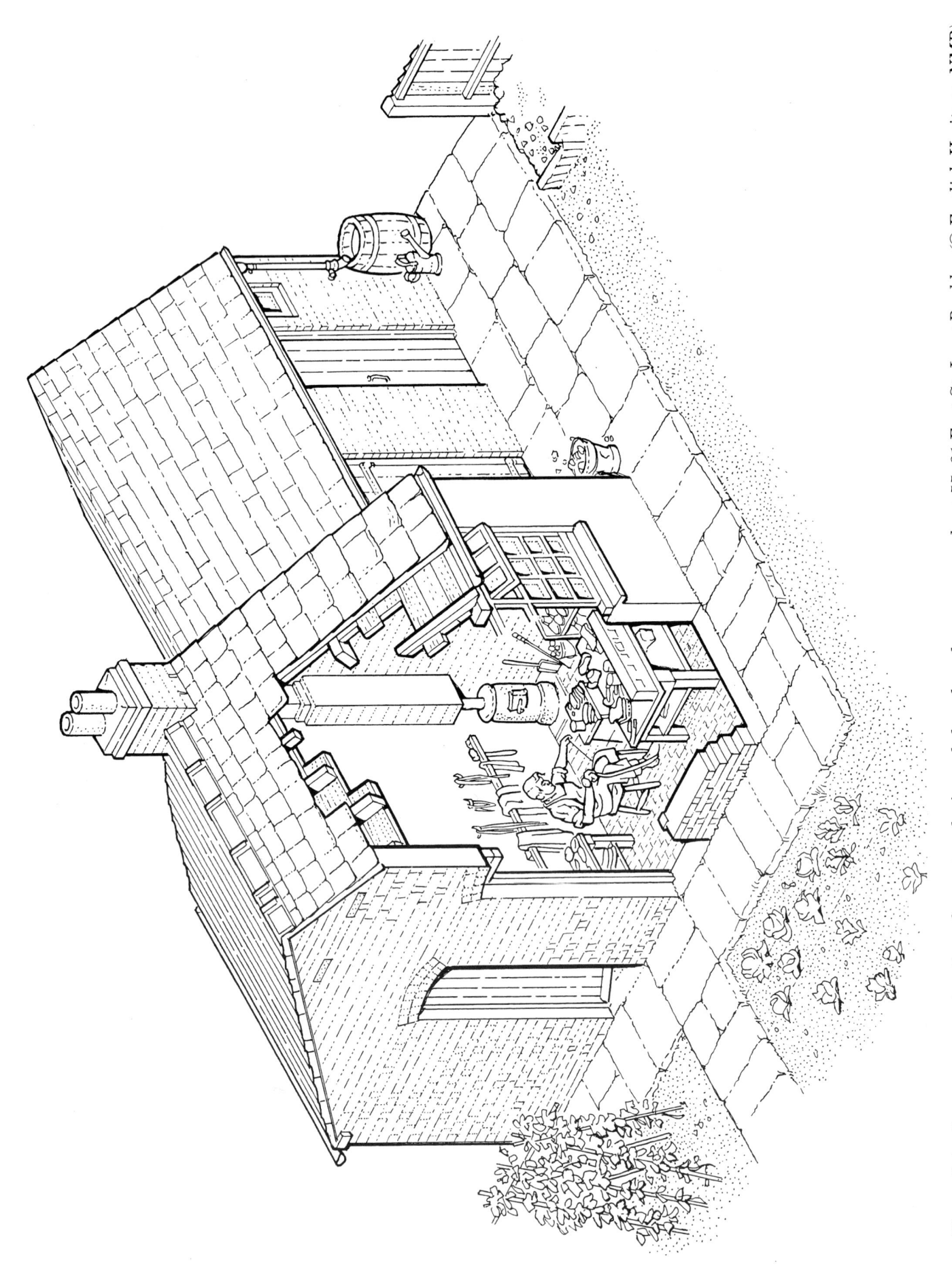

Figure 9.4 Cutaway reconstruction of an outworker's workshop, based on an example at 55–61 East St, Long Buckby. (© English Heritage. NMR)

nisation probably stimulated outworking for some considerable time, before eventually supplanting it. At a time of generally rising living standards the response was the construction, on a huge scale, of purpose-built accommodation. Kettering has workshops in greatest abundance, and in perhaps the simplest form, built between the 1860s and shortly after 1900. Many – perhaps the majority – were built by local manufacturers at the same time as the houses they serve. They are particularly well represented in the Havelock Street and Wood Street area of the town, where their proximity to a number of shoe factories is apparent (Fig 9.3). Known colloquially as 'barns', they vary very little, and were mostly built in the late 1870s and early 1880s. Nearly all back onto the rear wall of the garden plot, sometimes forming long rows, sometimes pairs interrupted by rear entrances from the back alley, or reached from the front via a tunnel between the houses. They have pitched or lean-to roofs, a corner or rear-wall fireplace or stove, and a large timber window looking out onto the garden. Besides Kettering, where their popularity may reflect the noisy practice of riveting soles, they can be found in smaller numbers in Rushden, Wollaston, and Irthlingborough, and indeed most of the shoemaking towns and villages in the north-east of the county, sometimes in the immediate vicinity of factories (Fig 9.4).

Another, less common, solution was to raise workshops above a privy, coal shed, or other outbuilding. If built singly, they are striking because they stand two storeys high on a footprint perhaps no more than 3 or 3.6 m (10 or 12 ft) square. There are a number of single and paired examples at Wollaston. A particularly good row, a mixture of single and paired examples, was built by the local cooperative society at Long Buckby around 1890 and extended in 1898. Raising the working floor gave better light, but there is also a modest economy to be made in roofing materials by building up rather than along. Most of these workshops were intended for the use of a single craftsman, but a few, occupying similar garden-plot locations, are quite substantial, and must signify the employment of a number of hands. The smallest are perhaps four tiny examples in Raunds, built onto the gable of a terrace, also of four houses, called Rotton Row. The variation in the roofing material betrays the fourfold division. Each had its own entrance and ladder stair, and there were originally four identical windows. Seeing their dimensions, one can well appreciate how the craftsman of an earlier period, working in his own home, might be architecturally invisible.

Some workshops continued to be provided within the domestic envelope. Characteristically this is located in a rear range, typically a first-floor room or garret, the externally distinguishing feature being a larger than normal window, probably of casement or horizontally sliding form. This arrangement may be much commoner than we can demonstrate at present. The detached back-yard workshop is uncommon in Northampton, where workers' housing of the period is laid out without back alleys, and thus with no public access to the rear of houses. Map evidence is only partially reliable as a guide.

Under pressure, not just from some employers but from the trade union, outworking diminished markedly after 1894 (Fox 1958), but workshops continued to be built for a few years after 1900 and their use was not uncommon up to the 1960s.

Flexible space

With so many potential variations in the organisation of shoe production, and with the disparate, independent nature of the processes involved, shoe manufacture calls for what modern architects might call 'loose-fit' buildings. This remains true of the traditional industry today. Though they vary in built form, reflecting the optimum requirements at the time of building, their design also embodies an in-built capability for variation. Interiors are unobstructed by fixed plant or masonry partitions. Any divisions required by a particular pattern of use are lightly built of studwork and planking – easily removed and replaced as needs change perhaps, though the spaces they define generally afford sufficient flexibility. The fixed points in a shoe factory – those which require substantial effort to move or remove – are the power plant (if there is one), the stair, the office (because it requires its own fireplace, and is nearly always distinguished architecturally on the exterior), and the external openings. Within those constraints there is a huge capacity for variation.

Once the extent and variety of outwork and specialist sub-contracting are appreciated, certain recurring features of the three-storey factory begin to make more sense. For example, the position of loading doorways varies. Among three-storey examples, some have them on the first floor, some on the second, and some on both; some originate with a single loading doorway and subsequently acquire a second. This is now not quite as mystifying as it might otherwise be. Despite the frequency with which the three-storey model is encountered, it is noticeable that the technical literature of the industry stops short of specifying on which storeys the main processes generally – or ideally – take place. The Goad Plans, which give a detailed picture of practice in central Northampton (but only from 1896 onwards), show considerable variation. Heavy machinery, such as rough-stuff presses or riveting machines, gravitated naturally to the ground floor or the basement. Clickers, who required good natural light to identify defects in the leather, were often located on the top storey where the windows were sometimes supplemented by roof-lights, but often their place was taken by finishing processes and packing. Closing was most commonly performed on the first floor, but naturally when a firm was putting out its closing work the arrangement would be different. The mere inclusion of an outwork or specialist-contractor element in the production chain called for more frequent transhipment of materials, part-made and finished goods, via a possibly greater number of loading doors, than does a regime keeping all processes in-house.

The landscape of workshops

The varied morphology of domestic and workplace accommodation, exemplified in the towns and industrial villages of Northamptonshire, gives expression to a number of contending forces, both social and economic. In a few cases, particularly on the more prestigious main thoroughfares, an arrangement can be found approximating to the frontage house and back-lot factory model familiar from many industrial contexts. On Billing Road, Northampton, for example, three substantial terraced houses are associated with a small three-storey factory in Denmark Road, a side street. In 1890 Thomas Evans was given as the proprietor of the factory and of 7 Billing Road. The house faces south and the factory, which stands at the far end of a long garden plot, faces east, so that to a passer-by there is no obvious connection between the two. At Nos 6 and 5 respectively lived William and Eli Evans, probably older relations of Thomas: in 1877 W & E Evans, boot and shoe manufacturers, were given as the occupants of the factory (Kelly 1877; 1890).

In the more densely built-up suburbs, which developed behind the main thoroughfares in the mid- and late 19th century, plots were rarely of a depth to favour this pattern, though some of the larger workshops mentioned above can be found, mostly taking advantage of corner plots. At 59–63 Moor Road, Rushden, around 1890, one manufacturer built a compact villa alongside a factory now of two storeys beneath a flat roof, but conceivably of three originally. In 1906 house and factory were occupied by Frederick Noble, boot and shoe manufacturer (Kelly 1906). At its most basic, the arrangement makes little concession to gentility, with its aim of rising above, or visually eliding, the source of wealth, and emphasises instead an uncomplicated pride of ownership. Elsewhere in Rushden, at 68–70 Harborough Road, the house (dated 1887) was built at the same time as the factory immediately alongside. Only modestly elevated above its neighbours by its slightly greater width and elaboration, it is more likely to be a manager's house than the owner's. In the late 19th-century boot and shoe industry, however, the proportion of owners who occupied large houses some distance from their works appears to have been relatively small.

It is principally among the smaller factories, and those which arguably we would still wish to call workshops, that direct communication between house and workplace is found. This arrangement has figured already in connection with closing factories. These usually take the form of an attached rear range, commonly taking advantage of sites on street corners in order to provide separate workshop entrances from the lesser thoroughfare. This represents a further gradation in the architectural expression of social relations, emphatically rooting the life and fortunes of the proprietor in his direct and daily involvement in the running of the business. Such proximity between master and man becomes increasingly restricted during the 19th century; beginning as a characteristic of most industries, regardless of scale, it ends as the hallmark of the small business. In the boot and shoe industry it can occasionally be found in connection with quite substantial houses, such as 41 and 43 Colwyn Road, built in the late 1880s in a comparatively prestigious location backing onto the former Northampton Racecourse (Fig 9.5a & b). Here the rear range to the left (43), and the one to the right (41) where the fenestration of the flank wall is not visible, were both attached first-floor workshops. No 41 was occupied by Ernest Remnett, described as a boot manufacturer in 1890, but perhaps more precisely as a manufacturer of closed uppers in 1896, while in the same period 43 belonged to John Letts, a machine closer (Kelly 1890; White 1896).

Relatively rarely, and apparently only in the 1870s, we find more substantial combinations of house and factory under one roof, for which the term 'house-factory' seems appropriate. No. 83 High Street South, Rushden, dated 1874, is a striking example of the type (Fig 9.6). The original occupier is not known, but two stone reliefs set in the gable wall facing the street depict a boot and bootmaker's tools. The distinction between the domestic and industrial elements has been slightly diluted by modern fenestration, but there are still plenty of clues to the internal organisation of this building, determined in large part by the narrowness of the plot, which limits side access to a single narrow alleyway. A further complication is the presence of steeply rising ground.

The building has three storeys, and there is in addition a basement confined to the roadside end. Here there are openings at basement- and second-floor level allowing goods to be taken in from, or put out to, the street using a surviving wall-mounted crane. The house occupies the front of the ground and first floors, sandwiched between factory space on the upper and lower levels. The use of a pale buff brick and a pedimented gable on the street elevation dignifies the residential end of the building, and the break between house and factory is signalled by a change in first-floor window levels on the return elevation. Further confirmation comes from the broad domestic stack on the same wall, containing too many flues for it to be serving a factory. Such buildings embody the same juxtaposition of domestic and production spheres as do the more conventional houses with attached workshops, but the architectural envelope is more nearly seamless and both the scale and the probable organisation of the production sphere proclaim it a factory in all essentials.

Figure 9.5 Substantial houses of the late 1880s at 41–3 Colwyn Rd, Northampton.
a (above): Front
b (below): Contemporary workshops attached at the rear.
(© English Heritage. NMR)

Figure 9.6 An unusual combination of house and factory under a single roof: 83 High St South, Rushden, built in 1874. (© English Heritage. NMR)

A speculative vernacular?

The extent to which the familiar mechanisms for the speculative development of building land influenced the course of the boot and shoe industry remains unclear. Some housing, with associated workshops, was built by manufacturers to establish a convenient pool of outworkers; some was also built by cooperatives, and some was doubtless the outcome of conventional speculation. More interestingly, some of the shoe factories appear to have been speculatively built. Where a single factory is thrown up this may be impossible to demonstrate on architectural evidence alone, but there are a number of paired factories which point to speculative origins. In Victoria Road, Northampton, a street developed to the rear of Wellingborough Road, there is a pair of matching houses and rear-range workshops facing each other across a side street, and probably dating from the early 1870s. To the east, 4 Victoria Road, was the shoe factory of Caleb Brockett in 1877, but by the 1890s was occupied by Thomas Roe, machine sole-sewer to the trade, another specialist process; the west (No. 3) was being used as a small boot and shoe factory in the 1890s. There are slight differences in the fenestration of the two buildings, suggesting that they were not precisely contemporary, but the general similarities decisively indicate a common origin. It is probable that some smaller production units such as these were true speculations, reflecting a growing demand for such premises in the 1870s. As discussed above, they were of a scale to fit comfortably into the kind of street grid adopted for predominantly residential development, and though corner sites were preferable for industrial use they were not essential.

The survey of boot and shoe industry buildings also identified a series of paired, or 'double', factories. In the absence of documentary confirmation it is less certain that these are truly speculative. It may be that builders with experience of the boot and shoe trade engaged clients and only set about building when they were assured of occupants. Nevertheless, the resulting building type is indicative of the builder's reading of the market rather than the occupant's self-projection. Henry Martin, described in 1884 as a bricklayer, stonemason, and builder, who lived at 63 Victoria Road and had premises in Dunster Street and Thenford Street, built a number of 'double' factories (Wright 1884).

The earliest in inception were probably 'Two New Shoe Warehouses / Shakespeare Road Northampton / for M[r] Henry Martin', for which designs by the architect Charles Dorman were submitted in May 1882.[3] The building has been converted to residential use, but the surviving ground-floor plan shows two essentially similar units, their differences in layout occasioned by their position where Shakespeare Road, Hervey Street, and Carey Street meet at a staggered junction. Each had a rough-stuff room and a riveters' room on the ground floor, and in each case there was no intercommunication between the two rooms, a lobby opening off the street providing access to both. Map evidence indicates that only the Carey Street 'warehouse' was built by 1884. The second appears to have been built by 1890, when the shoe-making firm of Eyre Brothers gave their address as Shakespeare Road, but it was not built entirely in accordance with the original design. It does, however, appear to have formed a separate unit, and dual occupation can be confirmed from directory sources for several decades.

The Unicorn Works, 20–26 St Michaels Road, Northampton, is the most straightforward expression of the type (Fig 9.7). Built shortly before 1896 on what had been laid out initially (but not built upon) as four plots, it is a reflecting pair of identical factory units, divided by a fire-break wall rising clear of the roof. In each case the entrance and loading doorway are placed in the end bay, on the rear of which a sanitary turret projects. In 1896 the building was occupied by two shoe manufacturers: Beale & Co in 24, and Wheeler, Hull & Co in what, owing to the origins of the plots, was numbered 20 and 22. By 1899, however, the works was in single occupation, and remained so.

On the corner of Artizan Road and Henry Street, Northampton, Martin built another 'double' factory (now Meadows House) to an unsigned design, approved on 27 March 1893.[4] Here the twin circumstances of a street-corner location and a relatively steep fall of ground combined to disguise the pattern.

Figure 9.7 The Unicorn Works, 20–26 St Michaels Rd, Northampton, a 'double' factory of the mid-1890s. (© English Heritage. NMR)

Again, two factory units are separated by a crosswall, but here they are additionally set apart by a change in floor levels. Owing to the irregularity of the plot the entrances and rear ranges are planned differently in each case but the accommodation is essentially the same. In 1896 only the shoemaking firm of Flack & Durrant was listed at the address – possibly an indication that factory units could be difficult to let – but the building formed the premises of two separate shoe manufacturers in 1906. Dual occupation ceased probably in 1912, shortly after the leather-dressing firm of J T Meadows & Sons took it over (White 1896; Kelly 1906).[5] Finally, it is worth observing that the phenomenon of purpose-built 'double' factories has only been noted in Northampton. However, in Kettering around 1897 a pair of two-storey pavilion-like factories were erected with frontages a few yards apart on Shaftesbury Street, but addresses in two side streets: 25 Harcourt Street and 28 Roseberry Street.

A culture of workshops

The 'house-factories' of the 1870s account for only a small proportion of the total number put up in that decade, but coupled with other arrangements in which domestic accommodation is provided in close proximity to the workplace, they indicate something of the enduring bond between the domestic and production spheres. The 'double' factories of the two succeeding decades are no more representative, but they conform in scale with the majority of contemporary factories on the three-storey model, and through their essentially speculative origins highlight the modest ranking of the majority of boot and shoe manufacturers in this period. In their different ways these building types draw attention to, and help to define, a particular and numerically dominant stratum of activity within the industry. The organisation of an industry around, or to include, smaller workshops tells us in addition something about the disparate nature of the processes involved. Together these varied building types have the potential to tell us a great deal about the broader socio-economic context of the industry, and prompt a question as to whether there is a distinctive *culture of workshops*.

One way in which this can be approached is by pointing to the very considerable fluidity that the numerous small and medium-sized workshops and small factories foster in the conduct of the trade. They belong to an economic stratum in which fixed capital is relatively small, or even insignificant, with the result that the costs of entry into the business are low. There is abundant anecdotal evidence that the industry was particularly fluid for just this reason (Anon 1916). A craftsman with initiative or good fortune might rise to a managerial position in which commercial skills could be learnt and contacts made. Then, with only a modest capital outlay in materials, he could establish a business of his own, typically in one of the larger workshops or smaller factories. Premises and machinery could all be rented. If he prospered he could expect to move to successively larger premises, or to enlarge his existing building. A number of sites illustrate the latter course particularly well. In Coleman Rd, Raunds, the firm of Tebbutt & Hall added and extended workshops several times on the rear of their house, between 1884 and c1900, when they added what is unequivocally a shoe *factory* at the far end of the extensions (and one of the last of the characteristic three-storey type to be built in the county). Burns Cottage, 7 Burns Road, Northampton, was built in 1883, as a date-stone records, with a rear-range workshop. By 1906 it had grown to include the neighbouring plot, and both frontages, which retain domestic sashes on the first floor, have the unlikely distinction of lying beneath a north-lit factory roof. Many small masters, and a few larger ones, failed in the process of self-betterment, but throughout the second half of the 19th century there is a constant replenishment of aspiring entrepreneurs, keeping this very finely graduated building stock in pretty constant use.

Only in the first decade of the 20th century does this dynamism falter seriously. The last three-storey factories were built about 1900 (thereafter multi-storey factories are mostly the product of inherited site constraints). By 1905, in Northampton, the Goad insurance plans showed a considerable number of former shoe factories of the three-storey type lying

Figure 9.8 This group of buildings on Robert St (left) and Connaught Rd (right) in Northampton typifies the mixed, modest-scale environment to which the boot and shoe industry gave rise in its late 19th-century heyday. (© English Heritage. NMR)

vacant (Goad 1905). By then the very large and heavily mechanised factory, following American practice and usually arranged (sometimes with the exception of the office accommodation) on a single floor, had become the dominant force in the industry, making little or no use of outworking. Manfield's new factory, built in 1893 on Wellingborough Road, Northampton, though not quite the first of its kind,[6] set a pattern which was rapidly adopted elsewhere in the county. The emergence of these factories coincides with the rise of the factory chains of shoe shops – Manfield's, Church's, Barratt's, and so on – itself a break with the earlier practice of leaving marketing to London merchants and their retail connections. This is perhaps more than coincidental, as the more elaborate new factories with their attractive office fronts tend to be invoked as part of the marketing of the firms' brands, their appearance in advertising and on letterheads symbolising the achievement of vertical integration.

By contrast the world of the workshop and the small factory, intermingled with the dwellings of the workforce, is one in which horizontal links, based on personal acquaintance and mutual obligation, still predominate; one in which many factories and workshops have no need of self-advertisement through showy architecture or the display of company names. At the opposite extreme to the signature factory, outworking is an almost entirely self-effacing system, in which the shoemaker makes his pitch in the labour market by presenting himself at the manufacturer's door. His own workplace has no need to announce its presence, since the marketing of the product is carried on by others at one or more removes, and his workshop may therefore be tucked away at the rear of a garden plot, or even in the garret room of a rear range.

The foregoing paragraphs move a long way away, perhaps, from the familiar preoccupation with identifying, analysing, and evaluating individual structures illustrative of an industry, and some way beyond even the development of typologies and the charting of the evolution of an industry through the evidence of its buildings. Yet the further step is a necessary one if the full potential of material evidence is to be realised, particularly where it relates to small- and medium-scale enterprises which typically leave quite scanty documentary evidence. Even if the case could be proved by documentary research, however, it is far from certain that the surviving documents, on their own, would prompt the same line of enquiry. Though the answers may falter, the questions are still worth asking.

A good impression of the culture of workshops is conveyed by a relatively well-preserved block in north Northampton, at the junction of Robert Street and Connaught St. Although Robert Street began to be developed in the late 1860s the buildings in Fig 9.8 mostly date from the 1880s and 1890s. They typify the generally modest scale of the shoe factories and workshops, their close connection with housing, and their continuing involvement with elements of outworking. Reading from left to right, there is first a three-storey cabinet-maker's works, later adapted to incorporate a shoe factory, then three two-storey houses, of which the left-hand example had a second front entrance leading to a machine closer's workshop at the rear. Next there is a three-storey currier's with the distinctive tall openings of the drying floor at the top of the building; this building was extended towards the right in the 1890s to engross a former machine closer's house and workshop, and this accounts for some of the anomalies in the fenestration. Then on the corner there is a house and contemporary rear range which directories describe as a shoe factory in the 1890s, though conforming to a typical plan for a machine closer's workshop; it has recently been rendered and formerly had large three-light windows to the upper floor of the rear range. Moving into Connaught Street, there is a more conventional three-storey shoe factory – known as the South Place Factory until about 1903 when the firm of Frederick Cook relocated to a new single-storey factory in Long Buckby, taking the factory name with them. Then follow a pair of houses, the long frontage of a substantial builder's yard and finally another three-storey shoe factory. Taken all together, the view typifies an industry which, for a transitional period stretching from the 1850s to about 1900, is organised very much around what may justly be termed industrialised houses on the one hand and domesticated factories on the other.

Notes

1. The work was undertaken with the financial support of Northamptonshire Heritage, the planning arm of Northamptonshire County Council. We are grateful for the support of past and present staff of Northamptonshire Heritage, particularly Ann Bond, Martin Ellison, and Jennifer Ballinger. The fieldwork and research have involved, at different periods, the author, Jonathan Cooke, Imogen Grundon, Kathryn Hilsden, Kathryn Morrison, and Andrew Williams. The photographs are by Patricia Payne and the drawing is by Allan Adams.
2. Advertisement in the *Northampton Mercury*, 13 September 1873. This reference was found in the archives of the Northamptonshire Industrial Archaeology Group (NIAG). I am grateful to Geoffrey Starmer and NIAG for permission to consult this material.
3. NRO, Northampton Borough Council Building Plans, D3.
4. NRO, Northampton Borough Council Building Plans, R94: 'Plan of 2 New Shoe Factories in Artizan Rd & Henry St for H. Martin Esq.'.
5. In 1916 Meadows & Sons were said to have acquired the factory in 1911 and to have doubled it in size the following year. Since there is no difference in the building's footprint as depicted on the 1899 and 1924 25 Inch Ordnance Survey maps it seems likely that the firm moved into one half of the building in 1911 and took over the other half in 1912. The fenestration, which incorporates two hopper lights in each opening, is characteristic of the thorough ventilation required by leather works, and was probably introduced by Meadows & Sons.
6. The Albion Works, Stamford Road, Kettering, was also built on a single storey, but two years earlier. It is now demolished. Of Manfield's only the office front survives.

10 Workshops of the Sheffield cutlery and edge-tool trades *by Nicola Wray*

In 1823 Sheaf Works (Fig 10.1) was built in Sheffield with the intention of '... centralising on the spot all the various processes through which iron must pass ... until fashioned into a razor, penknife, or other article of use' (Hunter 1869, 253). Built for the manufacturer William Greaves alongside the recently opened Sheffield and Tinsley Canal, it was the first fully integrated cutlery factory in the town, and is said to have been the first to have relied exclusively on steam power (Giles 1995, 1). Globe Works (Fig 10.2), built for Ibbotson and Roebuck, followed shortly afterwards, both sites distinguished by their imposing Classical-style offices of fine ashlar stone, fronting substantial complexes of furnace, forge, and workshop buildings. It might thus be thought that the early 19th century saw the rise of a system of large-scale urban cutlery and edge-tool factories, impelled by the introduction of steam power and an improved transport infrastructure.

First impressions can however be deceptive, and research into the buildings associated with the cutlery and edge-tool trades, supported by documentary evidence and contemporary accounts, reveals a much more complex story. In 1844, *The Penny Magazine* (Anon 1844b, 167–8) commented upon cutlery manufacture in Sheffield, stating that:

> ... there are several modes of conducting the manufacture, but the factory system is not one of them. By this we mean that there is no one large building, under a central authority, in which a piece of steel goes in at one door, and comes out at another converted into knives, scissors and razors. Nearly all articles of cutlery made in Sheffield travel about the town several times before they are finished.

Yet at Sheaf Works, and probably also Globe Works, the primary manufacture of steel was undertaken, as well as all subsequent processes from forging and grinding through to the assembly of finished articles for sale.

It is that apparent contradiction which forms the main theme of this chapter, which will suggest that industrial growth was achieved not by the factory

Figure 10.1 Sheaf Works, built in 1823 as the first fully integrated cutlery factory in Sheffield. This mid-19th-century view clearly shows the proximity to the new transport infrastructure, and the chimneys allude to the use of steam power. The depiction of cementation and crucible furnaces indicates that primary steel manufacture was undertaken on site as well as all subsequent manufacturing processes required to produce finished goods. (© Bob Hawkins)

Figure 10.2 Globe Works, built in 1825 as a cutlery and edge-tool works, has an imposing, ashlar office range with workshops hidden behind in a similar manner to Sheaf Works, again presenting the impression of a unified complex to the bystander. (© English Heritage. NMR)

system becoming dominant, but by the expansion of the traditional, established, small-scale workshop culture. Technological factors, such as the development of machinery, were relatively insignificant, many of the manufacturing processes continuing to be undertaken using hand-skills, and organisational factors, such as supervision of the workforce, were not a catalyst for the development of factory working. Cutlery and edge-tool factories in Sheffield were, rather, the assemblages of different workshop types and associated buildings on one site, not always, or perhaps even commonly, under the control of a single manufacturing employer. The group of often independently occupied workshops was known in the local terminology as a 'works', rather than a 'factory', a term redolent of capitalist masters overseeing the manufacture of an article by a directly employed labour-force. It can therefore be argued that cutlery and edge-tool workshops were not defined by size, location, or lack of power, but by working practices: a workshop may constitute part of a powered works or be a single unpowered building, the common factor being the provision of work space for individual manufacturers, often working independently of large-scale employers.

Local history of the cutlery and edge-tool trades

Both cutlery and edge-tool manufacture had a long association with the Sheffield region having been established in the Middle Ages, encouraged initially by the presence of iron ore, timber for charcoal used as fuel for blast furnaces, and good sandstone for grindstones. By the 16th century Sheffield had become England's major provincial centre of cutlery manufacture (Hey 1991, 2) attracting comment from John Leland in 1540 (Hey 1998, 17). In the late 16th century the process of grinding blades, previously been undertaken using hand-turned grindstones, was mechanised. The fast-flowing rivers and streams were harnessed to provide power, giving Sheffield a lead over manufacturers in London and on the continent (Lloyd 1913, 44). A century later, the 1672 Hearth Tax Returns list about 600 metalworkers'

138 *The vernacular workshop*

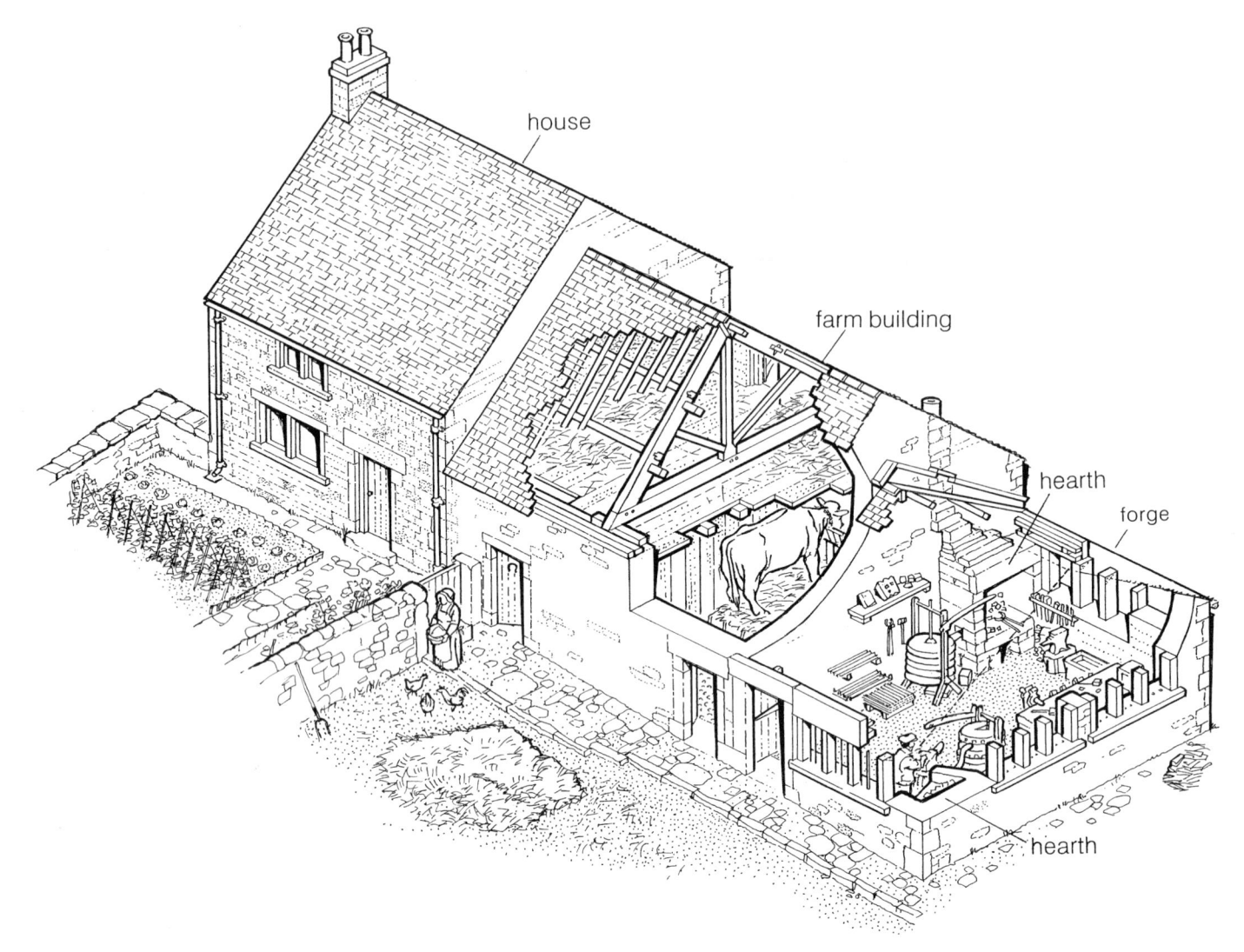

Figure 10.3 Cut-away reconstruction of Sykehouse, Dungworth Green, an early 19th-century rural complex comprising a house, an agricultural building and a forge, illustrating a dual economy of agriculture and metal-working. Later 19th-century rural workshops appear to have been independent from food production, indicating that metal-working had become a full-time occupation. (© English Heritage. NMR)

smithies in and around Sheffield, 224 of which were in the town itself, or one smithy for every 2.2 houses (Hey 1998, 60). In the early 18th century, Defoe described Sheffield as 'very populous and large, the streets narrow and the houses dark and black, occasioned by the continued smoke of the forges, which are always at work' (Defoe 1724–26, 482). Subsequently, the local innovation, by Benjamin Huntsman, of crucible steel, a material which was recognised world-wide as an improvement on any steel previously available, laid the foundation of Sheffield's steel industry (Barraclough 1976, 13). As the town prospered its population grew from 10,000 in 1736 to 45,000 in 1801, and to over 400,000 by 1901 (Barraclough 1976, 8); ten years later, Sheffield was the fifth largest city in England, behind only London, Birmingham, Manchester, and Liverpool (Hey 1998, 147). Its expansion was a combination of a spectacular growth in the traditional 'light trades' of cutlery and edge tools, and the establishment of the newer 'heavy trades' of bulk steel production, armaments manufacture, shipbuilding, and general heavy engineering, in which true factory production, in complexes of huge size and requiring great capital investment, was the norm.

The cutlery trades in Sheffield were initially regulated through the manor court, which issued marks and insisted upon common working practices, including a seven-year apprenticeship (Hey 1991, 55). In 1624 the craftsmen became self-governing, when an Act of Parliament handed jurisdiction over the cutlery trades in Hallamshire and six miles beyond to the Company of Cutlers. The new company was empowered to control the apprenticeship system, admit free men, make orders and act on behalf of the membership. Craftsmen, known as cutlers, originally had all-round proficiency, undertaking each of the three distinct aspects of the manufacturing process, namely, hand forging blanks; grinding the forged blades; and hafting, assembling and

Figure 10.4 Interior of Shepherd Wheel, a late 18th-century water-powered grinding workshop on the Porter Brook. In the foreground is a grinding trough, with the grindstone and 'horse' on which the grinder sat to sharpen the blades. The belt drive from the main drive shaft and the gearing from the waterwheel can be seen in the background. (© English Heritage. NMR)

finishing the goods ready for sale. Having served an apprenticeship, the cutler needed little capital to set himself up in business, only requiring somewhere to work which was equipped with a coal-fired hearth; bellows; an anvil set on a stone base, known as a stithy and stock; a coultrough for hardening; a 'workboard'; and various vices and hammers.

Urban cutlers, who practised metalworking as a full-time occupation, concentrated upon manufacturing higher-quality knives. Seventeenth-century probate inventories suggest that one in four urban cutlers had work chambers but no smithy (Hey 1991, 94), so that their effort was concentrated upon finishing goods to a high standard, rather than forging. In contrast, rural craftsmen, who generally produced common wares such as basic knives, scythes and sickles, also engaged in agriculture. Documentary evidence from land surveys and probate inventories describes early rural workshops as smithies of one bay, forming part of a farm complex (Hey 1972, 18–20). A rare surviving example is Sykehouse, Dungworth Green, an early 19th-century complex comprising a house, an agricultural building, and a smithy or forge (Fig 10.3). The forge contained two hearths in opposite corners, indicating that two men, perhaps more, worked there; the number depending upon the size of articles being made, since larger blades required two men for forging. The workspace was lit on three sides by large mullioned windows, possibly unglazed to aid ventilation and secured by square-section vertical bars.

Whilst individual craftsmen worked in humble workshops adjacent to or within their houses, the 16th century saw the development of a second type of workshop. This was the 'cutlers' wheel', a building which housed a number of water-driven grindstones used to make the cutting edge of blades (Fig 10.4). The cost of erecting and fitting out these much larger workshops, and the need for access to water, meant they were far beyond the resources of the artisan craftsmen and so they were erected by the landowners. Cutlers' wheels were probably first built during the time of George, Sixth Earl of Shrewsbury (c1528–90), the richest nobleman in the north of England, who owned the manor of Sheffield. He took an active interest in developing the mineral wealth of his estates,[1] and saw the cutlers' wheels as another way of raising revenue. In 1637, John Harrison, employed by the then lords of the manor, the Dukes of Norfolk, reported that the rivers were 'very profitable unto the lord in regard of the mills and cutler wheeles that are turned by theire streames, which weeles are imployed for the grinding of knives by four or five hundred Master Workmen' (quoted in Hey 1991, 26).

The wheels were not intended to challenge the existing manufacturing process by creating factories for wage labour, but to provide to the craftsmen with mechanised workshops. Initially, craftsmen engaged in the entire manufacturing process, taking their blades to a wheel, renting space, and grinding their own wares. A similar arrangement occurred in the woollen trade in Yorkshire where tenants undertook work for individual clients in public water-powered fulling, scribbling, and carding mills built by landowners, speculators, and wealthy clothiers. Contemporary commentators on the woollen industry also distinguished between this type of establishment, generally referred to merely as a 'mill', and a 'factory' where a manufacturer employed wage-earning labour and used mechanised processes to make up his own raw materials into yarn and later cloth (Berg 1994, 226). In the cutlery industry the formation of a Grinders' Sick Club in 1748 indicates that grinding had in general become a distinct trade (Hey 1991, 61). Grinders rented their own work space within a cutlers' wheel, and undertook work for small-scale craftsmen in other branches of the trade, meaning that such buildings were in effect in multiple tenancy.

Organisation of labour

Over the course of the 18th century the division of labour into specific processes developed markedly, increasing specialisation in a particular product resulting in complex networks of industrial organisation and articles passing between different types of craftsmen to reach completion.[2] Despite the division of labour, which is often seen as characteristic of the factory system, a high degree of craft skill was retained, a table-knife cutler, for example, 'undertaking up to forty distinct operations' (Lloyd 1913, 191). Workers who gained a high level of skill might become 'little mesters', or independent craftspeople who worked on a small scale, employing perhaps as few as one or two other workers. These working practices were described as 'democratie industrielle' by Leon Faucher, a Frenchman who wrote about manufacturing techniques in England, whilst Friedrich Engels called the little mesters neither genuine proletarians, since they lived in part upon the work of their apprentices, nor genuine bourgeois, since their principal means of support was their own work (Engels 1845, 207). A freeman of the Cutlers' Company had the right to set up as an independent master, to strike his own mark, and to take apprentices, provided that he was 'the owner of his work himself' (Lloyd 1913, 139–40). Those had served their apprenticeship but were financially unable to set themselves up as 'little mesters' were known initially as 'journeymen', a term subsequently abolished, and replaced by a broader useage of mester, with the result that, by the early 19th century, there were two classes of little mester. The first were factors who in many instances did not employ workmen directly, but subcontracted work to small manufacturers, some of whom formed the second kind – working craftsmen, who owned their own tools, rented working space, and employed a number of apprentices and men engaged by the week at a net wage. The perceived independence of the craftsmen was underlined by their provision of their own tools, and their payment of rent for work-space and power. Little mesters of this kind might rent space in a tenement factory, or work for one firm and be situated in its premises; if that firm did not provide them with enough work, their status as rent payers meant they were free to undertake work for another.

The small-scale undertaking of work for larger manufacturers or factors upheld the organisational forms of the domestic system of manufacture, albeit in a more complicated form. The perpetuation of the system was perceived to be mutually beneficial; the workers' skills, passed down through generations, secured them a quasi-independence and ability to manage their own work schedule as they saw fit. This was epitomised by the convention of a day of rest, known as 'Saint Monday', compensated for by an intensification of work towards the end of the week, and also 'Bull Week' immediately before Christmas when feverish activity made up the time and money which would be lost during the holiday. Irregular working hours had been established at an early date, since periodic excess or deficiency of the water supply made grinding intermittent, and conditioned working patterns even in the 19th century despite the regularity offered by steam power. In the 1860s it was recorded that many works stayed open for longer on Thursdays and Fridays, as well as during Bull Week when people might work for as long as from four in the morning to ten at night (BPP 1865, 45).

The factory system had few obvious advantages for the larger manufacturers as the processes continued to require long-established hand skills, even when, as in the case of grinding, steam superseded water power. The best-quality cutlery was made by hand, as it was said that 'the highest excellence can be attained only by the employment of intelligent hand labour' (Pawson & Brailsford 1879, 253), machinery only being employed for ancillary operations such as drilling and boring. There was also, perhaps, initially a collusion by the large manufacturers in the little mesters' belief that their work was best. File cutters, for example, showed a natural antipathy towards the machines used in Manchester and Birmingham, believing in the honesty of their handicraft as illustrated in the contemporary doggeral 'So unite well together, by good moral means, Don't be intimidated by these infernal machines; Let them boast as they will – and though the press clamour, After all, lads, there's nothing like wrist, chisel, and hammer' (Pawson & Brailsford 1862, 150).

This sentiment freed the manufacturers from the need to invest in machinery, while the little mesters' working practices enabled the large manufacturers to use independent labour and to hire work by the most economical means rather than having to tie up capital in taking on permanent employees. The putting out of work also allowed flexibility; large-scale manufacturers were able to offer an immense variety of types and designs of cutlery, which would have been impossible under the standardisation required by mechanised production.[3] In practice little mesters became increasingly beholden to the factors, and ruthless exploitation of little mesters often occurred during times of depression, when their numbers increased dramatically as, in an attempt to earn a living, individuals with no capital were often obliged to sell their goods at minimal prices to achieve a weekly income.[4]

Form of urban workshops

The 19th century saw a rapidly rising demand for cutlery and edge-tools, and consequently an increased scale of operation. In 1865 it was noted that, in the case of cutlery manufacture, 'House or garret work has been decreasing for the last twenty years and is now almost gone' (BPP 1865, 44), with independent little mesters finding organisational advantage in concentration within purpose-built workshops, situated close to other processes. In the town three main types of workshop were built, replicating the separation of processes brought about by the working practices of the little mesters – forges, grinding wheels, and cutlers' workshop ranges.

Figure 10.5 Hand forge, one of a row on the ground floor of the west workshop range at Portland Works. The forge shows the distinctive form of a split stable door and adjoining casement window under a single lintel. (© Crown Copyright. NMR)

Though one works complex might contain several processes they were kept apart, either in separate buildings, or more often, on different floors of the same building.

Urban hand forges generally comprised a row of individual rooms with hearths, offering a personal working space for each forger. Sometimes they were single-storied, as at Globe Works, where a row was built against the north-west boundary wall.[5] More commonly, space was an issue, and they were placed on the ground floor of a workshop range, as seen in the west workshop range at Portland Works, built in the late 1870s or early 1880s (Fig 10.5). These forges have a distinctive form consisting of a stable-type split door with an adjoining casement window, both under a single lintel. Variations are found at Trafalgar Works, which had individual doorways, though the large windows lighting each forge did not share their lintels, whilst Brooklyn Works and some of the smaller sites had individual forges with wide arched openings onto the courtyard.[6] Occasionally numbers of forges were housed in a single building, as at Alma Works, Barker's Pool, where 'instead of being each a small separate building, as used to be the case, [they] are open to each other for the purpose of ventilation through the whole length of the building, without anything to break the free current of air' (Pawson & Brailsford 1862, 158). An illustration of the hand forge at Cyclops Works (Fig 10.6) shows an open yard elevation, the roof being supported upon an arcade of cast-iron columns and shaped girders, in the manner of railway station architecture, though each pair of forgers retained their own working space with a hearth. No extant examples of this kind have been found, although one of the forge ranges at Brooklyn Works shows a similar principle, being a single room with five segmental arched openings into the yard, and six internal flues for hearths.

Grinding workshops, or 'wheels', had existed as separate premises since the 16th century, and despite the late 18th-century introduction of steam rather than water power to drive the grindstones, the general layout remained unaltered into the 20th century.[7] A deep room, or 'hull', was lit by large, closely spaced windows in the front wall, with an unfenestrated rear wall along which the line-shaft ran. The grinders worked facing the windows, the grindstones being hung on spindles over troughs set in the floor at right-angles to the line-shaft, from which they were driven via leather belts; a water-wheel or steam engine was located outside the room. Many of the steam-powered wheels in the town were much larger than their rural counterparts, which relied upon an uncertain water supply. In 1865 it was stated that '... in town, where space is valuable, the work-rooms are built back-to-back, and floor above floor, the lower rooms often being vaulted to support the weight of the machinery above' (BPP 1865, 4). Goad's 1896 *Insurance Plans of Soho and Union Wheels*, both now demolished, show that this resulted in a distinctive plan type (Fig 10.7). Soho Wheel had two long ranges of back-to-back hulls, linked by centrally placed engine and boiler houses and a 38m (125ft) chimney.[8] Union Wheel was in effect half the plan of Soho, with a single, two-storey range of double-depth hulls and centrally placed power plant projecting on one side.[9] The central location of the engine house ensured optimum distribution of power throughout the buildings, the line-shaft running along the spine walls between the hulls. At Union Wheel the power on the upper floor ran along a narrow spine corridor, transferred from the engine by a rope race. Urban grinding hulls might also be set on the lower floor or floors of workshop ranges. Lit by large, closely spaced windows, they sometimes have brick jack-arched ceilings to support the weight of machinery in the upper-floor hulls, and are clearly distinguishable externally by their blind rear walls (Fig 10.8). Though the physical working space and the grinding undertaken in both types of buildings was similar, separate grinding premises were called 'public wheels', while those located within a works where

142 *The vernacular workshop*

Figure 10.6   Open hand-forge range at Cyclops Works in the mid-19th century, praised by contemporary commentators for their superior ventilation in comparison to the rows of individual hand forges commonly built. No extant examples survive. (© Sheffield Local Studies Library)

other manufacturing processes also took place, were called 'private wheels' (BPP 1865, 4). The former, built as commercial speculations and owned by persons who had no interest in them beyond receiving the rent and supplying the power, are clear indicators of the working arrangements of grinders, the latter were generally found in the larger, powered works, though there too the manufacturer usually let off parts to individual grinders (BPP 1865, 4).

The resistance to the use of machinery for traditional hand-craft processes such as cutling is apparent from the form of unpowered urban workshop ranges, even in large, powered works. Such ranges were generic, utilitarian buildings, used interchangeably for a profusion of products. They were usually brick-built, and between two and four storeys high. Floors tended to be built of timber, as they required no great strength for machinery,

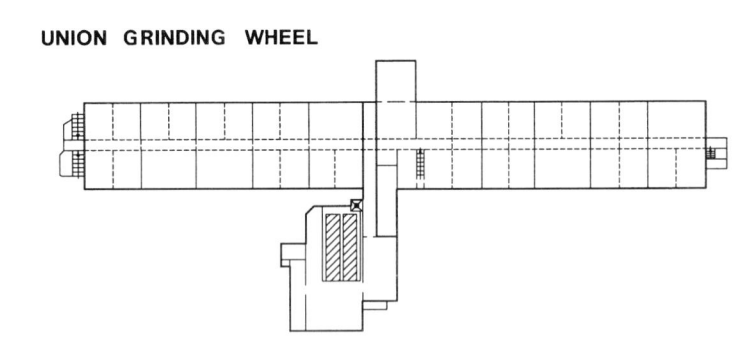

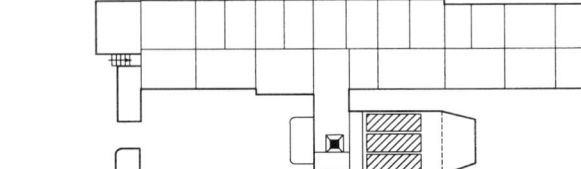

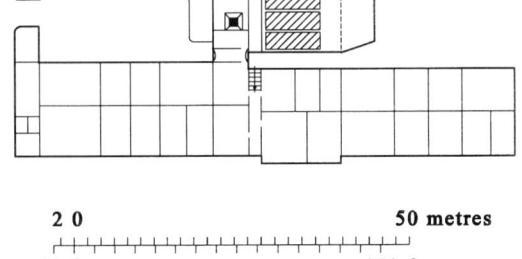

Figure 10.7 (right)   Soho and Union Wheels (demolished) showing the distinctive plan-type of urban grinding wheels, which were built with back-to-back work rooms (hulls) to save on space, with centrally-placed steam engine houses to ensure optimum distribution of power throughout the buildings. (© English Heritage. NMR)

Figure 10.8 Rear wall of workshop range at Beehive Works. The blind wall is indicative of grinding hulls on the lower floors, while the two closely-fenestrated upper floors would have been used as cutlers' workshops for the assembly and finishing of goods. (© Crown Copyright. NMR)

possibly indicating the undertaking of a specific process – in this case file-cutting, for which large windows lit the intricate cutting process.[10] Elsewhere however, file-cutting was undertaken in premises such as 35 Well Meadow Street, and Baltic Steel Works, with rows of closely spaced standard-size windows, like those in the upper floors of the range in Beehive Works. The lack of specific characteristics meant that the floors could be used by many different types of craftsmen, as contemporary trade directories show. In 1888, the workshop ranges at Venture Works in Arundel Street were occupied by six separate businesses, among them a scale cutter, a cutlery manufacturer, a pearl dealer, a brass turner, and a silver cutlery mounter (Kelly 1888, 55). Documentary sources make it clear that workshops were often in multiple occupation, even within larger integrated works. Craftsmen tended to change from year to year, and although they were generally involved in some branch of the metal trades, the specific type of work varied considerably. The prevalence of multiple occupation, often planned from the beginning, might be expected to find expression in provision of segregated access for different users. Often there are external steps, but this is generally where the ground floor has a different use, such as accommodating hand forges, and sometimes internal staircases were centrally placed, with a room to either side, as in the south range at Butcher's Wheel. Most separate doorways, however, were later adaptations, and access, segregation, and security must have been very much an *ad hoc* matter, with working spaces divided according to ever-changing circumstances.

Hand forges, grinding wheels, and general-purpose workshop ranges were built in a variety of combinations and capacities depending upon the size of the site, though the basic forms did not vary. Early integrated sites such as Sheaf Works and Globe Works, and the mid-19th-century Baltic Works, were all built for large cutlery and edge-tool manufacturers. The perceived benefits of the gathering together of various processes also resulted in the inclusion of crucible and cementation furnaces for primary steel production. While individual hand processes continued to be undertaken in workshops, a factory system was initiated for the process of steel production, which relied upon teams of directly employed men working in relays, often round the clock. The buildings were arranged round one or more secure yards entered through a covered cart entrance, which in the built-up urban environment also acted as light wells. Furnaces and grinding wheels were generally located towards the rear of sites, with the cleaner, quieter, unpowered processes adjoining, or partially contained within, the front ranges. The status of these works was emphasised by the inclusion of a front office and showroom of some architectural distinction, designed to suggest the business acumen of the owner to the outside world, and to screen the utilitarian workshop ranges from view.

though this left them open to the risk of fire from the hearths used to heat metal and for space-heating. Flues from the hearths either rose above the eaves, or above the higher rear wall in narrow workshops which had single-pitch roofs. Narrow workshops were a response to the restrictions of urban sites, enabling the interior to be well lit despite it only being possible to fenestrate the front wall due to the presence of buildings on an adjacent plot. Windows were generally small-paned wooden casements, with L-shaped iron strapping to the corners. Unlike workshop windows in Birmingham, the material was wood, despite the metalworking context, probably because it was cheaper. The lower levels of workshop ranges might contain space for hand forging or grinding, but sometimes the ground floors had particularly wide casement windows, as in the rear range of the main yard at Beehive Works,

Figure 10.9 The Garden Street area, on the west side of Sheffield, was characterised in the 19th century by the close association of working-class houses with contemporary purpose-built workshops, arranged round narrow yards. (© Crown Copyright. NMR)

Though large urban complexes, like Beehive Works, Eye Witness Works, and Portland Works, continued to be built during the second half of the 19th century, renewed fragmentation of the processes also occurred, with primary steel production no longer included on site. The majority of surviving crucible furnaces are in small-scale buildings erected at the same time as independent specialist steel works. For the cutlery manufacturer, this removed the expense of having directly to employ the steel workers, and, as with the rest of the process, it created the freedom to buy in raw steel from the most appropriate, or cheapest, source.

The building of integrated works by large cutlery and edge-tool manufacturers in turn stimulated outworking and encouraged the building of numerous smaller, often unpowered works. Trade directories show that these works were frequently multiple occupation, and also that their line of business changed numerous times. Most little mesters would have been unable to raise the capital required to erect purpose-built workshop ranges and, though a large proportion of owners remain unidentified, the majority were from occupations outside the cutlery and edge-tool trades (Beauchamp 1996, 128). This suggests that there was much speculative building of tenement works for the little mesters who supplied larger manufacturers and factors. It is noticeable that during the first half of the 19th century the smaller urban works lacked the uniformity of layout found amongst the large works. Many of them grew up piecemeal over time and were relatively poorly built. Often there was no distinct front office and showroom range, a building which would not be needed if a site contained a series of tenement workshops for small-scale craftsmen.

The smallest surviving urban works comprise workshop ranges associated with contemporary working-class housing, built in the second quarter of the 19th century in the Garden Street area (Fig 10.9). In some formerly respectable residential areas houses were converted for industrial use, Venture Works on Arundel Street originating in the late 18th century as the northernmost of a terrace of three houses before becoming a tenement works in the 19th century. John Watts's Cutlery Works on Lam-

Figure 10.10 Anglo Works, built in the second quarter of the 19th century, comprises a single workshop range with an office at one end. (© English Heritage. NMR)

bert Street began life in the late 18th or early 19th century as five independent residential properties, possibly with workshops in the rear gardens like those in Garden Street. As the area became primarily industrial the yards were gradually filled with further workshops and workers' housing, and ultimately some of the original frontage houses were either rebuilt or converted to industrial premises, resulting in the complex layout shown on the 1850 25 Inch Ordnance Survey map. Leah's Yard, on Cambridge Street, also developed piecemeal, from a site occupied by a horn merchant, a trade related to the production of knife and cutlery handles. The original purpose-built workshop range which incorporated a mainly open ground floor for the storage of horn, was altered, and the complex extended as the number of occupiers rose. In 1883 there were eight tenants comprising a silver and electro-plated goods manufacturer, a horn and bone merchant, an ivory dealer and cutter, a sportsman's knife manufacturer, a penknife manufacturer, a spring knife manufacturer, a silver buffer, and a table knife hafter (Kelly 1883, 69). In the following year the mention of Henry Hobson, engine tenter, amongst the occupants, indicates the introduction of steam power to the previously unpowered site (Giles 1998c, 1–2). A different arrangement was found among a few earlier unpowered works occupied by either a single manufacturer or a factor, as at Anglo Works, Trippet Lane (Fig 10.10) (Giles 1998a, 1), and Lion Works, Arundel Street (Giles 1998d, 1), both built in the second quarter of the 19th century. A single workshop range, constructed end-on to the street, also incorporated an office or showroom in an echo of the large manufacturers' works.

Smaller works of the second half of the 19th century tended to follow the conventions of the large works much more closely, being laid out from inception with a front office range and a covered cart entrance through to workshop ranges disposed round a yard to the rear. Some works provided power in an auxiliary role to hand processes, in the form of small steam engines, or later, oil or gas engines, with electric motors being installed from the early 20th century. Typical examples of these smaller premises include Montrose Works, Harland

Street, Challenge Works, 94 Arundel Street (Fig 10.11), Clifton Works, John Street, and Surrey Works, Heeley. The imitation of larger works, rather than the earlier haphazard development, may have been due in part to an increasing ease in obtaining finance, but may also be seen as an indication of the rise of the factor. Challenge Works, with its imposing office and warehouse range on Arundel Street, is particularly indicative. It was built in the 1880s for Louis Osbaldiston and Company, a merchant and manufacturing firm dealing in steel, saws, and files, and it replaced earlier buildings on the site (Giles 1998b, 1). Whilst such firms may have carried out their own manufacturing, it is as likely that they occupied the front range of what was otherwise a tenement works, let off to individual little mesters.

Rural workshops

The 19th-century metalworking expansion was not, however, merely an urban phenomenon. Integrated rural complexes, such as Abbeydale Works, were also built with a full range of processing buildings, though the urban display frontages were not replicated, perhaps because of the nature of the goods manufactured; common agricultural wares bought by farmers rather than high-quality table cutlery; or because separate showrooms were located within the town. On a practical level, some articles, such as scythes, required more power in their manufacture than cutlery and so it made sense to manufacture them next to the rivers which supplied the water power. This did not, however, mean that individual cutlers were confined to the town. In 1830 William Cobbett observed that 'the ragged hills all around this town are bespangled with groups of houses inhabited by working cutlers' (Cobbett 1830, 495). In fact the majority of surviving purpose-built rural hand forges and small workshops are contemporary with the urban workshops, indicating that the growth of metalworking within Sheffield did not suppress the small-scale work occurring in the surrounding villages, perhaps because they were at least initially producing different items. The buildings, despite their humble size, were an integral part of the 19th-century expansion of the cutlery and edge-tool trades, and are another indicator of the working practices of the little mesters. Despite the earlier tradition of dual occupation, the craft had become sufficiently profitable to allow independence from food production. Most sites therefore had no agricultural buildings, and, though forge workshops were still invariably built in association with domestic buildings, they were detached from the house, enabling access to be gained quite independently. The houses were larger than the contemporary urban working-class housing associated with hand forges and workshops such as that on Garden Street. Most rural workshops were of a standard type, with the exception of file-cutting

Figure 10.11 Challenge Works, Arundel Street, was built in the 1880s for the merchant Louis Osbaldiston. The firm sold steel saws and files. (© Crown Copyright. NMR)

workshops, which were clearly identifiable from their distinctive fenestration. As with urban workshop ranges, the majority require documentary evidence to identify the particular type of article being manufactured. They comprise small, single-storey vernacular buildings, built of local sandstone with a pitched stone slate or Welsh slate roof, and casement windows, often closely spaced. Extant examples usually combine hearths against each gable wall with working space between; workboards beneath the windows are still partly *in situ* at 1 Stepping Lane, Grenoside. This indicates that the separation of processes was not clear-cut in these small rural buildings which were in effect both forges and workshops under one roof. Such workshops were either used by little mesters working in the traditional manner on their own account, and employing a few men to assist, or more commonly as the 19th century progressed, by out workers for a large urban manufacturer or factor. Franklin House, Stannington (Fig 10.12), built in the 1820s, was reputedly first used to manufacture cut-throat razors, but later came to be occupied by five outworkers for Wolstenholmes, manufacturers of double-bladed hunting knives for export to America (Bayliss 1995, 42).

Figure 10.12 Franklin House, Stannington, a contemporary early 19th-century house and rural workshop. (© English Heritage. NMR)

Working conditions

Within the town the fragmentary working practices of the little mesters encouraged both a proliferation of tenement works and sub-letting by large manufacturers. Rate books suggest that between 1820 and 1850 only about 10% of workshops were owner-occupied, and by the end of the 19th century 60% of owners were unconnected with cutlery or related trades (Beauchamp 1996, 84, 128). In 1897 such owners were described as 'persons who never see [the tenement works], who recognise no obligations and who are represented locally by an agent who remits the rent and an engine tender' (Quoted in Beauchamp 1996, 148–9). This, combined with naturally hazardous processes, often resulted in very poor working conditions, exacerbated by the lack of industrial muscle of the diverse trades on account of their fragmentary nature. This was particularly apparent amongst urban grinders, whose lifespans were considerably shortened by silicosis, or 'ginder's lung' brought on by the inhalation of dust. A campaign was waged through most of the 19th century to improve ventilation systems in grinding wheels, but with little success. In 1865 it was reported that where owners of wheels put up fans the men might be charged more rent, and that the men either could not, or would not, pay for one themselves (BPP 1865, 11). It was the opinion of Engels that grinders did not encourage the installation of fans as the poor working conditions discouraged others and consequently kept wages high, resulting in a short, but merry life (Engels 1845, 212). Although by 1895 the proprietor of a workshop was charged with the responsibility of providing a fan, enforcement, particularly in tenement works, proved difficult (Lloyd 1913, 230), and little clear evidence of ventilation systems exists. A few grinding hulls, like those at Sellers Wheel, Arundel Street, have ventilation grilles in the blind rear walls. At Truro Works, Matilda Street, a regular pattern of four brick-sized openings occurs below the windows of a late 19th-century range incorporating grinding, which suggest a ventilation or extraction system on each floor. Also absent from the majority of workshops is any evidence for the provision of artificial lighting; this is surprising within the urban context, although perhaps it is explained by the ephemeral nature of the fittings. Nineteenth-century accounts only tend to mention artificial light with regard to grinding, where its provision was felt to be an important safety issue. In 1857 a number of workers interviewed for a treatise on 'Sheffield Grinders' Disease' stated that gas was only provided if the grinders paid for it themselves, the expense discouraging many despite poor lighting resulting in an increased risk of injury.[11] If this was the case for grinders it is probable that gas was not routinely supplied to other types of urban workshops, at least at this date. Thus the apparent lack of interest in safer working conditions appears to be directly attributable to the fact that the majority of workers were tenants, and led many to endure conditions described by one cutler in the 1860s as 'crude and sordid . . . [where] the dirty shops, the disregard of sanitary demands, and the arbitrary way the workmen are treated, all tended to low ideals of life' (Quoted in Tweedale 1995, 162–3).

Conclusion

Such contemporary written and built evidence serves to highlight the often appalling working conditions endured particularly by Sheffield's urban workers. The reasons were complex, but at its root was the phenomenal expansion of a trade which still operated in a craft tradition. Cutlery and edge-tool production became a major industry during the 19th century, with Sheffield developing global trade networks especially in America, through its export of Bowie ranch and specialist hunting knives, and countries where Britain had built up its Empire. For example Joseph Rodgers, Sheffield's largest cutlery firm, exported widely to America, but also secured a reputation for quality in India and the Far East (Symonds 2002, 5). Whilst the market for Sheffield's goods expanded rapidly, the methods of production remained largely unchanged. Even large-scale complexes were in effect merely an agglomeration of individual workers on one site each carrying out a single element of the entire manufacturing process. Rather than large factories gaining a stranglehold upon the industry, a complex structure of mutual dependence prevailed between the large manufacturers and little mesters, with the putting-out of various aspects of the work being widely practised as a means of keeping down production costs and providing a wide diversity of goods. This approach is manifest in the concurrent building of large multi-purpose complexes, smaller works, separate premises, urban and rural sites, and powered and unpowered workshops, all of which co-existed throughout the 19th century.

Perhaps the most radical change in working practices for the majority of workers was the largely 19th-century adoption of purpose-built workshops in which to undertake their craft. Power was not an issue for many, but the proximity to other workers and processes, which the workshops afforded, was seen as an advantage, of time and therefore money. While little mesters appreciated this saving they were generally unable to finance such buildings themselves, depending instead upon finding a workspace to rent. This encouraged a large amount of speculative building.

The proliferation of tenement works, together with the retention of old-fashioned hand skills, resulted in conservative building forms and poor working conditions. The latter were exacerbated by the rapid expansion of little mesters, particularly in times of recession, as they bid to survive in the harsh economic climate, so that output increased at times when wages and prices were depressed (Lloyd 1913, 342). Workshops built in the early 19th century generally appear little different from those constructed at the end of the century. Building quality was often low, with little pretence of architectural embellishment, as there was little incentive to improve such buildings, which were seen by their owners purely as distant income generators, with no duty of care attached to their occupiers. Nevertheless, or perhaps because of this *laissez-faire* approach, surviving cutlery and edge-tool workshops are generally held in affection by the residents of Sheffield. There is little in the way of the ambivalent attitude, for example, held by local residents towards the textile mills of Yorkshire and Lancashire with their perceived repressive influence upon the community. Despite the workshops' shortcomings, they represent a social and economic work structure which enabled the 19th-century workforce to manufacture a quality and quantity of cutlery and edge tools using traditional methods so successfully that the cachet 'Made in Sheffield' secured the city's reputation throughout the world.

Notes

1. George, Sixth Earl of Shrewsbury, brought Frenchmen or men of French descent from the Sussex Weald to erect charcoal blast furnaces and forges at Attercliffe, Kimberworth, and Wadsley, exploiting coal reserves under Sheffield Park (Hey 1991, 22–3).
2. 'The principle of sub-division of labour is very fully carried out in the cutlery trades. Not only is each department, as forging, grinding, etc, carried out by separate workmen, but the man who grinds or forges one particular class of blades, such as for penknives, does not work at table knives; and so on throughout all the different branches' (Pawson & Brailsford 1862, 135–6).
3. In 1865 Mr Wilkinson, a cutlery manufacturer interviewed for a report by the Children's Employment Commission, stated that 'these small makers can get cheaper labour than a

manufacturer can, and sell him goods of a common kind cheaper than he can make them, eg we can buy common scissors from them 20% cheaper than we could make them ourselves'. Another manufacturer commented that 'much of our work, probably half, is done off our premises by outworkers in small places. Most large cutlery manufacturers, I should say, have part of their work done out in this way' (BPP 1865, 47).

4. In 1872 the *Sheffield Independent* commented that 'in quiet times merchants are able to barter the 'little mesters' as they are called, almost to starvation prices, and thus compete on most unfair terms with the larger manufacturers, who continue to pay ordinary prices' (Kidd & Nicholls 1998, 47).

5. Globe Works had a row of single-storey hand forges which are clearly identifiable on the 6 Inch Ordnance Survey map, Sheffield Sheet 12, surveyed 1851, published 1853, and in an 1862 engraving in Pawson and Brailsford, though they have since been demolished.

6. Arched openings for forges are found on the ground floor of the small workshop range at 52–6 Garden Street and the diminutive Lion Works on Arundel Street.

7. A steam engine was first used to power grindstones in 1786 (Hey 1972, 14), and by 1865 there were about 96 grinding wheels in and around Sheffield, of which 80 were steam driven and sixteen used water wheels (BPP 1865, 12). The early 20th-century hulls at Butchers Wheel were laid out in a similar manner to those in earlier wheels, although the troughs were made of concrete and the grindstones were driven by electric motors.

8. There were three boilers, which suggests that two steam engines may have been used to produce the 60-horse-power specified. A contemporary feasibility study recommended 'two steam engines of 30-horse-power each at the centre of the building' to reduce the risk of loss of earnings should one engine break down (Beauchamp 1995, 56).

9. Union Wheel had a 30-horse power engine, two boilers and a 27 m (90 ft) chimney (Goad 1896).

10. Goad's 1905 Fire Insurance plan shows that the ground floor of the rear range at Beehive Works was used by file-cutters.

11. Mr Jonathan Wragg, secretary to the table-blade grinders, stated that 'There would not be half of the accidents if all wheels were well lighted by windows in the daytime, and particularly at night by gas ... working by a bad light is bad for the eyes, but men must put up with it because of the expense. A man cannot well have gas and a meter for himself alone, and others might not be willing to share the expense' (BPP 1865, 21). In the same report another man interviewed said that some grinders had gas if they paid for it and the fitting themselves (BPP 1865, 17).

11 The workshops of Birmingham's Jewellery Quarter *by John Cattell*

Introduction

Birmingham's Jewellery Quarter differs from many other historic industrial areas in that it survives as a working urban industrial quarter. It is still the main centre for gold jewellery production in Britain with around 6000 people employed in the trade. Although jewellery of every description remains the main product, the area has long been a focus for the manufacture of all manner of small metal items ranging from babies' teething rings, to pen nibs, coffin fittings, and even police whistles. Many of the Quarter's buildings are today used much as they were up to 150 years ago and this has provided us with an unparalleled opportunity for study, to learn in detail about the ways in which buildings have been operated; the tools, machines and processes they house, and also business practices. Thus continuity forms one of the principal themes of this paper. Another defining characteristic of the Jewellery Quarter is the persistence of the small scale; evident both in the high proportion of small specialist firms, and in the size of the historic buildings in which they operate. The longevity of the combined house and workshop unit is also fundamental to a detailed understanding of the development of the area. Houses with workshops were being constructed in the Quarter as late as the mid-1880s some 50 years after the construction of the first factories there, and until the 1950s outworking was still being undertaken in back-to-backs in courts. This paper also addresses the development of the jewellery factory, a legitimate field of enquiry in a book on the vernacular workshop given that, the domestic element aside, there is very often little difference between larger house and workshop units and small jewellery and metalworking factories in terms of scale, the virtual absence of powered machinery, and the processes and functions performed.[1]

Origins of the Jewellery Quarter

The Jewellery Quarter occupies a sandstone ridge approximately 10–15 minutes walk north and north-west of Chamberlain Square in the centre of the City, and encompassing around 1000 sites within a 94-hectare area (Fig 11.1). Principal features include St Paul's Square, a development of predominantly three-storey townhouses arranged around St Paul's Church, dating from the 1770s; the Birmingham and Fazeley Canal, completed in 1789; the 1836 General Cemetery at Key Hill; the Church of England Cemetery laid out on the site of a worked-out sand quarry in 1846; and the Birmingham, Wolverhampton, and Dudley Railway Line of 1854. The main thoroughfares are the main road to Dudley and Great Hampton Street leading to Wolverhampton.

The area that by the early 20th century would become the Quarter originated in the late 18th century as a sparsely populated residential zone centred on St Paul's Square. Initially the townhouses in the Square were occupied by moderately successful industrial masters and professionals. Within a few years, detached and semi-detached villas were built for wealthy industrialists, landowners, and leading professional men, in the areas immediately north and west of St Paul's Square on other parts of the Colmore family's extensive Newhall Estate. Such larger houses continued to be built into the 1830s, and together represent a pattern of development that took place in other towns during this period. The villas offered a pleasant retreat away from the noise and grime of the burgeoning industrial areas located on lower ground closer to the town centre. These houses were invariably surrounded by sizeable gardens and usually had coach houses and stables. A few villas survive, though nearly all have been hemmed in to varying degrees by later development.

By the 1820s smaller houses, some built with workshops, began to appear in the streets leading out from St Paul's Square, a development made possible by the absence of restrictive covenants in the Newhall Estate leases (Crisp-Jones 1981, 135). Nos 41–2 Caroline Street, originally a pair of two-bay houses each built with a workshop range to the rear in around 1826, are particularly good examples. The extent of this domestic industrial development is evident in an excerpt from Pigott Smith's survey of Birmingham of 1824.[2] With the improving economic conditions of the 1830s, and increasing specialisation, as well as the rapid expansion of the jewellery trade proper from the 1850s, the pace of development quickened eventually resulting in the heavily built-up Jewellery Quarter we see today (Fig 11.2) with its rich tapestry of former houses, houses built with workshops, factories without domestic accommodation, and buildings of varying degrees of specialisation that support the trade.

Historical development of the Birmingham metalware and jewellery trades

To understand what lay behind this rapid expansion of the small metalware and jewellery trades and the physical development of the Jewellery Quarter it is necessary to go back to developments in the 18th

Birmingham's Jewellery Quarter 151

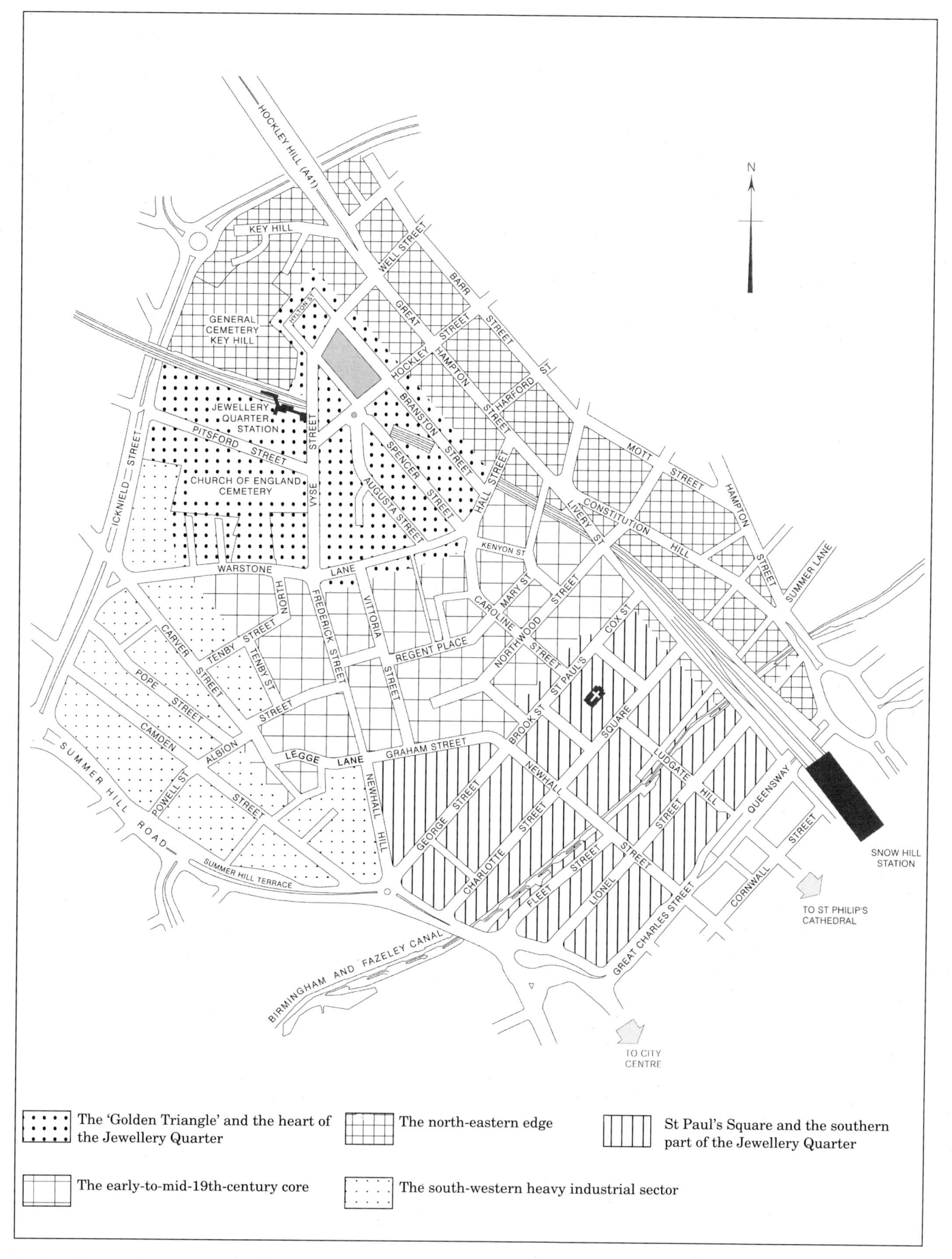

Figure 11.1 Map of the Jewellery Quarter and its principal features. (© English Heritage. NMR)

152 *The vernacular workshop*

Figure 11.2 View, from the south, of part of the centre of the Jewellery Quarter, showing the typically dense pattern of former houses, workshops, and factories. (© Crown Copyright. NMR)

century.[3] Birmingham had long been known as an important metal manufacturing centre, but it was in the 18th century that its reputation as 'the workshop of the world' was confirmed. It owed its success to the manufacture of toys, which were not children's playthings, but rather all manner of small personal accessories made of metal, including cheap jewellery, snuff boxes, buttons, and buckles. Button and shoe buckle manufacture formed major branches in their own right. Birmingham toys and other metal goods found their way to all parts of the world, the export trade taking on particular importance during the last quarter of the 18th century. In the early 19th century the onset of the Napoleonic wars coupled with changing fashions, the latter resulting in the collapse of the buckle and gilt button trades, acted as a check on further expansion. However with the improving economic conditions of the 1830s, production levels surged again with toymakers, many of whom possessed the requisite skills, increasingly shifting over to jewellery making. As the demand for jewellery and metal goods grew so these trades became increasingly subdivided with employees leaving their masters to set up on their own, often in highly specialised branches. This in turn resulted in

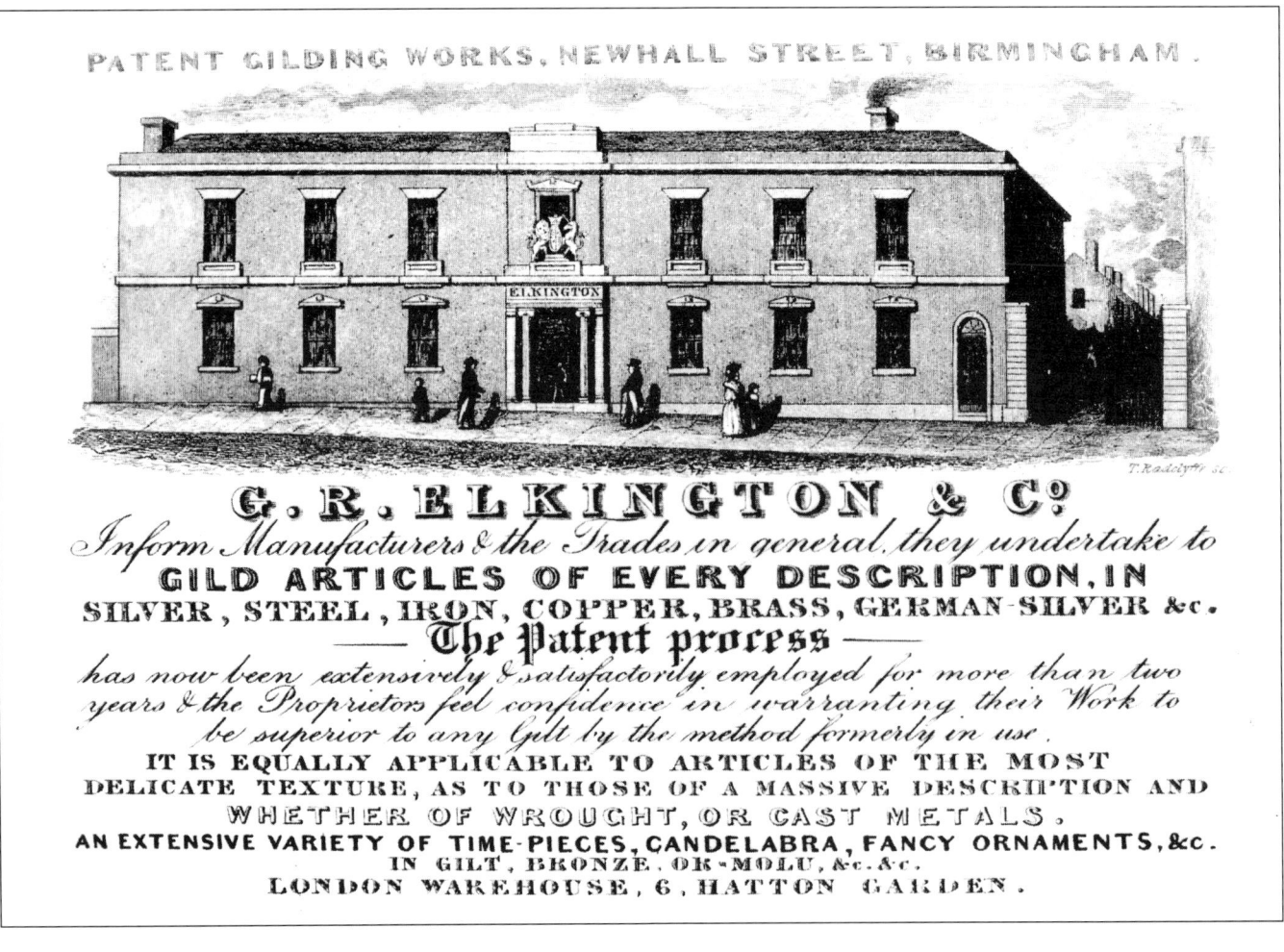

Figure 11.3 Engraving of c1843 showing the original frontage of Elkington and Co's electroplating and gilding factory on Newhall Street. (© English Heritage. NMR)

Figure 11.4 Two-storey workshop range added to the rear of a former house on Warstone Lane near the centre of the Jewellery Quarter. (© Crown Copyright. NMR)

an increase in the number of firms and an almost insatiable demand for workshop space.

The jewellery and metal working trades were given further impetus by the commercial exploitation of electroplating and gilding processes pioneered by the firm of Elkington and Company in the late 1830s from its premises on Newhall Street in the Quarter (Fig 11.3). Electroplating involved the use of an electric current to deposit a thin but durable layer of silver onto the surface of a base metal object. This was distinct from the older Sheffield Plate produced by rolling together a thin sheet of silver with a thicker layer of copper. Electroplated goods were comparatively cheap to produce, had the appearance of a sterling silver item, and were easily replated if the surface wore through. The technique brought gilt and plated jewellery products within reach of all but the very poorest sections of society.

The jewellery trade received its greatest boost in the 1850s, aided by the discovery of gold in Australia and California. In 1854 the passage of the Lower Standards Act also had a profound effect. It involved the introduction of three inexpensive gold alloys of 9, 12 and 15 carat. Pure gold at almost 24 carat is too soft and marks easily so alloys combining base metal and gold are used to both reduce the price of the item and increase its durability – the higher the carat number the greater the percentage of gold. The combined effect of these developments was a massive expansion in the trade that was to result in the employment of more than 50,000 people in jewellery manufacture in Birmingham at its peak in the years leading up to the First World War, with an estimated further 20,000 involved in collateral trades. Much of this activity was concentrated in and around the Jewellery Quarter making it the single largest jewellery manufacturing district in the world at that time.

Houses and workshops

The types of buildings erected in the Jewellery Quarter during the 19th and early 20th centuries can be divided into a number of fairly distinct categories. The first of these comprises houses of varying types built without workshops. With a few exceptions large houses of the kind touched on earlier ceased to be built in the area after around 1840, though some were able to survive in purely domestic use until around 1900, in most cases their gardens having been sold off to accommodate yet more workshops and factories. Sometimes workshops and even factories were built in the front gardens of houses as, for example, at Century Buildings at 35–38 Summer Hill Road.

154 *The vernacular workshop*

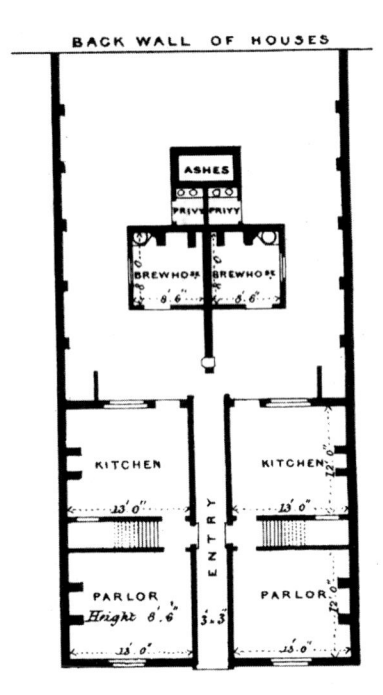

Figure 11.5 Elevation and plan of 1842 of a pair of 'three-quarter' houses. (© English Heritage. NMR)

Figure 11.6 Workshop range at the back of a former house at 94 Vyse Street. Originally of two storeys, the workshop range was subsequently heightened and extended to the north-east (left). (© English Heritage. NMR)

There are also smaller, terraced houses built without workshops between around 1820 and 1860. They may originally have incorporated a small workshop within the body of the house and many were converted to combined domestic and industrial units almost from the outset, with workshops built in the rear gardens. The workshops, or 'shopping' as they were known locally, were attached at right-angles to the backs of the houses, leaving a narrow yard to one side (Fig 11.4). As well as houses with direct entry from the street there were also passage-entry houses, three-quarter houses as they were called in Birmingham, the plans of which facilitated easy access via the shared passage for those working in added rear workshops (Fig 11.5). This was in contrast to direct entry houses where the workforce would have to troop through the house of the master and his family at the front of the plot to get to the shopping at the rear. As these small firms grew, the workshops might be heightened by the addition of extra storeys and the yard roofed over to provide additional shopping (Fig 11.6). In time part or all of the house might be taken over for use as offices, showrooms, or warehouses, the master and his family moving to other premises, and eventually adjoining houses might be acquired and linked to the original premises by a labyrinthine arrangement of internal and external stairs and passages. This very ad hoc pattern of expansion can be observed to varying degrees throughout the Quarter.

At the lowest level in the social scale were the back-to-back and blind-back houses arranged in courts and built throughout Birmingham. They were built in large numbers in the southern part of the Jewellery Quarter from around 1820 until the 1870s and some survived until the 1950s. The usual pattern was to have back-to-back houses fronting the street with a communal passage, marked up with the number of the court, leading to a yard at the back, around which were usually arranged a series of small houses, blind-backs, built against the boundary walls. The blind-backs and the back-to-backs which faced into the yard were separately numbered within each court. It is safe to assume that outworking was carried out in these houses of just two or three rooms, but the paucity of surviving examples and a lack of documentary source material makes this very difficult to prove. The best remaining court in the area is on the outskirts of the Quarter in Summer Lane (Fig 11.7). It was built by an American merchant, Alfred Harrold, in 1844 and originally consisted of two three-storey double-pile houses between which was a passage leading to Court 3 to the rear, which contained four blind-backs.

Figure 11.7 Former court of blind-back houses on Summer Lane, looking towards the rear of the court and showing a two-storey house running across the back of the plot and three houses adjoining the side boundary (right). The latter have been reduced in height from three storeys to one. (© English Heritage. NMR)

Figure 11.8 House of 1818 (far right) and adjoining workshops completed by 1827, on Mary Street. (© Crown Copyright. NMR)

The second main category of building type is the house built with shopping. As with other trades in other areas this combination of domestic accommodation and shopping in Birmingham dates back to the medieval period. Early and mid-19th-century examples are often very similar in appearance and plan to houses with added shopping, and they can sometimes only be identified by a close inspection of the brickwork of the workshop range where it meets with that of the house. However, as the 19th century progressed these mixed-use developments became increasingly sophisticated, and the resulting buildings came to represent an interesting hybrid between housing proper and small-scale purpose-built factories without a domestic element. Through a process of gradual expansion a few house and shopping developments grew to exceed some factories in size and production levels. For example, a button works, built in 1824 on Regent Street as a house and shopping development employing around 40 people, had by the 1850s grown into a large complex employing 250 staff and outworkers.

The earliest combined house and workshop unit identified in the Quarter is that shown in Figure 11.8. It is located not far to the north of St Paul's Square and dates from 1818–27. Here the plot had a wide frontage but very little depth so the workshops were built onto the side of the house in phases. They represent an early example of a speculative development incorporating workshops for multiple occupancy.

Nos 119–21 Branston Street is a speculative house and shopping development of around 1857 (Fig 11.9). There is a shared entrance passage between the two houses at the front of the plot, leading to a separate yard adjoining a shopping range to the rear of each house. Typically a long open-plan first-floor workshop oversails a kitchen and wash house, earth closets and a small stamp shop at the back of the plot. The domestic services are lit by sashes as distinct from the multiple pane cast-iron framed windows utilised in the workshop areas. The workshops of 119 were first occupied by Robathan & Pendleton, goldsmiths, jewellers, and manufacturers of fancy gem and signet rings. The firm employed three men and nine boys. The house was occupied by one of the partners, William Pendleton, his wife, father-in-law, and two sons, who probably also worked for the firm.

One of the last house and shopping developments in the Quarter was built on Legge Lane in 1885 (Fig 11.10). It has a highly evolved plan and occupies a plot with a curving street frontage. The development

Figure 11.9 Rear view of 119–21 Branston Street, showing the workshop range of 119 to the left and that of 121 to the right. Evidence for the dividing wall that once separated the yards of the two properties can be seen in the paving. (© English Heritage. NMR)

156 *The vernacular workshop*

consists of two pairs of three-quarter houses with each pair divided by a through passage leading to a yard containing workshops to the rear of each house. Each workshop range is of three storeys with a basement, and the two centre workshop ranges are positioned back-to-back.

Jewellery and metalworking factories

With the exception of Matthew Boulton's Soho Manufactory built in 1762–7 on a greenfield site at Handsworth north of what was to become the Jewellery Quarter, the factory came quite late to Birmingham – the factory being defined as a purpose-built industrial premises with a clear division between administrative and production areas and without a significant domestic element. The first factories erected in the Quarter were large complexes dating from the late 1830s and built adjoining or in close proximity to the Birmingham and Fazeley Canal. One of the most important of these large factories was the Victoria Works, a pen manufactory built for Joseph Gillott who had invented a method of mass-producing steel pen nibs. In the 1850s the firm was producing around 120 million pens per year

Figure 11.10 Two of the shopping ranges forming part of a speculative house and workshop development of 1885 on Legge Lane and looking towards the rear of the housing at the front of the complex. (© English Heritage. NMR)

Figure 11.11 Two small factories of 1870–71 on Warstone Lane. The building on the left was originally a private refining and assaying works, while that on the right was a jewellery manufactory. (© English Heritage. NMR)

Figure 11.12 A state of the art jewellery factory built in 1882 on Warstone Lane. The offices and warehouses are in the taller corner block and the workshops are housed in the two-storey range to the left. (© English Heritage. NMR)

using steel from Sheffield. Like the Elkington electroplating works the factory consisted of narrow three-storey buildings incorporating offices, warehouses, and workshops and arranged around a series of courtyards.

The first jewellery factories in the Quarter date from the 1850s. A gold-chain-making factory built in 1853 by Benjamin Goode in St Paul's Square was probably the first. It used newly invented specialist machinery and employed 400 staff in an integrated works which concentrated all of the necessary processes on the one site. These larger integrated factories were, however, relatively rare and most jewellery and metalworking factories were small in scale reflecting the craft nature of the trade, the size of the objects being produced, the smallness of the firms, and a continuing reliance on outworkers for the provision of certain often highly specialised processes. Thus these smaller factories (Fig 11.11), had more in common with many combined domestic and industrial units than with the few larger factories. The purpose-built factory often facilitated the improved and more efficient layout of the street range, as well as providing the manufacturer with an opportunity to promote his business by imbuing the façade with a greater degree of architectural elaboration. However, these advantages were rarely so great that factories were built in place of domestic-industrial developments. Instead they tended to be built in place of dilapidated workers' houses or in the former gardens of large houses. The workshops of the new factories were generally utilitarian and little different in form and plan from those of mixed domestic-industrial developments.

A state of the art jewellery factory constructed in 1882 on the corner of Warstone Lane and Tenby Street North was described by the *The Jeweller and Metalworker* journal in 1889 as 'certainly the handsomest building devoted to the manufacture of jewellery which has yet been erected' (Anon 1889, 173) (Fig. 11.12). Built on the site of a court of workers' houses, the factory has a tall three-storey corner block originally containing an elaborate entrance hall, offices, and warehousing and an equally distinguished workshop range fronting the long elevation to Tenby Street North. The building's office block was provided with concrete floors and a sophisticated central heating system. This factory was about as large as jewellery factories got. Perhaps more typical is a small jewellery factory of 1892 built for the firm of Alabaster & Wilson and still operated by the same family firm (Fig. 11.13). The building occupies a restricted corner plot with inadequate space for rear shopping so the main jewellery workshop is positioned above the entrance and warehouse on the ground floor. Purpose-built metalworking factories in the Quarter were very often of similar scale and sometimes quite plain, as in the case of a coffin furniture factory built in Fleet Street for Newman Brothers in around 1892.

In addition to houses, houses with workshops, and factories of differing scale, are a variety of building types providing specialist supplies and services to the trade. These include buildings like the Birmingham Assay Office where gold, silver, and platinum items are assayed (or tested for the quantity of precious metal they contain) and hallmarked; and the School of Jewellery, which for over a century has provided students with the requisite design and craft skills. There are also the warehouses of merchants and factors (Fig.11.14), as well as printing works producing catalogues, trade journals, and ornate letterheads for manufacturers. Then there are large engineering works producing specialist tools and heavier presses.

Organisation of the Birmingham jewellery trade

Having looked at the origins of the Jewellery Quarter and the kinds of buildings constructed in the area, it is necessary to look in a bit more depth at the organisation of the trade and in particular the reasons for the development of the Quarter as an industrial cluster. The typical working unit in the Birmingham jewellery trade in the 19th century was the family firm, employing a relatively small number of people (often only the master his wife and children and perhaps an apprentice or journeyman) and

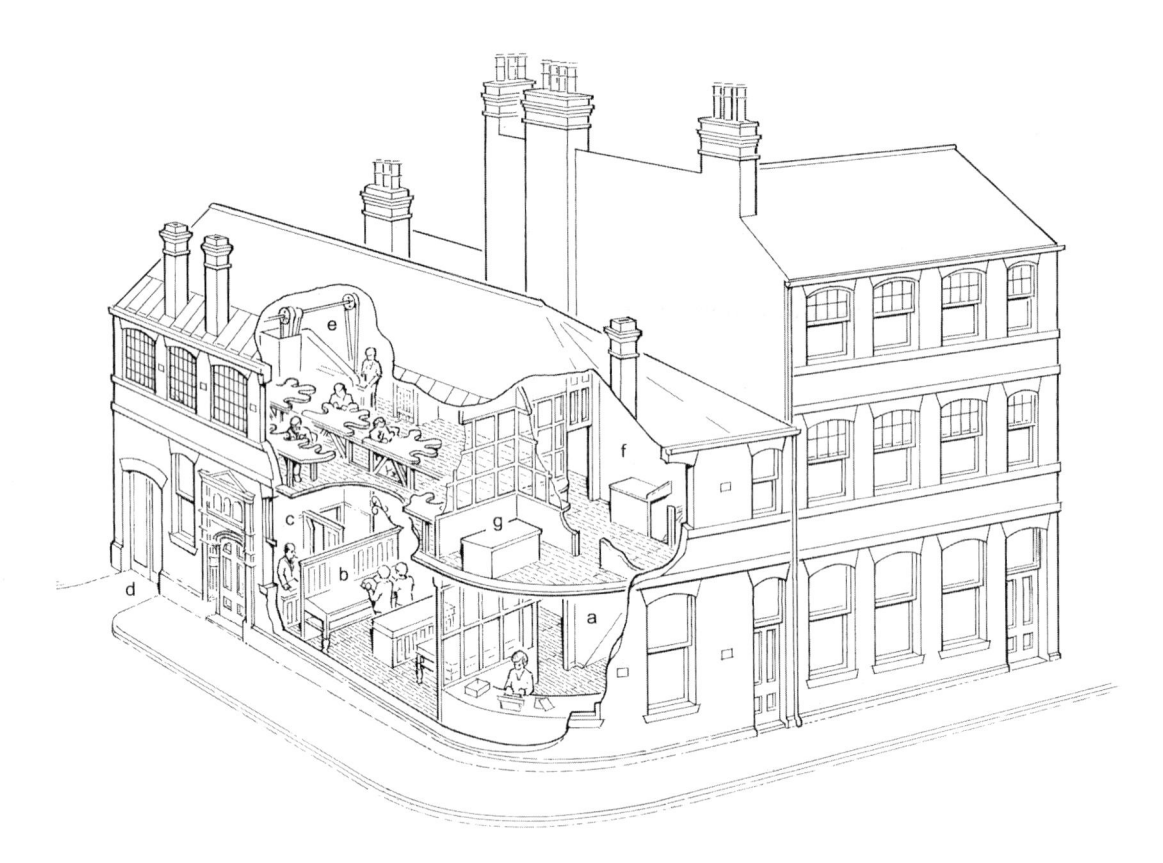

Figure 11.13   Cut-away drawing of a late 19th-century purpose-built jewellery factory in the Quarter, showing a stock room, warehouse, and reception/transaction area on the ground floor (a–c) and a jewellery workshop, rough warehouse, and office on the first floor (e–f).(© English Heritage. NMR)

generally occupying houses with workshops or small factories. The proprietors of these firms were known as small masters, Birmingham's equivalent to Sheffield's 'Little Mesters' (Wray, this volume). Firms were often connected through marriage or through long association in the trade. Even today 85% of firms involved in the jewellery trade in the Quarter employ 10 or fewer staff, while 47% comprise just one or two (Metra Martech 2001, 41). Although the family firm is no longer pre-eminent, and the proprietor now lives elsewhere instead of in front of the shop, many small firms continue to occupy former houses. In this respect the small master is alive and well in Birmingham. Many of these small firms tended to be highly specialised, concentrating on one or a small number of processes and this is often still the case. Although independent, these small firms might undertake work for larger manufacturers and factors as well as making some items on their own account. This state of affairs was described by *The Penny Magazine* in 1844 as follows:

> There are very few large factories, properly so called, in which an article goes through the entire

Figure 11.14 (right)   Former factor's warehouse of around 1839 on Regent Parade. (© English Heritage. NMR)

range of manufacturing processes; but there is a vast number of workshops, more or less extensive, in each of which portions of the works are done. One manufactured article, which is sold retail for a penny, may go through twenty workshops before it is finished; some having forty or fifty workmen; some four or five, while some are simply the garrets of workmen who ply their trade by their own fire-side. With the exception of the metropolis, there is perhaps no town in England where there are so many persons combining in themselves the characters of master and workman, as Birmingham, and none in which there is more observable a chain of links connecting one with the other (Anon 1844, 465–6).

The last part of this description highlights the high degree of interdependence existing between the various firms and helps explain how jewellers and small metalworking firms came to be colocated as part of a highly specialised and distinct industrial zone. The warehouses of merchants and factors also acted as a focal point: the small firms would collect their raw materials from the warehouse, and the finished goods would be returned there prior to being packaged and despatched to retailers around the country and abroad. Forming another strand of this localised network were those businesses, such as bullion dealers, jewellery case makers, toolmakers, and the Assay Office, that acted as suppliers and providers of specialist services. Together this mélange of small firms, a few larger businesses, and a wide range of support services resulted in a sense of collective security, particularly important in an area dealing in the use of precious metals and gems. Thus we begin to get a sense of the Jewellery Quarter in the 19th century as a self-contained and extremely complex industrial community where few outsiders had reason to enter unless they were in some way connected with the trade.

The jewellery trade is characterised by relatively low investment, since the jewellery-making process can be undertaken in a single room using little and or no machinery, a fact observed by a writer on the trade in 1866:

> All that is needed for a workman to start as a master is a peculiarly-shaped bench and a leather apron, one or two pounds worth of tools (including a blow-pipe), and a few sovereigns, and some ounces of copper and zinc. His shop may be the top room of his house, or a small building over the wash-house, at a rent of 2/- or 2/6 per week, and the indispensable gas jet, which the gas Company will supply on credit (Wright 1866, 454).

Thus with little capital investment in equipment, raw materials, and premises, a master could set up in business with relative ease, which helps to account for the great proliferation of small jewellery firms in the Quarter in the second half of the 19th century. In boom times these small businesses could make a very good living indeed with those employed in the trade being among the best paid artisans. In the 1860s for example it was possible for an enameller to make as much as £5 per week. With little capital tied up in costly fixtures and machinery, the small master could more easily ride out periodic economic downturns. There is very little evidence of small masters sharing a source of motive power, presumably because many workshops had little or no need of it. Unlike those in the jewellery trade, those involved in the manufacture of metal goods would need to invest in expensive dies, stamps, and presses as well as a source of power. Generally speaking, however, the capital outlay involved in establishing businesses of this kind was lower than that in many other trades, as Chambers *Edinburgh Journal* observed in 1844:

> Factories, which one now hears so much about, are of two classes; one, which embraces the production of cotton, silks, and other tissues, being conducted on a magnificent scale, with large buildings and the most expensive machinery, consequently involving the outlay of enormous capital – usually from £100,000 to £200,000 in one concern: the other, not by any means imposing, and which, requiring a union of operative skill with the labour only of small machines, can be carried on by a limited capital – from £20,000 to £30,000 at the utmost. To this second class the manufactories of Sheffield and Birmingham belong (Chambers & Chambers 1844, 369).

Manufacturing processes and the influence on the planning and design of workshops and factories

The processes employed in the production of jewellery and small metalwares can be divided into two broad categories, firstly those that are essentially bench-based crafts and secondly those that utilise manually-operated or powered machinery. In jewellery making, activity is centred on the wooden workbenches known as 'jewellers' boards'. These have scalloped out sections where each craftsman or woman works. In the centre of the board is a wooden work block known as a peg or a pin, while attached to the side is a kind of horizontal gas jet known as a Birmingham sidelight used in conjunction with a brass blowpipe to facilitate the precision soldering of jewellery. Leather pouches hold the various tools and hang below the work area to catch precious filings that are subsequently recycled. The process, fixtures, and tools associated with jewellery making have changed little over many centuries (Figs 11.15 and 11.16). Hand-operated and sometimes powered machinery is also used but usually as an adjunct to the basic process. Examples include wire-drawing machines used to produce gold wire of varying gauges and hand-operated rollers for rolling pieces of gold into sheets.

Those firms that concentrated on the production of

160 *The vernacular workshop*

Figure 11.15 Illustration of a Parisian jewellery workshop, from Diderot's L'Encyclopédie . . . , *1763, showing many of the fixtures and processes that can still be observed in the Jewellery Quarter. (© English Heritage. NMR)*

Figure 11.16 Two craftsmen working in a small workshop on Spencer Street. They are working at jewellers' boards of the same shape as those illustrated in Diderot. (© English Heritage. NMR)

Figure 11.17 Stamping battery in operation at 94 Vyse Street. (© English Heritage. NMR)

metal goods made extensive use of three main processes, stamping, pressing, and metal spinning. Stamping uses a heavy weight contained within an iron frame to stamp patterns into a sheet of metal or blank. The weight is dropped onto an engraved hardened steel block known as a die. The metal is forced into the incisions in the die to create the required pattern. Stamps were in use in Birmingham in the first half of the 18th century. Initially they were unpowered, with the weights being hauled to the top of the frame manually. However, they could be easily connected to a source of power via overhead line shafting allowing an individual to operate a large stamp with comparative ease. Where more than one stamp was required these would be grouped together to form a stamping battery (Fig. 11.17). The operatives would stand in a pit alongside the stamp, this arrangement permitting the base of the stamp to be at a level where the worker could reach it with ease. Alternatively, the stamp would be placed on a plinth. Stamps, some of which date from the late 19th century, are still in widespread use around the Quarter.

Pressing involves the use of a hand-operated press known as a fly press. The presses come in various sizes and are capable of being affixed to benches. Each press has a cast-iron frame used to exert pressure on the blank by means of a central screw thread. Presses could be used in conjunction with small dies to produce pressings, or with punches and jigs to cut out particular shapes and trim off excess metal (Fig.11.18). Manually operated presses are employed in virtually every metalworking shop and many jewellery workshops in the Quarter. Steam-powered coining presses were first used by Matthew Boulton at Soho in 1788 and heavier electrically-powered presses were developed in the 1920s. However, in most businesses power presses never really took over from manually operated fly presses, which very often are able to produce a more precise pressing. Some metals needed to be heated or annealed prior to pressing or stamping and for this reason hearths are often located alongside the stamps and presses.

Metal spinning using a lathe is a process of ancient origins still conducted in workshops in the Quarter. Spinning enables metals such as brass to be shaped over a wooden mould or chuck to form objects of hollow or raised profile. Casting was quite widespread in the Quarter, particularly in larger works, and the process was essentially the same as that conducted elsewhere. A specialist form of the ancient technique of lost wax casting known as 'centrifugal lost wax casting', the latter derived from dentistry techniques of the 1920s, is employed in the jewellery trade to produce batches of very precise identical castings. Electroplating firms are still operating in the Quarter and plating shops are distinguished by a series of metal vats. The objects to be plated are suspended from titanium trees, which are then lowered into the vats, through which an electric current is passed.

So how did the need to accommodate these processes and the more generic administrative, storage, dispatch, and sales functions associated with manufacturing influence the design and planning of workshops and factories? In the first place there was a basic division between the administrative and storage areas with their greater degree of contact with the outside world and the often noisier and dirty production areas. Thus offices, warehouses, and sometimes showrooms would be accommodated in a former house or a purpose-built range of the factory aligned parallel to and abutting the street line. The small scale of many house and workshop developments, and the fact that many smaller firms produced lines for middlemen, often obviated the need for extensive administrative and storage areas. However, where these facilities were required, they might be accommodated in the parts of the works between the house and the production areas, although this sometimes gave rise to what today seem unusual arrangements (Fig 11.19). The workshops would normally be located to the rear of the house or office and warehouse block at the front of the plot, creating a requirement for a dedicated means of access to allow the workshop employees to reach the rear of the complex without disturbing

Figure 11.18   Top-floor press shop at 94 Vyse Street. (© English Heritage. NMR)

activities in the street range. Corner plots provided an advantage in that it was possible to obtain direct access to workshops from a side street.

The offices, warehouses, and showrooms accommodated in the front range of the factory were often highly specialised and might be reached by means of a fine entrance hall and stair. Offices would be provided for the proprietors, as well as for the clerks who administered the daily business of purchases, sales, distribution, and labour. There were also secure private interview rooms or transaction booths where employees could conduct business with suppliers and agents from the other side of a high counter. Not surprisingly the need for security was particularly important and strongrooms and large

Figure 11.19 (right)   Variety Works, of 1881–82, on Frederick Street, originally incorporating a first-floor warehouse sandwiched between the living room and bedrooms of the proprietor's house at the front of the plot. (© English Heritage. NMR)

Figure 11.20   Engraving of 1844 of a double-width press shop forming part of William Elliott's button-making factory on Regent Street. (© English Heritage. NMR)

fireproof safes are still a common feature within the office and warehouse areas.

Warehouses were equally specialised, and included packing warehouses, usually positioned alongside a cart entrance, 'rough' warehouses used for the storage of goods part way through the production process, and what might be termed 'giving-out rooms'. The latter are located alongside jewellery workshops and are secure storage facilities designed to allow the usage of precious metals and gemstones to be closely monitored. The necessary raw materials would be weighed out to each artisan at the beginning of the day and this was expected to tally with the combined weight of any finished goods and leftover materials returned at the end of the day. Other types of warehouse might include those dedicated to the storage of raw materials, sometimes known as metal warehouses. Goods would be moved between the various warehouses in the street range by means of small internal hoists or later lifts akin in scale to the domestic dumb waiter.

Showrooms were once a relatively common feature of converted houses and middling- to larger-scale factories, but they are now very rare. They usually contained a great deal of valuable merchandise arranged on display shelves or in glass cases. For this reason they were nearly always located on the first floor of the street range where there was a reduced risk of theft. Showrooms tended to be well-lit by tall sashes so as to show off the various products to the best advantage.

The production areas, the workshops, are generally accommodated in two- or three-storey ranges attached at right angles to the rear of the former house or office and warehouse block. These red-brick workshop buildings are typically very narrow, often with an internal width of around 4–5m (12–15ft), and are built against one of the long side-boundaries of the plot. They are usually built back-to-back with the workshops of the adjoining property and many have mono-pitch roofs, this kind of simple wooden roof structure being ideally suited to spanning such narrow buildings and averting the need for difficult-to-maintain valleys along the boundaries. If the

Figure 11.21 An exceptionally well-preserved stamp shop on the ground floor of the workshop range at the former coffin furniture factory of Newman Brothers on Fleet Street. (© English Heritage. NMR)

site was of sufficient depth, a short return range might be built along the back of the plot. The workshops would normally face onto a narrow yard taking up the remainder of the plot. The yard acted as a circulation space for goods and people, and it was also the principal means of providing natural light to the workshops hemmed in on all sides by adjoining buildings. With their blind back walls, the yard elevations of the workshops were of pier and panel construction and lit by regularly spaced windows at each level, the yard thus forming a kind of giant light well. The workshop windows have multiple-pane cast-iron frames with small opening sections to allow the necessary ventilation without blowing valuable filings around the shop. A few factories and houses with a sufficiently wide frontage might have space for three ranges of shopping built around the boundaries and completely enclosing the yard. Where a workshop fronted the street it could be lit both from the front and from the yard to the rear, which allowed for the construction of much wider shops. One of the earliest surviving examples was constructed in 1837 as part of William Elliott's button-making factory (Fig 11.20).

More noxious processes, such as casting, which also carried with it the risk of fire, and plating, might be accommodated in rooms completely separated off from the rest of the workshops, or more typically housed in separate structures in the centre or to one side of the yard. Casting shops would have louvred clerestoreys, vents, or simple steeply-pitched roofs to aid the dissipation of harmful fumes, and were usually of a tall single storey so as not to impede the supply of light to the upper floors of the main workshop range.

Within the main workshop range there was a fundamental division between the location of the heavier processes, such as stamping and metal rolling, on the ground floor, and the more delicate processes, such as jewellery making, pressing, burnishing, and the assembly of finished items, on the upper floors. This basic separation was commented on by Harriet Martineau writing in Charles Dickens's magazine *Household Words* in 1852, in connection with gold chain making:

> Few things in the arts can be more striking than the contrast between the murky chambers where the forging and grinding – the Plutonic processes of machine making – are going on and the upper chambers, where the delicate fingers of women and girls are arranging and fastening the most cobweb

links of the most delicate chain-work (Martineau 1852a, 451).

Stamp shops were always located on the ground floor owing to the weight of the stamps, the need for substantial foundations and the noise and vibration associated with their use (Fig 11.21). Those artisans on the upper floors made use of the better light – jewellers prefer an even north light – to undertake finer work

Conclusion

Finally, what can the Jewellery Quarter tell us about industry in the 19th century? In the first place it provides evidence for the continuation of a craft system based on the domestic workshop, which paralleled the development of the factory, and was as much a feature of our towns and cities as of rural areas. Compared with the large factory and mill, the great importance of small domestic workshops and manufactories has until quite recently received relatively little attention in the literature. The Jewellery Quarter represents the other side of the coin comprising as it does numerous small firms together producing an enormous range of goods in great volume using processes, fixtures, and tools that have remained largely unchanged for centuries. An important facet of this sense of continuity is the sheer persistence of the house and workshop unit – long after proprietors in other areas had moved away from their place of work the Birmingham small master still preferred to live alongside his workshops. The Quarter has survived for so long partly because of the continuing existence of a highly sophisticated local network which helps knit the area together. This is reflected in physical terms in the surviving medley of specialist historic buildings, a particular combination which in the context of the jewellery trade, and in terms of its extent and architectural quality, does not appear to exist anywhere else in the world.

In the context of the jewellery and metalworking trades the distinction between the domestic workshop on the one hand and the small factory on the other is by no means clear, and at what point in the development of a house and shopping unit does it cease to be a workshop and become a factory? Nor is it simply a question of the degree of mechanisation, as in the jewellery and metal trades it is possible to have very large complexes in which there is very little exploitation of motive power. This problem of definition is also an issue in relation to the textile trade where the loomshop occupies an indeterminate middle ground between the workshop in the narrow sense and the factory. Also, in the jewellery and metalworking trades the 'workshop' is the part of the house, shopping, or factory complex where the production processes take place. All of these considerations call for the broadest possible definition of what is meant by the 'vernacular workshop' that takes into account both the grey area between the humble small workshop and the factory, and differences in scale and production method both within and between trades.

Notes

1. Much of the information presented here derives from a study of the buildings of the Jewellery Quarter undertaken by English Heritage between 1998 and 2001. For a general introduction to the area see Cattell & Hawkins 2000, and for more detailed analysis see Cattell, Ely & Jones 2002.
2. Map by J Pigott-Smith, surveyed 1824–25, printed in 1828. Birmingham Central Library, LSH 996269.
3. For more on the history of the Birmingham jewellery and metalworking trades, see Mason 1998 and Hopkins 1998.

12 The Furness iron industry *by Mark Bowden*

Introduction

Furness is an area rich in hematite, woodland, and water – bringing together high-quality iron ore with plentiful supplies of fuel (wood), a source of power (water), and means of transport (also water).[1] It was therefore able to support a vibrant charcoal-based iron industry for several centuries (Fell 1908). Throughout the 1990s the RCHME undertook a series of investigations into industrial landscapes in Cumbria, culminating in a major project on the iron industry and related woodland industries of Furness and south-west Cumbria (Bowden 2000). The area covered by the RCHME project amounts to about 500 square km (190 square miles), mainly between Ambleside and Barrow (Fig 12.1). Much of this area constitutes historic Furness (Lancashire North of the Sands) and is divided between High Furness or Furness Fells, between Coniston and Windermere, and Low Furness to the south. Additionally the Project included some remains of the iron industry in south-west Cumbria (formerly Cumberland), particularly Eskdale.

Whether many of the structures associated with this industry can be described as 'workshops' is perhaps debatable. Certainly, as far as I know, the term 'workshop' was never applied historically within the industry. However, if the workshop, as opposed to the factory, is defined by the autonomy of the workforce in deciding their own time and rhythm of working, then the bloomeries – early direct-process smelting works – could certainly be described as workshops. For those working in the closely related woodland industries of the area, the woods were their workshop.

Cabins in the woods

The 'archaic sod hut' (Cowper 1901) is as vernacular a piece of architecture as you could hope for. In its simplest form – the charcoal burners' hut – it is a transient, even mobile, form of architecture (Fig 12.2).

The existence of broadleaved woodland was an essential factor in the establishment of an iron industry in Furness by providing a reliable source of charcoal fuel. Charcoal was produced on pitsteads – circular platforms – in the woods in very much the way described by Arthur Ransome in his novels (eg 1930). Contrary to what was once popularly believed, the iron industry protected and promoted the woodlands of the area, which were carefully managed by coppicing. The woods also supplied the raw materials for a number of other industries: bark for tanning; greenery (leaves, twigs, and bracken) for potash; coppice poles for many uses – nothing was wasted. All this work was done by the same people at different times of the year; bark peeling, for instance, was done in spring and early summer while charcoal burning took place in late summer and autumn.

The woodland craftsmen worked from home or, frequently, occupied temporary cabins in the woods. There are two more-or-less distinctive types of woodlanders' huts, the first being the well-known charcoal burners' hut described graphically by Ransome (1930, chapter 13) and constructed on the wigwam principle with a turf covering which has generally left no archaeologically recognisable trace. The second is a more substantial structure incorporating a stone-built hearth and chimney, and stone- or turf-built walls (Figs 12.2 and 12.3). The latter type has come to be called by historians, following Cowper, the 'bark peelers' hut'. The theory behind the distinction is that when burning charcoal the men ('colliers'), being on duty 24 hours a day tending the stack, had their food brought out to them and did not require a cooking hearth, whereas when peeling bark they cooked on site:

> The charcoal burners' huts are inhabited for a month or two, and the work engages the attention of the colliers both day and night. As a rule and to save trouble, food ready prepared is brought from neighbouring farms; and the hut is, therefore, unprovided with hearth or chimney. This, however, is different with the bark peelers' huts, for this occupation gives more leisure, and the dwellings being intended to stand longer, are of more advanced type ... four strong poles are selected, and the tops being lashed to a short ridge pole ... the four feet are planted on the ground at the four angles of a parallelogram of about 13 by 8 feet. Side walls with rounded corners, and constructed of two faces of wattle packed between with earth, are then raised to a height of two feet. On the top of this wall lighter poles of elder, birch and ash are then placed close together, with their top ends supported against the ridge-pole. The sodding is then proceeded with as in the colliers' huts, but it only extends down to the top of the wattle wall. On one side a door is left 2½ feet wide, and 3 feet 10 inches high, with a closing door of wattle; and opposite this is a stone-built hearth projecting externally from the hut about 5 feet, and about 5 feet in height.
>
> This hut ... is for four persons, and is much roomier and more comfortable than the colliers' hut. Moreover, it has the great addition of a hearth for cooking, from which, unlike many savages'

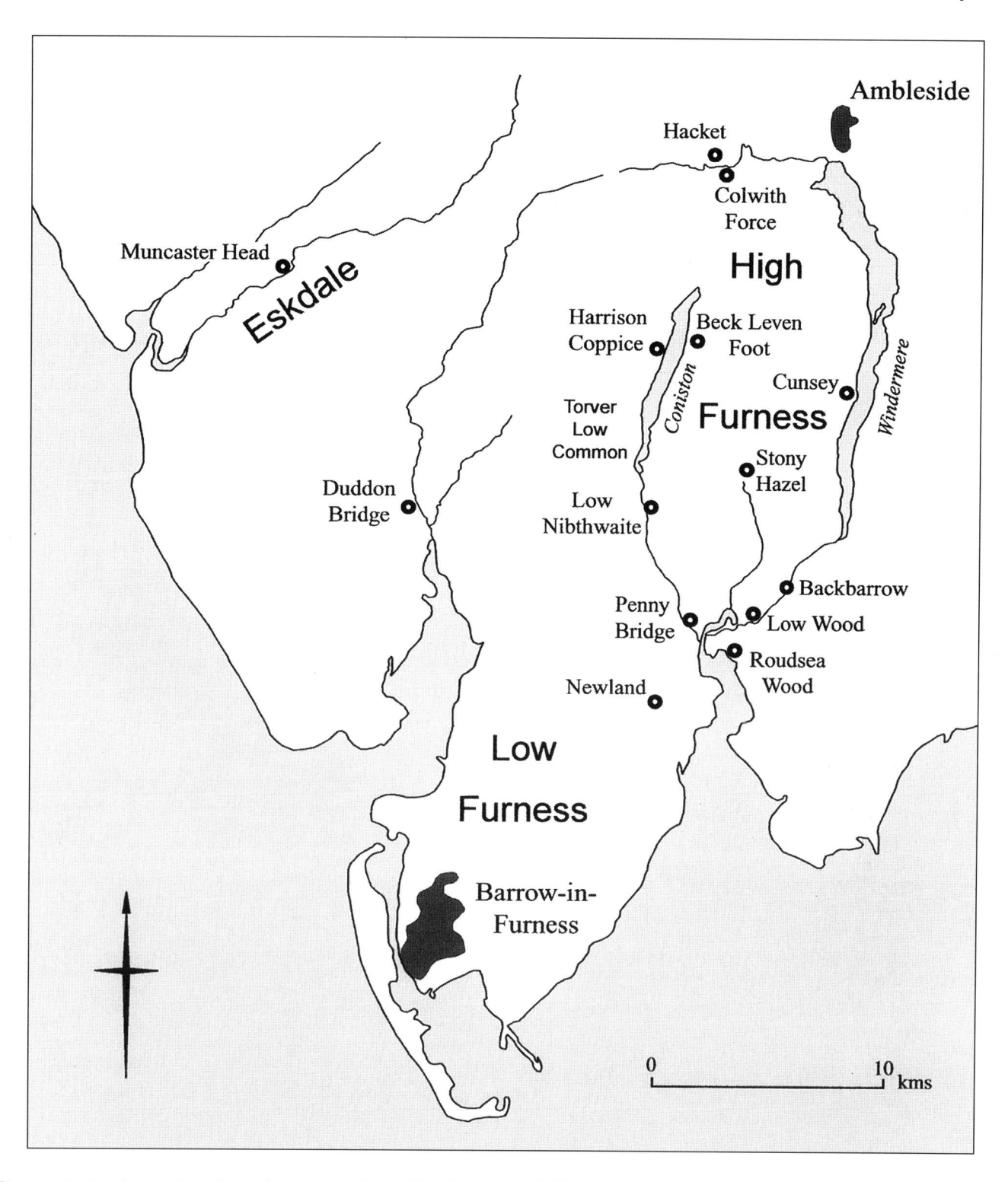

Figure 12.1 Map showing places mentioned in the text. (© English Heritage. NMR)

huts, the smoke escapes from a specially-constructed chimney, and not from a mere hole in the roof (Cowper 1901, 142–3).

Although it is clear that Cowper's descriptions and dimensions are taken from huts in contemporary use, he does not give any reference for his comments on Furness-style 'cookshop culture'. Whether the differing habits of the woodsmen in their spring and autumn occupations was a matter of record or of Cowper's own inference is not clear. There is, as many people have pointed out, an apparent illogicality about this account and there is evidence that charcoal burners, sometimes at least, cooked on site, on external hearths (Lambert 1991, 33). However, the archaeological evidence deduced from our survey tends to support the distinction between the two types of hut. The distribution of bark peelers' huts and pitsteads is quite different; some woods with many pitsteads have few, if any, bark peelers' huts

168 *The vernacular workshop*

Figure 12.2 Drawings of charcoal burners' (1,2,3) and bark peelers' (4,5,6) huts, after Cowper 1901.

and within any wood bark peelers' huts are usually placed at some distance from pitsteads. Even in the few cases where they occur together the huts face away from the pitsteads, showing that they are not associated with the charcoal burning (Bowden 2000, figs 2.10, 2.11, 2.12, 2.14).

'Workshops'

Bloomeries

It requires several tons of charcoal to smelt and refine one ton of iron ore and charcoal is friable, so the ore was brought to the charcoal, by water wherever possible, and the processing sites were all established among the woods of High Furness. Many examples, as at Beck Leven Foot on the east side of Coniston Water, lie only yards from the shore, emphasising the importance of water transport. There is also the possibility that there may have been deposits of bog ore in High Furness, in suitable quantities for pre-industrial smelting, especially in locations such as Throng Moss on Torver Low Common, on the west side of Coniston.

Until 1711, when the first blast furnaces were established in Furness, all iron in the region was smelted by the direct process in bloomeries. These could take a variety of forms but generally consisted of a small cylindrical furnace in which iron oxide in the ore is reduced, leaving metallic iron which forms a mass or 'bloom'. Slag can be tapped off from the bottom of the furnace and the bloom is removed and hammered to drive out remaining slag. The terminology for different types of bloomery is confused and disputed but classification depends to a large extent on the application of water power to the plant – or its absence – for driving bellows and hammers (Bowden 2000, 3). In the field some bloomeries exhibit evidence of water power, as at Muncaster Head, Eskdale. Muncaster Head was, according to its excavators (Tylecote & Cherry 1970), a bloomforge with powered bellows and, possibly, hammers. Other bloomeries are in positions where they may have been water-powered though direct evidence is lacking, while others – due to their topographical location – could never have been water-powered. None of the Furness bloomeries is dated. The site excavated at Muncaster Head was equated with a documented bloomforge of 17th-century date, and 17th-century finds were recovered (Tylecote & Cherry 1970). This interpretation was accepted, perhaps too uncritically, during the RCHME project (Blood & Lofthouse 1995; Bowden 2000, 45–7). Cranstone has since thrown doubt upon the identification and suggested that the documented site is actually at Forge House on the other side of the valley (pers comm).

Some bloomery sites, as at Harrison Coppice near Coniston and Colwith Force on the River Brathay, for example, have remains of stone buildings adjacent to them – which may or may not be relevant – but most are just heaps of slag with no distinguishing surface features. The tumbled remains of a rectangular dry-stone building at Harrison Coppice lies in close proximity to the larger of two slag heaps (Blood 1996; Bowden 2000, 42, fig 3.3b). This building would have measured approximately 5.6 m (19ft) by 4.8 m (30ft) internally. At its north end a mound of tumbled material possibly suggests the position of a chimney, though there is no visible trace of burning and this may only be the remains of a gable. At the south end, opposite the slag heap, is a gap containing a light scatter of stones, which may define the entrance. At Colwith Force (Lax 1998; Bowden 2000, 42–3, fig 3.3d) there are two buildings, one a relatively substantial rectangular structure of similar dimensions to the one at Harrison Coppice just described. The other is a poorly defined rubble structure measuring approximately 5.5 m (18ft 4 in) by 4.4 m (14ft 8 in) overall and adjacent to a slag dump, which appears to have been cleared from the interior. Furthermore, geophysical survey within this building has produced very exciting results. There are two strong anomalies, apparently two well-preserved furnaces, one with indications of its slag-tapping channel, at the north end of the building. These might be furnaces of successive

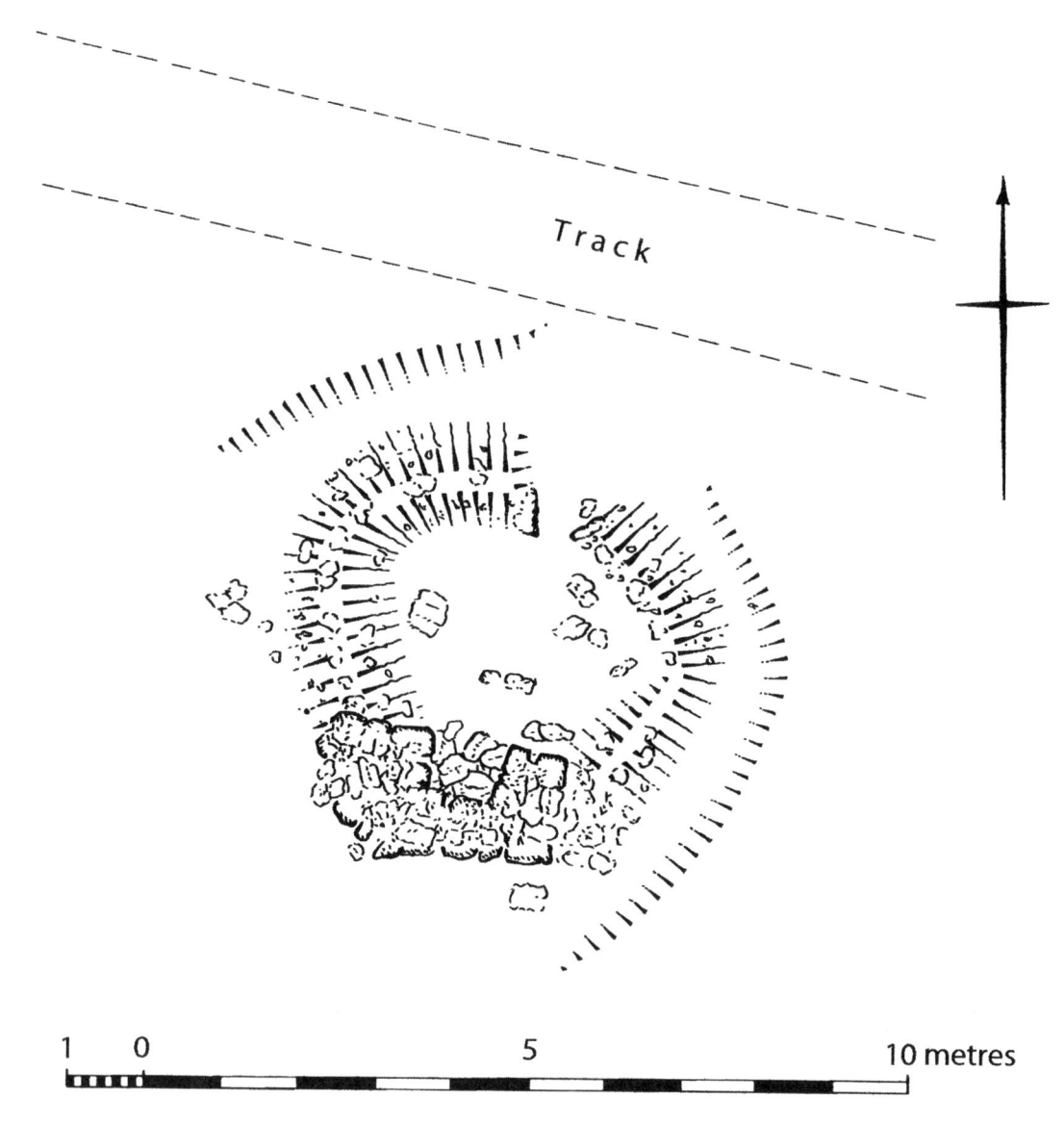

Figure 12.3 Plan of a bark peelers' hut in Roudsea Wood. (© Crown Copyright. NMR)

dates but they might also be contemporary with each other and operated alternately, one being the furnace and the other a hearth for refining (Price & Crew 1999). Other structures are rare and where they do exist, can be misleading. At Beck Leven Foot a neat stone platform alongside the bloomery mound turned out to result from experimental smelting undertaken at the site by Clare in the 1980s.

Otherwise our only understanding of what these sites might actually have looked like in operation comes from the work of experimental archaeologists, such as Crew. It seems clear that the bloomery furnaces must have been sheltered in some way and not simply open to the elements (as sometimes suggested by reconstruction drawings). However, these shelters may have been in many cases as insubstantial as the 'archaic sod huts' of the woodsmen, if a little larger. The provision of stone-built, or at least stone-founded, buildings at Harrison Coppice and Colwith Force suggests longer occupation and/or greater investment.

Blast furnaces

In 1711 the industry was transformed by the construction of the first blast furnaces in Furness and by 1750 there were eight. The first were at Backbarrow and Cunsey; Leighton (near Carnforth, not shown on Fig 12.1) followed in 1713; Low Nibthwaite and Duddon Bridge in the 1730s; and Newland, Low Wood, and Penny Bridge in the 1740s. Three companies, Backbarrow, Cunsey, and Newland, dominated the industry (Bowden 2000, 7–10). The stimulation for this revolutionary development in the Furness iron industry came from some of the major ironmasters of the West Midlands. Their motivation was the fine provision of ore, charcoal, and water, but particularly the latter (Bowden 2000, 78). They were ably abetted by local entrepreneurs – who also entered into competition – and the Furness companies formed their own daughter companies in the west of Scotland. The origins of the relationship between the locals and the outsiders is unknown but

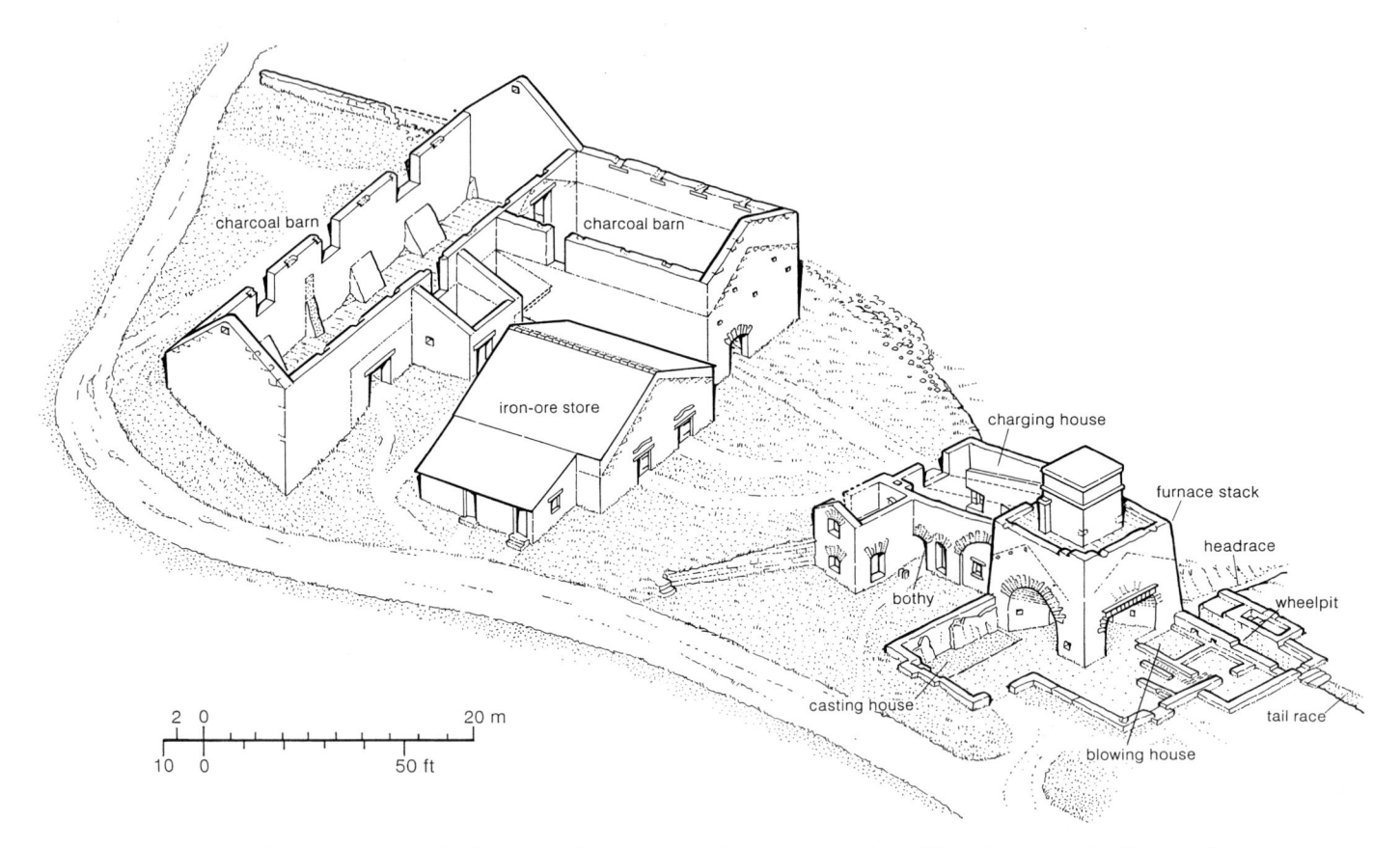

Figure 12.4 Bird's eye view of Duddon Bridge iron works as it is today. This drawing indicates the enlargements of the charcoal barns and ore store, to the left. The charging house and furnace stack are downslope to the right, with the excavated remains of the casting house, blowing house and wheelpit (extreme right). (© Crown Copyright. NMR)

close links between Furness and the West Midlands were maintained throughout the history of the industry.

Three of the Furness furnaces continued to work into the 19th century and Backbarrow did not close until the 1960s, though it had converted from charcoal to coke, and from water power to steam power, in 1921. Survival of the blast furnaces is excellent in Furness, with substantial building remains at four of the sites (Bowden 2000, 47–66). There is a respectable survival of documentary evidence for the industry (eg Marshall *et al* 1996) but very little of this deals with the physical and topographical aspects of the production sites; only the surviving physical remains can inform reconstruction of how the industry worked.

Each furnace is a series of related buildings linked by a common process. This is now best demonstrated at Duddon Bridge (Fig 12.4), the most completely surviving complex, retaining furnace, ore store, charcoal barns, cottages, and the structure of its water supply (Dunn 1998; Goodall 1999a). At the core of the complex is the stack. Attached to the left is the bridge house and charging house, on the right the blowing house, and in the foreground the casting house. The furnace stack is a tower-like structure with battered walls. Rubble voussoired arches, one of them rebuilt after a collapse, open through the base of the stack. Inside, the furnace shaft is a double cone in section. Extremes of heat and stress led to frequent re-linings, and this is evident on the surviving long-lived Furness stacks. The blowing arch opened into a roofed blowing house with double bellows, originally conventional leather, but here replaced by cylinder bellows in the late 18th century. Details of the casting house have been confirmed by excavation. At Duddon the charging house was two-storeyed, the ground floor apparently used as a bothy and perhaps as a store. The charge was mixed and prepared on the upper floor, and then tipped into the mouth of the shaft.

The layout of the site allows gravity to aid the movement of materials while allowing sufficient water supply to the wheel. The ore store is terraced into the slope so that the ore was unloaded through high-level doors at the rear and brought out at a lower level at the front and led downhill to the charging house entrance.

Charcoal is a demanding material. It is friable and fragile; if reduced to dust it is useless in the furnace. The size and evolution of the charcoal barns at the different furnaces reflect their output. Those at Duddon and Newland are the most extensive. The original barn at Duddon, gable end-on to the furnace, was extended across its upper end. It was rebuilt after a serious fire and the original barn heightened.

The storage capacity therefore grew from 600 cubic metres to 2000 cubic metres (785 to 2616 cubic yards). At Newland the charcoal barns are even larger, beginning with a capacity of 1400 cubic metres (1830 cubic yards), finally enlarged to 5000 cubic metres (6540 cubic yards). Again there are high-level loading doors at the rear and low-level doors at the front.

Work forces were small. When a furnace was in blast it was recharged constantly and kept in operation for a campaign which could last many months. The cottages at Duddon (not shown on Fig 12.4) were constructed as a pair of one-room deep single-fronted cottages, subsequently doubled in depth and thrown together, with a stable and shippon added. Duddon had a chief furnaceman, called the keeper, with probably two assistants who took charge of 12-hour shifts, overseeing the fillers. Were the two cottages intended for the assistants, with the furnaceman living off site? Did the fillers occupy the bothy below the charging house?

There was no question of autonomy for the workforce in the speed, rhythm; or intensity of their work but here the tyranny was imposed not by the iron company owners or managers – who tended to live at a distance from the plant, unlike some 18th-century industrialists elsewhere – but by the process itself. While in blast the furnace had to be fed with ore, fuel and, when necessary, flux on a continual 24/7 cycle for months at a time. The worker 'watching over the sleepless furnace himself slept 'scarcely at all" (Wertime 1962, 71). It was also dangerous:

> Against the danger of explosion there was no defence. For workmen and plant alike, eruptions are the most terrible danger. They bring death to those nearby and spread fire far and wide. In a sudden explosion, a furnace will throw up all its contents, molten and solid. It also becomes a volcano vomiting flaming fragments from every opening' (Diderot 1755b, I, caption to pl 87).

The blast furnace at Leighton is said to have blown up in 1806.

Iron products were occasionally cast directly at the blast furnaces, but more often the pigs of iron were taken away to forges for further refining. The majority seems to have been exported to the West Midlands but some local water-powered forges were operated.

Forges

The later forges with surviving structures, at Hacket and Stony Hazel, are well dated by documents – to about 1720 in the case of Stony Hazel – but great debate surrounds their classification. Were they very late examples of the direct process bloomery forge or were they refining forges designed to work with the blast furnaces? The answer to this question is crucial to the 'workshop' debate. If they were built as bloomeries at this late date then they are an example – perhaps a classic example – of 'resistance' or at least 'inertia'. In the Furness iron industry there is no question but that the blast furnace was more efficient than the bloomery (Bowden 2000, 77–8), so there is no possibility that resistance in this case was justified by good industrial practice.

Stony Hazel had a chequered history (Bowden 2000, 73–6). It may hardly ever have been worked and suffered three disastrous fires in quick succession, so raising the possibility of industrial sabotage or fraud. The forge was bought up by the Cunsey and Backbarrow Companies in collaboration, and terminally mothballed. In recent years it has been excavated twice (Davies-Shiel 1970; Cranstone 1985a; 1985b), hence the debate over its interpretation. Neither excavation has been fully published.

There were finery and chafery forges built in direct association with the blast furnaces, but they do not seem to have survived, with the possible exception of that at Backbarrow (Bowden 2000, 68–71).

The bar iron produced by the local forges, like the pig from the furnaces, was often taken away to the West Midlands, and sometimes to south Wales, for conversion into finished products; a further reflection of the relationship between the local industries and its sponsors (or exploiters?). One of the themes of this conference was the relationship between workshop and factory. It is doubtful if 'factory' is an appropriate word for any plant in Furness. However, Furness was one end of a 'distributed relationship' and the links between Furness and the West Midlands are certainly worthy of further research.

Ancillary buildings

There were a number of ancillary structures in the region, more-or-less directly related to the iron industry. At Newland, an industrial hamlet, there was a rolling mill, unique to the region, later converted to a blacking mill, with an adjacent store/stable. This is of some architectural interest because of its 'fireproof' cast-iron roof structure (Goodall 1999b; Bowden 2000, 64–5). In some cases the blast furnace structures were later converted for different uses. At Nibthwaite the blast furnace was later converted into a bobbin mill, and then a saw mill (Goodall 1999c; Bowden 2000, 54–5).

Conclusion

Much more research is needed in this area, and it was always our hope that the RCHME Project would form one step in a ladder. This is already happening, as shown by the fact that our information has fed into English Heritage's Monuments Protection Programme for the iron industry, and that (as mentioned above) the Lake District National Park has commissioned a series of geophysical surveys of bloomery sites (Price & Crew 1999).

One major problem with the remains of the early industries in Furness is the almost total lack of absolute chronology; this is particularly true for the bloomeries. In 1898 Cowper remarked that 'we have not one tittle of evidence that any hearths in the fells of Lancashire date from Roman or pre-Norman times' (101). Sadly this is still true today; there is no secure date for any bloomery site in Cumbria. Though this is an aspect of research which the RCHME Project could not directly address, it was flagged up so that others may carry research forward in this area. Only excavation can provide the data to resolve this issue. Full publication of the excavations at Stony Hazel is also clearly essential if the significant issue of the interpretation of this key site is to be resolved.

Notes

1. This paper draws on the work of many colleagues. In particular I owe a huge debt of thanks to Dr Ian Goodall. This also gives me an opportunity to rectify a previous omission by acknowledging the work undertaken by Adam Menuge, Nigel Fradgley, Garry Corbett, Jennifer Deadman, and Allan Adams at Backbarrow Furnace and elsewhere in Furness. Fig 12.1 was prepared by Deb Cunliffe, Fig 12.3 by Amy Lax, and Fig 12.4 by Allan Adams.

13 Workshops and cottages in the Ironbridge Gorge
by Barrie Trinder

Introduction

To suggest that 'workshops' are significant in the context of the coal and iron industry may seem paradoxical. The working of iron and the exploitation of mines that could supply ironworks demanded the investment of capital on a large-scale, in blast furnaces, steam engines, rolling mills, and the sinking of shafts. Ironmasters and coal-mining entrepreneurs have traditionally been seen as controllers of the lives of their employees, whose power has been expressed through the housing they owned, the sinuous terraces that stretch up the valleys of South Wales, the long rows that comprise the pit villages of County Durham, the Garden City-style estates built in the 1920s to accommodate those who worked the newly-sunk collieries of the Dukeries. This paper is concerned with the Coalbrookdale Coalfield in Shropshire, a region that was the source of many innovations in the 18th century, and that for a few decades at the end of the century was in quantitative terms the most productive iron-making area in Britain. The manufactures that were traded from the Coalfield were not, for the most part, the works of individual craftsmen, but pig iron for foundries and forges, iron castings, various forms of semi-finished wrought-iron, and coal in boat loads or wagon loads.

Workshops are, rightly, most closely associated with the manufacture of relatively small artefacts, with weaving, knitting, watch-making, the carving of wooden toys, the forging of nails, locks or chains, the stitching of leather gloves, or the making of felt hats. The culture of communities of this kind is memorably captured in the reminiscences of Samuel Bamford, who grew up in a weaving household in Middleton near Manchester in the opening years of the 19th century (Bamford 1893, 36–7). He recalls a self-regulating society, in which periods of intensive working activity, as in the weeks before Christmas, were interspersed with spells when manufacturing was abandoned, as it was during the twelve days of Christmas and the annual summer wakes. Every fortnight the head of the household delivered on foot the family's output to a Manchester merchant, and Bamford recalls the rather laboured social relations with the merchant, and the cameraderie of the Middleton weavers as they returned home together. Such a lifestyle seems to have little in common with those of miners or furnacemen, yet the fundamental nature of most workshop communities was determined by informal patterns of settlement, and such patterns were commonly found in coalfields.

The Coalbrookdale coalfield

The history of iron-making in Shropshire has been depicted in celebratory terms, as a succession of epoch-making innovations, and in a deferential manner, that puts at the centre the role of the Darby dynasty. This tradition is continued in a recent study of the family (Thomas 1999). The significance of the series of developments between 1708 and 1755 by which Abraham Darby I (1677–1717), Abraham Darby II (1711–63), and their partners demonstrated that iron for both the forge and the foundry could be produced economically using coke as the fuel of the blast furnace cannot be exaggerated. Nor can the impact made on the imaginations of contemporaries by the construction of the Iron Bridge in 1777–81 be in any way diminished (Cossons & Trinder 2002, 33–9). Nevertheless other 'Coalbrookdale firsts' including the patent granted to the brothers Cranage for the use of mineral fuel in forges, and the use of simple iron castings as rails in 1767, prove on closer examination to have been of less consequence. A deferential approach to the social history of the Coalfield naturally draws attention to the houses built by entrepreneurs, and in particular to those erected, or thought to have been erected, by the Darby family. A more detached view shows that the relatively few 'rows' built by the Darbys can only ever have accommodated a small proportion of their workforce and that many of those who toiled in their ironworks and mines lived in houses of different kinds. It is also evident that many of the families who lived in informal settlements in the 17th, 18th, and 19th centuries were to some extent self-sufficient, and that communities of this kind housed many self-employed craftsmen whose skills were essential to the operation of the great iron- and coal-working companies.

Understanding of the nature of settlement in the Coalbrookdale Coalfield has steadily enlarged over the past three decades, a development that is reflected in the successive editions of an economic and social history of the region (Trinder 1973, 1981 and 2000). Two volumes of the Victoria County History have described the inheritance of parishes and townships, landed estates and field patterns present in the area in the 17th century before the advent of large-scale industrialisation (VCH 1985 and 1999). A study of one particular settlement, Holywell Lane in Dawley parish, was based on an architectural survey, an excavation, wide-ranging documentary research, and on extensive use of oral evidence (Hunt *et al* 1982). The Nuffield Survey of the archaeology of the Ironbridge Gorge in the late 1980s analysed several areas of informal settlement, most notably Broseley Wood (Alfrey & Clark 1993). Two published volumes of probate inventories have revealed details of the households in informal settlements in Ketley and Wrockwardine Wood in the north of the Coalfield, as well as in the Ironbridge Gorge (Trinder & Cox 1980; 2000). Some aspects of settlement and of working class culture have been analysed by graduate students of the Ironbridge Institute, most notably the role of the brewhouse (or wash house), which has been contrasted with similar establishments in other kinds of community (McDonald 1989). Ward has recently set settlements of this kind in a national context (Ward 2002).

The Coalbrookdale Coalfield extends rather more than 16 km (10 miles) from north to south, and no more than 6.5 km (4 miles) from east to west at its widest point. Towards its southern end it is riven by the gorge formed by the River Severn during the melting of the Devonian ice sheet. The parochial, administrative, and tenurial pattern of the area is complex (Trinder 2000, 1–6), but contrasts between the patterns of housing that developed in enclosed and unenclosed areas can be seen throughout the region. Informal patterns of settlement, whether created by squatting, or by landowners allowing tenants to erect tenements, can be seen in Wrockwardine Wood, a detached portion of the parish of Wrockwardine, extending over some 200 ha (500 acres), that was never enclosed; the extensive manor of Ketley, the 14.5 ha (36 acres) of Snedshill Common in Shifnal parish, on Lawley Common in Wellington parish; where the untidy pattern of cottages contrasted with the Coalbrookdale Company's ordered rows alongside the Horsehay ironworks on the other side of the boundary with Dawley; in the western parts of Little Dawley township that included Holywell Lane; on either side of the River Severn in the Ironbridge Gorge; and to the south of the river in Broseley Wood.

The nature of informal settlement

Evidence from probate records provides many insights into the ways in which such settlements had grown up. The will of John Bayley, a collier from the riverside community of Madeley Wood, made in 1710[1] shows that the cottage in which he lived had been purchased from the assignees of the late lord of the manor, and subsequently divided into three parts. William Crippin, a collier who died in 1795 bequeathed to one son a pair of houses in Madeley whose gardens and brewhouse had been built on the waste, and to another a group of three houses with a pig sty also situated on the waste land.[2] Thomas York, a charter master (ie a sub-contractor who worked mines) who died in 1811, left money to his descendants for building on the waste adjacent to his freehold land in Madeley Wood.[3] The precise nature of tenure differed from place to place across the Coalfield, and the ways in which land was administered changed over time. The appointment in 1812 of the celebrated James Loch (1780–1855) as agent to the estates of the Leveson Gower family, for example, brought dramatic changes to the ways in which the scattered cottages of the manor of Ketley were managed (Trinder 2000, 140–1). Nevertheless it is clear that squatting on commons and the acquisition by tenants of leases or small freeholds from unassertive lords of manors, did much to shape the growth of settlement in the region, and the occupations and ways of life of the inhabitants (Figure 13.1).

Pictorial maps of the 1720s of Jackfield, the portion of the parish of Broseley that borders the River Severn,[4] show many terraces made up of dwellings of unequal size, apparently built at different dates, and standing within small enclosures of irregular shape. In some cases individual houses stand in the corners of plots in which the main house occupies the central part. Similar groups of house can still be observed in areas of informal settlement throughout the Coalfield. Wills provide evidence of this process. John Bedware, a carpenter from Madeley Wood who died in 1761 had a terrace of three cottages held by lease from the lords of the manor. He lived in one and his widowed daughter-in-law occupied another while the third was let to a tenant.[5] William Botteley, a collier who died in 1762, divided his house on the edge of the waste in Madeley Wood between two sons, one of whom inherited the kitchen, cellar, and parlour, while the other had a 'little room', the room above it, and the brewhouse (Trinder & Cox 2000, 327–8). William Lloyd, a Broseley collier who died in 1766, left to his wife 'that little houses lately erected at ye Top of ye Garden'.[6] Laurence Brown, a Broseley blacksmith who made his will in 1771,[7] bequeathed to his son John the north end of his house, consisting of one room upstairs, and a room and a buttery downstairs, to his wife the middle part and the new end that included his shop and a 'penthouse', and to his second son the south end that was occupied by a tenant. When the son John Brown made his will in 1783,[8] the building was still divided into three dwellings, left to his wife and two of his sons, but he also bequeathed to two other sons land on the property on which he wished them to build houses.

The will of John Brooke of Madeley, made in 1719 sets out the specifications for a house that was to be built by his son to accommodate his wife in her old age:[9]

a good, firm and substantial dwelling house in the Lower Yard ... with good and well-burnt bricks ... to contain 16 foots in length, 13 foots in breadth within the walls, and 12 foots high in the wall from the ground to the wall plate, with two good and sufficient fire-places ... and also a shear (ie a lean-to shed) to go the length of the said building and an over for the use of the same. The roof of the said house and all timber to be therein used to be all good sawd timber and to be covered with good and sufficient tiles (Fig. 13.2).

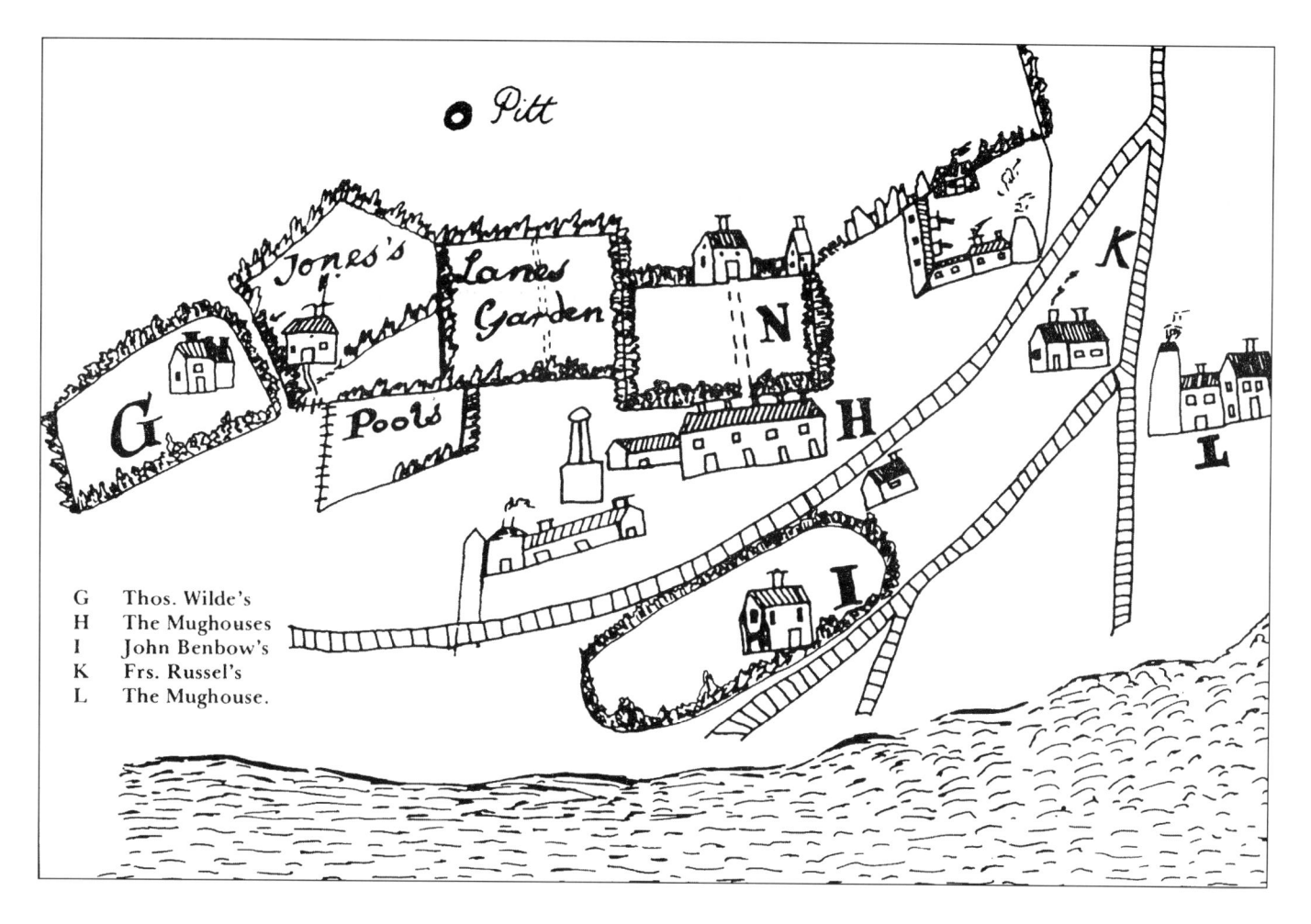

Figure 13.1 Squatter cottages, some with workshops attached, at the Calcutts in the Ironbridge Gorge in the mid-18th century. Redrawn from the Broseley Estate Book (SRR 6001/2365); reproduced from Trinder 2000. (© Barrie Trinder)

Figure 13.2 Landscape of open settlement at Madeley Wood on the north bank of the River Severn in the Ironbridge Gorge. (© Barrie Trinder)

Self-sufficiency

Map evidence and wills show that many houses of this kind stood in plots of land that were large enough to provide grazing for a cow, space for a pig sty, or ground sufficient for the growing of patches of flax or hemp, or small quantities of grain. Many testators gave precise instructions for the division of such plots, obviously anxious that their descendants should retain access to wash houses (or brew houses), privies, and wells, as well as enjoy their shares of land used for crops or grazing. Timothy Roper, a Broseley collier who made his will in 1766,[10] left part of his house to one son and part to another, while providing land on which a third son might build a house. He gave instructions for the division of his garden between the three sons, using as landmarks a pear tree and a Dunsweet apple tree, and specifying that his children were all to retain access to a well. The will of John Dyer, a barge owner from Benthall, made in 1795, provides further evidence of this kind of concern.[11] His whole estate was left to his wife, after whose decease it was to be divided between three sons.

His son John was to receive the dwelling house that he himself occupied, with the 'land from the upper end of the main house down to the Benthall Brook, the flower garden near the house, the cistern for holding wash and grain, and the nearest pig sty'. His son William was to inherit 'the brewhouse adjacent to the dwelling house assigned to John Dyer, the land from the corner of the house where the brewhouse door is, to the brook, and the rest of the ground above the brewhouse except the cistern and pig sty,' his brother to have a road through the flower garden to the brook, and the other pig sty. A third son, Richard, was to have the lower garden adjoining the house of Widow Barnes, together with £15 in cash, and, the father added, 'if I should build another sty, my son Richard is to have it which will prevent all disputes arising among my sons'. He further added that all his children were to have 'free ingress and egress to and from the Necessary House, without suit hindrance or interruption'.

Probate inventories show that many of those who lived in cottages of this kind kept a cow or a pig, and grew some crops. John Harris, a Broseley coal miner who died in 1674 (Trinder & Cox 2000, 153–4),[12] had a single cow, worth £1 13s 4d, and from the evidence of yarn in his house, that his will shows to have been highly valued, also grew some flax and hemp. Edward Darrall, a collier from Holywell Lane, Little Dawley, who died in 1726 (Trinder & Cox 1980, 180)[13] also had just one cow together with vessels with which to process its milk, as well as linen yarn. Another Dawley collier, George Hewlett, who died the previous year, kept a cow and a pig (Trinder & Cox 1980, 179). Many cottagers in the Ironbridge Gorge kept a pig. Of the 151 pig keepers in the four parishes in the Gorge, about a quarter kept only one pig (Trinder & Cox 2000, 49). One such animal is tellingly described on the probate inventory of James Weaver in 1735 as 'a small sow at the Door'.[14]

The self-sufficiency of many households of his kind is well-illustrated by the inventory of Richard Vickers of Wrockwardine Wood who died in 1705. He was a man of limited resources whose moveable possessions were valued at just over £30, in a house that consisted of two rooms downstairs and upstairs, with a buttery (a synonym for brewhouse) on the ground floor. He made part of his living from 'two aged horses' employed in carrying coal, valued, with their panniers and other tackle, at only £2 10s. Vickers also had 'four little cows, too of them very ancient' together with four heifers and two calves that were valued at £15. He had no pig at the time of his death, but bacon as well as beef joints were hanging in one of his bedrooms. He had four cheeses in the other chamber, and dairy equipment in the buttery that could have been used to make them. Vickers grew crops of 'corn' (probably a mixture of wheat and rye, used for bread-making) and barley. Growing crops of flax and hemp were not normally listed in inventories, but the presence of harvested flax and hemp in one of his chambers suggests that Vickers probably grew them.

Inventories show that flax and hemp were processed into linen yarn in many households whose heads were miners, ironworkers, bargemen, or craftsmen. The yarn was woven by 'custom weavers', nine of whom can be identified through their inventories in the four parishes of the Ironbridge Gorge (Trinder & Cox 2000, 41). Flax, and particularly hemp, were grown on odd plots of land in the district rather than on the principal arable fields. A map of the parish of Little Wenlock of 1727 shows ten small plots called hemp butts in and around the centre of the village (*ibid* 2000, 73). Harvested flax is itemised on 26% of the inventories for the four parishes of the Ironbridge Gorge made between 1700 and 1764, and spinning wheels on 21% (*ibid* 2000, 73–4). While weaving was the work of local craftsmen, and some hemp- and flax-dressing was done by itinerant specialists, the processing of hemp and flax was generally regarded as women's work, part of the duties of 'huswifery', a term that was commonly used in south Shropshire. The domestic manufacture of linen in this manner continued across much of the Midlands well into the 19th century (Trinder 1996, 134–6). George Eliot refers to it in novels set in the Coventry region in the 1820s, and it was still sufficiently commonplace in the early 1840s for Parliamentary Commissioners investigating the textile industry to find it necessary to define the term 'custom weaver'. The presence of wool and great wheels on some inventories and of 'woollen gears' on those of weavers suggests that small quantities of woollen cloth were made in this way in the Coalbrookdale Coalfield.

Many inventories include a buttery, brewhouse, or wash house on the ground floor. Rooms of this kind are evident as parts of dwellings on 18th-century pictorial maps, and fieldwork shows that they can still be identified, some of them lean-to structures, some detached. Rooms serving the same purposes were incorporated into rows of cottages built by the ironworking companies, and were often, like those in terraces extended by families, shared between several households. In Carpenters' Row, Coalbrookdale, for example, built by the iron company in the 1780s, ten front doors gave access to eight dwellings and two wash houses, each shared by four families. The various terms used to describe rooms of this kind are evidence of the different functions they served. They were used for laundry work; for brewing, equipment for which is listed on about 50% of the 18th-century inventories from the Ironbridge Gorge parishes; for the preparation of dough for bread-making; and for making butter and cheese. The evidence relating to this kind of room was assessed in 1989 by Miriam McDonald who concluded that it is found in many societies, in Clydeside tenements and in the Scottish Highlands for example, and that it is characteristically 'a reserved part of the domestic space used by women ... an easily slopped-out area' (McDonald 1989) (Fig. 13.3).

Figure 13.3 Characteristic cottage built of coal measure sandstone at Hodge Bower, Madeley, in the Ironbridge Gorge. (© Barrie Trinder)

Occupations and workshops

Probate records are a rich source of information on the occupations of those who lived in the informal settlements in the Coalbrookdale Coalfield. There are probate inventories for 67 miners in the Ironbridge Gorge parishes dating from the period 1662–1764. Some of their wills show that they lived in dwellings that had originated as squatter holdings on the waste or as small leaseholds or freeholds, and had been extended into short terraces, as do many wills from the following half-century. Inventories show that many miners were in part self-sufficient. 10 had cows, 16 had pigs, 7 made milk or cheese, 37 brewed their own beer, 12 had spinning wheels, and 7 had yarn in their homes (Trinder & Cox 2000, 17–20). Fewer probate documents related to employees at ironworks, but some, like John Thomas, the moulder brought to Coalbrookdale from Bristol by Abraham Darby I, and his brother George, acquired small freehold plots on which they built houses (Trinder 2000, 144; Trinder & Cox 2000, 327). Probate inventories survive for 73 bargemen for the same period, and show that they, like the miners, were in part self-sufficient, while their wills indicate that they lived in similar kinds of house. Nine bargemen kept cows, most of them single animals tended for their milk, 29 kept pigs, 32 had brewing equipment, 11 had spinning wheels, and 7 had yarn or unspun hemp in their homes. It is obvious that neither miners, nor ironworkers, nor bargemen plied their trades in workshops, but the settlements in which they lived were not, for the most part, created by entrepreneurs, but had much in common in social terms with the informal communities that produced textiles, nails, or watches.

If the principal occupational groups in the Coalfield made no use of workshops they depended on other craftsmen who did. The surviving account books of the ironworking companies show their reliance on a variety of craftsmen who provided services for them: carpenters who erected the headstocks of mines; tallow chandlers who provided candles for use underground; ropemakers; and families who kept packhorses. The best evidence for the role of such craftsmen is provided by the accounts for the construction and equipment by Thomas Botfield of the Old Park ironworks in Dawley parish in 1788–91 (Botfield Papers, John Rylands University Library, Manchester). Botfield called on the services of several brickmakers and a variety of builders to construct the ironworks, the collieries that supplied it, and the houses where its workers were accommodated. From a carpenter he ordered wheelbarrows, helves for hewing pikes, air troughs tarred and flannelled for mine ventilation systems, and horse gins for winding coals. He purchased ropes from several sources, water barrels from a local cooper, and baskets, in which coal and iron ore were handled, from a basket maker.

Probate records provide some evidence of the workshops in which such goods were produced. Mary Clemson, a widow, was operating a rope-making business at the time of her death in 1753, and left to her married daughter 'all the tools belonging to rope-making, and the spinning house, rope yard and piece of land adjoining, provided she follows that employment' (Trinder & Cox 2000, 322). Samuel Edwards, a Broseley tallow chandler who died in 1793,[15] left 'the workshop on the south side of the Delve' to his nephew Thomas Adams who followed the same trade. Charles Gwynn, a Broseley basket maker who made his will in 1798,[16] left to one son the 'Over Little House' with the little shop adjacent, and to another 'the old house . . . and the over part of the garden and basket shop, together with a little shed adjacent, and all the tools and stock, cistern, and backside, and all the twigs and the twig land'. Two more sons received other parts of the property. Baskets, like ropes, barrels, and candles, were essential in the operation of the economy of the region. They were the receptacles in which coal, iron ore, and limestone were moved between the mine workings and quarries in which they were cut, and the parts of ironworks where they were coked, calcined, or broken up. Hampers made by basket makers were also used for the despatch of ceramic products to customers

A relatively small proportion of those who lived in the Coalbrookdale Coalfield manufactured consumer products in workshops, principally ceramics of various kinds. The pictorial maps of the riverside parts of Broseley of the 1720s,[17] depict several short terraces on the ends of which were kilns, for the firing either of pots or tobacco pipes. The will of one pipemaker, Samuel Roden, refers to a 'new house with tenement and shop and garden which I builded' located in Broseley.[18] John Bell, a potter who made

178 *The vernacular workshop*

his will in 1790, left his house to his son, also John, on condition that his three daughters were to enjoy occupation of 'the upper part called the shop'. Similar 'shops' are mentioned in the wills of other potters and pipemakers.

Conclusions

The contrasts between the 'rookeries' of the Coalbrookdale Coalfield and the rows built by the ironmasters were pointed out in a paper written 30 years ago (Trinder 1974), and this chapter has been a means of assessing what has been learned over the past three decades through investigations based on a variety of sources, on maps, probate records, estate and parish documents, census enumerators' returns, and above all through the study of buildings and landscapes in the field and an awareness of the ways in which industrial communities were housed elsewhere. Nevertheless many tasks await completion. Much may be learned in due course from family reconstitution based on parish registers, and from the integration of data from registers with that from other documentary sources that modern information technology makes possible. Fieldwork can still be rewarding, for ancient cottages still lurk beneath more recent exteriors in the Ironbridge Gorge, the manor of Ketley, and elsewhere, and study of cartographic evidence may identify some sites of 17th- and 18th-century dwellings that are suitable for excavation. Not least, there is much understanding to be gained by reviewing the patterns of settlement in the Coalfield in the context of 'workshop communities' elsewhere in Britain, and, indeed, further afield. While there are many obvious differences between the Ironbridge Gorge and Saddleworth, Prescot, or Headington Quarry, there are also basic similarities, and we gain understanding both from the similarities and the differences (Fig. 13.4).

The study of settlement patterns has transformed the significance of the history of the Coalbrookdale Coalfield. It should no longer be seen as a series of 'Coalbrookdale firsts', the achievements of the Darby family, but as the development of a range of communities that grew in size, and in some respects in prosperity, while enduring the pains of large-scale industrialisation. Berthold Brecht asked 'Where did the bricklayers go? The evening the Great Wall of China was finished?' Investigation in the late 1970s showed that the stone-built cottage that was then No. 4 Holywell Lane, documented as the home of members of the Dorrall family from 1763 until at least 1871, was probably that described in the inventory of Edward Dorrall in 1726, when it consisted of a kitchen, a little room and a buttery on the ground floor, and two chambers above, and Dorrall's moveable possessions were valued at less than £5. It was probably this Edward Dorrall who in 1709 provided coal for Abraham Darby I's blast furnace at Coalbrookdale, and 'charcked' it into coke (Trinder 2000, 26). The study of settlements provides some of the answers to Brecht's question.

Figure 13.4 Well-documented squatter cottage built in 1798 alongside the recently opened Shropshire Canal at Stocking, Little Dawley, about 1.5 km (1 mile) north of the Coalbrookdale ironworks. (© Barrie Trinder)

Notes

1. HRO ex. 8 April 1712
2. HRO ex. 17 July 1795
3. HRO ex. 15 March 1811
4. SRR 6001/2365–6
5. HRO ex. 14 Sep 1761
6. HRO ex. 6 Aug 1766
7. HRO ex. 18 July 1776
8. HRO ex. 10 June 1783
9. HRO ex. 27 March 1721
10. HRO ex. 27 July 1767
11. HRO ex. 6 May 1806
12. HRO ex. 18 April 1674
13. LRO ex. 21 Oct 1762
14. HRO ex. 2 June 1735
15. HRO ex. 27 April 1793
16. HRO ex. 28 Jan 1799
17. SRR 6001/2365–6
18. HRO ex. 20 March 1762

14 Workshops, industrial production and the landscape *by P S Barnwell*

Although this volume does not claim to approach comprehensive coverage of workshop-based industries, it nevertheless represents a significant step towards correcting an imbalance in the study of buildings connected with the processes of production, which has hitherto largely been concentrated on factories. A similar imbalance exists in contemporary accounts of industrialisation, comment and wonder being attracted largely by its most novel feature, the great factory with its steam engines and machinery which ruled the lives of hitherto unimaginable concentrations of workers (King & Timmins 2001, 10–20, 49). The first generation of historians of the industrial economy also saw the adoption of the steam engine and advent of the factory system as the defining characteristics of an age which began, quite suddenly, around 1780, and viewed them as containing the origins of the social ills of their own times, the turn of the 19th century (Toynbee 1884; Webb & Webb 1911). Although the contemporary accounts have ensured that factories and the factory system have remained central to discussion of industrialisation, historical discourse has long-since brought to attention other themes, particularly the importance of changes in the structure of investment; it has also adduced a more refined and gradualist understanding of the chronology and effects of the application of power to different processes, and comprehended the phase of proto-industrialisation discussed by Palmer in Chapter 1.[1]

The study of industrial buildings has, in a more compressed period, followed a broadly similar path to that of historical enquiry, but for different reasons. Systematic interest in the subject began in the 1970s when one of the early consequences of the transition to a post-industrial economy was the closure of factories and mills on an unprecedented scale. The buildings thus made redundant were often massive, visually dominant in their locality, landmarks; their demolition had an immediately obvious effect on their surroundings. This was the spur to a wave of research aimed at understanding the historical significance of the buildings, and led to a recognition that some are amongst the most architecturally innovative and significant of their period, as well as monuments to a phase of human achievement and a way of life which was about to disappear. The fate of workshops, by contrast, has not been so stark, so sudden, or so noticeable. Countless buildings, such as Yorkshire weavers' cottages, which once combined working and living space have long-since lost their industrial functions, former working areas simply having been absorbed into the domestic arena with little change in outward appearance. Elsewhere the erosion of often relatively small and architecturally undistinguished buildings has been gradual, its cumulative effect scarcely noticed until after the event. Appreciation of what has been lost, and of what still could be lost, has informed, and been informed by, appreciation of the ways in which 'ordinary' buildings create distinctive built environments and lend to places their individual character.

The interest of building historians in these smaller manifestations of the period of industrialisation has also been stimulated by economic historians' re-evaluation of the significance of workshops for the industrial economy and industrialising process of the 18th and 19th centuries. With the publication of this corpus of material relating to the physical evidence, behind some of which lies considerably more detailed research, there is an opportunity for economic historians and those who work with the historic environment to bring their insights together to create a new understanding of the organisation and evolution of particular industries, of methods of production, and of the ways of work and life of those engaged in them. Buildings, as much as texts and documents, are primary sources, often illuminating what actually happened on the ground in a particular place at a particular time in a way which, even for the relatively recent past, complements the evidence supplied by contemporary commentators and by documents; in particular they can contribute significantly to understanding the kinds of environment in which former generations lived and worked.

Only in recent years has it been appreciated quite how many workshop buildings still exist in large parts of the country, ranging from the Gloucestershire and Somerset textile areas to those of Lancashire and West Yorkshire, and from the metal-working towns of Birmingham and Sheffield to the furniture-making parts of east London, to single out but a few. One of the most surprising realisations has been of the survival of the highly significant but fragmentary evidence of the silk workshops of Spitalfields discussed by Guillery. These relatively neglected elements of the historic fabric of England in their day provided work space for a far larger proportion of the population than did the factories which have attracted so much attention.[2] It has, for example, been calculated that in 1833 there were two and a half outworkers to every one of the 1000 workers in the textile mills of Trowbridge (Palmer & Neaverson 2003, 135); according to an estimate of the 1860s, Tillie's shirt factory at Londonderry employed 1000 operatives but no fewer than nine times that number outside the factory (Marx 1887, 462).

Much of the reason for the continued importance of extra-factory production is related to differing rates of mechanisation both between industries and within the range of trades which came together to form a single industry. The earliest and best-known examples are those of the cotton and woollen industries, in which power was applied to spinning almost a generation before a way was found of harnessing it to weaving. The result was that, from the 1780s, domestic spinning was rapidly rendered uncompetitive by machines of such unprecedented sophistication, size, and cost that they required new forms of building to house them, financed by significant new concentrations of capital, and necessitated new kinds of labour, driven by the speed and rhythm of the machines themselves (Ure 1835, 6–9). The vast quantities of yarn created by the new spinning machines caused equally fundamental changes in weaving, as manufacturers strove to turn the thread into cloth and then finished articles. The change in weaving was not however primarily technological, and, although there were some improvements in looms, by far the greater part of the increase in production was achieved by hand weavers, whose hours of work became longer and whose numbers rose. At the end of the 1820s, when power looms had begun to occupy a significant place in the production of cotton and worsted cloth, Carlyle characterised the time as one in which 'On every hand, the living artisan is driven from his workshop, to make room for a speedier, inanimate one. The shuttle drops from the fingers of the weaver, and falls into iron fingers that ply it faster' (Carlyle 1829). However, even in the 1830s and for long after, the action of steam-driven machinery was too violent for weaving more delicate fabrics including gingham, muslin, cambric, and lace. The quantity of such materials required was so great that the number of hand-loom weavers went on rising after powered looms were introduced for coarser cloths (Place 1835). It was this machine and factory-impelled intensification of domestic and workshop production which accounted for the particular misery associated with non-factory workers and called forth the especial horror of social commentators and political reformers alike (e.g. Taylor 1842, 145–6; Engels 1845, 149–50; Marx 1887, 462–9; Royston Pike 1966, 203–04). It was the same impelling force which created the need for the vast number of weavers' cottages built in Lancashire and Yorkshire between the end of the 18th and the middle of the 19th century (cf Smith 1971).

For entrepreneurs there were some financial advantages in continuing to use home-based labour, for they did not have to pay for looms or work space, and outworkers were more easily and cheaply laid off in lean times than were factory hands (King & Timmins 2002, 53, 56; Palmer & Neaverson 2003, 144–6). Not all industrialists, however, took this view, and there arose other, non-domestic, kinds of workshop in which labour was centralised. One kind perhaps evolved from earlier, 18th-century, clothiers' houses in which there was space for a few paid workers (Smith 1971, 251–4; RCHME 1985, 97–8): as the pace and scale of production increased, many such clothiers managed to expand their businesses and establish loomshops on a larger scale, often separate from their houses. Another kind of loomshop was that created by factory owners on their own premises, the additional capital costs perhaps offset by the advantages of better supervision and control. All three kinds of working arrangement were consequences of the factory system: although the last was within the factory, since none of these kinds of work place was mechanised, all can be considered as different elements within the broad category encompassed by the term 'workshop'. The persistence of domestic production was also found in other textile trades, such as lace, and in the garment-making industry (eg Engels 1845, 197–202), one of the last of this group of trades in which production entered the factory being stocking knitting (Palmer 2000, 59). The processes involved in making other garments, such as suits and shirts, were hardly susceptible to mechanisation until the middle of the 19th century, and even in the great tailoring centre of Leeds most work remained home or workshop-based until the end of the 19th century (Honeyman 2000, 4–5), often carried out in houses with no identifiably distinct work space. Long before then, however, seamstresses, for all that they might have appeared to retain control over the speed of their work, had been reduced to little more than the physically remote human agents of the spinning machine. As Thomas Hood put it in his relentlessly mechanical 1843 account of the fate of a shirt-maker:

Work — Work — Work,

Like the Engine that works by steam,
A mere machine of iron and wood
That toils for Mammon's sake —
Without a brain to ponder and craze
Or a heart to feel — and break!
            (Hood 1843, lines 83–8)

This unfortunate woman worked at home and by hand, for the sewing machine was still a thing of the future, but the advent of the machine did nothing to ease the lot of her children's generation, for it led to a concentration of workers in workshops, or 'manufactories', where the machines, beyond the financial means of most workers, were supplied.[3] The degree of over work in such premises was no less than in domestic situations (Marx 1887, 472–3), partly as entrepreneurs had to cover the costs of the machines and premises, and partly as supervision and control of workers was much greater. As Menuge shows, much of this is equally applicable to the Northamptonshire boot and shoe trade.

For Marx, mechanisation and the factory system might stimulate hand production, but only until the reservoir of human labour was drained and the peak of human efficiency reached: the transition from hand-driven domestic production to the mechanical factory was almost inevitable (Marx 1887, 470–1). Such was indeed the course taken by many branches of the textile trades, but the future was to show that the logic did not apply equally to all industries, at least in the age of steam. The Birmingham metal trades, for example, never achieved the scale of factory-based centralisation found in the cotton industry by the last quarter of the 19th century. The buildings which accommodated the industry reveal much of the story. As Cattell shows, trades originally conducted in houses or in small workshops associated with houses, created a critical mass which led to the transformation of a once high-class residential area into an industrial quarter. It contained businesses of varying size ranging from the domestic through a variety of workshop premises (some, but not all, associated with domestic accommodation) to small factories. Many of the workshops might be characterised as manufactories, with workers brought together by small masters. Such masters provided premises and the costly raw materials which were worked by hired labour; concentration of the workforce was less related to a need for machinery than to the value of both the raw materials and the finished products, which might easily be pilfered. In Sheffield too, a high proportion of the metal working industry was conducted in workshops, or in agglomerations of workshops ('works'), run by small masters. There, however, the reason was less to do with supervision than with the bringing into close proximity of complementary elements of the trade, coupled with investment needed for machinery, and economies of scale in relation to supplies of power and heat. The only real exception to the pattern of workshop-based industries in the region was steel-making, where the scale of the enterprise demanded large investment in plant and a significant concentration of labour (King & Timmins 2001, 88–9).

If factories, 'manufactories', and workshops of all kinds formed parts of a spectrum in which the precise balance varied with time, place, and trade, so too did even less formal work places, including those for charcoal burning and smelting, which took place out of doors. Such trades were no less subject to the pressures of machine-driven industry than those which were accommodated in special buildings: mining for coal, the fuel which powered the machines, was even more notorious than domestic weaving for its increasing and inhuman demands on men, women, and children alike as, hardly aided by mechanical aids of their own, they strove to produce ever more (Samuel 1977, 149). Even in Cumbria, some distance from the main concentrations of industry, charcoal-burning and iron-smelting were, as early as the 18th century, stimulated by the demands and investment from the Black Country iron masters, so that, as Bowden shows, parts of the county became for a time significant industrial landscapes.

The effects of ever-increasing demand upon the kinds of production conducted in places other than factories are hard to over estimate. The fact that some older industries, of the kinds reviewed by Grenville and Alston, continued to be conducted in domestic or workshop premises suggests a greater degree of similarity than may in fact have been the case. Although the domestic Suffolk weaver of the 15th or 16th century and his Yorkshire counterpart in the early 19th century both used hand-looms, there was little in common between their ways of life and conditions of work (cf Marx 1887, 461–2). The impact of the shift from work conducted at the natural and uneven pace of hand- and water-power to a pattern of labour driven by inexhaustible artificial power was fundamental, part of a wider cultural shift from seeing human endeavour as part of the natural order to seeing it as mastering and bettering nature (Thomas 1983, esp. 17–50). The resultant quest for ever greater efficiency and productivity saw increasing division of labour, each individual worker often only performing a single operation rather than creating a complete product, practice making the operation fast and perfect (Martineau 1852b): even a needle might pass through the hands of 120 different people (Samuel 1977, 51).

It is in charting the pace and location and the specific local nature of such new modes of production that the evidence of the built environment is particularly valuable. For the period before the 18th century much of the evidence has to be drawn from excavation, and the particular industries discussed by Grenville are not the most likely to have taken place in substantial and durable buildings, even where their predominantly urban or suburban sites have not been redeveloped. For other trades, however, buildings with specialist spaces can be found, often, as Alston indicates, not recognised or understood. They may be concentrated in rural areas such as Suffolk and Sussex where early industrial activity, large-scale for its day, left a legacy of substantial buildings of types which could be adapted to primarily domestic use, enabling their survival. Such buildings are however, only the clothiers' premises, and there is no evidence for where other activities, including the majority of weaving, were performed. While many weavers' houses may have succumbed to the vicissitudes of time, it is possible that much weaving was conducted in quite ordinary houses without special, or at least identifiable, work space: looms and spinning apparatus could have been set up in a chamber at one end of the hall without leaving any physical trace in a building. It may even be quite likely that some kind of craft activity was conducted, at least on a part-time basis, in many medieval and early-modern houses, perhaps supplying a supplement to agricultural income which enabled a substantial house to be built. The use for weaving of now unidentifiable space in houses also seems characteristic of 17th- and early 18th-century Gloucestershire and Wiltshire (Palmer & Neaverson 2003), though there the continuation of the industry into more recent times may have swept away some of the evidence, including early clothiers' houses.

The earliest houses so far identified which were of a form to indicate their association with weaving are those in London. That is not surprising, for London was the largest and most advanced town in the country in the late 17th and the 18th century, and, as Clifford notes, the place where the critical mass required for the true division of labour was first achieved. Pursing Guillery's thought that some features of later weavers' cottages elsewhere could have been derived from London, as well as the evidence from Wiltshire, Gloucestershire, and the West Riding of Yorkshire, it seems that the arrival of distinctive weavers' cottages in an area was a consequence of a shift in the mode of production from the truly domestic to the later kind of factory-driven system described above. In other industries, changes in the types of building which accommodated non-factory production are similarly indicative of intensification and change: in Sheffield, for example, the mid-19th century saw the replacement of now lost (or at least unidentified) work spaces in houses and garrets with agglomerations of workshops, or 'works', and in Northamptonshire the advent of the workshop-factory marked a significant moment in the development of the boot and shoe trades.

Division of labour was intended to achieve a peak of efficiency. Its effect, however, was that, as both Cattell and Wray demonstrate from contemporary evidence, unless production was concentrated in a single workshop or manufactory, articles had to be moved, often many times, from one workshop to another during the course of manufacture. For this to be economically sustainable required a density of businesses within a restricted area, so that the network of inter-dependent workshops created a kind of dispersed factory, with the specialist workers working like a dispersed machine. The result was the creation of tight-knit communities with a sense of common purpose, fate, and identity, living in areas dominated by the buildings, often individually undistinguished, of the local trade: the mass of such buildings often transformed the local landscape and, where they still exist, create a dominant sense of local distinctiveness. In Birmingham, for example, the early houses, various generations of workshop, and more specialised 19th-century buildings of the Jewellery Quarter are not only artefacts of every stage through which the metal trades have passed since the late 18th century, but fundamentally transformed the once elegant residential area, creating a dense small- and medium-scale urban grain which can still be appreciated as distinctive today. Although the effect is not always so noticeable, the same is true of the Northamptonshire boot and shoe towns, with their end of street warehouses, sometimes attached to masters' houses, and their street patterns created by the sometimes scarcely consciously noticed back-of-plot workshops. As Campion shows in relation to Nottinghamshire, different circumstances, some of which can now only be surmised, led to variations over quite small areas, so that each settlement underwent its own particular development and had its own peculiar physical character, very probably also reflected in its social composition and culture. The transformative effect of workshops on the landscape was felt even in areas where factories or mills are the most obvious features. In the West Riding Pennines, weavers' cottages form as distinctive an element of the valley towns as the mills and loomshops which catch (or caught) the eye by virtue of their scale. The combination transforming once relatively insignificant settlements into hubs of the 19th-century economy. The concentration of weavers' cottages in smaller places such as Mirfield and Hartshead fundamentally changed the settlement pattern, joining up dispersed settlements within the townships to create nucleated, or semi-nucleated, ones in areas where they had not previously existed (Roberts & Wrathmell 2002, 90–2).

It is in this, the constitutive effect on the buildings, settlements, and spaces which still surround us that workshops, even for industries which have long closed or moved away, still affect our lives today. For those who built them and lived and worked in their surroundings they were the vital means to earning a living, whether good or wretched. For other, more dispassionate contemporaries however, they were the backbone of the national economy: it may have been steam power which drove Britain's economic dominance, but a large part of what was driven was not new machines in new factories, but human beings in the great range of workshops, domestic and outdoor industries, who strove to keep up. It was perhaps not for nothing that Disraeli, speaking in 1838 on international envy of the preeminence of the national economy, described England not as the factory, but as 'the workshop for the world' (Hansard 1838, 939/2).

Notes

1. For discussion of the historiography to the early 1980s, see Cannadine 1984; some of the more recent trends are scrutinised in Berg 1994.
2. Even in the most advanced industries related to textiles, fewer than half the workers in 1850 were in factories – see Freedgood 2003, 1–2. For the variable application of powered machinery in other trades, which is to some extent an index of the degree to which they came to be based in factories, see Samuel 1977.
3. For a similar development in Leicestershire stocking knitting, where new machines were too large to be accommodated in knitters' houses, see Palmer 2000, 66–70.

Bibliography *compiled by Peter Neaverson*

Agricola, G, 1556 *De re metallica*, H C Hoover & L H Hoover (eds and trans) 1912. Reprinted 1950. New York: Dover Publications

Alfrey, J, & Clark, K, 1993 *The Landscape of Industry: Patterns of Change in the Ironbridge Gorge*. London: Routledge

Angerstein, R R, [1753–55] *R R Angerstein's Illustrated Travel Diary 1753–5. Industry in England and Wales from a Swedish Perspective*, T Berg & P Berg (eds) 2001. London: Science Museum

Anon, 1742–43 *Commons' Journals*, 3 March 1742/3, **24**, 448

Anon, 1844a A Day at the Birmnigham Factories, *The Penny Magazine (of the Society for the Diffusion of Useful Knowledge)*, New Series **13**, 465–72

Anon, 1844b A Day at the Sheffield Cutlery Works, *The Penny Magazine (of the Society for the Diffusion of Useful Knowledge)*, New Series **13**, 161–8

Anon, 1853a *The Builder*, 23 April, 28 May and 4 June 1853, 257–8, 337–8, 360

Anon, 1853b Saint Crispin, *Household Words*, **7**, 76–80

Anon, 1889 *Jeweller and Metalworker*, 1 June 1889, 173–4

Anon, 1916 *Shoe and Leather News Biographical Supplement*. London: Shoe & Leather News

Anon, 1917 *The Modern Boot and Shoe Maker*, 4 vols. London: Gresham

Anon, 1971 *Ruddington 120 years ago – The Framework Knitters*. Ruddington: Hassell & Lucking

Anon, nd *A Stroll Though Calverton's Past – A History of Local People for the William Lee Celebrations*

Ashurst, D, 1987 Excavations at the 17th and 18th-Century Glasshouse at Bolsterstone, Yorkshire, *Post-Medieval Archaeol*, **21**, 147–226

Atkinson, F (ed), 1956 *Some Aspects of the 18th-Century Woollen and Worsted Trade in Halifax*. Halifax: Halifax Museums

BPP, 1840–41 Royal Commission Report and Reports of Assistant Commissioners on Hand-Loom Weavers in the United Kingdom 1840–1 (IUP, *Industrial Revolution, Textiles*, **10**)

BPP, 1845 Report From the Commissioner Appointed to Inquire into the Condition of the Frame-work Knitters with Minutes of Evidence, Appendices and Index, (IUP, *Industrial Revolution, Textiles*, **8**)

BPP, 1864 Third Report of the Commissioners Appointed to Enquire into the Employment of Young Children in Trades and Manufactures (IUP, *Children's Employment*, **14**)

BPP, 1865 J E White, Report upon the Metal Manufactures of the Sheffield District, in *Fourth Report of the Children's Employment Commission*: London

Baker, M, 1995 Roubiliac and Cheere in the 1730s and 40s: Collaboration and Sub-Contracting in 18th-Century English Sculptor's Workshops, *Church Monuments*, **10**, 90–108

Bamford, S, 1844 *Walks in South Lancashire and on its Borders*. Reprinted 1972. Sussex: Harvester

Bamford, S, 1893 *Early Days*. H Dunkley (ed). Reprinted 1967. London: Cass

Barke, M, 1979 Weavers' Cottages in the Huddersfield Area: A Preliminary Survey, *Folk Life* **17**, 49–59

Barker, D, 1999 The Ceramic Revolution 1650–1850, in G Egan & R L Michael (eds), *Old and New Worlds*. Oxford: Oxbow, 226–34

Barraclough, K C, 1976 *Sheffield Steel*. Buxton: Moorland Publishing

Barre, J, 2001 *La Colline de la Croix-Rousse*. Lyons: Éditions Lyonnaises d'Art et d'Histoire

Barrell, J, 1992 Visualising the Division of Labour: William Pyne's Microcosm, *The Birth of Pandora and the Division of Knowledge*. London: Macmillan, 89–119

Bartlett, K S, 1971 Excavations at Potovens, near Wakefield 1968, *Post-Medieval Archaeol*, **5**, 1–34

Bayliss, D (ed), 1995 *A Guide to the Industrial History of South Yorkshire*. Ironbridge: Association for Industrial Archaeology

Beardsmore, J H, 1909 *History of Hucknall Torkard*. Mansfield: J. Linney

Beauchamp, V, 1996 The Workshops of the Cutlery Industry in Hallamshire 1750–1900. Unpubl PhD thesis, University of Sheffield

Beckett, J V et al (eds), 1997 *A Centenary History of Nottingham*. Manchester: Manchester University Press

Beier, A L, 1986 Engine of Manufacture: The Trades of London, in A L Beier & R Finlay (eds), *The Making of the Metropolis: London, 1500–1700*. Harlow: Longman, 141–8

Bennet, J A, 1986 The Mechanics: Philosophy and the Mechanical Philosophy, *History of Science*, **24**, 22–39

Bennett, J M, 1996 *Ale, Beer, and Brewsters in England*. Oxford: Oxford University Press

Beresford, M, & St Joseph, J K, 1979 *Medieval England: An Aerial Survey*. 2nd edn. Cambridge: Cambridge University Press

Berg, M, 1994 *The Age of Manufactures, 1700–1820: Industry, Innovation and Work in Britain*. 2nd edn. London: Routledge

Berg, M, 2001 French Fancy and Cool Britannia: The Fashion Markets of Early Modern Europe, *Proc of the Istituto internazionale di storia economica F. Datini*, 519–56

Berg, M, Hudson, P, & Sonenscher, M, 1983a *Manufacture in Town and Country Before the Factory*. Cambridge: Cambridge University Press

Berg, M, Hudson, P, & Sonenscher, M, 1983b Manufacture in Town and Country Before the Factory, in Berg, Hudson & Sonenscher 1983a, 1–32

Berry, C, 1994 *The Idea of Luxury: A Conceptual and Historical Investigation*. Cambridge: Cambridge University Press

Betterton, A, & Dymond, D, 1989 *Lavenham Industrial Town*. Lavenham: Dalton

Bewick, T A, 1762 *Memoir of Thomas Bewick Written by Himself*. I Bain (ed), 1975. Oxford: Oxford University Press

Blair, J, & Ramsay, N (eds), 1991 *English Medieval Industries: Craftsmen, Techniques, Products*. London: The Hambledon Press

Blood, N K, 1996 Harrison Coppice Bloomery Forge. RCHME Archaeol Investigation Report, NMR, NMR No SD 29 SE 18

Blood, N K, & Lofthouse, C, 1995 Muncaster Head Bloomery Forge. RCHME Archaeol Investigation Report, NMR, NMR No SD 19 NW 15

Bodey, H A, 1971 Coffin Row, Linthwaite, *Ind Archaeol*, **8**, 381–91

Boulton, J, 2000 London 1540–1700, in Clark (ed) 2000, 315–46

Bowden, M C B (ed), 2000 *Furness Iron: The Physical Remains of the Iron Industry and Related Woodland Industries of Furness and Southern Lakeland*. Swindon: English Heritage

Brears, P, 1967 Excavations at Potovens, near Wakefield 1968 *Post-Medieval Archaeol*, **1**, 1–43

Brooke, A J, 1993 *The Handloom Fancy Weavers c1820–1914*. Sharlston: Workers' History Publications

Brunskill, R W, 1971 *Illustrated Handbook of Vernacular Architecture*. London: Faber and Faber

Burnett, J, 1986 *A Social History of Housing 1815–1985*. 2nd edn. London: Methuen

Burritt, E, 1868 *Walks in the Black Country and its Green Borderland*. London: Sampson Low & Co

Byng, Hon. John, [1794] *The Torrington Diaries Containing the Tours Through England and Wales of Hon. John Byng (later fifth Viscount Torrington) Between the Years 1781 and 1794*. C B Andrews (ed), 1935. 4 vols. London: Eyre & Spottiswoode

Caffyn, L, 1986 *Workers' Housing in West Yorkshire 1750–1920*. London: HMSO

Caldwell, D H, & Dean, V E, 1992 The Pottery Industry at Throsk, Stirlingshire, in the 17th and Early 18th Century, *Post-Medieval Archaeol*, **31**, 61–119

Calladine, A, & Fricker, J, 1993 *East Cheshire Textile Mills*. London: RCHME

Campbell, R, 1747 *The London Tradesman*. Reprinted 1969. Newton Abbot: David and Charles

Campion, G, 1996 People, Process and the Poverty-Pew: A Functional Analysis of Mundane Buildings in the Nottinghamshire Framework-Knitting Industry, *Antiquity*, **70**, 847–60

Campion, G, 1999 'People, Process, Place and Power': An Archaeology of Control in East Midlands Outworking 1820–1900. Unpubl PhD thesis, University of Leicester

Campion, G, 2001 'People, Process, Place and Power': An archaeology of Control in East Midlands Outworking 1820–1900, in Palmer & Neaverson (eds) 2001a, 75–84

Cannadine, D, 1984 The Present and the Past in the English Industrial Revolution, *Past and Present*, **103**, 131–72

Carlyle, T, 1829 Signs of the Times: The Mechanical Age, *Edinburgh Rev*, **49**, 441–4

Cattell, J, Ely, S, & Jones, B, 2002 *The Birmingham Jewellery Quarter: An Architectural Survey of Manufactories*. Swindon: English Heritage

Cattell, J, & Hawkins, B, 2000 *The Birmingham Jewellery Quarter: An Introduction*

Chadwick, E 1842 *Report on the Sanitary Condition of the Labouring Population of Great Britain*. M Flinn (ed), 1965. Edinburgh: Edinburgh University Press

Cayez, P, 1978 *Métiers Jacquard et hauts fourneaux aux origines de l'industrie Lyonnaise*. Lyons: Presse Universitaire Lyonnaise

Chalabi, M, *et al*, 2000 *L'Orfèvrerie de Lyons et de Trévoux du XVe au XXe siècle*. Paris: Éditions patrimoine

Chambers, W, & Chambers, R, 1844 Two Days in Birmingham, *Chambers' Edinburgh J*, 15 June 369–73

Chapman, S D, 1963 Working-Class Housing in Nottingham During the Industrial Revolution, *Trans Thoroton Soc*, **67**, 67–92

Charleston, R J, 1991 Vessel Glass, in Blair & Ramsay (eds) 1991, 237–64

Chesterfield, Lord, 1984 *Letters to His Son and Others*. London & Melbourne: Dent (Everyman's Library)

Clapham, J H, 1916 The Spitalfields Acts, 1773–1824, *The Economic J*, **26**, 459–71

Clark, D, 2000 The Shop Within? An Analysis of the Architectural Evidence for Medieval Shops, *Architectural History*, **43**, 58–87

Clark, P (ed), 2000 *The Cambridge Urban History of Britain. Volume 2, 1540–1840*. Cambridge: Cambridge University Press

Clark, P, & Slack, P, 1976 *English Towns in Transition 1500–1700*. Oxford: Oxford University Press

Clarke, L, 1992 *Building Capitalism: Historical Change and The Labour Process in the Production of the Built Environment*. London: Routledge

Clifford, H, 1990 The Organisation of an 18th-Century Goldsmiths' Business, *The International Silver & Jewellery Fair and Seminar*. London: IS & JF, 16–22

Clifford, H, 1998 The Vulliamys and the Silversmiths 1790–1817, *The Silver Society J*, **10**, 96–102

Cobbett, W, 1830 Rural Rides. 2nd edn, 1853, in G Woodcock (ed), 1967. Harmondsworth: Penguin

Cooke, J; Hilsden, K; Menuge, A, & Williams, A, 2000 *The Northamptonshire Boot and Shoe Industry: A Summary Report*, English Heritage Architectural Survey Report, NMR

Corfield, P, 1990 Defining Urban Work, in P J Corfield & D Keene (eds), *Work in Towns 850–1850*. London: Leicester University Press, 207–30

Cossons, N, & Trinder, B, 2002 *The Iron Bridge: Symbol of the Industrial Revolution*. 2nd edn. Chirchester: Phillimore

Cowper, H S, 1898 Excavations at Springs Bloomery (Iron Smelting Hearth) near Coniston Hall, Lancashire, With Notes on the Probable Age of the Furness Bloomeries, *Archaeol J*, **55**, 88–105

Cowper, H S, 1901 A Contrast in Architecture, *Trans Cumberland & Westmorland Antiq Archaeol Soc*, **1**, 129–43

Cranstone, D, 1985a Stony Hazel Forge: Interim Report 1985. Typescript Report for the Lake District National Park Authority

Cranstone, D, 1985b Stony Hazel Forge: Second Interim Report, Autumn 1985. Typescript Report for the Lake District National Park Authority

Cranstone, D, 2001 Industrial Archaeology – Manufacturing a New Society, in R Newman, *The Historical Archaeology of Britain c1540–1900*. Stroud: Sutton Publishing, 183–210

Craske, M, 1999 Plan and Control: Design and the Competitive Spirit in Early and Mid-18th-Century England, *J of Design History*, **12** (3), 187–216

Crisp-Jones, K C, 1981 *The Silversmiths of Birmingham and Their Marks: 1750–1980*. London: NAG Press

Crossley, D, 1967 Glass making in Bagots Park, Staffordshire, in the 16th century, *Post-Medieval Archaeol*, **1**, 44–83

Crossley, D, 1975 *The Bewl Valley Ironworks c1300–1730*. London: Royal Archaeological Institute

Crossley, D (ed), 1989 *Water Power on the Sheffield Rivers*. Sheffield: University of Sheffield Division of Continuing Education and Sheffield Trades Historical Society

Crossley, D, 1990 *Post-Medieval Archaeology in Britain*. Leicester: Leicester University Press

Crossley, D, & Ashurst, D, 1968 Excavations at Rockley Smithies, a Water-Powered Bloomery of the 16th and 17th Centuries, *Post-Medieval Archael*, **6**, 107–59

Crump,W B, & Ghorbal, G, 1935 *A History of the Huddersfield Woollen Industy*. Huddersfield: Tolson Memorial Museums Publications

Culme, J, 1987 Attitudes to Old Plate 1750–1900, *The Directory of Gold & Silversmiths Jewellers & Allied Trades 1838–1914*. Woodbridge: Antique Collectors' Club

Dahlström, E. 2001 The Swedish Eengineering Industry During the 19th Century: From Diversity to Mass Production, in Palmer & Neaverson (eds) 2001a, 85–92

Davies, A, 2002 Ancillary Buildings on Lead Mining Sites in the Yorkshire Dales. Unpubl MA dissertation, University of York

Davies-Shiel, M, 1970 Excavation at Stony Hazel, High Furnace [sic], Lake District, 1968–1969: An Interim Report, *Bull Hist Metallurgy Group*, **4**(1), 28–32

Dearden, W, 1834 *Dearden's History and Directory of the Town of Nottingham and Adjacent Villages*. Nottingham: W Dearden

Defoe, D, 1724–26 *A Tour through the Whole Island of Great Britain*. P Rogers (ed), 1971. Harmondsworth: Penguin

Defoe, D, 1726 *The Complete English Tradesman*. London: Charles Rivington

Diderot, D, 1755a *Encyclopédie ou dictionnaire raisonné des sciences, des arts et des métiers*. Paris

Diderot, D, 1755b *A Diderot pictorial encyclopedia of trades and industry: manufacturing and the technical arts; in plates selected from 'L'Encyclopédie, ou dictionnaire raisonné des sciences, des arts et des métiers' of Denis Diderot*. C G Gillespie (ed), 1959. New York: Dover Publications

Dunn, C J, 1998 Duddon Bridge Ironworks: an archaeological field survey of the immediate environs. RCHME Archaeol Investigation Report, NMR, NMR No SD 18 NE 14

Dyer, C, 2002 *Making a Living in the Middle Ages: The People of Britain 850–1520*. New Haven & London: Yale University Press

Dymond, D, 1998 Five Building Contracts from Fifteenth-Century Suffolk, *The Antiquaries J*, **78**, 269–87

Ekwall, E, 1960 *The Concise Oxford Dictionary of English Place-Names*. 4th edn. Oxford: Oxford University Press

Engels, F, 1845 *The Condition of the Working Class in England*. D McLellan (trans), 1993. Oxford: Oxford University Press

Fairbanks, J, 1984 Crafts Processes and Images; Visual Sources for the Study of Craftsman, in I M G Quimby *The Craftsman in Early America*. New York and London: W W Norton & Co, 299–30

Farge, A, 1993 *Fragile Lives: Violence, Power and Solidarity in 18th-Century Paris*. Cambridge: Cambridge University Press

Felkin, W A, 1844 *An account of the Machine-Wrought Hosiery Trade: Its Extent, and the Condition of the Framework Knitters. Evidence Given under the Hosiery Commission Inquiry*. London: W Strange

Fell, A, 1908 *The Early Iron Industry of Furness and District*. Ulverston: Hume Kitchin

Felibien, A, 1676 Des Principes de l'architecture, de la sculpture, de la peinture, et des autres arts qui en dependent. Avec un dictionnaire des terms propres à chacun de ses artes. Paris: Jean-Baptiste Coignard

Firth, G, 1981 The Bradford Trade in the 19th Century, in D G Wright & J A Jowitt, *Victorian Bradford: Eessays in Honour of Jack Reynolds*. Bradford: City of Bradford Metropolitan Council, 7–36

Firth, G, 1990 *Bradford and the Industrial Revolution: An Economic History 1760–1840*. Halifax: Ryburn Publishing

Forty, A, 1986 *Objects of Desire: Design and Society since 1750*. London: Thames & Hudson

Fox, A, 1958 *A History of the National Union of Boot and Shoe Operatives 1874–1957*. Oxford: Blackwell

Fox, C, 1987 Images of Artists and Craftsmen in Georgian London, *Apollo*, May, 357–6

Freedgood, E, 2003 *Factory Production in Nineteenth-Century Britain*. New York & Oxford: Oxford University Press

Gaimster, D, & Nenk, B, 1997 English Households in Transition c1450–1550: The Ceramic Evidence' in D Gaimster & P Stamper (eds), *The Age of Transition: The Archaeology of English Culture 1400–1600*. Society for Medieval Archaeol Monograph **15**, Oxbow Monograph **98**. Oxford: Oxbow, 171–96

Garden, M, 1970 *Lyon et les Lyonnais au XVIIIe siècle*. Paris: Les Belles Lettres

Garrioch, D, 1986 *Neighbourhood and Community in Paris, 1740–1790*. Cambridge: Cambridge University Press

Gavin, H, 1848 *Sanitary Ramblings; Being Sketches and Illustrations of Bethnal Green. A Type of the Condition of the Metropolis and Other Large Towns*. London

Geddes, J, 1991 Iron, in Blair & Ramsay (eds) 1991, 167–88

George, M D, 1925 *London Life in the 18th Century*. Reprinted 1964. New York: Harper & Row

Giles, C, 1995 Sheaf Works, Maltravers Street, Sheffield. RCHME Architectural Investigation Report, NMR, NBR No 65044

Giles, C, 1998a Anglo Works, Trippet Lane, Sheffield. RCHME Architectural Investigation Report, NMR, NBR No 95123

Giles, C, 1998b Challenge Works, Arundel Street, Sheffield. RCHME Architectural Investigation Report, NMR, NBR No 98220

Giles, C, 1998c Leah's Yard, Cambridge Street, Sheffield. RCHME Architectural Investingation Report, NMR, NBR No 95122

Giles, C, 1998d Lion Works, Arundel Street, Sheffield. RCHME Architectural Investigation Report, NMR, NBR No 98303

Giles, C, & Goodall, I H, 1992 *Yorkshire Textile Mills: The Buildings of the Yorkshire Textile Industry 1770–1930*. London: HMSO

Giles, C, & Hawkins, B, forthcoming 2004 *Storehouse of Empire: Liverpool and its Historic Warehouses*. Swindon: English Heritage

Giles, K F, 2000 *An Archaeology of Social Identity: Guildhalls in York, c1350–1630*. British Archaeological Reports, British Series **315**. Oxford: BAR

Goad, C E, 1896 *Fire Insurance Plans*, Sheffield. London: Chas. E Goad

Goad, C E, 1905a *Fire Insurance Plans*, Northampton. London: Chas. E Goad

Goad, C E, 1905b *Fire Insurance Plans*, Sheffield. London: Chas. E Goad

Goldberg, P J P, 1992 *Women, Work and Life Cycle in a Medieval Economy: Women in York and Yorkshire c1300–1520*. Oxford: Clarendon Press

Goodall, I H, 1999a Duddon Furnace, Duddon Bridge, Millom Without, Cumbria. RCHME Architectural Investigation Report, NMR, NBR No 95780

Goodall, I H, 1999b Newland Furnace, Egton with Newland, Cumbria. English Heritage Architectural Investigation Report, NMR, NBR No 95778

Goodall, I H, 1999c Nibthwaite Furnace, Colton, Cumbria. English Heritage Architectural Investigation Report, NMR, NBR No 95779

Grady, K, 1989 *The Georgian Public Buildings of Leeds and the West Riding*. Publications of the Thoresby Society, **62** (for 1987), **133**

Gregory, D, 1982 *Regional Transformation and Industrial Revolution: A Geography of the Yorkshire Woollen Industry*. London: Macmillan

Grenville, J, 1997 *Medieval Housing*, London and Washington: Leicester University Press

Grenville, J, 2001 Out of the Shunting Yards: One Academic's Approach to the Recording of Smaller Vernacular Buildings, in S Pearson & B Meeson (eds), *Vernacular Buildings in a Changing World*, CBA Research Report **126**. York: CBA

Guillery, P, 2000 Another Georgian Spitalfields: 18th-Century Houses in Bethnal Green's Silk-Weaving District. English Heritage Survey Report, NMR

Guillery P, 2004 *London's Smaller 18th-century Houses: A Social and Architectural History*. London and New Haven: Yale University Press

Guillery, P, forthcoming, Housing the Early Modern Industrial City: London's Workshop Tenements, in A Green & R Leech (eds) *Cities in the World 1500–2000*. Society for Post-Medieval Archaeology monograph

Halls, Z, 1973 *Machine Made Lace in Nottingham in the 18th and 19th centuries*. 2nd edn. Nottingham: The City of Nottingham Museums and Libraries Committee

Hansard 1838 *Hansard's Parliamentary Debates*, **41**. London: Hansard

Harcourt, E W, 1938 *The Harcourt Papers, 2*. Oxford: Oxford University Press

Hargrave, E, & Crump, W B, 1931 The Diary of Joseph Rogerson, Scribbling Miller of Bramley, 1808–14, in W B Crump (ed) *The Leeds Woollen Industry 1780–1820*. Leeds: Publications of the Thoresby Society **32** (for 1929), 59–166

Harris, J, 1992 *Essays in Industry and Technology in the 18th Century: England and France*. Aldershot: Ashgate

Hatcher, J, 1993 *The History of the British Coal Industry. 1. Before 1700: Towards the Age of Coal*. Oxford: Clarendon Press

Hazlitt, W, 1902 *Table Talk*. London: John Murray

Healey, F, 1963 The Enlightenment View of 'Homo Faber', *Studies on Voltaire and the 18th Century*, **25**, 837–59

Heine, G, 1996 Fact or Fancy? The Reliability of Old Pictorial Trade Representations, *Tools & Trades, J of the Tool and Trades History Society*, **9**, 20–7

Hervier, D, & Ferault, M-A, 1998 *Le Faubourg Saint-Antoine, un double visage*. Paris: Cahiers du patrimoine, **51**, Editions de l'Inventaire

Hey, D, 1972 *The Rural Metalworkers of the Sheffield Region, A Study of Rural Industry before the Industrial Revolution*, Department of English Local History Occasional Papers, Second Series **5**. Leicester: Leicester University Press

Hey, D, 1991 *The Fiery Blades of Hallamshire. Sheffield and its Neighbourhood, 1660–1740*. Leicester: Leicester University Press

Hey, D, 1998 *A History of Sheffield*. Lancaster: Carnegie Publishing

Heyl, C, 2002 We are not at Home: Protecting Domestic Privacy in Post-Fire Middle-Class London, *The London J*, **27** (2), 12–33

Honeyman, K, 2000 *Well Suited: A History of the Leeds Clothing Industry 1850–1990*. Oxford: Oxford University Press

Hodgson, J, 1879 *Textile Manufacture and other industries in Keighley*. Facsimile reprint, G Cookson & G Ingle (eds), 1999. Stamford: Shaun Tyas

Homer, R F, 1991 Pewter, in Blair & Ramsay (eds) 1991, 57–80

Hood, T 1843 *The Song of the Shirt*, in W Jerrold (ed), 1906 *The Complete Poetical Works of Thomas Hood*. London: Oxford University Press, 625–6

Hopkins, E, 1998 *The Rise of the Manufacturing Town. Birmingham and the Industrial Revolution*. 2nd edn. Stroud: Sutton

Horriben, E,?1973 *Hucknall: 'of lowly birth and iron fortune'*. Nottingham: TBF Printers

Hudson, P, 1983 From Manor to Mill: The West Riding in Transition, in Berg, Hudson & Sonenscher 1983a, 124–44

Hudson, P, 1986 *The Genesis of Industrial Capital: A Study of the West Riding Wool Textile Industry, c1750–1850*. Cambridge: Cambridge University Press

Hughes, S, Malaws, B, Parry, M, & Wakelin, P,?1994 *Collieries of Wales: Engineering and Architecture*. Aberystwyth: Royal Commission on Ancient & Historical Monuments in Wales

Hunt, M, Jones, K, Malam, J, & Trinder, B, 1982 Holywell Lane: A Squatter Community in the Shropshire Coalfield, *Ind Archaeol Rev*, **6**, 163–85

Hunter, J, 1869 *Hallamshire: The History and Topography of the Parish of Sheffield and the Surrounding District*. London: Pawson and Brailsford

Jenkins, D T, 1975 *The West Riding Wool Textile Industry 1770–1835: A Study of Fixed Capital Formation*. Edington: Pasold Research Fund

Jenkins, D T, & Ponting, K G, 1982 *The British Wool Textile Industry 1770–1914*. London: Heinemann

Jennings, B (ed), 1992 *Pennine Valley: A History of Upper Calderdale*. Otley: Smith Settle

Jenstad, J A, 1998 'The Gouldsmythes Storehowse', *Silver Society J*, **10**, Autumn, 40–3

Joy, E 1955 Some Aspects of the London Furniture Industry in the 18th Century. Unpubl MA dissertation, University of London

Kean, H, & Wheeler, B, 2003 Making History in Bethnal Green: Different Stories of 19th-Century Silk Weavers, *History Workshop J*, **56** (1), 217–30

Keene, D, 1985 *Survey of Medieval Winchester*, Winchester Studies, **1**. Oxford: Oxford University Press

Kelly & Co, 1877 *Kelly's Northamptonshire Directory*. London: Kelly & Co

Kelly & Co, 1883 *Directory of Sheffield & Rotherham and Neighbourhood*. London: Kelly & Co

Kelly & Co, 1888 *Directory of Sheffield & Rotherham and Neighbourhood*. London: Kelly & Co

Kelly & Co, 1890 *Kelly's Northamptonshire Directory*. London: Kelly & Co

Kelly & Co, 1895 *Kelly's Nottinghamshire Directory*. London: Kelly & Co

Kelly & Co, 1906 *Kelly's Northamptonshire Directory*. London: Kelly & Co

Kermode, J, 1998 *Medieval Merchants: York, Beverley and Hull in the Later Middle ages.* Cambridge: Cambridge University Press.

King, S, & Timmins, G, 2001 *Making Sense of the Industrial Revolution: English Economy and Society 1700–1850.* Manchester: Manchester University Press

Kirkham, P, 1969 Samuel Norman: A Study of an 18th-Century Craftsman, *Burlington Magazine*, **145**, 501–13

Lambert, J, 1991 Charcoal Burners and Woodcutters of the Furness Fells, 1701–1851, *Univ Lancaster, Centre for North-West Regional Studies: Regional Bull,* **5**. 32–6

Lax, A, 1998 Colwith Force Bloomery. RCHME Archaeol Investigation Report NMR, NMR No. NY 30 SW 58

Leech, R, 1981, *Early Industrial Housing: the Trinity area of Frome.* London: HMSO

Linebaugh, P, 1991 *The London Hanged: Crime and Civil Society in the 18th Century.* Harmondsworth: Penguin

Lloyd, G I H, 1913 *The Cutlery Trades. An Historical Essay in the Economics of Small-Scale Production.* London: Longmans, Green, and Co

Magnusson, G (ed), 1995 *The Importance of Ironmaking: Technical Innovation and Social Change.* Stockholm: Jernkontorets Bergshistoriske Utskott

Malster, R, 2000 *A History of Ipswich.* Chichester: Phillimore

Marshall, J D, Helme, J, Wignall, J, & Braithwaite, J C, 1996 The Lineaments of Newland Blast Furnace, 1747–1903: An Historical Investigation, *Trans Cumberland & Westmorland Antiq Archaeol Soc*, **96**, 195–213

Martineau, H, 1852a An Account of Some Treatment of Gold and Gems, *Household Words*, **4**, 449–55

Martineau, H 1852b What there is in a Button, *Household Words*, **138**, 106–12

Marx, K, 1887 *Capital, I: A Critical Analysis of Capitalist Production. Translated from the Third German Edition by Samuel Moore and Edward Aveling and Edited by Frederick Engels.* London: Swan Sonnastein, Lowrey & Co.

Mason, S, 1994 *Nottingham Lace – 1760s–1950s: The Machine-Made Lace Industry in Nottinghamshire, Derbyshire and Leicestershire.* Stroud: Mason/Alan Sutton

Mason, S, 1998 *Jewellery Making in Birmingham 1750–1995.* Chichester: Phillimore

McDonald, M R, 1989 The Wash-House: An Archaeological and Functional Evaluation with Special Reference to the 'brew'us' of the Ironbridge/Coalbrookdale Area. Unpubl MSocSci dissertation, Ironbridge Institute, University of Birmingham

McKendrick, N, 1961 Josiah Wedgwood and Factory Discipline, *Historical J*, **4**, 30–55

Mende, M, 2001 Places of Proto-Industry Revisited: Architectural Remains of the 18th and 19th-Century Woollen and Worsted Industries in the Eichsfeld Region of Germany, in Palmer & Neaverson (eds) 2001a, 57–64

Mendels, F F, 1972 Proto-Industrialization: The First Phase of the Industrialization Process, *J of Economic History* **32**, 241–61

Menuge, A, 2001 Technology and Tradition: The English Heritage Survey of the Northamptonshire Boot and Shoe Industry, in Palmer & Neaverson (eds) 2001a, 101–10

Metra Martech, 2001 A Survey of the Businesses in the Jewellery Quarter. Report for Birmingham City Council Economic Development Department

Miller, E M J (ed), 1983 *A Walk Through Barrowford.* Barrowford: Friends of Park Hill

Mitchell, D (ed), 1995 *Goldsmiths, Silversmiths and Bankers: Innovation and the Transfer of Skill, 1550 to 1750.* Stroud: Allan Sutton

Money, J H, 1971 Medieval Iron-workings in Minepit Wood, Rotherfield, Sussex, *Medieval Archaeol*, **15**, 86–111

Morgan, N, 1990 *Vanished Dwellings.* Preston: Mullion Books

Morrison-Low, A D, 1995 The Role of the Subcontractor in the Manufacture of Precision Instruments in Provincial England during the Industrial Revolution, in I Blanchard (ed), *New Directions in Economic and Social History, Papers presented at the 'New Researchers' Sessions of the Economic History Society Conference held at Edinburgh.* Avonbridge: Newless Press , 13–20

Moxon, J, 1678 *Mechanick Exercises or the Doctrine of Handyworks.* Reprinted 1970. New York & London: Praeger

Nevell, M (ed), 2003 *From Farmer to Factory Owner: Models, Methodology and Industrialisation. Archaeology North-West* **6**. Manchester: CBA North West

Newman, R, 2001 *The Historical Archaeolgy of Britain c1540–1900.* Stroud: Sutton Publishing

Palmer, M, 1989 Houses and Workplaces: The Framework Knitters of the East Midlands, *Knitting Internat*, **96**, 1150, 31–5

Palmer, M, 1990 The Transition from Domestic to Factory Production in the Hosiery Industry of the East Midlands, *Knitting Internat*, **97**, 1154, 31–35

Palmer, M, 1994 Industrial Archaeology: Continuity and Change, *Ind Archaeol Rev*, **16** (2), 135–56

Palmer, M, 2000 Housing the Leicestershire Framework Knitters: History and Archaeology, *Trans of Leicestershire Archaeol and Hist Soc*, **74**, 59–78

Palmer, M, & Neaverson, P, 1992 *Industrial landscapes of the East Midlands.* Chichester: Phillimore

Palmer, M, & Neaverson, P (eds), 2001a *From Industrial Revolution to Consumer Revolution:*

International Perspectives on the Archaeology of Industrialisation. Ironbridge: Association for Industrial Archaeology

Palmer, M, & Neaverson, P, 2001b The Social Archaeology of the Textile Industry, in Palmer & Neaverson, 2001a, 47–56

Palmer, M, & Neaverson, P, 2003 Handloom Weaving in Wiltshire and Gloucestershire in the 19th century: The Building Evidence, *Post-Medieval Archaeol*, **37** (1), 126–58

Palmer, M, & Neaverson, P A, 2004 Home as Workplace in 19th-Century Wiltshire and Gloucestershire', *Textile History* **35** (1), 25–57

Parker, V 1971 *The Making of King's Lynn: Secular Buildings From the 11th to the 17th Century*. London: Phillimore

Parson, W, & White, W, 1830 *Directory of the Borough of Leeds and the Clothing Districts of Yorkshire*. Leeds: Edward Baines & Son

Pawson, H, & Brailsford, J, 1862 *Illustrated Guide to Sheffield and Neighbourhood*. Reprinted 1985. Otley: The Amethyst Press Limited

Pawson, H, & Brailsford, J, 1879 *The Illustrated Guide to Sheffield and The Surrounding District*. Sheffield, Pawson & Brailsford

Pigot 1842 *Pigot's Directory of Nottinghamshire*. London: Pigot & Co

Place, F, 1835 *Handloom Weavers and Factory Workers: Letter to James Turner, Cotton Square, from Francis Place*. J A Roebuck (ed). London: C. Ely

Porter, S (ed), 1994 *Survey of London*, **43**. *Poplar, Blackwall and the Isle of Dogs, the Parish of All Saints, Poplar*. London: Athlone

Pound, J (ed.), 1986 *The Military Survey for Babergh Hundred*. Suffolk Record Society **28**. Woodbridge: Boydell Press

Prest, J, 1960 *The Industrial Revolution in Coventry*. Oxford: Oxford University Press

Price, J, & Crew, P, 1999 Geophysical Survey of Ironworking Sites, April 1999. Report by Engineering Archaeological Services Ltd for the Lake District National Park Authority

Pyne, W H, 1808 *Microcosm, or, A Picturesque Delineation of the Arts, Agriculture, Manufactures & c of Great Britain*. 2nd edn. 2 vols. London: W Miller

RCHME 1985 *Rural Houses of the Lancashire Pennines, 1560–1760*. By S Pearson. London: HMSO

RCHME, 1986 *Rural Houses of West Yorkshire 1400–1830*. By C Giles. London: HMSO

Raistrick, A, 1953 *Dynasty of Ironfounders*. London: Longman

Ramsay, N, 1991 Introduction, in Blair & Ramsay (eds) 1991, xv-xxxiv

Ransome, A, 1930 *Swallows and Amazons*. London: Jonathan Cape

Reach, A B, 1849a *Manchester and the Textile Districts in 1849*. C Aspin (ed), 1972. Helmshore: Helmshore Local History Society

Reach, A B, 1849b *The Yorkshire Textile Districts in 1849*. C Aspin (ed), 1974. Blackburn: Helmshore Local History Society

Roberts, B K, & Wrathmell, S, 2002 *Region and Place: A Study of English Rural Settlement*. London: English Heritage

Rogers, K H, 1976, *Wiltshire and Somerset Woollen Mills*. Edington: Pasold Research Fund

Rothstein, N, 1977 The Introduction of the Jacquard Loom to Great Britain, in V Gervers (ed), *Studies in Textile History*. Toronto: Royal Ontario Museum, 281–304

Rothstein, N K A, 1961 The Silk Industry in London, 1702–1766. Unpubl MA thesis, University of London

Rouquet, J A, 1755 *The Present State of the Arts in England 1755*. Reprinted 1960. London: David & Charles

Rowe, R, 1869 Toiling and Moiling: Some Account of our Working People and How they Live, VI: The Northampton Shoemaker, *Good Words*, 1 Nov 1869

Rowlands, M B, 1975 *Masters and Men in the Small Metalware Trades of the West Midlands*. Manchester: Manchester University Press

Royston Pike, E, 1966 *Human Documents of the Industrial Revolution in Britain*. London: George Allen and Unwin

Safley, M, & Rosenband, L N (eds), 1993 *The Workplace Before the Factory: Artisans and Proletarians, 1500–1800*. Ithaca & London: Cornell University Press, 1993

Saint, A, 1987 Detailed Note on the History of the Former Silk Mill, Streatham High Road, London SW16. English Heritage, London Historical Research File, LAM 44

Salaman, R A, 1986 *Dictionary of Leather-working Tools, c1700–1950, and the Tools of Allied Trades*. Mendham, New Jersey

Samuel, R, 1977 Workshop of the World: Steam Power and Hand Technology in Mid-Victorian Britain, *Hist Workshop J*, **3**, 6–72

Schofield, J, 1987 *The London Surveys of Ralph Treswell*. London Topographical Society Publication, **135**

Schofield, J, and Vince, A G, 1994 *Medieval Towns*. London: Leicester University Press

Schwarz, L, 1992 *London in the Age of Industrialisation: Entrepreneurs, Labour Force and Living Conditions, 1700–1850*. Cambridge: Cambridge University Press

Schwarz, L, 2000 London 1700–1840, in P Clark (ed), 641–71

Sewell, W H, 1986 Visions of Labor: Illustrations of the Mechanical Arts Bbefore, In and After Diderot's Encyclopedie, in Kaplan & Koepp (eds), *Work in France, Representation, Meaning and Organisation*. London: Cambridge University Press, 258–86

Shackle, R, & Alston, L, 1998 The Old Grammar School: The Finest Merchant's House in

Lavenham, *Historic Buildings of Suffolk*, **1**, 31–49

Sheppard, F H W (ed), 1957 *Survey of London, 27. Spitalfields and Mile End New Town*. London: Athlone

Shrimpton, D, 1989 *The Parkers of Rantergate – Framework Knitters*. Ruddington Framework Knitters' Museum Trust

Shure, D, 1959 *Hester Bateman, Queen of English Silversmiths*. New York: Doubleday

Sigsworth, E, 1958 *Black Dyke Mills. A History*. Liverpool: Liverpool University Press

Smith, A, 1776 *An inquiry into the Nature and Causes of the Wealth of Nations*. 2 vols. London

Smith, D, 1965 *Industrial Archaeology of the East Midlands*. Dawlish: David & Charles

Smith, W J, 1971 The Architecture of the Domestic System in South-East Lancashire and the Adjoining Pennines, in D Chapman (ed), *The History of Working-Class Housing*. Newton Abbot: David & Charles, 247–75

Snodin, M, 1990 Charles and Edward Crace and Rococo Coach Painting, in M Aldrich (ed), *The Craces: Royal Decorators 1768–1899*. London: John Murray, 33–41

Southwick, L, 1997 William Badcock, Goldsmith and Hilt-Maker, *Silver Society J*, 584–9

Stafford, B M, 1994 *Artful Science: Entertainment and the Eclipse of Visual Education*. Massachussetts: MIT Press

Steer, F W, 1969 *Farm and Cottage Inventories of Mid-Essex 1635–1749*. Chichester: Phillimore

Stenning, D F, 1985 Timber-Framed Shops 1300–1600: Comparative Plans, *Vernacular Architecture*, **16**, 35–9

Strong, R, 1999 *The Making of a West Riding Clothing Village: Pudsey to 1780*. Wakefield: Wakefield Historical Publications

Strong, R (ed), 2000 *Israel Roberts 1827–1881 Autobiography*. Pudsey: Pudsey Civic Society

Styles, J, 1993 Manufacturing, Consumption and Design in 18th-century England, in J Brewer & R Porter (eds), *Consumption and the World of Goods*, London: Routledge, 142–58

Summerson, J, 1945 *Georgian London*. 8th edn, 2003, revised H M Colvin. New Haven and London: Yale University Press

Swanson, H, 1989, *Medieval Artisans: An Urban Class in Late Medieval England*. Oxford: Blackwell

Swanson, H, 1999 *British Medieval Towns*. Basingstoke: Macmillan

Swaysland, E J C, 1905 *Boot and Shoe Design and Manufacture*. Northampton: Tebbutt

Symonds, James (ed), 2002 *The Historical Archaeology of the Sheffield Cutlery and Tableware Industry 1750–1900*. Arcus Studies in Historical Archaeology 1. Sheffield: Arcus

Taylor, R F, 1966 A type of handloom-weaving cottage in mid-Lancashire, *Ind Archaeol*, **3**, 251–55

Taylor, W C, 1842 *Notes of a Tour in the Manufacturing Districts of Lancashire*. London: Duncan & Malcolm

Thomas, E, 1999 *Coalbrookdale and the Darbys*. York: Sessions

Thomas, K, 1983 *Man and the Natural World: Changing Attitudes in England 1500–1800*. Harmondsworth: Penguin

Thompson, E P, 1967 Time, Work-Discipline, and Industrial Capitalism, *Past and Present*, **38**, 58–97

Thornes, R C N, 1981 *West Yorkshire: 'A Noble Scene of Industry': The Development of the County 1500 to 1830*. Wakefield: West Yorkshire Metropolitan County Council

Thornes, R, 1994, *Images of Industry: Coal*. London: RCHME.

Timmins, J G, 1977 *Handloom Weavers' Cottages in Central Lancashire*. Lancaster: University of Lancaster

Timmins, J G, 1979 Handloom Weavers' Cottages in Central Lancashire: Some Problems of Recognition, *Post-Medieval Archaeol*, **13**, 251–72

Timmins, J G, 1988 Early Building Societies in Lancashire, in S Jackson (ed), *Industrial Colonies and Communities*. Lancaster: Conference of Regional and Local Historians

Timmins, J G, 1993a *The Last Shift: The Decline of Handloom Weaving in 19th-Century Lancashire*. Manchester: Manchester University Press

Timmins, J G, 1993b The Evolution of the Two-Up, Two-Down House in 19th-Century Lancashire, in A Crosby (ed), *Lancashire Local Studies*. Preston: Lancashire County Books, 101–22

Timmins, J G, 2000 Housing Quality in Rural Textile Colonies, c1800–c1850: The Ashworth Settlements Revisited, *Ind Archaeol Rev*, **22**, 21–37

Toynbee, A, 1884 *Lectures on the Industrial Revolution in England*. London: Rivingtons

Trinder, B, 1973 *The Industrial Revolution in Shropshire* (also 1981 & 2000 edns), Chichester: Phillimore

Trinder, B, 1974 Industrial Rookeries in Shropshire, in J Tann (ed), *Industrial Communities: The Proceedings of a Symposium on Industrial Colonies, Settlements and Planned Communities*. Birmingham, University of Aston

Trinder, B, 1981 see Trinder 1973

Trinder, B, 1996 *The Industrial Archaeology of Shropshire*. Chichester: Phillimore

Trinder, B, 2000 see Trinder 1973

Trinder, B, 2003 Recent Research on Early Shropshire Railways, in M Lewis (ed), *Early Railways 2*. London: Newcomen Society

Trinder, B, & Cox, J (eds), 1980 *Yeomen and Colliers in Telford: The Probate Inventories of Dawley, Lilleshall, Wellington and Wrockwardine*. Chichester: Phillimore

Trinder, B, & Cox, N (eds), 2000 *Miners and Mariners of the Severn Gorge: The Probate

Inventories of Benthall, Broseley, Little Wenlock and Madeley. Chichester: Phillimore

Tweedale, G, 1995 *Steel City: Entrepreneurship, Strategy and Technology in Sheffield 1743–1993*. Oxford: Clarendon Press

Tylecote, R F, 1986 *The Prehistory of Metallurgy in the British Isles*. London: Institute of Metals

Tylecote, R, & Cherry, J, 1970 The 17th-Century Bloomery at Muncaster Head, *Trans Cumberland & Westmorland Antiq Archaeol Soc*, **70**, 69–109

Uglow, J, 2002 *The Lunar Men, The Friends who made the Future 1730–1810*. London: Faber and Faber

Ure, A 1835 *The Philosophy of Manufactures*. London: Charles Knight

VCH, 1906 *The Victoria History of the County of Northampton*, **2**. London: Archibald Constable & Co

VCH, 1985 *The Victoria History of Shropshire, **11**. Telford*. Oxford: Oxford University Press

VCH, 1998 *The Victoria History of the County of Middlesex, **11**. Early Stepney with Bethnal Green*. Oxford: Oxford University Press

VCH, 1999 *The Victoria History of Shropshire, **10**. Wenlock, Upper Corve Dale and the Stretton Hills*. Oxford: Oxford University Press

Veblen, T, 1914 *The Instinct of Workmanship and the State of the Industrial Arts 1914*. Reprinted 1964. New York: W W Norton & Company

Vernon, R W, McDonnell G, & Schmidt A, 1998 An Integrated Geophysical and Analytical Appraisal of Early Ironworking: Three Case Studies, *Hist Metallurgy* **32** (2), 67–81

Vitali, U, 2000 Beyond the Secret Tradition: The Evolution of Style and Techniques in the Art of the Goldsmith, *The Silver Society Jnl*, **12**, 8–17

Ward, C, 2002 *Cotters and Squatters: Housing's Hidden History*. Nottingham: Five Leaves

Warwick University, 1999 *Exercising Taste: Luxury and the Education of the Senses. An Anthology of Texts for the Winter Workshop, 26 February 1999*. Coventry: Warwick Eighteenth Century Centre

Webb, S, & Webb, B, 1911 *The History of Trade Unionism*. 2nd edn. London: Longman

Wedgwood 1903 *Letters of Josiah Wedgwood 1771 to 1780*. London: E J Morton.

Wendeborn, F A, 1791 *A View of England Towards the Close of the Eighteenth Century*. Dublin: University College

Wertime, T A, 1962 *The Coming of the Age of Steel*. Chicago: University of Chicago Press

White, W, 1832 *White's History, Gazetteer and Directory of Nottinghamshire*. Sheffield: Francis White & Co

White, W, 1865 *White's History, Gazetteer and Directory of Nottinghamshire*. Sheffield: Francis White & Co

White, W, 1896 *White's Directory of Northampton*. Sheffield: William White

Williams, M, & Farnie, D A, 1992 *Cotton Mills in Greater Manchester*. Preston: Carnegie Publishing

Wilson, H, 1902 *Silverwork and Jewellery: A Textbook for Students and Workers in Metal 1902*. Reprinted 1978. London & New York: Pitman

Wilson, R G, 1971 *Gentlemen Merchants: The Merchant Community in Leeds 1700–1830*. Manchester: Manchester University Press

Wray, N, Hawkins, B, & Giles, C, 2001 *'One Great Workshop': The Buildings of the Sheffield Metal Trades*. Swindon: English Heritage

Wright, C N, 1884 *Commercial and General Directory and Blue Book of Northamptonshire*. Leicester: C N Wright

Wright, C N, 1887 *Directory of Nottinghamshire*. Nottingham: J Bell

Wright, C N, 1891 *Directory of Nottinghamshire*. Nottingham: J Bell

Wright, C N, 1904 *Directory of Nottinghamshire*. London: Kelly's Directories

Wright, J S, 1866 The Jewellery and Gilt Toy Trades, in S Timmins (ed) 1866, *The Resources, Products, and Industrial History of Birmingham and the Midland Hardware District*. London: Robert Hardwick, 452–62.

Wrigley, E A, 1990 Urban Growth and Agricultural Change: England and the Continent in the Early Modern Period, in P Borsay (ed), *The 18th-Century Town 1688–1820*. Harlow: Longman, 41–7

Yeo, E, & Thompson, E P, 1971, *The Unknown Mayhew*. New York: Schocken Books

Index

Page numbers in italics refer to illustrations and tables and/or captions

Abbeydale Works, Sheffield 146
Adam brothers 18
Adams, Thomas 177
Agricola, Gnaeus Julius 31
Alabaster & Wilson 157
Aleame, Jacques 20
Alma Works, Sheffield 141
Almondbury 80
Ambleside 166
Angerstein, Baron Reinhold Rucker 3, 17
Anglo Works, Sheffield 145, 145
'apartment' 2
apprenticeship 2
Arkwright, Sir Richard 16, 65
Armitage Bridge Mills 84, 86
artisan production 3–7, 9, 16
Ashurst, Dennis 36
Ashworth, Cornelius 75
Augsburg 20, 21

Backbarrow 169, 170
Bacon, Sir Francis 20
Badcock, William 20–1, 22
Badly Hall, Suffolk 40
Bagot's Park, Staffordshire 35
Baker, M 19
baking 30
Balaam, Master of 20
Baltic Steel Works, Sheffield 143
Bamford, Samuel 97, 173
Barker, D 33
Barratt's 134
Barrell, John 18, 21
Barrow 166
Barrowford 98
Bartlett, K S 34
Bateman, Hester 19
Bath 33
Bayley, John 174
Beale & Co 132
Beardsmore, J H 113
Beaumont, Joseph 83
Beck, Joseph 15
Beck Leven Foot 168, 169
Bedware, John 174
Beehive Works, Sheffield 143, 143, 144
Belgium 11, 12, 13
Bell, John 177–8
Belper 9, 109
Benthall 175
Bentley Grange iron pits 30
Bentley, Thomas 27
Berner, John 39

Bewick, Thomas 26
Bildeston 48
Bildeston Hall 43, 44, 45, 46
Birmingham:
  Assay Office 157
  metalworking 33
  population 60
  School of Jewellery 157
  see also following entries
Birmingham and Fazeley Canal 156
Birmingham Jewellery Quarter:
  Branston Street 155, 155
  casting 161, 164
  Century Buildings 153
  coffin furniture factory 157, 164
  employment 153
  exports 152, 153
  factories 155–7, 157, 158, 165, 181:
    design 161–5
  family firms 157–8
  Fleet Street 157, 164
  gold chain making 164–5
  historical development 150–3
  jewellers' boards 159, 160
  Legge Lane 155–6, 156
  machinery 159
  manufacturing processes 159–61
  map 151
  Mary Street 155, 155
  metal spinning 161
  Newhall Street 152, 153
  offices 161, 162
  organisation 157–9
  outworking 154, 157
  photograph 152
  plating 164
  power and 159, 161, 165
  pressing 161, 162, 163, 164
  Regent Parade 158
  Regent Street 155
  residential area transformed 182
  rollers 159
  St Paul's Square 157
  security 162–3
  showrooms 153, 162, 163
  small masters 3, 158
  Soho works 27, 29, 156, 161
  Spencer Street 160
  stamping 161, 161, 164, 164, 165
  Summer Lane 154, 155
  survival of 150
  'toy' trades 3
  Variety Works 162

Birmingham Jewellery Quarter (*cont.*)
   Victoria Works 156–7
   Vyse Street *162*
   warehouses 161, *162*, 163
   Warstone Lane *153*, *156*, 157
   wire drawing 159
   'workshop of the world' 152
   workshops:
     design 161–5
     garden 154
     houses and 153–6, 165, 182
     longevity of 150
     origins of 150
     outworking 150
Black Country 12
Blackburn 91–2, 96
Blair and Ramsey 37
blast furnaces 31–2, 33
bloomeries 30, 32, 33
bobbin-net machines 101
Bolsterstone Glasshouse 36, *36*, 37
Bolton *99*
boot and shoe industry *see* Northamptonshire boot
   and shoe industry
Botfield, Thomas 177
Botteley, William 174
Boulton, Matthew 19, 24, 27, 29, 156, 161
Bradford 75, 76, 79, 83, 87, 88
Bradford-upon-Avon 7, 9, *14*
Bradley Green, Wotton-under-Edge 10, *10*
Bramley 79
Brathay River 168
Braunche, Elizabeth 39, 42
Brears, P 34
Brecht, Berthold 178
brewhouses 53–4
Bristol 60
broadcloth industry:
   decline of, East Anglia 53
   geography of 75
   looms larger 88
   marketing 7
   tenter hooks 52
Brockett, Caleb 132
bronzeworking 32
Brooke family 84, 86
Brooke, John 174
Broseley Wood 174, 175, 176, 177
Brown, John 174
Brown, Laurence 174
Browne, John 39
Brownlow, Lord 18
bruk system 8
Brunskill, R W 1
buckle factory 17
building society movement 90
Bures St Mary 39, *41*, 57
Burritt, Elihu 12
Burslem 29
Bury St Edmunds 39, 43, 49, 54, 55–7
Bushloe End 13, *15*
buttons 17

Byng, John 26–7
Byrkenott 31

Caffyn, L 10
Calcutts *175*
Calder Valley 75, 87, 88
Caldwell and Dean 34
Calne 13, *14*
Calverton 98, *102*, *107*, *108*, 109, 113, 116, 118, *120*
Cam 15
Campbell, R 17
Campion, G 1–2, 101, 109
cannon making 32
capitalist production 7–15
Cardmakere, John 54
Carlyle, Thomas 180
Carr, John 35
Cash Brothers *15*
Cattell, J 182
Cellini, Benvenuto 20
census evidence 94, 100, 103, *103*, *107*, 109, 110,
   111, 115, *120*, *121*
ceramics *see* pottery
chain industry 11, 12
Challenge Works, Sheffield 146, *146*
Chambers, Ernest 127
charcoal 170
charcoal-burning 181 *see also* charcoal burners'
   huts *under* Furness iron industry
Chesterfield, Lord 24
Children's Employment Commission 12
china manufactory 26
Ching, John 9, *9*
Chingley 31
Chorley *92*, 93, 96
Church's 134
Civil War 122
Clare 49, 54
Clark, D 38
Clemson, Mary 177
Clifford, H 182
Clifton Works, Sheffield 146
cloth halls 5
cloth industry:
   collapse of 49
   dyehouses and 54
   finishing 75
   processes 7
   putting-out system 9 *see also verlagsystem*
   see also broadcloth industry; East Anglian
     workshops; Lancashire, domestic weaving;
     loomshops; silk weavers; silk-weaving
     workshops, London; weavers; weaving shops;
     West Riding, Yorkshire; worsted industry;
     Yorkshire wool textile
clothiers 5–8, *5*, 39
   houses *6*, 7, 8
coach making 17
coal industry 1
coal-miners 115
Coalbrookdale 176
Coalbrookdale Coalfield 173–4, 177, 178

194 *The vernacular workshop*

Coalbrookdale Company 174
Cobbett, William 146
Cock, Joseph 81
Coggeshall 40, 49, 54–5, *56*
Colchester 48–9, 55
Coles, George 127
Colmar, Alsace 3, *4*
Colne Valley 79, 80, 81, 83
Colwith Force 168–9
Commissioners 13
Congleton 61
Coniston Water 166, 168
Cook, Frederick 135
cotton: cellar workshops 11, 90, 95, 96, 98
Coventry 15, *15*
Coventry ribbon industry 2
Cowper, H S 166, 167, 172
craft guilds:
    decline, 18th century 3
    medieval 2
    'mysteries' controlled by 20
craft industries:
    economic conditions and 37
    feudal 29
    rural 29
    specialisation 17–19, 37
    urban 29
    see also under names of individual craft industries
Cranage brothers 173
Cranstone, D 32, 33, 168
Crippin, William 174
Critoft, Roger 39
Cromford *8*, 9
Crosley, Thomas 76
Cross, Jonathan 81
Crossley, D 30, 33, 34, 35, 36
Crossley and Ashurst 30, 37
Crowther family 83
Culme, John 18, 19
Cumbria 166, 172
Cunsey 169, 171
cutlers 138–39
Cyclops Works, Sheffield *142*

Dale, David 16
Darby family 173, 178
Darby, Abraham I 173, 177, 178
Darby, Abraham II 173
Darling, John 20
Daventry 122
Dawley parish 173
Debenham 46, 54, 57–8, *57*, *58*, 59
Defoe, Daniel 3, 5, 24, 77, 78–9, 138
Delaune, Etienne 20, *21*
Delph 96
Derby 61, 109
Desborough 122
Diderot, Denis 2, 21, *160*
Dilton Marsh 15
directory evidence 104, *105*, 109, *109*, 111, 113, *114*, 115, *119*

Disraeli, Benjamin 182
Dorman, Charles 132
Dorrall family 178
Dorrall, Edward 176
Dossie, Robert 24
Dounton, Thomas 32
Duddon Bridge 169, 170–1, *170*
Dungworth Green *138*, 139
dyehouses 39, 53, 54
Dyer, C 32
Dyer, John 175–6
Dyer, Richard 176
Dyer, William 176

Earls Barton 122
East Anglia:
    economic success 38
    poverty 38
East Anglian workshops:
    builders 43
    cloth manufacture 38
    clothiers 39
    documentary evidence 38–40, 52, 58
    entrances 43, 44
    export 53
    finishing 39
    gablets 53
    houses 40–9:
        location in 39
    jetties 49, 54
    'lock-up' rooms 49, 54, 58, 59
    loom ownership restricted 39
    merchants' courtyards 49–54
    multi-purpose units 43
    outworkers 39
    pentice roofs 52
    retail counters 40, 41
    retail outlets 38–9, 54:
        stalls 54, 55–7, *57*
    shops and 38, 58, 59
    survival 39
    tenter yards 52
    two-cell houses 44
    undercrofts 49
    uniformity 43
    versatility 59
    warehouses 49
    weaving 39
    windows 40, 41, 42–3, 52, 55, 58
Edwards, Samuel 177
Eliot, George 176
Elkington and Co *152*, 153
Elliott, William *163*, 164
Encyclopedie (*see* Diderot)
Engels, Friedrich 140, 147
English Heritage 1, 3, 122
English Heritage Monuments Protection Programme 171
Eskdale 166
Essex 38
Etruria 26, 27
Evans, Eli 130

Evans, Thomas 130
Evans, William 130
Evelyn, John 20
Exeter 3
Eye Witness Works, Sheffield 144
Eyre Brothers 132

factories:
   workers' discontent 13
   workers' loss of control and 15
   workers' resistance to 13, 16
   see also under Birmingham Jewellery Quarter;
      Lancashire, domestic weaving premises;
      Northamptonshire boot and shoe industry;
      Sheffield cutlery and edge-tool trades
Faucher, Leon 140
Felibien, André 20
Felkin, W A 109
Flack & Durrant 133
flax 11, 176
Flint, Alfred 127
flying shuttle 79
Forest of Dean 32
Forge House, Furness 168
Forty, A 27
Fox, C 19
Fox family 36, 37
framework knitting:
   domestic, persistence of 180
   invention of 11, 105
   lace industry, comparison with 101, 116–18
   move to Nottingham 60
   wide frame 105–07, 110, *110*, 116
   workshops 11, *11*
France 16, 35
Frome 2–3
Furness iron industry:
   bark-peelers' huts 166, 167, 168, *168*, *169*
   blast furnaces 169–71
   bloomeries 166, 168–9, 172
   charcoal burners' huts 166–8, *169*
   chronology 172
   documentary evidence 170
   forges 170
   map *167*
   pitsteads 167, 168
   power 168
   resources 166
   West Midland ironmasters and 169, 170, 171
   woodland protected by 166
   woodlanders' huts 166–8, *168*
   work forces 170
   workshops 168–71
furniture making 18

Gaimster and Nenk 33
Gainsborough Old Hall, Lincolnshire 40
Garden, Phillips 26
Geddes, J 31, 32
George, M D 64
Giles, C 37
Gillott, Joseph 156

glass production 35–7
Globe Works, Sheffield 136, *137*, 141
Gloucestershire 12–13, 97, 181
Glover, Robert 34, *34*
Goad Insurance Plans 127, 129, 133, 141
Golcar 81, *81*, *82*, 83, 84, 85
gold 153
goldsmiths 18, 19, *21*
Goldsmiths' Company 21, 23, *24*
Goldsmythes Storehouse 20
Goode, Benjamin 157
Gott, Benjamin 86
Gourley, Holly 28
Graham, James 83
Greaves, William 136
Greene, Daniel 77
Grenoside 146
Grenville, J 1
Grinders' Sick Club 139
Gully 83
Gwynn, Charles 177

Hacket 170
Halifax 75, 76:
   Piece Hall 5, *5*
Harris, John 176
Harrison, John 139
Harrison Coppice 168
Harrold, Alfred 154
Hartshead 182
hatmakers 26
Haughley 43
Haverhill 38, 57
Hazlitt, William 19
Headington Quarry 178
Heap, George 81
Heap, John 84
Heathcoat's bobbin-net machine 101
Heaton, Robert 76
Hedon 33
Heming, Thomas 19
hemp 176
Heptonstall *77*, *78*
High Furness 166, 168
Hill, Samuel 76
Hobson, Henry 145
Hodge Bower 177
Holme Valley 79, 80, 81, 83, *83*
Holmfirth 81, 83
Holt *6*
Homer, R F 32
Honley 79, 81, *83*, 84, 85, *85*, 86, *86*
Hood, Thomas 180
Horsehay ironworks 174
hosiery industry:
   collective workshops 12
   wide frame 13
   workshops 11, 12, 13
   see also framework knitting
Hounslow 33
Household Words 164
Hucknall *102*, 109, 113–16, *114*, 116, *117*, 118, *120*

Huddersfield 75, 79, 80, 83, 86, 87, 88, 89
Huddersfield Cloth Hall 83, 84
Hudson, P 3, 4
Huntsman, Benjamin 138
Hutton-le-Hole 35
Hymen, Isaac 26

Ibbotson and Roebuck 136
Icornshaw 79
Improved Industrial Dwellings Company 69
India 138
Ipswich 38
Iron Bridge 173
iron smelting 30
Ironbridge Gorge:
    bargemen 177
    cottages 173–8, *175*, 176, 178, *178*
    miners 177
    Nuffield Survey 173–4
    rope-making 177
    self-sufficiency 175
    settlements 173–4, 177, 178
    workshops 173–8
Ironbridge Institute 174
ironworking:
    ores 30
    peasant ironmasters 32
    rural sites 32
    technological advances 30–31, 32
    see also Furness iron industry
Irthlingborough 129

J and J Craven 79
J T Meadows & Sons 133
Jack of Newbury 12, 59
Jackfield 174
Jacquard loom 3, 65, 68–9, 71
Jalland map 101
Joy, E 18

Kames, Lord 24
kaufsystem 3, 9, 16
Kedington 57
Keene, D 38
Keighley 79
Kentwell Hall 53
Kersey 38, 46, *48*, 57
Ketley 174, 178
Kettering 122, *125*, 126, *127*, 129, 133
King's Lynn 39
Kingswood *10*
Kirkham, P 18
Knole 35

lace industry 101–05, 180:
    decline 101, 118
    factory system 101
    framework knitting, comparison with 101, 116–18
    primacy of 104
Lake District National Park 171

Lancashire: weavers' workshops in 11, 93
Lancashire, domestic weaving premises:
    accommodation standards 90, 96–9, 100
    agriculture and 94
    cellar workshops 90, 93, 95
    cottages 90, 91, 93, 94, 95, 96, 100, 180
    factory colonies 94
    loomshops 91, 92, 94, 95, 96, 97, 99, 100
    map *90*
    rural 93, 96
    settlement and 90–6, 100
    space 95, 96–7, 98, 99
    urban 93, 96
    weavers' colonisation 90, 93, 94–5, 96
    windows 95–6, 98
Lavenham 38, 39, 43, 49, 52, 59:
    Barn Street, Old Grammar School 53
    Hall 53
    High Street 52–3, *52*
    Market Place *40*, *41*
    Prentice Street *44*
    timber mined 53
Lawley Common 174
Leah's Yard, Sheffield 145
Leech, R 2
Leeds 75, 76, 79, 83, 86, 88, 180
Leek 61
Leicester 109
Leicestershire 122
Leighton 169, 170
Leland, John 137
Letts, John 130
Leveson Gower family 174
linen 11, 90, 95
Linthwaite 83, *84*, 85
Lion Works, Sheffield 145
List of Buildings of Architectural and Historic Significance 38
Little Dawley 174, 176
Little Wenlock 176
Littleborough *95*
Liverpool: population 60
Livesey 93–4, *94*, 96, 99
Lloyd, William 174
Loch, James 174
Lodgemore Mill 8
London:
    advantages of 19
    clothing industry 60
    disadvantages of 19
    house building 65
    manufacturing 60
    population 60
    putting-out system 60 *see also verlagsystem*
    working classes 60
    see also luxury goods workshops, London; silk-weaving workshops, London
London Building Act, 1774 61, 65
Londonderry 179
Long Buckby 122, *125*, 126, *128*, 129, 135
Long Eaton 101
Long Melford 39, 49, *49*, 53

loomshops:
  cellar 90, 91
  collective 13
  development of, 1800–50 85–6
  discontent and 13
  photograph *14*
  workers' control 12
  workers'concern about 12–13
Loughborough 109
Louis Osbaldiston and Company 146
Low Furness 166
Low Nibthwaite 169
Low Wood 169
Lower Standards Act, 1954 153
luxury goods workshops, London:
  advertising 26
  consumers and 24–7
  makers' writings about 19–21
  retailers 26
  specialisation 17–19
  sub-contracting 17–19
  trade cards 26, *26*
Lyons, France:
  La Croix-Rousse 3, *4*
  silk weaving and workshops 70–2, *70, 71, 72*
  silk workers of 2, 3

Macclesfield 26, 61, 98, 99
McDonald, Miriam 176
Madeley Wood 174, *175, 177*
Malmesbury 9
Malmesbury Abbey 12
Manchester:
  loomshops 92
  population 60
'Manchester Methodology' 9
Manfields 134
Mansell, Sir Robert 36
Marshall, Alfred 1
Martin, Henry 132
Martineau, Harriet 164
Marx, Karl 18, 180
Medieval Archaeology 28, 29
Medieval Britain 37
Melksham *6*
Melton Mobray 109
Mende, M 8
Mendels, F F 3
metalworking:
  blast furnaces 31–32, 33
  bloomeries 30, 32, 33
  dating 33
  guilds 32
  ores 30
  organisation 32
  power and 31
  putting-out 33 *see also verlagsystem*
  rural sites 32
  smelting 30
  social factors 32
  technological changes 30, 32
  urban 32–3

  see also Birmingham Jewellery Quarter; Furness iron industry; Ironbridge Gorge; ironworking; nail industry; Sheffield cutlery and edge-took trades
Metropolitan Association for Improving the Dwellings of the Industrious Classes 69
Middle Ages:
  craft guilds 2
  workshops 2
Middleton 97, 98, 173
Mile End colony 96
Miles, W A 13, 15
Minepit Wood *32*
Mirfield 182
Mitchell, D 18
Money, J H 32
Monschau, Germany 7, 8
Montagu, Elizabeth 21–4, 27
Montrose Works, Sheffield 145–6
Morgan, N 90, 91
Morris, Henry *25*, 26
Morrison-Low, A D 18
Mortimer, Thomas 24–6
Moxon, Joseph 20, *20*
Muncaster Head 30, 168

nail industry:
  organisation of 2, 11–12
  putting-out system 16 *see also verlagsystem*
  workshops *12*
Nayland 38, 39, 44–46, *47, 48, 50–51, 53,* 54
Needham Market 54
Newbridge 31
Newland 169, 170, 171
Newman Brothers 157, *164*
Nibthwaite 169, 171
Noble, Frederick 130
Norfolk, Dukes of 139
Norman, Samuel 18
Northamptonshire boot and shoe industry:
  Artizan Road, Northampton 132
  Bailiff Street, Northampton 127
  Billing Road, Northampton 130
  Burns Road, Northampton 133
  Carey Street, Northampton 132
  clicking 124, 129
  closing 124, 126, 127, 129
  Colwyn Road, Northampton 130, *131*
  Connaught Road, Northampton *134,*134–5
  Denmark Road, Northampton 130
  exports 122
  factories 124–26, *125,* 126, 127, 129, 130, 132, 133, 134
  Henry Street, Northampton 132
  history of 122–4
  house-factories 130, 133
  making and manufacturing distinguished 122
  mechanisation 126, 127–9
  offices 126, 129
  origins of 122–24
  outwork, persistence of 126–9
  power and 127, 129

198 *The vernacular workshop*

Northamptonshire boot and shoe industry (*cont.*)
    Robert Street, Northampton 134–5, *134*
    St Michael's Road, Northampton 132, *133*
    sewing machines 124, 127
    Shakespeare Road, Northampton 132
    South Place Factory 135
    space 126, 129–30
    Unicorn Works 132, *133*
    Victoria Road, Northampton 132
    warehouses 126
    Wellingborough Road, Northampton 134
    windows 126
    workshops 122–4, *123*, *128*, 129, 130, 182:
        culture of 133–5
        speculative building 132–3
Norwich 33, 49, 60
Nottingham:
    lace industry 101:
        Mansfield Road area 101–05, *102*, *103*, *104*, 105, *105*, *106*, 109, *119*
        North Sherwood Street 101, *103*, *104*, 105, *106*, *119*
    slum development 101
    stocking frames 3, 101
    Nottingham Lace Market 101

Old Park ironworks, Dawley, Ironbridge Gorge 177
Osbaldiston, Louis *146*
Owen, Robert 16

Paddock 81
Palmer, M 28, 101, 109
Palmer and Neaverson 95
Paris 60, *160*
Parker and Wakelin 19
paternalism 8, 9, 16
Peltzner family 12
Pendleton, William 155
Pennington Brass Foundry, Exeter 32–3
Penny Bridge 169
Penny Magazine, The 136, 158–9
pewter workshop 32
Phelps, John *6*
Piggott-Smith, J 150
pin manufacture 2, 17
placenames 33, 34
Portland Works, Sheffield 141, *141*, 144
Post-Medieval Archaeology 28, 29
Post-Medieval Britain 37
Potovens 34, *34*, 35
pottery 33–5
Poultar, Thomas 40
Prescot 178
Preston 90, *91*, 92–3
Preston St Mary 53
probate inventories 78, 139, 174, 176, 177
proto-industrialisation 3–7
Provins 49
Pudsey 79, 88
putting-out system 3–7, 9–15 see also *verlagsystem*

Rathbone, Gamaliell 40
Raunds 122, 127, 129, 133
RCHME (Royal Commission on Historical Monuments of England) 13, 166, 168, 171, 172
Reach, Angus Bethine 83, 98
Remnett, Ernest 130
Ribble Valley 94, *95*
Ricardo, David 69
Rievaulx 32
Rise Farm, Lavenham 53
Robathan & Pendleton 155
Rochdale 97
Rockley smelting complex 30, *31*
Roden, Samuel 177
Rodgers, Joseph 148
Roe, Mr 26
Roe, Thomas 132
Rogers, K H 13
Rogerson, Joseph 79
Roper, Timothy 175
Rosedale, Yorkshire 35–6, *35*, *36*
Rothwell 122
Rounsea Wood *169*
Rouquet, Jean André 17, 24
Rowlands, M B 33
Roxwell 39, 40
Ruddington *102*, 109–113, *110*, *111*, *112*, 116, 118, *120*
Rushden 122, 129, 130, 132

Saddleworth *5*, 178
Saffron Walden 40
Sanderson map *102*
Scheemaker, 19
Scheibler family 7, 8
Schofield and Vince 30
sculpture trade 19
Sellers Wheel, Sheffield 147
Severn River 174, *175*
Sheaf Works, Sheffield 136, *136*, *137*
Sheffield:
    expansion 138
    metal production 33
    population 138
Sheffield cutlery and edge-tool trades:
    Abbeydale Works 146
    agriculture and 146
    Alma Works 141
    Anglo Works 145, *145*
    Baltic Steel Works 143
    Beehive Works 143, *143*, 144
    Brooklyn Works 141
    'Bull Week' 140
    Butcher's Wheel 143
    Challenge Works 146, *146*
    Clifton Works 146
    cutlers 138–39
    Cutlers' Company 138, 140
    'cutlers' wheel' 139, 140
    Cyclops Works *142*
    documentary evidence 139
    exports 148

Eye Witness Works 144
factories 136, 137, 140
forges 138, 146
Garden Street 144, *144*
Globe Works 136, *137*, 141
grinding 137, 139, *139*, 140, 147
grinding wheels 140, 141–2, 147
journeymen 140
knives 139, 148
labour, organisation of 139–40
Leah's Yard 145
lighting 148
Lion Works 145
'little meesters' 3, 140, 144, 146, 147, 148
local history of 137–9
Montrose Works 145–6
out-working 144
Portland Works 141, *141*, 144
power 136, 137, 139, 140, 141, 145, 146, 148:
   resistance to 142–3
regulation of 138
Saint Monday 140
Sellers Wheel 147
Sheaf Works 136, *136*, 137
smithies 137–8
Soho Wheel 141, *142*
Surrey Works 146
Trafalgar Works 141
Truro Works 147
Union Wheel 141, *142*
Venture Works 144
Well Meadow Street 143
'works' 137
workshops:
   expansion of 136
   forges 140
   multiple occupation 143, 144
   purpose-built 140–1, *144*, 149
   rural 146
   speculative building 144, 148
   urban 140–6, 147
   ventilation 147
   working conditions 147–8
Sheffield cutlery and edge-tool trades: Union Wheel 141
Sheffield Grinders' Disease 148
Sheffield and Tinsley Canal 136
Shepherd Wheel 139
Shepsted *10*, 11
Shetland shawl manufacture 115, 116
'shop': term 38, 58
Shrewsbury, George, Sixth Earl 139
Shrimpton, D 109, 110
Shure, D 19
silk weavers:
   combination 64, 67, 68, 72
   French 61
   immigrants 61
   Irish 61
   journeymen 64
   largest group in industry 60
   machine breaking 61
   poverty 61, 69
   religion 61
   riots 61
   throwsters 60, 61
   see also following entries
silk weaving workshops, Coventry 15
silk-weaving workshops, London:
   18th century 64–5
   19th century 65–8
   Bethnall Green 61–2, *68*, 69
   Bethnall Green Road *61*, *63*
   Brick Lane 67
   decline 64, 68, 69
   domestic use and 64
   dyers 60
   employment 60, 68
   immigrants 69
   Lyons, comparison with 72
   multiple occupation 62–4, 65
   Sclater Street *62*
   skill 64
   Spitalfields 60–1, *63*, 64, 65, *66*, 67
   staircases 61–2, 62–4, 65
   Streatham 68–9
   survival 179
   technological advances 65
   tenement blocks 65
   timber construction 61, 65
   transport costs 64
   weavers' cottages 65, 67–8, *68*, 69
   winders 60, 61
Silsden 79
silver trade 19
Simpson, George 39
small metal industries 2, 7, 15, 150
Smith, Adam 17, 18
Smith, Laurence 43
Smith, W J 95, 97
Smyth, John 39, 52
Snedshill Common 174
Soho Works, Birmingham 27, 29, 156, 161
South West England:
   weavers' houses 9
   weaving shops 7
   woollen industry 75
Sowerby Bridge Mills *87*
spinning 16, 75, 78, 180
spinning jennies 13
spinning, mechanised 96
Spitalfields Acts 64–5, 68, 69
Staffordshire potteries 34
Stannington 146, *147*
Staveley and Wood's map 101, *103*
steam engines 2, 79
steel industry 17, 136, *136*, 138, 181:
   crucible steel 138, 143
Steer, F W 40
Stenning, D F 38, 40
Stocking *178*
Stockport 61
Stocksbridge 36, *36*
Stoke-by-Nayland 43–4

Stony Hazel 170, 172
Strutt, Jedediah 9, 16
Stumpe, William 12
Sudbury 39
Suffolk 38:
  woollen industry 2, 39
Surrey Works, Sheffield 146
Sutcliffe family 77
Sutton 79
Swanson, H 2
Sweden 8, 16
Sykehouse *138*, 139
Sykes, Joseph 81

tanning 3, *4*
Taylor, R F 96
Tebbutt & Hall 133
Tewkesbury 11
textile industries *see* cloth industry
Thackley 88
Thaxted Guildhall 54, 55, *55*
Thomas, John 177
Thongsbridge 84
Throng Moss 168
Tillie's shirt factory 179
Timmins, J G 11
Torrington, Viscount 26
Trafalgar Works, Sheffield 141
Treswell, Ralph 49
Trippe, Robert 52
Trowbridge *6*, 7, 9, *9*, 179
Truro Works, Sheffield 147
Turc, Le 17

Union Wheel 141
Unicorn Works, Northamptonshire 132, *133*
United States of America 16, 148
Uppermill 96

Vaucanson, Jacques de 71
Veblen, Thorstein 18
Venture Works 144
verlagsystem 3–7, 9–15, 16 *see also* putting-out system
Verviers 12, *13*
Vickers, Richard 176
Vulliamy brothers 18

Wakefield 33, 34, *34*, 35
water power 31
Watts, John 144–45
Weald, The 32
Weaver, James 176
weavers:
  houses 9, 10, *10*, 15, 18, 79–84, *85*, 86–8, 180, 182:
    builders 10
  loom ownership restricted 2, 39
  numbers of 79, 88, 180
  poverty 13–15, 180
  thread spun elsewhere 2
  Weavers' Company 61

weaving: mechanised spinning and 180
weaving shops:
  builders 9, 10
  domestic 11, 182
  see also Lancashire, domestic weaving premises
Webb, Edward 26
Wedgwood, Josiah 27, 29
Wednesbury 17
Wellingborough 122
Wendeborn, Pastor 19
West Midlands 11, 169, 170, 171
West Riding, Yorkshire:
  loomshops 13
  woollen industry 3–5, 7, 13, *76*
  workshops 9–10, 11, 182
  see also Yorkshire wool textile industry
West Yorkshire: pottery 34
Wheeler, Hull & Co 132
White, J E 12
Wigston Magna *16*
Willans, Joseph 34
Willett and Co 79
wills 38, 39, 54
Wilson, Henry 18
Wilson, Stephen 68, 69
Wiltshire 12–13, 181
Winchester 38
Windermere 166
Wollaston 129
Wolstenholmes 146
Woodbridge 38, 44, *46*, 52
Wood's map 101
woollen industries 2, 11, 79 *see also* East Anglian workshops; Lancashire, domestic weaving premises; Yorkshire wool textile industry
woollen industries: mills 79
workshops:
  agriculture and 3, 5, *5*, 7, 37
  cellar 11
  collective 15
  company mills 5
  consumer and 24–7
  definition 1–2, 28
  domestic arena, absorbed into 179
  in domestic buildings 1, *6*, 7, 7–8, 10, 15, 37
  economic organisation 29
  erosion of 179
  factories, differentiating from 2
  illustrations of 20–1, 27
  landscape and 179–82
  mechanical power and 2, 180
  as primary sources 179
  re-evaluation of 179
  research agenda 28–37
  retail shops and 1
  rural production 3–7, 37
  separate buildings for 2
  settlement pattern and 182
  shops and 28
  significance 179
  social organisation 28, 29
  space 28, 29

study of 179
surviving 179
term first used 59
urban 28, 29, 37
urban artisan production 2–3, 7
as vernacular buildings 1
work organisation and 2–15
workers' control of 2, 9, 12, 28
see also East Anglian workshops; Lancashire, domestic weaving premises; loomshops; luxury goods workshops, London; silk-weaving workshops, London; weaving shops; *and under* Birmingham Jewellery Quarter; Furness iron industry; Ironbridge Gorge; Northamptonshire boot and shoe industry; Sheffield cutlery and edge-tool trades

worsted: mill 79
worsted industry:
  combing shops 75
  marketing 7
  mills 79
  organisation 9, 16, 75–6
  power looms 79, 88, 89
  putting-out system 88 *see also verlagsystem*
  Yorkshire 75
Wray, N 182
Wrigley, John 79, 86
Writtle 40
Wrockwardine Wood 174, 176

York 2
York, Thomas 174
Yorkshire wool textile industry:
  domestic system 75
  dominance of 75
  factory production 88
  history 75–9
  importance of 76–7
  landscape and 182
  loomshops 85–6
  map *76*
  organisation of 75, 77
  power 79, 139
  power looms 79, 87, 88, 89
  putting-out system 77
  weavers' cottages 79–84, *80, 85,* 88, 89
  weaving 78